Object Relations Psychotherapy

Object Relations Psychotherapy

AN INDIVIDUALIZED AND INTERACTIVE
APPROACH TO DIAGNOSIS
AND TREATMENT

Cheryl Glickauf-Hughes
and
Marolyn Wells

A JASON ARONSON BOOK

ROWMAN & LITTLEFIELD PUBLISHERS, INC.
Lanham • Boulder • New York • Toronto • Plymouth, UK

A JASON ARONSON BOOK

ROWMAN & LITTLEFIELD PUBLISHERS, INC.

Published in the United States of America
by Rowman & Littlefield Publishers, Inc.
A wholly owned subsidiary of The Rowman & Littlefield Publishing Group, Inc.
4501 Forbes Boulevard, Suite 200, Lanham, Maryland 20706
www.rowmanlittlefield.com

Estover Road
Plymouth PL6 7PY
United Kingdom

British Library Cataloguing in Publication Information Available

The hardback edition of this book was cataloged by the Library of Congress
as follows:
    Glickauf-Hughes, Cheryl.
        Object relations psychotherapy : an individualized and interactive approach
    to diagnosis and treatment / Cheryl Glickauf-Hughes, Marolyn Wells.
            p. cm.
        Includes bibliographical references and index.
        ISBN-13: 978-0-7657-0518-1 (pbk. : alk. paper)
        ISBN-10: 0-7657-0518-4 (pbk. : alk. paper)
        1. Object relations (Psychoanalysis)   2. Psychotherapy.   1. Wells, Marolyn
    Clark.   II. Title.
    RC489.025G58   1997
    616.89'14—dc21   97-8531

Printed in the United States of America

♾ ™ The paper used in this publication meets the minimum requirements of
American National Standard for Information Sciences—Permanence of Paper for
Printed Library Materials, ANSI/NISO Z39.48-1992.

To George and Richard

Our partners in life who have learned,
grown and changed with us

*To Virginia, Marion, Harry, Mahlon, Jacob,
Mackenzie, Emma, Sam and Ben*

Our past and our future
from whom we learned and continue to learn about
the complexities of the parent-child bond

*To Susie, Susan, Sheila, Nivine, Ilana, Marcia, Eileen,
Kathy, Deirdre, Carol, Cyndy, Becky and Cathy*

The special women in our lives from whom we have
learned the meaning of friendship

And to each other

Contents

Foreword

Perhaps the most unusual and important thing about this wonderful book is that its authors do not pledge allegiance to any particular theoretical orientation. They are dedicated to the task of practical, effective patient care, and they take from any and all sources what they find to be useful to their project of formulating an integrated, comprehensive approach to psychotherapy with the wide range of patients who come for help.

In a way, the volume's title is almost misleading. By "object relations," Glickauf-Hughes and Wells don't intend merely to indicate a set of propositions deriving from the work of Klein, Winnicott, and so forth, but to underline that their conception of the therapeutic encounter is completely grounded in thinking about a relationship between two people, each of whom brings to the clinical situation his or her own wishes, fears, values, and theories about the world. And by speaking of "psychoanalytic treatment," Glickauf-Hughes and Wells certainly aren't invoking the orthodoxy all too often associated with that term; rather, they are acknowledging their use of certain fundamental perspectives, developed by Freud and his followers, that are by now generally well understood in our culture and brought to bear by clinicians across the board.

In keeping with this approach, Glickauf-Hughes and Wells offer a diagnostic scheme emphasizing attachment styles and based on the broad categories of "normal," "neurotic," "preneurotic," "borderline," and "psychotic" that is down-to-earth and phenomenological. Any experienced clinician will immediately recognize the distinctions drawn and will understand their relevance to common, crucial treatment decisions. The theoretical assumptions that underlie the authors' nosology are simple and explicit. What Glickauf-Hughes and Wells offer us is an innovative frame of reference for assessing psychopathology that is at once sensible and sophisticated. I need hardly mention that their diagnostic scheme is helpful to the clinician in his or her daily work in exactly the way that *DSM-IV*, say, is not.

The chapter on Treatment Contracts and Goals is, in my opinion, an invaluable contribution in and of itself. Glickauf-Hughes and Wells go right to the heart of what dooms so many psychotherapies from the outset. Their sections on impossible contracts, covert contracts, no contract, and on translating bad contracts into good contracts should be required reading in every training program for mental health care providers.

I won't go over in further detail the inventory of treasures to be found in the pages to follow, since the authors' introduction provides an excellent reader's guide, a kind of annotated table of contents. But I will note that— as one would expect, given the shrewd user-friendliness that is the cornerstone of the approach to psychotherapy taken by Glickauf-Hughes and Wells —they illustrate their ideas with evocative, cogent clinical examples at every turn. This is a very personal book. It's aimed at people who want to be helpful to other people, and it reaches its mark.

Owen Renik, M.D.

Acknowledgments

We would like to express special appreciation to Jason Aronson for his intelligence, warmth and wisdom in editing and publishing our work.

And, again, to George and Richard, for their continued support and faith in us, and their participation in the challenge and rewards of being lifelong partners.

Introduction

We are pleased to write this introduction to the second printing of our book. It has provided us with the opportunity to discuss the current trends in the field of mental health that are of particular concern to practitioners and to relate those concerns to the theories and techniques described in this book.

We are now in an era of accountability with a value on specificity and hard, scientific facts. Two particular trends in mental health have emerged from this zeitgeist.

The first trend is the increased emphasis on the biological basis of behavior. This includes (1) viewing the etiology of psychological problems (e.g., depression, obsessive-compulsive disorder) as biological; (2) the growth of neuropsychology with its focus on biologically based disorders, such as attention deficit disorder (ADD); and (3) the consequent increase in the use of psychotropic medications. The second trend is the advent of managed care and the proliferation of health management organizations (HMOs) and preferred provider organizations, which emphasize cost cutting and encourage treatment approaches such as brief psychotherapy and psychotropic medications.

As a result of both trends, many clinicians, especially those who specialize in long-term psychodynamic treatment, often feel like an endangered species. They experience significantly increased pressures to justify the use of psychotherapy, particularly long-term psychotherapy, as a legitimate means of treatment, even with patients whose chronic and severe characterological problems require this approach.

We suspect that many clinicians' current sense of insecurity may be exacerbated when they are not knowledgeable about the etiology and treatment for behavior disorders and are not facile at formulating diagnostically based treatment plans that clearly necessitate the use of long-term psychotherapy. Ironically, in order to succeed financially, competent clinicians whose gift is their use of intuition must develop some of the same skills required to be effective attorneys. We believe that the conceptual approach described in this book, if mastered, can facilitate this process.

We think that one reason for the current emphasis on biological aspects of behavior is the tendency in our culture to want a fast fix. It is reassuring to believe that if something is wrong with us, someone can fix it. Many people think that, apart from maladies such as AIDS and cancer, there is a specific, effective treatment for most physical symptoms or diseases. It is not widely known that in general medicine, only about 5 percent of problems brought to physicians are easily diagnosed and have a simple, effective cure. The remainder of the problems presented to doctors are nonspecific and if cured are usually done so by trial and error.

This principle is further exemplified in the field of psychopharmacology. Unlike the use of antibiotics for treating patients with streptococcus, the relationship between serotonin reuptake inhibitors (SRIs) and depression is not clearly understood. Many medications that are biochemically different facilitate the reuptake process of serotonin, thus alleviating depression. On average, patients try two SRIs before discovering one that reduces their symptomatology without causing excessive adverse side effects. Some patients need to experiment with as many as five or six. Furthermore, there are some medications prescribed for depression in which the mechanism that produces change is unexplained. Many of the psychiatrists with whom we have discussed this topic have expressed the belief that knowing which medication to prescribe to a patient for depression is somewhat of an art form (i.e., a decision based on an intuitive hunch rather than a precise scientific formula).

Clinical experience informs us that many patients who take SRIs without receiving effective psychotherapy aimed at changing underlying negative character traits (e.g., lack of relatedness to others, anxious attachment, a deficient sense of self) and reducing environmental stressors (e.g., remaining in abusive relationships or stressful jobs that lack intrinsic meaning) often find that SRIs begin to lose their initial effectiveness after a period of time. This phenomena is informally referred to as "Prozac poop-out." When this occurs, patients often begin to increase the dosage of their medication or switch to a new SRI in an often unsuccessful attempt to rekindle the medication's initial effectiveness.

More specifically, we have experienced SRIs providing many depressed patients with a window of opportunity in which they have increased internal strength to begin to change their lives and their negative character patterns. When SRIs are combined with psychotherapy, motivated patients are in an optimal position to benefit from the therapeutic relationship. Because they do not have a "bad feeling inside themselves," they are often less defensive and more likely to perceive and be impacted by the therapist's concern, have less shame about understanding their problems, and experience less separation anxiety about literally or emotionally leaving abusive or dysfunctional attachment relationships. Finally, supported by the therapeutic relationship, many patients are better able to internalize an accurate image of the therapist that can be used as a new good-enough internal object. Corrective real-world interactions with the therapist, coupled with mental interactions with the good-enough internalization of the therapist, can help these patients develop a healthier mental template about themselves and human relationships. They are thus less likely to repeat past relational traumas and are better able to make decisions leading to reparative human relationships.

Finally, disorders with a strong biological component such as ADD that have historically been treated by psychotropic medications such as Ritalin are now beginning to be viewed less simplistically. Current experts such as Sears and Thompson (1998) believe that what is referred to as ADD is a biologically based phenomenon that ranges from a challenging temperament to a neurobiological disorder or deficit. They think that even when psychotrophic medications are advised, they should be temporary and replaced as quickly as possible with interventions such as education and psychotherapy.

Thus, there seems to be a contemporary resurgence of the age-old nature–nurture controversy with a leaning in the direction of nature. We would thus like to clarify the philosophical assumptions in this area that underlie the theory that we have described in this book.

We propose that children are born with an innate temperament as well as other innate features of psychological importance (e.g., sexual identity development). We believe that to the extent that a child's nature is compatible with that of his or her parents and culture, the development of self is more likely to evolve as a relatively uneventful process. However, if there is a significant mismatch, there is a higher likelihood of the child developing a disorder of the self. In other words, the degree of parent–child "fit" and cultural fit is as important to the healthy development of the self as, for example, the lack of parental attunement to the child's needs (Winni-cott, 1965) or parents' facility at empathy and mirroring (Kohut, 1971, 1977).

For example, when the popular belief that gay men manifest a prepon-derance of narcissistic features was examined (Beard & Glickauf-Hughes, 1994), the authors maintained that if, in fact, this belief is true, then it is not the result of gay men having what Freud (1914) describes as primary narcissism or even the pressure to conform to a narcissistic gay subculture. Rather, sexual identity may be innate and related to gender-nonconform-ing behavior that occurs early in life. As gender-nonconforming behavior, particularly in boys, has been considered unacceptable in American cul-ture, the child is unlikely to receive sufficient acceptance, mirroring, and admiring of his true self, leading to narcissistic disturbances (Kohut, 1971; Miller, 1981; Winnicott, 1965).

The same may be true for ADD. Even if a child is impulsive and has low frustration tolerance and difficulty concentrating, the child's parents, teachers, and culture may be more or less effective at helping a child with ADD to mature. Thus, whether an individual develops a disorder or learns to channel his or her temperament into socially productive behavior (as did Albert Einstein and Franklin D. Roosevelt) may depend both on the temperamental fit between the child and the parents and on the parents' ability to teach the child how to constructively regulate his or her impulse patterns. Moreover, the quality of the parents' social support system is par-ticularly important in the process of raising psychologically healthy chil-dren.

It is beyond the scope of this book to discuss the relationships between innate temperament, parent–child fit, and implications for psychotherapy. Further theory and research in this area are needed for both prevention and treatment. For example, are individuals with regressive narcissistic characteristics more innately sensitive and perceptive, as Alice Miller (1981) maintains? Are obsessive-compulsive characteristics, in part, a learned approach for managing ADD?

In addition, we would like to address the impact of HMOs, which seem to be causing a crisis in medicine in general and in mental health in partic-ular. It has always been true that human resources are limited and that peo-ple compete for them. In primitive times, this process was obvious. In civilized society, where value is not placed on straightforward competition, self-interest is rationalized.

Unfortunately, psychologists who operate intuitively and employees of

HMOs who think in terms of treatment plans and cost-benefit analyses do not speak the same language. To survive economically, clinicians need to learn to be informed, articulate, and political in their transactions with HMOs. They must be able to discuss the treatment that a patient needs with HMO representatives in a clear and convincing manner, including what is likely to occur if the patient does not receive the recommended treatment (e.g., a psychotic break, suicide attempt, loss of employment, relationship breakup, chronic and severe depression, anxiety leading to increased physical illness). This enables health care providers to be more cognizant of the ethical, financial, and potentially legal issues involved if they refuse to authorize the treatment and the clinician's predictions transpire.

We believe that this book provides clinicians with an excellent model for making and documenting diagnoses, providing treatment plans that are clearly and specifically related to the patient's presenting problems and their underlying disorder and doing so in an operational, jargon-free manner that health care providers can understand. When this approach is used consistently, writing up treatment plans becomes second nature, and paperwork begins to require reasonable time and effort.

Finally, the issue of culture and object relations therapy warrants address. Object relations theories are culturally sensitive in that all of them are based on the premise that psychic structure depends on the internalization of the individual's relationships with significant others. The interpersonal environment, including cultural group values, are thus of central importance in an individual's psychic development. Furthermore, we believe that the interpersonal environment and the individual's innate or genetic constitution interact with the individual's own use of will to help form and maintain the individual's ongoing patterns of relating to self and others.

While culturally sensitive in their emphasis on internalization, it should be noted that the American object relations school of theories (e.g., Kernberg, Mahler, Kohut) can be criticized for being culture bound. Specifically, American object relations theories are based on Western culture's heterosexual, separation/individuation paradigm (Mahler, Pine, & Bergman, 1974), which promotes the primary goal of self-reliance. Consequently, the mental health goals of these theories, which reflect Western culture's idealization of rugged individualism, are incongruent with the values embraced by other cultures that emphasize collectivism or valuing the group's needs over the individual's. Moreover, feminist authors (e.g.,

Jordan, 1991) have argued that interdependence is a more appropriate goal for women, who tend to value the connectivity of friendship and family over individualism.

Interdependence as a general mental health goal also appears to be more congruent with our underlying value on mutuality, which permeates the therapeutic premises of this book. That is, we believe that therapists and their clients learn from one another, that neither has absolute authority over the truth, and that change occurs in the intersubjective learning space between therapist and client. Additionally, we believe that corrective relating experiences that are potentially healing and transformational for clients are not simply provided to a client by a therapist but are co-created by two participants exercising and allowing influence with one another.

We emphasize understanding the client's perceptions of his or her early and current interpersonal relationships and cultural environments and the client's coping or protective strategies as well as internal resources, including psychic structure, resilience, and motivation, for change. We believe that the mental health goal for any particular client needs to take into consideration the values held by that client, including those that reflect his or her unique personhood and cultural group identifications. For some minority clients, the ultimate mental health goal may not be initially clear as they struggle to reconcile bicultural or multicultural values. For example, one thirty-two-year-old Hispanic American client who lived with her husband at her parents' house exemplified the socially normative values of this pattern within the Hispanic culture. Both client and therapist assessed the situation in this case as unrelated to an inability to achieve a desirable level of separation/individuation.

In addition, we do not believe all women value interdependence over individualism and self-reliance. Nor do we believe all Caucasian, heterosexual men value self-reliance over interdependence. Understanding the client's value system and goals for change is paramount. However, so is helping clients appreciate their options so that they can make informed decisions about the direction they want to set for themselves. For example, clients with more self-defeating character structures may benefit from appreciating the cost to themselves of their self-sacrificing, other-oriented ways of relating in order to ensure relationships. Balancing self-interest with the interest of others may be an option. Thus, for these clients, interdependence may be a healthier goal than giving more than taking.

On the other hand, if the individual's cultural value system promotes self-esteem garnered through self-sacrifice for the benefit of the group (even at the expense of self-development) and the individual wishes to respect that value system, the goal of therapy needs to reflect that value and may change to helping the individual become a more effective contributor to the group. A more detailed discussion of cultural implications for object relations therapy is beyond the scope of this book but warrants serious consideration in applying the constructs discussed within the following pages.

Finally, while we will be presenting guidelines to help clinicians identify patterns of relating that can direct diagnostic efforts, therapists must continuously know when to let go of theory and listen for the unique personhood of the client. It is through the exploration and examination of the client's unique personhood in the intersubjective space surrounding the therapist and client that learning and healing, mutual understanding, and transformation occur.

In conclusion, while these are challenging times, the informed dynamic psychotherapist need not look for another vocation. Biological and environmental theories regarding the development of and treatment for psychopathology are rivals. When clinicians are informed about the uses for and limits of psychopharmacological treatment and the interaction of nature and nurture, an integrative treatment plan can be formulated that is more effective for patients than one approach alone.

Finally, a compelling argument can be made for long-term treatment if clinicians use diagnosis-centered models of treatment and can operationalize treatment plans and goals when communicating with representatives of HMOs and patients. When clinicians are also able to effectively execute these plans, we believe that they are likely to be successful in their work and no longer feel like an "endangered species." We believe that this book, which clearly relates diagnosis to treatment and which specifically outlines related treatment goals and methods, can be helpful in this process.

REFERENCES

Beard, J., & Glickauf-Hughes, C. (1994). Object relations and gay identity: Rethinking male homosexuality. *Journal of Gay and Lesbian Psychotherapy, 8,* 39–53.

Fairbairn, W. R. D. (1952). *An object relations theory of the personality.* New York: Basic Books. (Original work published 1941)

Freud, S. (1914). On narcissism: An introduction. *Standard Edition, 14,* 67–102.

Hallowell, E. M., & Ratey, J. J. (1994). *Driven to distraction: Recognizing and coping with attention deficit disorder from childhood through adulthood.* New York: Simon & Schuster.

Jordan, J. V. (1991). The meaning of mutuality. In J. V. Jordan, A. G. Kaplan, J. B. Miller, I. P. Stiver, & J. L. Surrey (Eds.), *Women's growth in connection* (pp. 81–96). New York: Guilford Press.

Kernberg, O. (1976). *Object relations theory and clinical psychoanalysis.* New York: Jason Aronson.

Kohut, H. (1971). *The analysis of the self.* New York: International Universities Press.

Kohut, H. (1977). *The restoration of the self.* New York: International Universities Press.

Mahler, M., Pine, F., & Bergman, A. (1974). *The psychological birth of the human infant.* New York: Basic Books.

Miller, A. (1981). *The drama of the gifted child.* New York: Basic Books.

Sears, W. & Thompson, L. (1998). *The A.D.D. Book.* Boston: Little, Brown.

Winnicott, D. W. (1965). *The maturational process and the facilitating environment.* New York: International Universities Press.

Object Relations Theories of Personality

This book should appeal to a wide range of readers, from analytically oriented therapists who are already familiar with object relations theory to those therapists who are less familiar with psychodynamic theories, in general, and with object relations theories in particular. This chapter defines object relations theory and the most commonly used terms, and introduces the reader to several of the most influential object relations theorists. The chapter provides readers with some basic conceptual tools to facilitate their understanding of the theory of object relations therapy outlined in the remainder of this book.

DEFINING OBJECT RELATIONS THEORY

In the broadest terms, object relations theories represent a psychoanalytic approach to studying and understanding the internalization of interpersonal relationships and its impact on behavior. More specifically, object relations theories have focused on the child's internalizations of early interactional patterns with his or her parents or primary caregivers (Kernberg

1975, 1980, Masterson 1996). The resulting intrapsychic template or mental map constructed in the mind of the child is composed of an image of the self in relation to internal objects. Internal object representations are primarily based on the individual's experience of caregivers from early childhood.

Object relations theories assume that if we know a person's mental template, we can better understand and predict the person's behavior in interpersonal relationships. The inner world of object relations determines in a fundamental way the individual's relationships with people in the external world. Object relations theory thus emphasizes understanding and modifying the patient's intrapsychic template (e.g., self and object representations and their related affects).

What underlies object relations theory is the assumption that the primary human motivation is to have relationships with other people rather than to gratify sexual and aggressive drives as is postulated in classical psychoanalytic theory. Reliance on the pleasure principle (i.e., drive gratification) is viewed by some object relations theorists as a substitute for relationships when real relationships become too depriving or abusive.

Humans are pack animals by nature who seek the intrinsic meaning in knowing and being known in a relationship. Sex is thus viewed by object relations theorists as one of many ways of relating to another person. Sullivan (1953) and Kohut (1971) believe that when people's satisfaction of sexual and aggressive impulses is their primary motivation and not related to a specific other (e.g., casual sex), it is an indication of psychopathology due to unsatisfying interpersonal relationships.

OBJECT RELATIONS TERMINOLOGY

The terminology associated with object relations theory has been criticized for being overly complicated and depersonalized. The interchangeability of terms (e.g., *self* and *ego*) as they are used by different object relations theorists is especially confusing. The language and complexity of object relations theory has thus deterred or offended many readers who otherwise would have been interested in the therapeutic applications of this approach, given its substantial contributions to understanding and treating patients with borderline, schizoid, and narcissistic disorders. Thus, before we introduce readers to theorists who have laid the foundation upon which our theory of object relations therapy is based, the most commonly used terms will be defined.

The Object

The term *libidinal object* was first coined by Freud (1915) and referred to that which satisfies a person's drives. Thus, the first object was thought to be the mother's breast. Freud (1926) believed that the particular object used to gratify the drive was of no particular importance. Human beings just happened to be a good, convenient source for drive gratification. However, while Harlow's (1958) wire monkeys should have been able to just as adequately serve the purpose of reducing oral drives as the mother, they were not.

Hamilton (1988) believes that many people feel somewhat offended by the term *object* in object relations theory as it feels too dehumanizing (i.e., why not say person if you mean person). The reason is that an *object is not always a person*. Rather, Hamilton describes an object as "a loved or hated person, place, thing or fantasy" (p. 5). For example, one patient was passionate about cars. He often had several cars, read about them, frequently thought about them, spent money that he did not have on them, and spent most of his free time washing, waxing, and polishing them. For this patient, cars were his primary love object. Other people's most significant object may be their pet, the city where they grew up or went to college, or their computer. This is why the term *object* is used in *object relations theory* rather than calling it *interpersonal relations theory*.

Part of what is confusing in object relations theory is that objects can be *internal* or *external* and many authors fail to clarify which type of object they are referring to. Internal objects are mental images. Thus, when we hear our parent's voice in our head, we are relating to an internal object. In contrast, external objects actually exist in the world.

Internal objects have several functions. They provide an ① anticipatory image of what other people expect from the person. For example, a patient with an internal object based on a narcissistic mother expected other people in her current life to be self-absorbed, demanding, and requiring solicitous and accommodating behavior from her.

Internal objects also provide individuals with a ② sense of moral values that they feel inspired to live up to. For example, a patient's father, whom he greatly respected, expected him to be honest and fair. Thus, in his business dealings with other people, he would remember his father talking to him about those principles and do his best to abide by them.

Good-enough internal objects provide a person with a sense of security. Thus, when one patient was anxious she remembered an image of her mother's warm face or her father's patient guidance and as a result felt much calmer.

In sum, objects may be good and bad, anxious or calm, exciting, rejecting, or gratifying, split or whole, and internal or external. What object relations theory attempts to explain is how an individual can simultaneously live
in a world of internal and external objects.

The Self

Several authors view the self as being initially based on one's *awareness of
bodily sensations.* Freud (1923) said that the self was first and foremost a "bodily
self" (p. 26) in that individuals gain an initial sense of their own existence
in the world through their awareness of sensations in their body. "The word,
self, has historically meant a body, [and] a bundle of perceptions in constant flux" (p. 9). Moore and Fine (1990) explain that an individual's self-
image is "the encoding of the self in a sensory (visual, auditory or tactile)
mode of thinking" (p. 174).

   Other theorists view the self as a *psychic structure.* Psychic structures are
the use of models or hypothetical constructs to explain enduring, organized,
and interrelated aspects of mental functioning (Moore and Fine 1990).
Piaget (1936) sees self-representations as enduring mental structures or
schemas. It generally takes a long period of time for an individual's self-
representations to develop (Jacobson 1964).

   Kohut (1971, 1977), who also viewed the self as a mental (i.e., psychic)
structure, defined the self as an *independent center of initiative.* Moore and Fine
(1990) agree and believe that the self includes an individual's ambitions,
ideals, talents, and skills. They believe that an individual's sense of self also
provides "a central purpose to the personality and . . . a sense of meaning
to the person's life" (p. 177).

   Moore and Fine (1990) also define the *self-concept* as *"the view one has of
oneself* at a particular time" (p. 174). Sullivan (1954) makes a distinction between the personality (i.e., how one is perceived by others) and the self (i.e.,
what one takes oneself to be). These two concepts are not entirely unrelated,
however, as what one takes oneself to be is highly influenced by how one is
perceived by others. Winnicott (1960) describes this phenomenon as the
difference between an individual's *true self* (i.e., the child's inherent dispositions and experience of sensory-based feelings and sensations) and the *false
self* (i.e., the self that perceives him- or herself as the parents viewed the child
and conforms to the parents' wishes).

   Object relations theorists maintain that there is no self without an other.
Thus, Winnicott (1965a) states that there is no such thing as a baby, only a
nursing couple. Likewise, Sullivan (1940) believed that a self "can never be

isolated from the complex of interpersonal relations from which the person lives and has his being" (p. 10).

Another important construct related to the self is *self constancy*. When individuals have a sense of self constancy, they experience themselves as having continuity in time and space (i.e., they experience themselves as more or less the same person today as yesterday). Thus, for example, individuals without a sense of self constancy might perceive themselves as being a very kind person one day and a selfish person on another day. In contrast, individuals with self constancy would experience themselves on both occasions as a generally giving person who sometimes gets needful, self absorbed, and less attuned to the needs of others.

Several other concepts were developed by Kohut (1971). The *nuclear self* is the nascent or beginning organization of the self during the first years of life. *Cohesion of the self* is the sense of primitive psychic glue that holds together an individual's discrete and unrelated experiences, enabling him or her to feel a coherent sense of self. This perception of the child as a unified self is initially provided by the parents who perceive their child's body, laughter, anger, hunger, temperament, preferences, and eye color as parts of a unified being. Through identifying with the parent's perceptions, the child begins to conceptualize his or her different attributes, feelings, and sensations as connected to one another and part of a whole integrated picture rather than as discrete entities (e.g., "My black hair, toes, feeling hungry, liking yellow, feeling angry, long legs, feeling joyful, and being active are all me").

Integration is the synthesis of discrete parts of the self. Early integration is between good and bad self experiences. Later integration is the conscious awareness of all the major aspects of a person's self experiences at one point in time that allows for a basic sense of identity. In contrast, *fragmentation* is the lack of simultaneous awareness of ego-dystonic (i.e., unacceptable) parts of the self and ego-syntonic (i.e, acceptable) parts of the self. For example, the "kind me" has difficulty acknowledging the existence of the "jealous me."

Object relations theorists attempt to define how a child develops a separate, autonomous sense of self in his or her relationships with other people. For example, Winnicott (1960) believes that a child develops a sense of self through the mother's attunement to the infant's needs and her nonimpingement on the infant when he or she is contented. Kohut (1971) thinks that the child develops a sense of self by being seen, heard, understood, and valued by the parents. The process of self-development is addressed in greater detail later in the chapter when the theories of Kohut (1971, 1977), Winnicott (1965a), and Mahler and colleagues (1975) are discussed.

Selfobject

Developmentally, the earliest object relations unit is a symbiotic selfobject where the distinction between self and object is not clear. The child's experience at this time is that "Mommy and I are one being." The concept of selfobject originated with Kohut (1971), who describes selfobjects as objectively separate people whom the child believes that he or she can use as though the object were an extension of his or her self. For the child, selfobjects don't exist in their own right. Rather, they serve several functions such as mirroring, empathy, and soothing that will later be performed by the individual's self. Kohut believes that the child merges with his or her selfobjects and experiences the selfobject's feelings (e.g., positive regard) as though they were his or her own. Kohut believes that the need for selfobjects is a normal part of development, that the infant needs (1) mirroring selfobjects to admire his or her evolving abilities, and (2) idealized selfobjects (i.e., an idealized image of a parent with which to identify).

Kohut thinks that when a child's selfobject needs are met adequately by parents, then the parents and their selfobject functions are internalized by the child. Other people are then related to as *whole objects* (i.e., autonomous beings with needs of their own). When individuals do not get these needs met adequately, they continue to overuse other people for their selfobject functions (e.g., narcissistic personalities). For example, one patient talked "at" the therapist as though she weren't there. Unless the therapist made a comment that was admiring or empathic, he interrupted the therapist. At the end of the session, the patient continued to bring up new topics (even when the therapist had told the patient twice that their time was up). This patient thus related to the therapist as someone without any needs or responsibilities other than to listen to and support him.

Overuse is a key term here, because Kohut also maintains that even individuals who have had adequate parenting in this regard never completely outgrow their needs for selfobjects. For example, this need is met to some extent by priests during confession. In such situations, the individual wants to feel soothed and absolved of guilt and is not usually thinking, "I wonder if the priest is getting tired. It must be hard sitting in that booth all day."

Transitional Object

Winnicott (1951) introduced the concept of a transitional object, which he defined in terms of a highly valued object (e.g., toy, blanket) to which the infant attributes the mother's caregiving functions. It may even have the mother's smell on it. The transitional object thus serves as a stimulus cue, helping the child recall the emotionally soothing behaviors or qualities of the mother. For example, one child had a stuffed rabbit for a transitional object that he called "Munny" (i.e., mommy-bunny).

Furthermore, transitional objects are neither self nor object but a space in between. An important aspect of a transitional object is that both the mother and the infant agree that it is under the infant's control as he once believed that his or her mother was.

Internalization

Internalization represents the process by which aspects of need-gratifying others (e.g., A. Freud, 1936, Hartmann 1950) are psychologically taken in and preserved as one of the patient's psychic structures (i.e., internal objects) or part of the individual's self representation. This can include three processes with varying degrees of maturity. They include incorporation, introjection, and identification.

Incorporation

Incorporation is the most primitive form of internalization. It is thus a global, undifferentiated, and literal experience that occurs before an individual has established a selfother boundary. Incorporation implies a sense of psychological eating, swallowing, or oral ingestion. Thus, one of the authors observed that her 6-month-old son (who previously only ate her hair and chewed her fingers) began to attempt to eat her face (i.e., mouth, nose, and cheeks). Furthermore, he did this most often after a separation. However, incorporation does not completely disappear after infancy. For example, a form of incorporation for normal individuals is the Catholic tradition of eating the wine and wafer and thus symbolically ingesting the blood and body of Christ. However, incorporation is more often seen in more troubled patients. It is generally manifested in dreams and regressed states.

Introjection

Introjection is generally regarded as a more differentiated and less primitive process than incorporation as it lacks the implication of potential destruction of the object through ingestion that incorporation entails. There is controversy, however, among different theorists about the relative degree of primitiveness of this process.

For example, Kernberg (1976, 1984) defines introjection in terms of the earliest most primitive level of internalization. In contrast, Moore and Fine (1990) believe that introjection is a more differentiated and less primitive process than incorporation. Hamilton (1988) also believes that "when introjection supplants incorporation, self and object images are somewhat internally differentiated so the internalized object can be held as an object-image rather than merged with the self-image" (p. 69). Sandler and Rosenblatt (1962) believe that when an object is introjected, the internalized object has sufficient power in the internal world to be taken in and held intact, rather than devoured. An example of an introject is what the personality theory called transactional analysis refers to as "the parent" (i.e., an internal representation of the parent in the individual's mind that guides and, at times, praises or criticizes the individual). Finally, in introjection "the internal object introjected does not correspond exactly to the external object, but is colored by projections onto the external object before it is introjected" (Hamilton, p. 70).

Identification

Identification is regarded as a developmentally advanced form of internalization, which reflects the individual's cognitive ability to recognize the role aspects of interpersonal interactions (Kernberg 1976). The process of identification includes (1) the image of the object adopting a role in interaction with the self, (2) the image of the self more clearly differentiated from the object than in introjection, and (3) a more modulated emotional experience during the interaction. For example, the child builds up memory traces of her mother assuming the role of protective and concerned instructor in helping her to dress herself. The image of child and mother is differentiated and the affect is one of excitement and pride as the child acquires more mastery over the task. The child identifies with the mother's caregiving role, learning to care for his or her self as the mother does.

What is most important in the process of identification is that the object is not swallowed whole as it is in introjection. Rather, particular aspects of the object are internalized as part of the self and eventually the association with the object may even disappear.

For example, an individual admires a jacket worn by someone whom he respects, and he looks for a similar jacket for himself. He tries it on, feels attractive in it, and decides to buy it. He has a feeling of confidence when he wears this jacket due to its association with the original owner. Years later, he thinks of this type of jacket as representative of his style of dressing. By now, he has forgotten where he first saw the jacket (John Nardo, personal communication).

Object Relations Unit

An object relations unit is an enduring mental template or schema that represents the internalization of the child's relationships with significant others. This unit consists of a self representation and an object representation, linked together by the predominant emotion that characterized the child's original interactions with objects (Masterson 1996).

For example, an *all-bad object relations unit* is bad self hates bad object (e.g., like a hungry, unfed infant). An *all-good object relations unit* is good self loves good object (e.g., like a fed, soothed, contented infant). These two templates are common in personality types at the borderline level of ego and object relations development (e.g., schizoid, hysteroid).

A *devalued object relations unit* is good self devalues bad object (e.g., "I am wonderful and you are contemptible"). An *idealized object relations unit* is bad self admires good object (e.g., "Humble or contemptible me greatly admires extraordinary you"). These two templates are common in the narcissistic personality disorder.

Object relations units develop and become more clearly articulated with the individual's continuous experiences in relationships with other people. Thus, the object relations template of one patient was "bad, narcissistic men seduce, use, and hurt helpless women." This template was based on her father's behavior toward both her and her mother, and her tendency to date narcissistic boys as an adolescent. This template then became the template through which she viewed and interpreted the behavior of all men.

Ego

The *ego* is a confusing term in psychoanalytic theory as Freud originally used it to mean *the self* as well as a psychic structure that has *a set of mental functions* that mediates between the individual's drives, conscience, and reality (i.e., "the system ego"). In modern usage, the term usually refers to Freud's (1923) redefinition of the *system ego* (i.e., mental functions). However, various theorists, as will be seen in the latter part of the chapter, still use this term inconsistently. In this book, we will refer to the ego according to Freud's (1923) definition, and when other theorists are using it differently we will indicate that this is occurring. In discussing Fairbairn, for example, when we refer to the libidinal ego, we will bracket it (i.e., the needful self).

We begin our definition of the ego by quoting Gregory Hamilton (1988) because of his particular ability to express complex phenomena clearly:

> The ego cannot be experienced subjectively. The ego perceives, integrates, thinks, and acts. It is central to our personalities, yet unknowable. Its functions can be measured and observed from the outside but it can never be known (i.e., experienced by the self) firsthand. During introspection, the ego remains the observer (not) the observed. . . . [The] ego can never be known subjectively, because it is not a person, place, thing, idea or fantasy. The ego is an abstraction denoting a set of functions. [p. 21]

Hartmann (1939, 1950) describes the ego as an organizer or a system. Hartmann (1964) believes that further knowledge about ego functions would provide the eventual link between psychology and biology. Thus, one of our colleagues in neuropsychology has speculated that there may be a relationship between the ego and the frontal lobes of the brain.

Thus, the ego is defined here as a set of functions, the main purpose of which is to achieve optimal emotional gratification while maintaining a good relationship with the superego (i.e., the conscience) and the external world. Ego functions include (1) defense mechanisms (e.g., intellectualization, rationalization, repression, reaction formation); (2) autonomous functions (e.g., intelligence, perception, intention, speech, thinking); (3) adaptive functions (e.g., reality testing, impulse control, frustration tolerance); and (4) the psychic mapping of self and object representations.

Good-Enough Mother

Winnicott (1958b, 1965a) introduced the terms *good-enough mother, primary maternal preoccupation,* and *average expectable environment.* The concept of the good-enough mother refers to a maternal caregiver who offers a holding (i.e., protective) environment attuned to the baby's evolving needs. Through primary maternal preoccupation, or the mother's devotion to her infant and the creation of an average expectable environment, the good-enough mother provides an optimal (although not perfect) amount of consistency, responsiveness, nurturing, and comfort for the infant who is wholly dependent on her.

Thus, when the infant cries, the good-enough mother is intensely attuned to the infant's nonverbal behaviors for clues about what the infant needs. Through trial and error, she eventually soothes or gratifies the infant. In the future, she recognizes what the infant needs from remembering what his or her particular nonverbal behaviors generally meant in the past. On some occasions the mother is too tired to attend to the infant, unavailable or unable to determine what the infant needs. Winnicott believes that these disappointing times are nonproblematic as long as the mother meets the child's needs with sufficient regularity.

Holding Environment

During early childhood, the mother creates a holding environment by availing herself and organizing the setting so the infant feels secure, protected, and not excessively frustrated. The holding environment might be the mother's good-enough soothing of the child or literally organizing the environment (e.g., "baby proofing" the child's room to provide safety and optimal frustration). The holding environment provides sufficient security so that after a while the infant is able to tolerate the inevitable failures of empathy or excessive frustration that result in rage and terror when the holding is lost. The holding environment prepares the infant for later phases of development. The holding environment also refers to the nonspecific, consistent, empathically attuned, and supportive environment provided by the therapist (Modell 1968, Winnicott 1965a).

Containment

Bion (1962, 1967, 1970) discusses the importance of the mother's bearing the infant's anxiety and frustration so that her child feels contained. By identifying with and introjecting the mother's tolerance of his or her anxiety, the infant learns to contain (i.e., tolerate, rather than act out) these feelings in him- or herself. In Bion's concept of containment, projective processes are not damaging to the mother (i.e., the mother is not hurt by experiencing the infant's emotions), and introjective processes are growth promoting for the child (i.e., the mother's calm response to the infant's frustration is internalized by the infant who learns to become less frustrated over time) (Glickauf-Hughes and Cummings 1995).

An example of containment is soothing an infant who is screaming uncontrollably at night because he or she is overstimulated, frustrated, and unable to eat or sleep. When the mother approaches the infant with a bottle to feed him or her, the infant kicks the mother and bangs his or her head. In such instances, the mother may swaddle the infant in a blanket (so that he or she cannot hurt the mother or him- or herself). The mother may then rock and sing to the infant, and even attempt to feed the infant again until he or she falls asleep. In such instances, it is important for the mother not to personalize the infant's behavior (e.g., believe that she is a bad mother) and to soothe herself during this process.

Object Constancy

This concept, introduced by Hartmann (1952), refers to the capacity to maintain a predominantly positive emotional connection to a significant other independent of one's need state or the object's immediate ability to gratify one's needs. Object constancy requires several developmental achievements, including (1) object permanence (i.e., the cognitive ability to remember the object's existence when it is out of sight); (2) evocative memory (i.e., the ability to have an emotional memory of the object, particularly a positive emotional memory); (3) the ability to differentiate oneself from the other; and (4) the ability to integrate good and bad aspects of oneself and the other. Mahler (1968) notes: "By object constancy we mean that the maternal image has become intrapsychically available to the child in the same way as the actual mother had been available—for sustenance, comfort, and love" (p. 222).

With the establishment of object constancy, the relationship between mother and child becomes more stable and durable and persists despite frustrating experiences.

A female patient with a secure sense of object constancy was laid off from her job and was understandably distressed. She called her partner to talk with him and get his support. However, as he was out of town, she had difficulty reaching him. While the patient was disappointed, she was able to emotionally recall the many times in the past when he was consoling to her and thus maintained a predominantly loving internal image of him. Furthermore, she began to soothe herself in the way that both he and other people with whom she had good-enough relationships had done for her in the past (i.e., cry, empathize with how she felt, do soothing activities, and reassure herself that she had an excellent employment history and would most likely not remain unemployed for long).

When an individual has mastered the task of object constancy, his or her interactions with others are described as *whole object relations*. In whole object relations, other people are perceived in a realistic manner and are loved and accepted even when they have needs of their own that preclude them from being emotionally available at times.

Transmuting Internalizations

This term was introduced by Kohut (1971) and represents the process by which an individual gradually internalizes the selfobject's functions (e.g., empathy, admiring, mirroring, soothing, being an auxiliary ego). Thus, something that was once attributed to an object becomes a part of the self. This is different from the process of incorporation in which the object is internalized but experienced as an internal object that is separate from the self.

The process of making transmuting internalizations of the object's functions is facilitated by optimal, nontraumatic frustrations that induce the individual to do for the self what the mother has previously done for the child because the mother is either unavailable or currently unempathic. Thus, with sufficient internalizations of good-enough objects the self is able to perform vital selfobject functions such as empathy, soothing, gaining perspective in the object's absence. Thus, at the beginning of treatment, one patient was unable to empathize with himself. Over time, he introjected the therapist and would imagine what the therapist would say to him when he was unhappy. Eventually, he identified with the therapist and began to empathize with himself without calling to mind the image of the therapist.

Projection

Projection is a defense mechanism whereby an unacceptable and/or intolerable impulse, feeling, or thought is externalized and attributed to others. For example, one patient from a fundamentalist religious background repeatedly told her analyst that she knew that he wanted to ask her probing sexual questions as "that's how psychoanalysts are." He responded by telling the patient that "it seems as though when we're together, the topic of sex keeps coming up" (Steven Levy, personal communication). A particularly malignant form of projection is the experience of prejudice. In prejudice, an individual or group projects an ego-dystonic aspect of him- or herself onto an entire group. Projection is a common phenomenon and can range from normal to pathological forms.

Projective Identification

Projective identification is a defense mechanism introduced by Melanie Klein (1952a,b, 1957) and elaborated upon by Thomas Ogden (1982) and Otto Kernberg (Kernberg et al. 1989). Projective identification is a three-step mental process whereby the individual (1) projects an unwanted or intolerable aspect of the self or a bad internal object *onto* the other person; (2) behaves toward the object in such a way as to induce the feelings or thoughts *in* the other person that correspond with the projection (i.e., the object is induced to experience or enact the individual's own feelings or mental images); and (3) unconsciously identifies with the object's response as a potential model for managing the ego-dystonic (i.e., unacceptable) projected experience.

Defensive purposes of projective identification include (1) fusion with the external object to avoid separation; (2) control of the bad, persecutory object that is experienced as a threat to the individual; and (3) preservation of good portions of the self by splitting off the bad parts of the self, projecting them into the object (e.g., the therapist) for "safe keeping" (Moore and Fine 1990, p. 109).

> One patient projected onto the therapist her unacceptable feelings of inadequacy, shame, and helplessness that she acquired from being raised by a cold, contemptuous mother. She then treated the therapist as if the therapist were stupid and incompetent. Each time the therapist offered an intervention or response, the patient would roll her eyes like her mother had done to her, and make a devaluing comment under her breath. The patient's behavior induced a feeling state in the therapist that was very similar to the patient's ego-dystonic experience. At other times, the patient projected her contemptuous mother onto the therapist. She then behaved toward the therapist in such a way (i.e., coming late, whining, interrupting, repeating the same thing several times, accidentally breaking a piece of the therapist's pottery) that the therapist noticed that she was feeling a proclivity to behave in a contemptuous, rejecting manner toward the patient (as her mother did).

Repression

Repression is considered to be a neurotic or higher level defense mechanism. Higher level defenses are those that distort reality to a lesser degree and/or cause the individual fewer problems in his or her interpersonal relationships. In repression, an aspect of a patient's experience (e.g., a memory or a feeling) is excluded from consciousness (e.g., the birth of a sibling when the individual was 6 years old). Repression is sometimes referred to as unconsciously motivated forgetting. In repression one banishes part of one's experience to the unconscious. In denial, one semiconsciously and actively negates the existence of an experience (e.g., "I'm not jealous of this baby"), whereas in repression one simply does not remember.

Splitting

The splitting defense functions to keep contradictory, primitive affect states separated from each other. For example, splitting actively keeps apart the experiences of hating and loving the same person. Both states remain conscious (at different points in time), but they do not influence one another. It also keeps apart the internalized self and object representations that are linked with these affective states. Masterson (1996), Kernberg (1980), and Mahler and colleagues (1975) believe that splitting is normally present until the end of the separation-individuation stage of development, when it is replaced by repression.

A session with a paranoid patient whom the therapist had been treating for six months exemplifies the use of defensive splitting.

Throughout treatment, the therapist had never been late for an appointment. On one occasion, due to a misunderstanding about a change in the therapist's schedule, the therapist arrived 15 minutes later than the patient had expected. Until this incident, the patient had never expressed feelings of anger toward the therapist. On this occasion, however, the patient was completely enraged and told the therapist, "How can I ever trust anyone in the world if even my therapist is late for our appointment." During this interaction, the patient experienced herself, the therapist, and all objects as bad and was unable to emotionally recall previous occasions when she trusted the therapist and believed that she was dependable.

Psychic Structures

The concept of psychic structure refers to the enduring mental patterns or schemas that may be inferred from an individual's behavior and the analysis of his or her thoughts, feelings, and mental images as inferred from the individual's verbalizations. These structures develop through the internalizations of early relationships, learning processes, and the resolution of developmental conflicts. Typical structures include (1) the self representation, (2) the object representation, (3) the ego, and (4) the superego.

When we talk about how psychic structures develop, we mean how individuals organize the world into meaningful patterns for themselves. These patterns or schemas evolve over the first three to four years of life and are the basis for enduring mental configurations. In healthy development, these structures continue throughout life to be modified by experience. In pathological development, they are organized early on in a rigid and distorting manner that results in a fixation in the development of certain aspects of feeling, thinking, and behaving.

Therapeutic Alliance

The therapeutic alliance refers to the collaborative working relationship between the therapist and the patient and is evidenced by the patient's feelings of liking, trust, and respect for the therapist, and his or her commitment to the therapeutic process (Greenson 1967). The therapeutic alliance is differentiated from positive transference (i.e., the projection of good objects onto the therapist by the more childlike part of the patient). The therapeutic alliance represents the real (rather than wished for) relationship between the therapist and the more mature, self-observing part of the patient who has agreed to work with the therapist as a team to facilitate the patient's improvement. Zetzel (1956) thinks that the existence of a therapeutic alliance is dependent on the patient's maturity level and the integration of his or her ego functions. Thus, patients who have difficulty with neutral, self observing capacities will have difficulties in establishing an alliance with the therapist.

An example of a therapeutic alliance is illustrated in a session with a patient who felt extremely angry at the therapist as she had experienced the therapist as critical of her in the last session. As they went over the patient's recollections of the session, the patient began to realize that she had misunderstood the therapist's intent. She also realized how easy it was to feel criticized when she believed that she wasn't perfect due to her father's criticism of her when she failed to live up to his extremely high standards. Thus, the objective part of the patient was able to collaborate with the therapist in understanding her transference feelings toward the therapist.

The concept of the therapeutic alliance is debated frequently in the psychoanalytic literature (Brenner 1959). Objections to the term are most often found among traditional analysts who contend that distinguishing between the therapeutic alliance and transference is unnecessary, difficult, and perhaps impossible. Meissner (1992) believes that accepting a portion of the therapeutic relationship as reality based may protect therapist and patient from understanding the patient's unconscious fantasies and conflicts toward the therapist.

Transference

Transference represents a type of object relationship whereby patients displace and project onto the therapist their feelings and perceptions of important people from their childhood. For example, on one occasion the therapist rubbed her eyes (which were irritated from an allergy). The patient became angry at the therapist as he interpreted her behavior as boredom and inattentiveness (frequent behaviors of his mother). Freud (1905) viewed transference as a repetition of an old object relationship. Transference is largely a semi- or unconscious phenomenon. However, as demonstrated in the example in the previous section, with help from the therapist the higher functioning patient can differentiate the independent reality of the therapist as a separate person from the projected transference.

Transference is a type of stimulus generalization. It occurs with neurotics, psychotics, and healthy people, and does not only occur with the therapist but with other objects in the individual's life (Greenson 1967). All human relationships are a mixture of reality and transference (Fenichel 1941). What Freud (1912) thought was particularly important about a patient's transference reactions was that they offered the analyst an invaluable opportunity to understand the patient's inaccessible past.

Transference Acting Out

Freud (1914) and Fenichel (1945) believed that transference acting out were patients' attempts at wish fulfillment. Under this condition the patient directs feelings, thoughts, and desires onto the therapist that are really directed toward important objects from the patient's childhood. However, the patient is not able to differentiate these projections from the independent reality of the therapist. The patient thus behaves toward the therapist as if he or she were the projected object (usually a parent).

Transference acting out can be negative as well as positive. Greenson (1967) believes that negative acting out stems from underlying impulses of hatred and are often seen in perversions, impulse ridden characters, and borderlines. Anna Freud (1936) saw transference acting out as a type of resistance in which the patient repeats and relives a situation with the therapist as a defense against emotional involvement.

One patient physically cringed and said, in a panic, "Don't be mad," every time she voiced an opinion she thought the therapist would disapprove of. She canceled several sessions because she believed that the therapist was going to be very angry with her. She projected an image of her father onto the therapist, who used to take her to the garage and beat her with a stick whenever she "sassed him back" by speaking her mind. She could not directly tell the therapist about her feelings toward her father, but she could tell the therapist her story by acting it out with her.

OBJECT RELATIONS THEORISTS

Object relations theories do not represent a unified or integrated body of work, but rather a general area of evolving analytic thinking proposed by a number of psychoanalytically informed theorists who postulated that individuals were primarily motivated to have relationships with other people rather than to gratify their instinctual drives (as Freud had believed). These theorists were particularly interested in understanding how an individual's mental representations of self and others become enduring psychic structures. While object relations theorists at times use many of the terms of the classical psychoanalytic tradition, they all give particular emphasis to the study of object relations as opposed to instinctual drives.

We now present a brief summary of some of the most prominent theorists who have contributed to the development of object relations theory. This movement has its genesis in the later writings of Freud, and has continued to evolve through the British object relations school (e.g., Klein, Fairbairn, Guntrip, and Winnicott), the American object relations school (e.g., Mahler, Kernberg, and Kohut), and the American interpersonal movement (e.g., Sullivan). This background should help the reader unfamiliar with the evolution of object relations theory to better understand the models for psychotherapy and differential diagnosis presented in Chapters 2 and 3 and the descriptions of how to apply this model of treatment to working with the six different personality disorders described in later chapters.

Sigmund Freud: The Beginnings of an Object Relations Theory

Late in his career, Freud (1923) developed the beginnings of an object relations theory that has received much less attention than his drive theory. In these later writings he described how, following the loss of someone important to them, people often regress. In their suffering, they continue to seek a relationship with the lost person by assuming characteristics of the person. The grieving person does this, in part, by internalizing the lost person's image and relating to this now internal object as if it were the actual person. The introject is then treated as though it were the abandoned object. The individual may even reproach him- or herself as the lost object once reproached him or her.

In addition to introjecting the object, the grieving individual may identify with the object's characteristics, thus making the lost object a part of the self. By assuming the qualities or characteristics of the lost object, individuals retain their relationship with that object. Freud (1923) noted that the ego was, in fact, "the repository of abandoned objects," by which he meant that the ego internalizes the image of the lost object and assimilates its qualities through the process of identification. Identification thus becomes the substitute for object cathexes (St. Clair 1996).

For example, one patient who lost her mother at age 13 unconsciously assumed her mother's mannerisms and loquaciousness as a way of remaining close to her mother. Identification with her lost mother replaced the actual object relationship. In another way of describing this phenomenon, Freud (1921) noted that the idea of "I no longer have that dear friend" is replaced by the notion that "I am that friend, and I direct toward myself all the disappointment and anger I feel because of the friend's leaving" (p. 106).

British School of Object Relations

Melanie Klein: The Foundation of Object Relations Theory

Melanie Klein is credited with laying the foundation for the British object relations school. Although she presented her theories as simple extensions of Freud's original work, her ideas were sufficiently innovative (e.g., drives were relational) to split the British Psychoanalytic Society. She has thus emerged as "a key transitional figure between [Freud's] drive/structure model and the relational/structure model" (Greenberg and Mitchell 1983, p. 121) of object relations theory.

In her work, Klein wrote about the inferences that she made from her clinical observations of children. While Klein's writing is highly speculative and replete with technical jargon, it is also innovative and revolutionary in (1) emphasizing that sexual and aggressive drives in the form of passionate love and hate were always connected to objects, (2) proposing that infants actually formulated object relations during the preoedipal period (i.e., during the first few years of life), (3) extending Freud's concepts of fantasy and "internal objects," and (4) generating rich concepts such as projective identification and splitting.

Klein proposed several important revisions to Freud's classical drive theory, the most significant of these being her notion that instincts are intrinsically connected with objects. Mitchell and Greenberg (1983) believe that the revolutionary part of Klein's thinking was that individuals' drives are directed toward having object relationships. Klein (1952b) thus revised Freud's classic propositions that instincts or drives were originally objectless (e.g., the infant seeks pleasure in being fed) and objects merely served as vehicles to reduce tensions. Instead, she believed that every impulse was related to an object, albeit a part object (e.g., mother's breast) in the beginning because the infant's perceptual skills were so immature.

On the basis of her observational studies, Klein inferred that object relations were structured very early in the child's development. She thus moved the focus of inquiry in the understanding of patients from the oedipal period (which Freud believed to be the most significant period of development and personality formulation) to the preoedipal period. She emphasized (1) the infant's tendency to relate to part-objects (especially the mother's breast); (2) the active, innate nature of the infant's fantasy life; and (3) the role of defense mechanisms such as projection and introjection in establishing the infant's inner world of object relations.

Klein hypothesized that the infant's initial objects consisted of primitive feelings and innate images (e.g., the good and bad breast) that were projected onto the external object (i.e., the infant's real mother). Klein's concept of innate internal images resembles a more primitive version of Jung's concept of archetypes. After projecting these images on his or her mother, the infant reintrojects them. However, they are now modified by the external object's behavior (Grotstein 1982). For example, if the infant projects the bad breast onto the mother and the mother is warm and gratifying to the infant, the reintrojected image will be less harsh.

Introjection thus enables infants to formulate a mental map of the relationship of the self to the object. This map synthesizes (1) the infant's feelings and innate mental images that are projected onto the external world of real objects; and (2) the internalization of the original projected object (innate mental image), which is now modified by the parent's actual behavior. Klein (1948) thought that the infant's internal objects were an amalgam of the infant's projections and internalized real objects.

Paranoid-Schizoid and Depressive Positions

As a result of her observations and writings, Klein (1935) proposed two developmental positions, the paranoid-schizoid position and the depressive position. The movement from one position or developmental stage to the other was characterized by the infant's movement from relating to part-objects in the first four to five months of life to relating to whole objects. For example, the shift would go from valuing people for their part object functions, like a breast that provides needed milk, to appreciating people as whole objects or individuals with value beyond their ability to gratify needs (i.e., for their personal qualities, values, and attributes).

The *paranoid-schizoid* position is characterized by destructive impulses, fears of being destroyed, and persecutory anxieties. The primary goal of this position is to protect the self. What are sacrificed are good relationships with others. Defenses utilized during this period are thus aimed at self protection and include splitting, projection, and projective identification. During this phase the infant has violent fantasies of destruction and envy toward the good object (e.g., mother's breast), wishing to suck it dry, thus stealing its good contents and making it a part of the self (and, therefore, under the infant's control). The infant's aggression, like his or her love, is innate and unmodified at this stage of development.

According to Klein, the *depressive position* begins with the integration of object relations (i.e., object constancy) at approximately the fifth month of life. At this time the infant recognizes that the loved object is external to the self and begins to realize that the object that he or she loves is the same object that he or she hates. The infant now feels anxious, guilty, and depressed that the love object is endangered or hurt by the infant's own aggressive fantasies. Guilt over previous aggression toward the loved object turns to desires for reparation of the object. Klein suggested that "the infantile depressive position is the central position in the child's development" (1935, p. 310). Klein further suggested that we never fully overcome it, as we "remain concerned for the fate of our objects in the face of our own conflictual feelings throughout our lives" (Greenberg and Mitchell 1983, p. 126).

During the depressive position, the individual's primary goal is to maintain a relationship to the object. What is sacrificed in order to maintain this goal is the individual's self and self-esteem. Thus, the defenses used to accomplish this purpose are introjection, rationalization, and denial of the object's negative characteristics.

Envy

Another important contribution of Klein's is her focus on the concept of envy, which has offered substantial explanatory power to Freud's "negative therapeutic reaction" (patients who get angry at the therapist or regress as a result of the therapist making an accurate intervention). While Freud attributed the negative therapeutic reaction to the patient's unconscious guilt (i.e., "I don't deserve to get better"), Klein believed that some patients hated and wished to spoil the good object because that goodness, like mother's milk, is not completely accessible to them (i.e., in their control). The patient enacts this same pattern with other people in his or her life.

> One patient admired and envied his professor. He wanted to do research with him and when he had not had the opportunity to do so during his first year, he told the professor about his feelings of disappointment. The professor responded immediately to his request and invited him to join one or both of two research projects. The patient impolitely rejected the professor's offer because, like the infant, the "milk" (i.e., opportunity to collaborate with the professor) was under the professor's control. The patient, thus, felt compelled to spoil the milk (i.e., research activities) and the good but envied professor.

The envious patient, like the infant, thus resents the therapist's (i.e., maternal object's) control over the good supplies (e.g., soothing, nurturance, effectiveness), which seem doled out at the therapist's pace and not under the patient's control. It seems to the patient that the therapist is hoarding the good supplies for his or her own purposes. Thus, the envious patient resists treatment as a way of spoiling the therapist's powers.

The envious patient turns each interpretation into something useless or hurtful because the sense of hope with its inherent risk of disappointment, loss, and rejection is viewed as too painful and thus intolerable. To help resolve the envious patient's malicious and spiteful sabotaging of the therapy, the therapist must interpret the envy itself (Greenberg and Mitchell 1983).

However, while Klein was the first psychoanalytic theorist who believed that drives were object related, she also thought that psychopathology was primarily determined by the child's own aggression when the child's aggression is not modified by the nurturance or care of the child's real parents. Klein generally minimized how the strengths or deficits in the parents' personalities and their consequent behavior toward the child could affect the child's images of people and relationships. Parents were important as universal representatives (e.g., mother with breasts), stimulus cues for the infant's fantasies, projections, splitting, reparative strivings. "Character, for Klein, is constituted by phantasies concerning internal objects, derived from the inherent object-relatedness of love and hate" (Greenberg and Mitchell 1983, p. 150).

For Klein, the dangers of the human psyche reside within. The child's innately derived inner world of fantasy and aggression creates bad objects. Parental care may transform these bad objects into "more benign, whole objects" (Greenberg and Mitchell 1983, p. 146) but the child's own aggression is viewed as being more impactful than the parental environment. It was not until Fairbairn and Winnicott (who were less encumbered by loyalty to the drive/structure model) that the child's responses to the real behavior of his or her parents were emphasized (Greenberg and Mitchell 1983).

In summary, Klein proposed that (1) the primary motivation of development is the need for relationships rather than instinctual discharge; (2) drives represent an innate desire for nurturing contact with objects; (3) object relations exist from birth; (4) the greatest weight in the development of psychic structures is given to the infants' innate aggression, and use of fantasy, introjection, and projection; (5) the focus of therapeutic inquiry be shifted from the oedipal to the preoedipal period; and (6) the two basic developmental hurdles facing all infants (and adult patients) are represented by the schizoid-paranoid and the depressive positions.

Major Criticisms

While Klein's contributions to laying the foundation for the British object relations school are impressive, she has been soundly criticized on a number of accounts (Brody 1982, Jacobson 1964, Kernberg 1980). Major criticisms include (1) overemphasizing constitutional (i.e., innate aggression or innate images of bad objects) versus environmental factors (e.g., parent's behavior toward the child); (2) having an accelerated developmental timetable (she attributes cognitive processes to young infants that they are incapable of having due to their level of neurological development); (3) her use of odd terminology (e.g., phantasies); and (4) her recommendation to make deep interpretations early in treatment. Klein's work has also been criticized as being highly speculative and inferential, and overattributing to infants the thoughts and motives of older children.

Implications for Treatment

Implications for therapy based on Klein's ideas include (1) alleviating unresolved depressive and paranoid anxieties by analyzing the transferences
as they develop (e.g., "You feel frightened when you feel angry at me because you're afraid that your anger will somehow hurt me. Do you remember feeling that way with your mother?"); and (2) connecting current fantasy and feeling patterns with the patient's earliest object relations. One
patient had shared with the therapist her fantasy about eating up the therapist like a bowl of ice-cream. The therapist responded that she thought the
patient wished to keep the therapist inside her so that she'd have her there
whenever she needed her.

W. R. D. Fairbairn: A Pure Object Relations Model

In a series of papers written during the 1940s, Fairbairn developed a theoretical perspective that has provided the purest and clearest expression of
the shift from Freud's drive theory to a purely relational model (Greenberg
and Mitchell 1983). Unlike Klein who worked with infants and children in
London, Fairbairn worked in Edinburgh, Scotland with adolescent and adult
patients, many of whom had been exposed to excessively barren and harsh
childhoods. While Klein built her theory on the observations of children,
Fairbairn, like Freud, built his theory on the retrospective reports of his adult
patients. Even more than Klein, Fairbairn's overall contribution lies in his
efforts to describe the period of infancy and early childhood during which
internalized object relations foster self development. In Fairbairn's model,
the role of instinctual drives such as sex and aggression is replaced by the
need for relationships with others, both real and imaginary. Fairbairn believes that the individual's personality is derived from internal mental representations of interactions with real other people. Psychopathology is thus
attributed to unsatisfying (i.e., overly depriving) relationships with others.
    While Fairbairn was influenced by Klein, his own ideas, based predomi-
nately on his work with adolescent children of alcoholics and schizoid adult
patients, were independent and original. He elaborated upon many of the
concepts that Klein implied but, unlike Klein, he explicitly departed from
Freud, wholly rejecting Freudian drive theory. For Fairbairn, the ego (i.e.,
self) is object-seeking, and having satisfying relationships with others (not
gratifying sexual and aggressive drives) is people's main motivation.
    Fairbairn believes that children seek relationships with external real ob-
jects. If these relationships are predominantly satisfactory, presumably the

individual's ego (i.e., self) remains integrated. When external objects are excessively unsatisfying, frustrating, or abusive, however, children split the bad object into two bad objects (i.e., the *exciting object* that entices but does not gratify and the *rejecting object*) and one good object (i.e., the *ideal object*). To feel some sense of control over these objects, the individual internalizes them.

Fairbairn also believes that the object is inextricably tied to the self. Thus, when the object is split, so is the individual's self. The ego (self) thus splits off into the *libidinal ego* (i.e., the needy and hopeful part of the individual who still seeks gratification from the exciting object) and the *antilibidinal ego*, which feels contempt for the libidinal ego's naive hopes and hatred toward the exciting object for repeated disappointments. The *central ego* is the part of the self identified with the ideal object that is still able to have relationships with external objects.

The internalization of bad objects represents the child's attempt to purge his real external objects of their badness. The child hopes to make the objects good by internalizing their badness. Children thus maintain the illusion of the goodness of the object (i.e., outer security of the external environment) at the expense of internal security by internalizing the persecutory aspects of real objects. As Groucho Marx said, "The problem with going on a vacation is that you have to take yourself [i.e., your bad internal objects] with you." As a result of this defensive process the ego (self) is at the mercy of internal persecutors against which further defenses must be erected.

Fairbairn thought that the child, who feels possessed by these internalized bad objects, attempts to defend against them by banishing them to the unconscious through the mechanism of repression. When these psychic structures are repressed the ensuing conflicts between exciting and rejecting objects and their influence over the individual's self occur mostly outside of the patient's awareness. The central ego (conscious self) continues to relate to real people in the real world while the libidinal and antilibidinal egos and their internalized objects unconsciously affect how the person feels about him- or herself and other people.

The relationship of the antilibidinal ego to the libidinal ego is often expressed through need shame. Patients may say that when they feel needful, they feel ashamed or bad (e.g., one patient described herself at these times as "slimy"). At these times, patients frequently criticize themselves for being needful and thus weak, and often express the desire to rid themselves of these needs.

The relationship of the libidinal ego to the exciting object helps to explain intractable attachments to abusive objects. In essence, like an individual using a slot machine, the libidinal ego continues to attempt to get the exciting object to gratify him or her. For example, one patient said about her partner, "One week, he sends me roses and the next three weeks, he doesn't call."

Fairbairn thought that everyone was subject to a degree of ego (self) splitting. However, he believed that in ordinary healthy development, the central-ego (conscious self) remains dominant and the individual's primary relationships are with real other people rather than internal objects.

Fairbairn also proposed that the normal developmental progression in people is from a state of infantile dependence to a state of mature dependence (i.e., switching from a predominant interest in taking to giving). Fairbairn (1941) believed that there were three stages of normal development: (1) infantile dependence, characterized by the oral (e.g., greedy, demanding) attitude of taking from the object with whom the infant maintains a "primary identification" (p. 340) or undifferentiated relationship; (2) an intermediate stage, characterized by conflicts between the progressive urge to give up infantile attachments to objects and the regressive urge to remain dependent on them; and (3) mature relational dependency, which implies a predominance of giving and mutuality in a relationship between two independent persons who are completely differentiated from each other.

Implications for Treatment

Fairbairn proposed that the therapeutic task was (1) to focus on understanding patients' internal representational world through studying recurring patterns in their interactions with others; and (2) to provide patients with a relationship that enables them to resolve the splitting of their ego (i.e., self). More specifically, Fairbairn proposed that (1) therapy involves restoration of the capacity to make direct and full contact with others; (2) in therapy, the patient becomes conscious of, and thus releases, bad internal objects that once seemed indispensable; (3) the therapist becomes a good-enough real object so that the patient can give up attachments to bad internal objects; and (4) the therapist must not induce guilt or shame over the patient's fear of giving up bad objects when the prospect of doing so is too terrifying for the patient to face.

In sum, Fairbairn's theoretical principles are that (1) the ego (self) is object seeking from birth; (2) object and self are inextricably intertwined; (3) aggression is a reaction to frustration and is most intense during infancy; (4) infants cope with needed but frustrating objects by internalizing and repressing them; and (5) in healthy development, the central ego remains dominant over subsidiary egos (i.e., the libidinal ego, the antilibidinal ego), whereas in pathology the subsidiary egos can be dominant, especially when the patient is regressed.

Major Criticisms

Fairbairn has been criticized for a number of limitations in his theory. Like Klein, he believed all development occurred during a very brief early period, ignoring the differentiation between self and object representations during this period (Kernberg 1980, St. Clair 1996). In addition, while Fairbairn acknowledged how the individual's real, external parents fulfill the infant's dependency needs, he did not really account for parents' fulfillment of the infant's other developmental needs such as facilitating separation, maintaining appropriate boundaries, containing the child, mirroring infantile grandiosity, or enticing the child out of the symbiotic orbit and into the world (Greenberg and Mitchell 1983). In particular, Fairbairn (1944) minimized the unique developmental role of the father. Fairbairn also did not adequately account for the internalization of good object experiences and healthy identifications. Also, Fairbairn clearly implied that all pathology has its roots in parental deprivation. Even though Fairbairn admits that "total parental availability is impossible," he does not consider that "infantile dependence is, by its very nature, ungratifiable" (Greenberg and Mitchell 1983, p. 181). He suggested, instead, that parental psychopathology was responsible for infant deprivation. Finally, like Klein, Fairbairn imputed considerably complex and discerning mental processes to infants (Greenberg and Mitchell 1983).

Harry Guntrip: The Regressed Ego

Guntrip, an analysand of both Fairbairn and Winnicott, popularized the work of both these theorists by enthusiastically presenting his overview and synthesis of their work in a clear and effective style. While minimizing the changes he introduced, he nevertheless radically extended Fairbairn's theory of ego-splitting and object relations to fit his own ideas about the nature of the human condition (Greenberg and Mitchell 1983).

The Regressed Ego

Guntrip's innovations revolve around the concept of the "regressed ego" (i.e., self) (Greenberg and Mitchell 1983). Guntrip argues that the dominant drive in individuals is toward regression. He agreed that when individuals' real objects are depriving, they withdraw into a world of internal objects. However, as the internal objects reflect the exciting and rejecting aspects of parents, the individual further withdraws from an outer world of bad objects to an inner world of bad objects. For example, one patient withdrew from her partner when he was verbally abusing her. However, her internal objects also criticized her (i.e., told her that he was right about the things that he said to her). This made her feel a sense of yearning and separation-anxiety (i.e., as she was so bad, she would be terrifyingly alone for the rest of her life).

According to Guntrip (1961), Fairbairn's libidinal ego, which acts as the repository of all disappointed object needs, undergoes a "final split," with part of it remaining attached to the "exciting object" and another part (i.e., the regressed ego) splitting off from the exciting object and renouncing all object-seeking in order to secure some measure of psychic safety. A large portion of the self thus withdraws to "an isolated, objectless state" (Greenberg and Mitchell 1983, p. 211), which may be similar to the experience of dissociation. Thus, in the last example, the patient took a sleeping pill to fall asleep and in the morning began to get overinvolved in work to the point where she felt extremely detached from the world and remained there so that she would be safe from being hurt.

Guntrip thought that when hope still exists, the regressed ego, withdrawn into protective isolation, awaits rebirth into a more nourishing human environment. When hope is lacking, the regressed ego wishes for death.

Guntrip's concept of the regressed ego represents a clear departure from Fairbairn, as Guntrip thought that the predominant motivation within human experience is represented by schizoid withdrawal or a deep longing for a "return to the womb," which he depicted as a total retreat from others to a state of objectlessness. In contrast, Fairbairn thought that the self begins and remains inextricably related to objects (i.e., there is no self without an object).

Like Fairbairn, Guntrip believed that psychopathology is the result of severe parental deficiencies. The helpless, frightened, terrorized child is induced into hiding or lifeless withdrawal, waiting to be called back to life by a more nourishing environment. However, unlike Fairbairn, Guntrip thought that all forms of psychopathology represent defenses against the dangers associated with this regressive flight to an objectless state. Guntrip (1969) believed that proper parenting would result in "a perfectly mature person" (p. 425) capable of enjoying ongoing internal harmony and equilibrium, without anxiety or guilt.

Implications for Treatment

Guntrip (1969) notes that the "kind of parent love, which the Greeks called agape as distinct from eros, is the kind of love the psychotherapist must give his patient because he did not get it from his parents in an adequate way" (p. 357). As a result, Guntrip professes that it is largely through the maternal relationship with the analyst, which he calls "replacement therapy," that the patient is helped to relinquish defensive attachments to real and imagined bad objects in order to allow for the reemergence of the infantile self (i.e., the frightened child in retreat). The more nurturing therapeutic environment encourages the regressed ego (self) to become reborn and reintegrated into a more positive interpersonal matrix.

Major Criticisms

Despite Guntrip's stated position of agreement with Fairbairn, his focus on the primacy of withdrawal from real and imagined objects is at odds with Fairbairn's focus on the primacy of the need for relationships. Furthermore, Greenberg and Mitchell (1983) believe that it remains unclear why the womb represents an objectless state rather than the seeking of a perfect fantasy object. They suggest that Guntrip really regards the womb as an undifferentiated preobject, rather than an objectless state. We believe that while Guntrip's belief that all forms of pathology represent defenses against withdrawal is an overgeneralization, his concept of the regressed ego does explain the dynamics of particular patients who are in contentless, dissociated states.

D. W. Winnicott: The Good-Enough Mother

Donald Winnicott was a London pediatrician and psychoanalyst who, based on his observations of children with their parents, wrote about the emergence of the child's self out of the child's relationship with his or her mother. Unlike Fairbairn and Klein, Winnicott did not have a penchant for theory. Nevertheless, he applied his considerable intuitive and observational skills to understanding particular areas of child development (Greenberg and Mitchell 1983).

Winnicott believed that the infant enters the world with scattered and diffuse pieces of experience (Greenberg and Mitchell 1983). The infant initially organizes this experience by relying on the mother to organize it for him or her. The mother also provides a *holding environment* (a secure environment that enables an infant to tolerate frustration without hurting him- or herself or the mother). In this holding environment, the infant is "contained" or protected. Winnicott (1945) notes that "an infant who has had no one person to gather his bits together starts with a handicap in his own self-integrating task" (p. 150).

In addition to holding, Winnicott believed that it is of critical importance that the mother be attuned to the infant's needs, that when infants are needy they imagine an object gratifying their needs. When the mother is sufficiently attuned to the infant, she gratifies the infant's needs at the precise moment that this fantasy is occurring in the infant's imagination. Winnicott described this as the "moment of illusion" (i.e., when the infant's hallucination and the external object seem the same). This causes infants to feel omnipotent (i.e., to believe that they have the power to make the world gratify their needs). Winnicott believed that this experience is the beginning of the development of a healthy sense of self (i.e., "When I have a need, it is seen and responded to").

Winnicott believed that for a brief period it is necessary for the mother to be devoted and attuned enough to empathically anticipate the infant's needs and time gratification precisely. Winnicott called the state of devotion that characterizes the mother's willingness to attentively offer herself for the infant's growth the *primary maternal preoccupation.*

Attunement, thus, means being accurately sensitive to the infant's needs and gratifying the infant's needs at the moment that he or she is imagining these needs being gratified. This establishes a feeling in the infant of hallucinatory omnipotence. Under these circumstances, the infant becomes attuned to his or her own bodily functions and impulses, which becomes the basis for the infant's slowly evolving sense of self.

Winnicott also stated that it is important for the mother not to be *impinging* (i.e., the mother must be a nondemanding presence when the infant is not needy). He believed that the infant's learning to prematurely respond to the needs of others encourages false self development. In contrast, not interfering when the infant is not needful leads to a sense of comfort in being alone.

However, Winnicott believed that once hallucinatory omnipotence is established, it is important for the child to learn about reality (i.e., his or her limited abilities to control the world). Winnicott believed that during this period, it is necessary for the child to become *gradually disillusioned.* As the mother becomes more interested in her life, the child must come to terms with the reality of his limits to control his mother. Furthermore, there is a natural developmental urge toward separation-individuation in the child.

An important aspect of this process is the *transitional object* often represented by a child's favorite blanket or stuffed animal. A transitional object may have the mother's scent on it. It is neither self nor object but may be treated as if it were the mother and the self. Most important, the parent and child agree that the transitional object is something that is totally within the child's control.

Winnicott believed that there are two types of maternal failures that impede self development. When the mother fails to be attuned to the infant's needs when he or she is having them, the infant feels unresponded to (i.e., "My needs are not important") and eventually learns to become unattuned to his or her own needs. Furthermore, if the mother impinges on the child when he or she is not needy, the infant feels forced to respond to the needs of the mother. Winnicott believed that this leads to the child's becoming prematurely attuned to the needs of others.

As a result, the child develops what Winnicott called a *false (compliant) self* in which the child becomes the type of person that his or her mother desires. Thus, in order to avoid maternal rejection, the child gives up his or her *true (authentic) self,* the source of the child's spontaneous needs and behavior.

One patient reported that she was described as a very active, exuberant infant (e.g., she ran at 9 months). As an adult, she was told that when she was an infant, her impatient, short-tempered father would throw her across the bed when she was too noisy and hit her to the point of creating welts when he felt irritated by her behavior. Her mother, who feared for the child's safety, overcontrolled the patient's behavior from infancy on to prevent her from provoking her father. As an adult, this patient was overcontained, unmotivated, depressed, withdrawn, and cautious.

Winnicott (1960) believed that a healthy authentic sense of self is dependent on the experience of receiving *good-enough mothering,* which makes it possible for the infant to engage "by existing and not by reacting" (p. 148). This involves the mother's being durable, responsive, and nonimpinging, particularly during the earliest years of life. He believed that in a good-enough maternal environment, the infant develops from absolute dependence to relative dependence to independence. These correspond to three overlapping stages of parental care: "(1) holding; (2) mother and infant living together; and (3) mother, infant, and father living together" (Winnicott 1960, p. 43).

Implications for Therapy

Winnicott (1958b) believed that therapy should (1) simulate a good-enough mothering environment in order to reverse the environmental failure that led to the development of the patient's false self; (2) induce a controlled regression in which the patient returns to the period of unresolved early needs and environmental failures; (3) appropriately respond to those needs; and (4) provide good enough maternal or environmental functions that were missing during the patient's childhood. Winnicott believed that a therapeutic experience of this nature facilitates the growth of the patient's true self.

Winnicott (1958a) used the term *ego relatedness* to refer to the support provided by the mother to balance the immaturity of the infant's ego. "It is only when someone is available and present to the infant, without making demands, that the infant can discover its personal life (rather than a false self), can feel real, [and] can develop the capacity to be alone" (St. Clair 1996, p. 80). Winnicott thought the therapeutic environment called for the same kind of good-enough ego (i.e., self) relatedness in order for the patient to develop his or her true self.

For Winnicott, however, healing in therapy is not something that the therapist does. Rather, the patient, in the dependent relationship with the therapist, brings about a self-cure within the context of ego-relatedness. The individual feels confidence in the therapist because the therapist reliably and patiently provides a facilitative, nonimpinging environment that is attuned to the patient's needs (Winnicott 1960).

As therapy progresses, the patient experiences increased independence. During this period, the therapist helps the patient's true self to tolerate limited environmental failures without organizing his or her defensive false self. In the early stage of treatment, Winnicott attempted to foster a therapeutic climate where the patient would create the kind of therapist that he or she needed and the therapist would try to foster a regression by fitting into that role. To assist the therapeutic regression, the therapist was thus required to tolerate being the patient's hate object without taking revenge and/or being the patient's love object without acting out (Winnicott 1963). Winnicott used this therapeutic regression to learn more about the patient's inner world and to ascertain where and how the patient's needs were impaired. The therapist then attempts to provide the patient with good-enough mother functions to help the patient move from false to true self expression.

Major Criticisms

Winnicott has been criticized for a number of reasons, including (1) his casual use of terminology, (2) his idiosyncratic use of Freudian concepts to reflect his own ideas about psychopathology, and (3) the fact that his ideas do not constitute a unified theory. His ideas have also been criticized for their simplicity, although their simple but compelling eloquence is also what makes them appealing and powerful.

American Object Relations School

Margaret Mahler: Observational Studies of Separation-Individuation in Children

Mahler, born in Hungary and trained in Vienna, immigrated to the United States, where her studies of children at the Master's Children Center in New York City resulted in influential articles and books from the 1950s through the 1970s. Mahler used object relations concepts to focus on what she described as the psychological birth of the person. Empirical studies were conducted in order to better understand both normal development as well as how the clinical issues of child development could be predictive of later adult psychopathology.

Mahler made significant contributions to a generation of analytic theorists and practitioners by providing insights into the basic struggles of childhood development. In particular, she highlighted the child's psychological hatching from the symbiotic experience with the mother and the conflict between the child's autonomous strivings for an independent sense of self and the "equally powerful urge to surrender and reimmerse himself in the enveloping fusion from which he has come" (Greenberg and Mitchell 1983, p. 273). By articulating a developmental sequence for the psychological birth of the infant, Mahler contributed important, new organizing concepts such as symbiosis, separation-individuation, differentiation, practicing, and rapprochement.

In contrast to Winnicott (1962), who eschewed the adaptive false self that he believed developed from the child's unhealthy compliance to the needs of others, Mahler's theory of development acknowledged the importance of the adaptive capacities of the infant. She noted that the normal infant "actively takes on the task of adaptation in the mother–infant interaction" during separation-individuation (Mahler 1965, pp. 163–164).

More specifically, Mahler, who adopted a more biological or adaptational approach to development, claimed that the average devoted mother met the biological needs of the child but also imposed conditions to which the infant was required to adapt. For Mahler, the infant's psychological birth is thus partially achieved through his or her adaptation to the environment. In contrast, Winnicott, who assumed a more interpersonal approach, proposed that the good-enough mother is actively discerning and adaptively responding to the infant's nascent self. For Winnicott, the infant's true self is an innate given, encouraged by a facilitating environment.

Based on her observational studies of children's interactions with their mothers, Mahler described three stages of development over the course of the first four years of life: normal autism, symbiosis, and separation-individuation. She further described the separation-individuation stage as having four developmental subphases: differentiation, practicing, rapprochement, and on the way to object constancy.

Mahler believed that infants begin life in a state of relatively undifferentiated psychological insulation (i.e., the *autistic stage*), which she viewed as a state of mental disorganization. The infant's first few weeks of life are thus spent in a disoriented, primitive hallucinatory state. In this early stage, the child cannot differentiate between his or her own attempts to reduce tension (e.g., by urinating, eating) and the mother's attempts to reduce the infant's tensions (e.g., by changing a diaper, feeding). Mahler proposed that this first stage thus represented an objectless period for the infant in which the primary goals were satisfying needs and maintaining a sense of equilibrium. She thought that good mothering required attunement to the infant's emotional and biological needs. Mahler believed that the infant was born into chaos with physiological processes dominating, but with the ego potential to organize, relate, and develop into a personal self with an unquestioned sense of identity and value. Mahler thought that the infant's first psychic organizer is separating a global sense of distress from nondistress or pleasure from pain.

By the second month, when the *symbiotic stage* begins, Mahler noted that infants appear to move toward an experience of feeling merged with the mother (e.g., molding their body to fit her body). This stage begins when the child begins to explore the mother through sight and touch. The infant is now only dimly aware of the world beyond the mother. Mahler believes that the infant now develops a delusion of a common boundary, and within that psychological boundary enjoys the oceanic feeling of "Mommy and I are one."

The essential feature of symbiosis is the illusion of fusion with the representation of the mother. The infant continues to differentiate and organize pleasure from pain and good experiences from bad ones. During this stage the infant begins to build memory traces of good mothering and begins to make a nascent separation between good self and good object (e.g., "I feel good inside because my stomach is full" and "Here comes that good person again"). Bad experiences are still so chaotic, disorganizing, and overwhelming that the child is not remotely able to discriminate between "This is a bad experience because I feel bad internally" and "This is an anxious or unresponsive mother that is making me feel bad." The baby just feels bad.

Mahler believed that the primary developmental goals during the symbiotic stage are attachment and homeostasis. She believed that the smiling response, manifested by the infant at 3 months, is the beginning of a sense of reciprocity and relatedness. Good-enough mothering (1) pulls the child from autistic regression to an increased sensory awareness of the mother and the environment, (2) satisfies the infant's needs through attunement, (3) buffers and modifies internal and external stimulation in order to keep the infant feeling comfortable, and (4) provides auxiliary ego functions (e.g., reality testing) that the infant cannot provide for him- or herself.

Mahler thought that gross maternal failure during the symbiotic period led to disorders such as psychosis, autism, and psychopathy. Furthermore, when mothers provide infants with a small taste of symbiotic gratification without sufficiently and consistently meeting their needs, it results in a hunger for reunion with the symbiotic object, precocious ego development, and problems with dependency.

When symbiosis is optimally negotiated, the next developmental stage of *separation- individuation* is heralded. The child now begins the difficult process of physically and psychologically separating him- or herself from the primary parent and becoming an autonomous person. During the first subphase of *differentiation*, which begins at about 6 months, the primary goal for the infant is to differentiate self from other and mother from not mother. The second psychic organizer, recognition memory, develops during this period. By the eighth month in normal development, the symbiotic object has become so specific that she is no longer interchangeable and the child develops stranger anxiety. The primary goal of this period is to differentiate self from nonself.

During the *practicing* subphase of separation-individuation (10 to 16 months), the child becomes exhilarated by his or her new mobility, which helps propel him or her from the symbiotic orbit into exploring the world. Thus, this is a period of greater physical separation from the mother and emotional elation at mastery in the world. The child believes that the world is his or her oyster and seems oblivious to knocks, falls, and frustrations. The child also begins to turn toward the father as a new, more interesting object. The father's first role is to continue to draw and attract the child into the real world of people and things that are further out of the symbiotic relationship with the mother.

By 16 to 25 months, the child becomes increasingly aware of his or her vulnerability and separateness (i.e., he or she is not omnipotent but just a small child). This leads to an uneasy return to his or her mother and the conflict of the *rapprochement subphase.* The child now vacillates between clinging to his or mother and darting away from her to explore the world. During rapprochement, children feel conflicted between (1) their needs for autonomous experiences in the world versus symbiotic reunion with the mother; and (2) their desire to be separate, grandiose, and omnipotent versus their desire to have their mother magically fulfill their wishes without having to acknowledge that help is actually coming from her. Gradually, over this period the child begins the process of internalizing maternal functions through identification.

During the rapprochement phase, the child's attempts to divide the world into all good and all bad, nurturing and depriving, are redoubled. Splitting becomes the prominent defense mechanism. At around 18 months the child develops *object permanence* (i.e., the object still exists, although it is out of sight), *evocative memory* (i.e., the ability to feel an emotional connection to a mental image of an object), and the capacity for representational memory. These abilities are vital to the eventual establishment of object constancy in the next subphase. The child also begins to psychologically separate and become more autonomous through refusal to comply (i.e., saying no) which signifies that "I am different from you." Children also begin using transitional objects during rapprochement. Their relationship with the father becomes even more significant as the father facilitates the child's shift from being in an exclusive relationship with his or her mother to developing a sense of autonomy and independence. Children begin to have a mental image of the absent mother during this period, but are not able to do so consistently. This phase is thus represented by incomplete internalizations of the mother's caring for the child and a persisting reliance on her actual presence.

When the rapprochement stage is successfully negotiated, the child develops the capacity for object constancy during the next subphase. However, if the mother responds to the *separating* child with hurt, anger, or rejection or to the *returning* child with depression and withdrawal, then the child may become fixated at this stage with its conflicts between regressive longing for symbiotic attachment and the desire for autonomy.

Finally, the uneasy solution of rapprochement eventually evolves into the child's developing whole object relations (24 to 36 months) during the subphase called *on the way to object constancy*. Relationships are perceived by the child as being primarily good but as also having some less than optimal qualities. This period is hallmarked by the separation of self and object (i.e., the child now understands that he or she and the mother are different people with different needs) and the healthy integration of good and bad aspects of the self and the object. Thus, the child is now able to be ambivalent (i.e., simultaneously love *and* be angry) at his or her mother.

As a result of the child's integration of his or her feelings, object constancy develops. The child thus undergoes a shift from self-centered, demanding clinging behavior to more mature and realistic object relationships. During this period the child learns to (1) express affection, trust, and confidence; (2) show regard for the interests and feelings of others; (3) develop the ability to play cooperatively (i.e., sharing and taking turns); and (4) tolerate separation or aloneness. At this time, the child's core self stabilizes along with clear ego boundaries (i.e., knowing where he or she stops and the other begins) and more mature reality testing.

Mahler's developmental schemas establish the major landmarks of the preoedipal period. Her constructs of symbiosis, separation, and individuation are key organizing ideas for understanding the early development of the personality. Her developmental framework provided an empirically derived and testable model for the clinical observations and theoretical ideas of many other writers, including Winnicott, Jacobson, Masterson, and Kernberg. In addition to providing insight into the causes of preoedipal pathology in adults, particularly borderline and narcissistic disorders, Mahler's model has increased our understanding of normal development.

Implications for Treatment

With the clarity of her empirical findings, Mahler stressed that therapy must focus on the developmental needs of the patient. Like Winnicott, whose ideas she admired, Mahler proposed that helping a patient to reexperience the failed stages of development, with the therapist serving as a substitute mother or auxiliary ego, could help the patient achieve higher levels of object relations through the internalization of needed functions (Mahler and Furer 1968).

Major Criticisms

Mahler's studies have been found to be largely consistent with Spitz's and Piaget's studies of cognitive development. However, Emanuel Peterfreund (1978) criticized Mahler's tendency toward the adulto-morphization of the experience of infants (i.e., looking at the infant's world of experience from an adult standpoint and perhaps imputing adult motives to the immature mind of the child).

   In addition, her work has been criticized by Daniel Stern (1985), whose infant studies indicated that babies are born with rudimentary object relatedness and do not go through an initial autistic period. Stern (1985), himself, noted that "For Mahler, connectedness is the result of a failure in differentiation; for [Stern] it is a success of psychic functioning" (p. 241). In addition, Stern argued that the birth of the self went through four evolving phases that continued over the lifetime and were not set by the ages of 4 to 6 years.

   However, the developmental studies of Mahler and Stern, as well as Piaget, are similar in the sense that they focus on the interpersonal interaction of a system, not an isolated entity with pent-up drives. The similarities of Stern's work with Mahler's thus outweigh the differences.

Otto Kernberg: Synthesis of Object Relations Theory and Ego Psychology

It was through the work and influence of Otto Kernberg (1976) that object relations theory firmly achieved its place in American psychoanalysis and began to exert a growing influence over general psychiatry and psychology. Kernberg, also from Vienna, took medical and psychiatric training in Chile and continued further psychiatric work at the Menninger Clinic in Kansas until he moved to New York City. In the same way that Freud's theory stemmed from his clinical work with neurotics and Fairbairn's emerged from his work with schizoid patients, Kernberg's theory evolved in large measure from his work with borderline and severely disturbed narcissistic patients. Kernberg's theoretical work is based on inferences he has derived from the retrospective reports and characteristic transference reactions of his patients, especially severely disturbed borderline and narcissistic patients.

   His books and articles, which began to appear in the 1970s, reflect a synthesis of object relations theory and ego psychology and have generated considerable controversy. Kernberg acknowledges the influence of Jacobson, Mahler, Bowlby, Fairbairn, Klein, and Freud in his writings. In particular, his conceptual model was based on Jacobson's (1964) three-level developmental schema and Mahler's developmental timetable. Kernberg also applied the concepts of structure and development to a classification of character pathology that has become highly influential.

Kernberg's writing is often difficult reading for the beginner. Because of his desire to maintain a connection to Freud, Kernberg keeps but redefines the meaning and development of all Freud's psychic structures from an object relations perspective so that, at times, these concepts are somewhat confusing. However, while his object relations theory is sometimes unclear, it is replete with gems of psychological wisdom.

Like most great innovative writers, Kernberg's theories have evolved over time. His later theories sometimes contradict his earlier writings, which may account, in part, for some of the lack of clarity in his theory. Finally, Greenberg and Mitchell (1983) believe that Kernberg's goal (i.e., to develop a coherent and cohesive theory of object relations that integrates the essential elements of drive theory) is an impossible task as the underlying assumptions of each theory are entirely different.

Development of Psychic Structures

Kernberg (1982) broadly defines object relations theory as the study of an individual's internalization of interpersonal relations. He particularly concentrates on describing how intrapsychic structures such as the id, ego, and superego develop from internalized past relationships with others. In discussing the other theorists, we waited until the end of the section to discuss problems in their theory. However, as this chapter is geared to the needs of readers who are unfamiliar with object relations theory, we believe that Kernberg's theory of the development of psychic structures is sufficiently confusing to warrant discussing its problems as it is being described. We begin by reviewing some of the major concepts of drive theory so that it can be contrasted with Kernberg's work.

Freud (1940) stated that an infant is born with an *id*. Freud thought that at a later time, an individual's *ego* differentiates out of the id due to exposure to and the need to deal with reality.

Kernberg believes that the infant is born with an *undifferentiated id-ego potential* that is energized and responsive. Moore and Fine (1990) describe this undifferentiated matrix as "the genetically determined growth pattern of the central nervous system, the sense organs, and the body in general" (p. 59). Kernberg believes that this undifferentiated matrix has the potential to later develop into what Freud terms the id (i.e., the mental structure that is the source of sexual and aggressive drives) and the ego (the mental structure that deals and negotiates with reality).

As the ego is primarily a cognitive structure (i.e., that perceives, anticipates, thinks, and plans) that is likely to be influenced by the infant's neurological development, Kernberg's theory that the ego gradually develops from innate potential in the infant is convincing. It is confusing, however, how the id that Freud (1940) described as the container of everything that is present from birth (particularly instinctual drives) develops gradually over time.

Kernberg believes that the infant starts out with *ego forerunners*. With the development of internalization as a defense, the ego emerges as a psychic structure. Kernberg thinks that infants internalize the objects that they love and hate and that these internalized objects eventually develop into the ego as an integrated mental structure. We believe that it is somewhat unclear how and why internalized objects develop into a cognitive structure whose function is to negotiate with reality. Are parental ego functions internalized until the infant develops an ego structure of his or her own? Clarification is warranted in this area.

Kernberg believes that infants are born with the affect dispositions of love and hate. These feelings of love and hate organize infants' experiences into good experiences and bad experiences. However, self and others are not yet separated. The infant thus internalizes or introjects undifferentiated selfobjects (i.e, merged images of self and other) that are organized by the infants feelings about them (i.e., loved or good selfobject experiences and bad or hated selfobject experiences).

In contrast to Freud, who believed that sexual and aggressive drives are innate and non–object related, Kernberg believes that as these loved and hated internalized selfobjects accumulate and form an all-good and an all-bad selfobject world in the infant's mind, these accumulated good and bad experiences become organized into the traditional Freudian drives of sex and aggression. We believe that this is one of the more confusing aspects of Kernberg's theory of structural development as it is neither explained nor intuitively obvious why the accumulation of good and bad experiences with other people eventually develop into drives (which are typically thought of as innate). It is unclear how Kernberg is using the term *drive*.

Thus, this component of Kernberg's theory does not seem to add explanatory value. Rather, it appears to be motivated by Kernberg's desire to preserve a link to drive theory rather than truly integrating how innate drives *and* relationships with others both effect character development. Figure 1–1 illustrates Kernberg's model of the transformation of internalized object relations units into drives.

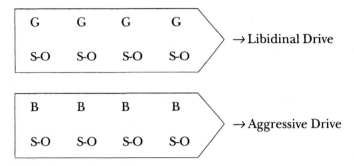

Figure 1–1. Kernberg's model of the transformation of internalized object relations units into drives. G = good (i.e., loved), B = bad (i.e., hated), and S-O = selfobjects.

Kernberg also thinks that the splitting of the infant's experiences into good and bad experiences originally occurs naturally as good and bad events occur separately. When the infant is hungry and uncomfortable, it is experienced as a separate event from when the infant is fed and satisfied. Splitting continues because the ego is still too weak to integrate these highly disparate experiences (i.e., infants are unable to understand that the mother who feeds them and makes them feel good is the same mother who does not respond to their hunger and thus makes them feel bad). At this stage of development, the infant actively uses splitting as a defense to protect good selfobject images (e.g., happy, fed mother–baby) from being contaminated by bad selfobject images (e.g., unhappy, hungry mother–baby).

Kernberg believes that the self-image now becomes differentiated from the object image within the good selfobject representation (i.e., the good happy self and the good feeding mother are separate people). As bad selfobject experiences are still too disorganizing, they continue to overwhelm the infant's ability to differentiate self from other.

Furthermore, as the ego matures and is more able to integrate contradictory experiences, there is a gradual lessening of the splitting defense. The infant gradually develops higher, more complex, and mature forms of positive introjections (i.e., good-enough objects that are generally loved and sometimes disliked when they frustrate the child). As more complex positive introjects become preponderant, the ego's synthetic (i.e., integrating) function replaces the splitting defense and the child's sense of self becomes more integrated.

As the infant's development continues, the ego continues to integrate part-object images into whole-object images (e.g., the breast that feeds is a part of the whole mother who does other things in addition to feeding the infant). Libidinal and aggressive drives (which developed out of feelings of love and hate) also become integrated. Kernberg believes that in the latter process aggression is neutralized, which provides energy for the development of the defense mechanism of repression. However, Kernberg does not explain how neutralized aggression provides energy or how and why the infant comes to specifically use this energy for the defense of repression as opposed to some other function.

Kernberg proposes that the structure of the id (i.e., the seat of unconscious drives) emerges with the use of repression as intolerable, hated, aggressive introjects can be banished into the unconscious. Repression now becomes the predominantly used defense mechanism. Kernberg views the id as the structure where unrepressed drives as well as repressed, disturbing self and object images are stored. However, Kernberg's use of the term *id* is ambiguous here as it is unclear how he defines it (e.g., the source of drives, the unconscious?). Furthermore, while Kernberg states that unrepressed drives are stored in the id, he does not explain how this process occurs.

The superego also emerges at this time as its own structure, combining the ego ideal (i.e., the individual's aspirations) with sadistic forerunners (e.g., "Don't do that, you bad girl") and realistic demands (e.g., "If you push your brother down the stairs, he can get hurt"). This structure continues to develop from approximately 2 to 5 years of age.

In summary, for Kernberg the emotions of love and hate serve as the major organizers of good and bad internal object relations and thus constitute the major motivational systems that organize internal experience. He believes that the integration of the affect and drive systems through the integration of good and bad object relations results in the modulation of the infant's primitive instincts and emotions. As the child's mental representations of self and other are differentiated and the good and bad aspects of self and object are integrated, the child achieves whole object relations, whereby both self and others are experienced as separate and viewed more realistically. As this developmental milestone is achieved, the child's perceptions of people become more complex.

Kernberg believes that the child develops the traditional structures described by Freud (i.e., id, ego, and superego). However, Kernberg also views the self as a psychic structure that both remains a substructure of the ego and is supraordinate to the ego (e.g., directs ego functions such as integrating the representational world).

Kernberg thinks that the disruption of these normal developmental processes leads to adult psychopathology. The severity of the disruption and the age at which the disruption occurs determines where and how the patient was impaired and the resulting type of character pathology. Unlike Fairbairn, Guntrip, and Winnicott, he believes that these disruptions emerged from either environmental failure or excessive innate aggression in the infant. His latter belief is similar to that of Melanie Klein. Thus, if infants have too much aggressive drive or too many bad experiences with others, they will be unable to neutralize their aggressive drive to develop energy for repression. Splitting will thus remain a primary defense.

However, while Kernberg believes that excessive aggressive drive is one important factor in the development of psychopathology, in Kernberg's system aggressive drives are not innate but develop from an accumulation of internalized bad relationships with others. When one looks at the derivation of aggressive drives in Kernberg's model, it essentially translates into psychopathology resulting exclusively from bad relationships with others.

Through his concept of units of internalized object relations, Kernberg attempts to develop a model that synthesizes drive theory and object relations theory. The two models become mixed by having the self and object representations built under the influence of the innate affects of love and hate. These loved and hated selfobject units are then transformed into libidinal and aggressive drives. In other words, the object-directed feelings of love and hate precede and build up the drives. This conceptualization is very different from Freud's proposition that drives are innate. Kernberg's model thus views the person as innately emotional and relational rather than innately sexual or aggressive (Greenberg and Mitchell 1983).

Internalization

Psychic structures are built through a continuous process of internalizing relationships with others. Kernberg believes that there are three levels in the process of internalization: (1) introjection, (2) identification, and (3) ego identity.

Kernberg defines *introjection* as the earliest, most primitive form of internalization. During the process of introjection, the infant takes in the least organized, least differentiated self and object images in the context of the most violent, least modulated emotions (e.g., rageful mother–child).

Kernberg defines *identification* as an object image in a specific social role and a self image in a complementary role. In the process of identification, emotions are more modulated than they are in introjection (e.g., "When

my mother teaches me to cook, she is nice and patient and I am cooperative and enjoy learning from her").

Kernberg uses Erikson's (1956) definition of *ego identity*: the organization
of identifications and introjections by the ego into a consistent conceptualization of an object world and a consolidated sense of self. Ego identity thus
organizes and integrates more primitive internalization processes.

Developmental Goals

Kernberg concurs with Mahler that infants develop from a state of objectlessness to a stage of need-gratifying object relations to a level of self-reliant
whole object relations. In contrast to Fairbairn, who believed that mature
dependence was the ultimate developmental goal, Kernberg emphasizes the
importance of the self-reliance that comes with the integration of good and
bad object relations and a resulting sense of object constancy. Their emphasis
is thus different (i.e., Fairbairn focused on developing a feeling of mutuality in a relationship between two differentiated individuals while Kernberg
emphasizes the importance of becoming independent from other people
through the internalization of their functions).

Classification of Character Pathology

Kernberg applies his model of development to a classification of character pathology. He proposes that there are three levels of severity in psychopathology that correspond to three levels of psychic structure (i.e.,
high, intermediate, and low). Kernberg then formulates specific criteria
for each of these levels with regard to drive maturation, superego structuralization, and object relations development. In general, he believes that
with character pathology that has more severely disturbed ego development and object relations (1) there are more primitive masochistic and
sadistic feelings, (2) the superego is harsher, and (3) the individual's object relations are more fragmented (i.e., part self representations relating
to part object representations).

Kernberg then classifies specific character pathologies according to their
typical object relations structure. For example, he thinks that the obsessive-
compulsive and hysterical personalities are typically structured at the high
level of character pathology (because of their development of self and object constancy and generally good ego functioning), while most narcissistic
and sadomasochistic personalities are structured at the intermediate level
of ego development and object relations.

Implications for Treatment

Kernberg offers specific suggestions for treating patients based on their level of character pathology. In his own work with patients, he focuses on the treatment of middle and lower level character disorders. Kernberg and his colleagues (1989) have thus articulated a two-phase approach to working with borderline ego organization.

In the first phase of treatment, the Kernberg group recommends helping patients to coalesce part self and part object representations in order to help them develop "images of themselves and others that are multidimensional, cohesive, and integrated" (Kernberg et al. 1989, p. 91). This is accomplished by (1) structuring the therapeutic situation to minimize the patient's acting out, and (2) confronting the patient's negative transference and primitive defenses (e.g., splitting and projective identification) as they occur.

Kernberg believes that a major component of treating borderline and narcissistic patients involves examining and confronting the patient's intense unmodulated aggression. He thus criticizes some of the British object relations theorists for neglecting the importance of aggression in borderline and narcissistic patients as aggression is manifested (1) in the patient's attempts to eliminate frustrating, dangerous, or competing objects; and (2) in the patient's expression of unconscious conflict (Kernberg 1975).

Major Criticisms

Kernberg's work is so comprehensive and complicated that it is difficult to summarize and still adequately capture the extent of his contributions. He is certainly one of the most innovative object relations theorists in America today. His work, however, is controversial and thus has not avoided criticism.

For example, his early focus on the etiological importance of excessive innate aggression in narcissistic and borderline pathology and the consequent focus in treatment of confronting these patients' expressions of aggression has been criticized for a number of reasons. The literature has provided no empirical evidence to support Kernberg's hypothesis that genetically based excessive aggression is associated with the development of narcissistic and borderline personalities. As a result, feminist writers who highlight environmental failures and the history of having traumatic experiences in borderline patients perceive Kernberg's focus on the patient's aggressive drives as victim blaming (Herman 1992). Most problematic is that in Kernberg's model the aggressive drive is not innate but is composed of internalized bad experiences with others that really reflect environmental failure.

We believe that Kernberg's most confusing subtheory is his attempt to explain the development of Freudian structures through object relations principles. In this theory, Kernberg attempts to make one large puzzle out of two smaller ones. The resulting picture lacks clarity due to gaps where pieces of the puzzle are missing or adjacent pieces don't quite fit together. Some of the gaps in the puzzle are how internalized objects develop into the ego, why loved and hated internalized object relations units develop into libidinal and aggressive drive, how the integration of libidinal and aggressive drives described in this theory produce energy, and why that energy is specifically used for repression. To follow Kernberg's theory, one has to accept a number of assumptions (which aren't intuitively obvious) as givens. Given Kernberg's general clarity of thinking, the best explanation for these gaps in his theory is that they are based on his desire to remain aligned with Freud and drive theory rather than on logical principles or his clinical observations.

Kernberg's theoretical writings have also been criticized for being too speculative and insufficiently research-based. In addition, Kernberg has not reconciled some of his earlier and later theories (St. Clair 1996). Despite these criticisms, however, Kernberg's writings have made a major contribution to a better understanding of severe personality disorders, including categorizing them on their level of ego development, which has greatly influenced our approach to differential diagnosis and treatment.

Heinz Kohut: Self Psychology

After receiving his medical degree from the University of Vienna, Kohut moved to Chicago and joined the professional staff at the Chicago Institute of Psychoanalysis. He is credited with developing self psychology, which was primarily based on his work with narcissistic patients. Kohut's (1977) theories evolved from his introspective, empathic immersions into the inner life of his narcissistic patients. Although criticized for not being sufficiently objective or scientific, Kohut is generally recognized for providing significant insights into the development and treatment of narcissism, in particular, and self disorders, in general.

Kohut's self psychology is an object relations theory because it emphasizes the development of personality through the internalization of relationships. It thus focuses on relational aims and de-emphasizes drive theory. However, despite his lack of emphasis on drives, Kohut developed two mixed-model strategies, initially believing that to fully understand human nature one needed to consider both relational and instinctual motivations.

Kohut's theory of self psychology emphasizes the development of the self as a psychic structure that is the center of initiative and the recipient of impressions. He thus considered the self to be an active agent like the ego rather than merely a mental representation or image.

Kohut believes that the infant originally requires the parent to provide self cohesion and self regulation. Through empathic attunement, the parent integrates and modulates the infant's experience. Self development, thus, requires participation by others who function as selfobjects to provide the self's needed sense of cohesion, constancy, and resilience.

It is through the interaction between the infant's innate potential and the responsiveness of adults who treat the infant as if he or she already had a self that the infant's self actually develops. Kohut's descriptions of self development are similar to Winnicott's descriptions of the good-enough mother's responsive encouragement of the infant's true self development.

Kohut defines selfobjects as a subjective phenomenon whereby the child experiences an objectively separate person like the mother as part of his or her self, providing needed self functions that will later be performed by the infant's own self (e.g., mirroring, soothing, admiration). The infant's immature self merges with the selfobject and by doing so enjoys need satisfactions and a more well-organized experience.

In the beginning of Kohut's theory building, he still relied on the construct of drives. In his first model, he utilized Freud's concept of libidinal energy (i.e., a form of mental energy that is directed toward objects who gratify the individual's desire for pleasure). However, Kohut's integration of Freud's concept of libidinal energy into his own theory about how an individual's sense of self (and self-esteem) develops in relationships with other people can be confusing. This is particularly the case if readers are unfamiliar with these theories, including the context in which they were conceived. We recommend that when reading Kohut's first model about the split in libidinal energy, readers not allow Kohut's confusing first attempt to mix drive and relational theory to distract them from understanding his theory about how adequate selfobject relationships lead to healthy narcissism.

Model One: Split in Libidinal Energy

In his first model, Kohut (1971) proposed that libidinal energy divides into object libido (i.e., Freud's realm of inquiry) and narcissistic libido (Kohut's realm of inquiry). Kohut believed that an individual's *object libido* (i.e., emotional investment in affectional and sexual relationships with other people) leads to the development of *object love* (i.e., reciprocal love for a separate, realistically perceived person).

In contrast, Kohut believed that an individual's *narcissistic libido* (attraction to an object to enhance one's self) relates to other people as selfobjects (Ornstein 1978). When the infant internalizes the functions that are provided by selfobjects (i.e., mirroring, admiration, idealizing, empathy), it leads to the development of self love or healthy narcissism.

Kohut discusses three types of selfobject relationships (i.e., relationships that are used exclusively for the needs of the self) that lead to healthy narcissism: the mirroring selfobject, the idealized selfobject, and the twinship selfobject. Understanding these relationships is important for clinicians in treating narcissistic personality disorders.

Type of Selfobject Relationships

In the *mirroring selfobject relationship*, the child exhibits his or her evolving abilities to make noises, turn over, walk, talk, and squeal, and requires recognition and admiration from the object. At this point in development, the child has a grandiose, exhibitionistic self image. The relationship that the child seeks from the mirroring self object can be stated as "I am perfect and you admire me."

In the *idealizing selfobject relationship*, the child forms an idealized image of the parent and merges with it. The relationship that the child seeks from the idealized selfobject can be stated as "You are perfect and I am part of you."

In the *twinship selfobject relationship*, the child searches for a soulmate or kindred spirit. Kohut thought that this experience was developmentally akin to selfobject experiences with peers during latency. In the twinship transference, the individual feels that the selfobject "shares the same basic experience of the world" (Karterud 1990, p. 620). The relationship that the child seeks can be stated as "You and I are exactly alike."

Kohut believes that when selfobjects are good enough and their failures to mirror the child or permit idealization occur gradually over time, a slow internalization of selfobject functions takes place through *transmuting internalizations* (i.e., identifications with the object's functions). This process gives rise to the development of two poles of the self: (1) the grandiose self pole, which becomes transformed into healthy ambition and assertiveness; and (2) the idealizing self pole, which becomes transformed into values and ideals. Disturbances in early selfobject interactions between parents and child result in the child's failure to develop at least one of these poles, which can result in the individual developing a disorder of the self such as narcissistic personality disorder. During latency, internalization of the twinship selfobject relationship with peers results in the individual's developing a sense of community.

Kohut states that (1) mature or whole object relations presuppose a stable self that is experienced as separate from objects, and (2) the development of a cohesive self is a prerequisite to negotiating the oedipal struggle (i.e., the wish to defeat one parent and exclusively possess the other parent).

In sum, Kohut believes that self psychology relates to preoedipal development (i.e., the development of a separate, cohesive sense of self during the first few years of life) while drive theory relates to oedipal development (i.e., the ability to compete, to share, and to make positive identifications during the fourth or fifth years of life). Narcissistic or preoedipal pathology is reflected in a defective sense of self and an inability to maintain stabilized self-esteem. Consequently, Kohut believes that self psychology describes narcissistic patients and Freudian theory describes neurotic patients.

Model Two: Theory of Complementarity

In his second model, Kohut (1977) directly stated his belief that drive theory is an outdated rather than an adjunctive theory to self psychology. He maintained that the self does not seek sexual gratification but relatedness to other people. Kohut no longer differentiated between disorders produced by narcissistic and object libido. Rather, he thought that all self disorders were caused by selfobject failures. Kohut proposed that the self disorders of Freud's day were produced by faulty selfobject responses in late childhood due to the parents' difficulties accepting and empathizing with the child's emerging sexuality. This resulted in what are referred to as oedipal conflicts and neurotic problems (i.e., conflicts between sexual needs and internalized moral prohibitions against sexual expression). Kohut thought that in his day and time, with the breakdown in the extended family system, selfobject failures took place earlier during the preoedipal period, resulting in more narcissistic disorders.

At this point Kohut was directly critical of drive theory and had developed a purely relational theory that he called the *psychology of the self.* In a confusing move (and despite his rejection of instinctual drives as the motivator of behavior), Kohut still attempted to retain a link between self psychology and Freudian drive theory. He thus argued that self psychology simply addresses a different, but complementary, aspect of human experience (i.e., the "tragic man" who struggles to develop a cohesive and integrative sense of self) than drive theory (which discusses the "guilty man," who represses his or her drives in the face of competing reality and internalized moral values).

Contributions

Kohut's contributions have been many. For example, like Fairbairn and Winnicott, Kohut emphasized the importance of relationships with others on the development of the self. He was the first theorist to discuss narcissistic pathology in regard to parental failures to provide adequate selfobject functions such as mirroring and empathy.

Kohut also contributed to the field by stressing the importance in normal self development of parents mirroring and admiring the infant's grandiosity and providing the infant with opportunities to idealize the parents. Since the parent performs a self-modulation function for the infant and yet is still an object, the parent serves as a selfobject until the child gradually internalizes his or her parents' functions. Kohut believed that, to some degree, normal adults continue to need sustaining selfobjects throughout life. Furthermore, Kohut entirely eliminated the concept of an organizing ego. Instead, he emphasized the self as a primary structure that is the center of the individual's initiative.

Kohut shifted the emphasis in treatment from interpretation to the provision of missing developmental experiences such as empathy and mirroring. While other theorists (e.g., Fairbairn, Guntrip, Mahler, Winnicott) believed that providing parental functions was important, Kohut was the first theorist to actually systematize this idea into a system of psychotherapy. He also contributed a great deal to examining the importance of timing and manner of delivery in addition to the content of interpretations.

Implications for Treatment

Self psychology's implications for therapy include (1) the establishment of a therapeutic alliance that facilitates reactivation of the patient's original developmental issues (i.e., allowing oneself to be idealized by the patient or used by the patient as a mirror or a soulmate); (2) the importance of empathizing with a patient's experience rather than merely interpreting it;

and (3) providing a greater understanding of the narcissistic personality disorder (including mirroring, idealizing, and twinship transferences).

In the mirroring transference, the patient seeks mirroring, admiration, and empathy from an attentive selfobject. In the idealizing transference, the patient seeks to merge with the ideal, omnipotent object. In the twinship transference, the individual seeks a soulmate or twin who is exactly like him or her. The task of therapy is thus to help patients become aware of and to acquire their needs for mirroring, idealizing, and twinship. Mastery is acquired through gradually internalizing the therapist's selfobject functions until they become functions of the patient's self. This process is encouraged by manageable, optimal frustration of the patient's needs for the therapist's authentic engagement with the patient and perfect provisions of selfobject functions (St. Clair 1996). Through internalization and insight the patient gradually gives up his or her primitive demands on the therapist (Kohut 1971).

Kohut encourages a neutral stand toward the patient's transferences, allowing the patient to express grandiose, idealizing, and twinship fantasies to the therapist, making them more conscious and thus amenable to treatment. Kohut characterizes these fantasies as reflecting the patient's fixation on specific normal developmental processes rather than representing a pathological defensive process that must be actively confronted as Kernberg does. Rather, he believes that the crucial components of treatment are facilitating insight and providing patients with missing developmental experiences.

Major Criticisms

Kohut's second theory of complementarity has been criticized for (1) minimizing the concept of the ego as the main organizer of experience, and (2) de-emphasizing the role of aggression. Focusing exclusively on the self structure allows for no autonomous, cognitive, organizing structure that matures with neurological consolidation and helps some infants cope with less carefully attuned parents. Furthermore, minimizing the importance of aggression and reinterpreting it as the patient's frustration at being "misunderstood" limits understanding of patients' problems where aggression may be an important component of their pathology and not necessarily derived from lack of empathic attunement.

In addition, the idea of complementarity is itself problematic because of the inherent contradictions between self psychology and drive theory

(Greenberg and Mitchell 1983). Kohut believed that for the more impaired "tragic man" of self psychology, relationships with others are primary, and nonrelational instinctual gratifications (e.g., casual sexual encounters) are pathological. In contrast, Kohut believed that for Freud's less impaired "guilty man" of drive theory, gratification of instinctual drives is primary and important for its own sake. Thus, the primary motivation of the higher functioning neurotic individual as described by Freud is considered a sign of pathology as described by Kohut. Furthermore, this contradicts Kohut's belief that drives are not primary motivators for people.

Greenberg and Mitchell (1983) believe that Kohut used the theory of complementarity to avoid making a choice between drive and relational models of personality (although his emphasis clearly seemed to be in the direction of relational motivation). In other words, the principle of complementarity seemed less designed to integrate two compatible, mutually enriching perspectives than to provide Kohut with a means to preserve a tie with the drive theory tradition.

Furthermore, Kohut has been criticized for proposing a theory that interprets human experience within too narrow a focus. In particular, as Fairbairn emphasized unmet dependency needs as the underlying problem for all patients, Kohut consistently interpreted narcissistic issues in his patients (e.g., the desire for empathy and the need to idealize) to the exclusion of other motivations (e.g., the desire to be liked or loved, the desire for self-expression, the desire for control or security, the desire to dominate). Kohut also gave secondary status to everything in life except joyful exuberance. He did not view greed, envy, and separation conflicts as an inevitable part of life.

Kohut failed to acknowledge the similarities of self psychology to the theories of Sullivan, Fairbairn, Guntrip, and Winnicott. He also never addressed and perhaps was unaware of the great similarities between self psychology and the client-centered therapy of Carl Rogers (1965).

American Interpersonal School

Interpersonal psychoanalysis was initiated in the United States during the late 1930s as an alternative to Freud's drive/structure model. The initiators of this movement (e.g., Harry Stack Sullivan, Erik Fromm, Karen Horney, Clara Thompson, and Frieda Fromm-Reichmann) worked together in various ways and influenced one another's writings. They shared a common set of beliefs about the importance of relationships with others, but they also held an abiding respect for social and cultural influences that set them apart from the British school of object relations theorists.

Harry Stack Sullivan: The Father of Interpersonal Psychiatry

Sullivan studied medicine in Chicago during the 1920s and ran a small ward for male schizophrenics between 1923 and 1930 in Towson, Maryland. Within the context of this experimental ward, Sullivan developed his interpersonal theory. While Sullivan has been called the father of American psychiatry and the co-parent (along with Melanie Klein) of object relations concepts (Havens 1976), his theory was largely ignored or derided during his lifetime and his work still goes largely unappreciated in the psychoanalytic community. This may be due in part to Sullivan's resistance to systematizing his concepts for fear of being misunderstood (Greenberg and Mitchell 1983).

Sullivan's early work with schizophrenics led him to several convictions that he later expanded into his theory of human experience. For example, he came to understand schizophrenia as a reaction to interactions occurring between the patient and his or her environment, rather than as an irreversible biological process. For Sullivan, the environment included both significant others and the larger social context or culture. As a result of this work, Sullivan defined the field of psychiatry as "the field of interpersonal relations" (1940, p. 10).

Sullivan's desire not to undermine Freudian psychoanalysis in the United States prevented him from directly addressing a full critique of Freud. However, Sullivan (1972) had several concerns about drive theory: (1) the limited usefulness of classical analytic techniques with lower-class or severely disturbed American patients; (2) too narrow a view of the therapeutic potential of treating schizophrenics; (3) Freud's postulation of universal principles, like castration anxiety (without sufficient empirical data), and proposed processes like the death instinct (which could not be observed, only inferred); and (4) Freud's underemphasis of the importance of interpersonal and cultural relations on individual functioning.

Sullivan believed that all of our knowledge about another person is mediated through our interactions with him or her. As a result, when the therapist gathers data about the patient, the therapist cannot be "an objective reporter, but is always a *participant-observer*" (Greenberg and Mitchell 1983, p. 90). Sullivan noted that "Personality is made manifest in interpersonal situations, and not otherwise" (1938, p. 32). We thus learn about each other by observing what the other person does in interaction with what we do and by listening to reports of their interactions with other people.

Sullivan objected to concepts such as superego, ego, and introjects, which he thought implied intrapsychic "quasi-entities." He also argued against the existence of psychic structures, thinking they portrayed the mind as being too static.

Sullivan further proposed that individuals are motivated by either the *need for security* or the *need for satisfaction* (e.g., food, oxygen, exercise, and needs for tenderness like affection and intimacy). Sullivan believed that the relative balance between these needs determined psychological health and influenced an individual's relationships with others.

Sullivan thought that only some of the infant's needs for satisfaction are present from birth. Others, like emotional intimacy, develop over time. The satisfaction of needs requires an exchange between the individual and the environment. Sullivan believed, however, that this was potentially a simple process as caregivers have complementary needs to meet the child's needs (e.g., the baby needs to be fed and the mother needs to feed him). Sullivan thought that what interfered with the simple satisfaction of needs was anxiety. He believed that the infant experienced anxiety through empathic linkage with the infant's caregivers (i.e., when the mother is anxious, the infant internalizes the mother's anxiety). While this process sounds somewhat mystical (e.g., what is the mechanism through which this occurs?), the author observed with her infant that after her dog ran away and she was feeling anxious, her baby began to cry and she was unable to soothe him. She remembered Sullivan, and hoping that empathic linkage was not caused by "bad vibes," kept the infant on her lap but turned him around so that he would not be able to observe worried expressions on her face. The baby immediately calmed down.

However, for mothers who are not so lucky as to have read Sullivan, circular problems evolve between the mother and child. The anxious infant arouses tenderness in the anxious caregiver, who then attempts to meet the infant's needs. Unfortunately, as the infant's anxiety is caused by the caregiver's anxiety, the caregiver's attempts to soothe the infant only make the infant more anxious, which further distresses the caregiver and, in turn, makes the infant more anxious.

Sullivan believed that the infant's earliest organizer of experience was the feeling and avoidance of anxiety. He believed that the infant learned to distinguish between anxious states (i.e., the bad mother) and nonanxious states (i.e., the good mother) (Greenberg and Mitchell 1983). Over time the child begins to observe that some of his or her behaviors increase or decrease the mother's anxiety (and thus the infant's anxiety). Sullivan thought the behaviors (or area of the child's personality) that didn't make the mother anxious and, in fact, evoked her approval and tenderness were experienced by the child as *the good me* part of the self. The behaviors and experiences that seemed to make the mother anxious were experienced by the child as *the bad me* part of the self. Lastly, behaviors in the infant or child that evoked intense anxiety in the mother and thus intense anxiety in the child induced infant amnesia for these transactions, which Sullivan labeled *the not me* part of the infant's self.

Sullivan thought infants used what he referred to as the *self system* of good me, bad me, and not me to organize experience and control anxiety by attempting to limit their self awareness to the good me part of the self. Sullivan believed that as children matured, the self system developed a set of security operations in order to minimize anxiety. These include behaviors or thoughts that make the individual feel powerful, special, or superior.

Implications for Treatment

Sullivan believed that the personal relationship between therapist and patient was the curative factor in treatment. He noted, specifically in relation to his work with schizophrenics, that "far more than any single action of the physician, it is his general attitude toward the patient that determines his value" (1924, p. 20). Sullivan also added the careful use of questions to Freud's technique of free association.

In his writings, Sullivan portrayed therapy as an ongoing and necessarily incomplete inquiry. In treatment, the therapist attempts the difficult task of understanding the ultimately unknowable reality of the patient's life (Greenberg and Mitchell 1983). Goals of treatment are helping patients develop a more unified self system and better interpersonal relationships, in part by examining and responding to their anxiety about anxiety, which Sullivan thought lay at the root of all psychopathology.

Major Criticisms

Sullivan objected to the reification of constructs implied by the British object relations theorists in their use of terminology. Nonetheless, he was also unable to avoid naming his hypothetical constructs. For example, his term *diagrammatic fragments* serves the same function as internal objects do in the British school. Furthermore, Greenberg and Mitchell (1983) believe that, like Fairbairn, Sullivan "fails to provide a framework for non-pathological functioning," in essence a "theory of health" (p. 114).

SUMMARY FORMULATIONS RELATED TO
OBJECT RELATIONS THEORIES

All of the object relations theories have in common an emphasis on the importance of the internalization of relationships with others that become enduring structures in people's minds, influencing their perceptions of self and others as well as their behavior. There are several important issues, however, about which these theorists do not agree: (1) the importance of instinctual drives versus relational needs, (2) the role of aggression in development, and (3) the existence of an autistic phase of interpersonal unrelatedness in the newborn.

Because object relations theory is an intrapsychic and interpersonal theory that primarily focuses on emotional interactions with others, cognitive and perceptual-motor factors have been relatively ignored. For example, there has been little consideration of the observation that splitting could result from a neurological deficit in cognition so that the patient is unable to hold opposites in mind at the same time.

Furthermore, object relations theories have been derived from and have made their most profound contribution to the understanding and treatment of severe character disorders. There is a need, however, for further investigation into how modern object relations principles such as providing missing developmental experiences from childhood (e.g., empathy, containment) can also be useful in the treatment of less severe disorders. We attempt to do this in Chapters 8 through 11 in this book as we apply the principles of object relations theory to the treatment of preneurotic and neurotic patients.

Finally, a criticism of a number of object relations theories is that they are too narrow in their focus. As in the story about the blind men and the elephant, each theorist bases his or her conclusions about the "whole elephant" by touching a part of the elephant (i.e., studying a specific subgroup of patients). Initially, Freud touched the elephant's eyes and concluded that the elephant needs insight through interpretation. Kohut touched the elephant's ear and concluded that the elephant needs mirroring, empathy, and someone to idealize. Kernberg disagreed with Kohut, when he touched the elephant's legs. He thought that the elephant needed confrontation of splitting.

Our own conclusion is that all these theorists are right about the treatment of patients with particular types of character disorders with their accompanying developmental and structural issues. Their theories are only deficient when they are viewed as describing the dynamics and consequent prescription for treatment for all patients. In this book, we attempt to integrate and apply what we believe are the most salient ideas and useful technical applications of the ideas of each of these theorists to the treatment of particular patient problems. In addition, we have added our own theories of, and clinical applications for, the treatment of each character disorder. All are organized under the umbrella of the theory of psychotherapy presented in the next chapter.

2

Object Relations Therapy[*]

While object relations theory is becoming an influential perspective in contemporary clinical work as a means of understanding patients, particularly those with narcissistic and borderline disorders, until recently its main impact on treatment had been limited to the modification of traditional psychoanalytic technique (Cashdan 1988, Glickauf-Hughes and Wells 1995b). Greenson (1967), for example, posits that while what is curative in treatment is the interpretation of transference, in order to interpret transference a working alliance must first exist between analyst and patient. Kleinian analysts believe that the manner in which interpretations are made can transform the relationship between patient and analyst (Greenberg and Mitchell 1983). Rucker (1968) similarly stresses that in interpreting the transference, analysts implicitly say to patients that they are not like their bad objects but are trying to understand them and to reach them. Pine (1993) believes that an "interpretation can have its maximum effect because the relationship (non-condemning) belies the patient's inner world" and that "additionally,

---

*This chapter repeats the discussion previously published in *Treatment of the Masochistic Personality: An Interactional Approach to Psychoanalytic Treatment* (Glickauf-Hughes and Wells 1995b).

the relationship factor has its maximum effect at precisely the moment of interpretation" (pp. 192–193).

In contrast, Sullivan (1953) de-emphasizes the value of interpretation altogether. Rather, he highlights the importance of the analyst as a new relationship in the patient's life. Fairbairn (1952) stresses the necessity of the analyst's being a good object in order to provide the patient with sufficient security to relinquish bad object ties. Winnicott (1960) thought that therapy should simulate a good-enough maternal environment in order to reverse the environmental failure of patients.

Kohut (1977) likewise believes that it is the actual interpersonal experience with the analyst that carries the treatment's therapeutic action. Furthermore, he suggests that specific analyst behaviors (e.g., empathizing, explaining, interpreting, mirroring, idealizing) are required as a corrective experience to heal the patient's developmental deficits. Guntrip (1961) states that in order to help patients, therapists must be the kind of person with whom patients can integrate their disparate fragments. Jacobs (1993) believes that while "many factors go into the development of rapport between patient and therapist including the matching of personalities and styles, employing the correct techniques of working from the surface down, tuning in to the patient's affects and interpreting these before one gets into deeper conflicts, [these factors] will not be effective or have meaning if the basic ingredient, the *mensch* factor ingredient is not present" (pp. 4–5). Jacobs defines a mensch as a genuinely "mature individual with sound values who can relate warmly and empathically to another human being" (p. 4).

THE CONCEPT OF A CORRECTIVE
EMOTIONAL EXPERIENCE REEXAMINED

The concept of a "corrective emotional experience" as outlined by Alexander and French (1946) has received substantial criticism within the analytic community. Alexander defined the corrective emotional experience in terms of the patient's reliving original traumatic experiences in the presence of a significant other (therapist, friend) with a more favorable resolution than in the original childhood conflict. Alexander recommended that the therapist "manipulate" the transference by assuming a role that would most readily evoke this corrective emotional experience (Horner 1979).

Greenson (1967) cautions against the use of essentially manipulative and antianalytic techniques, pointing out that, when such techniques are employed, "the patient does not learn to recognize and understand his resistances, there is no premium on insight as a means of overcoming resistances, and there is no attempt to change the ego structure" (p. 136). Horner (1991) agrees, noting that "antianalytic procedures can block or lessen the patient's capacity for insight and understanding" (p. 191).

The concept of a corrective emotional experience, however, seems to be experiencing a resurgence at this time. Renik (1993) discusses how an analyst's countertransference enactment can provide a corrective emotional experience that helps the patient to "re-create and master crucial pathogenic experiences" (p. 142). Furthermore, Norcross (1993) and Lazarus (1993) discuss tailoring therapeutic relationship stances to the patient's needs. Dolan and colleagues (1993) stress the importance of making the therapist's interpersonal stance contingent upon the patient's attachment style. Mahrer (1993) believes that crucial parts of the therapy relationship are uniquely tailored by and for each patient in each session. Weiss (1993) believes that patients seek corrective emotional experiences through their testing of the therapist, and that therapists should provide patients with the experiences that they seek. Weiss further believes that providing these experiences helps patients to disprove their pathogenic beliefs and, thus, to pursue important but forbidden goals.

We do not conceptualize the therapist's offering of a corrective emotional experience as a manipulation or even as a role assumption, but rather as a genuine engagement that emphasizes the particular aspects of the parental relationship that a specific patient has insufficiently received and are, thus, required to facilitate the patient's continued interpersonal and structural development. Much of the analytic community has recognized the validity of altering the analytic frame of neutral therapeutic abstinence for borderline patients who need the therapist to behave in a more warm, empathic, and authentic manner as well as to provide psychic functions these patients cannot provide for themselves (e.g., self-validation, self-soothing, selfobject differentiation, reality testing). We believe that therapists may be more effective by altering their stance with other patients as well.

This proposal finds support in Lazarus's concept of the therapist as an "authentic chameleon." Lazarus thinks that "it is important for the therapist to modify his or her participation in the therapeutic process in order to offer the most appropriate form of treatment for the client being seen as opposed to the situation where the therapist fits the person to the treatment" (Dryden 1991, pp. 17–18).

We believe that clinicians who utilize object relations theories to direct psychotherapy need to develop models of treatment that go beyond the mere modification of classical psychoanalytic techniques and instead specify the precise nature in which the therapist must be a new object for each patient, given his or her particular characterological makeup. While Kohut (1977) has proposed such a model, self psychology best serves as a corrective interpersonal experience for individuals suffering from narcissistic disturbances (Hedges 1983).

We are not advocating acting, role playing, or being a narcissistic object for patients. What is suggested is tailoring the therapeutic relationship to the patient's developmental and interpersonal needs within the confines of what the therapist is authentically able to provide for the patient. All therapists have limits. Therapists with schizoid tendencies may not be able to help schizoid patients learn to bond. Therapists with borderline mothers may have particular difficulty containing the projective identifications of their borderline patients. What is important to note is that therapists do not help patients resolve transference feelings when they subtly behave like the patients' internal objects. It is thus helpful for therapists to be aware of their strengths and limitations and their own countertransference issues, and to know which patients should be referred to another therapist.

CURRENT INTERPERSONAL AND OBJECT RELATIONS THEORIES OF TREATMENT

While there have been several excellent models applying object relations principles to the treatment of couples (Scharff and Scharff 1991) and families (Slipp 1984), the most thorough model to date of a theory of object relations therapy that deals with varied patient problems has been proposed by Cashdan (1988). The basic tenets of Cashdan's model of object relations therapy are that (1) emphasis in treatment is placed on the therapist–patient relationship; (2) the therapist focuses on the therapist–patient relationship in the here and now rather than on transference, defense mechanisms, and insight; and (3) the goal of therapy is to use the therapist–patient relationship as a vehicle for the patient's developing both healthier object relations and a more positive sense of self. Cashdan believes that interpersonal psychopathology is expressed through different projective identifications (e.g., dependency, power, sexuality, ingratiation) and that therapists can understand patients' pathology as well as derive a therapeutic strategy for treating that pathology by understanding their own countertransference reactions to the patient's projective identifications. Once therapists understand the patient's metacommunicative demands (e.g., "Take care of me," "Do what

I say"), they can treat the patient's interpersonal pathology by refusing to concede or conform to the metacommunicative demand.

This strategy appears to be similar to that proposed by interpersonal therapists who stress the importance of the therapist's not responding in a complementary fashion to the patient but instead providing the patient with an "asocial response" (Beier 1966). The basic modes of the asocial response are delay of response, reflection of content and feeling, labeling the style of interaction, and making a paradigmatic response (Young and Beier 1982).

The primary limitation of this approach is that while it is recommended that therapists not make complementary social responses to the patient's pathological and interpersonally self-defeating behaviors, and while alternate behaviors are recommended, a model of variable therapeutic response for treating patients with different interpersonal pathology (e.g., behaving in a more spontaneous, emotional way with obsessive-compulsive patients and being more logical and cognitive with hysterical patients) has not been articulated.

Alternative strategies have been proposed by Leary (1957) and Benjamin (1979). In Benjamin's structural analysis of social behavior (SASB) model, the therapist both refrains from emitting complementary behaviors and attempts to do the antithesis with the patient. For example, if the patient whines, defends, and justifies, the therapist confirms that the patient is acceptable just as he or she is. Through confirmation, it is hoped that the patient's defensiveness will give way to free and enthusiastic disclosure.

While Benjamin (1979, 1993) recommends therapeutic strategies tailored to modify particular maladaptive behaviors of patients, this approach does not, however, specifically address the more complicated remediation of developmental deficits, including the building of new psychic structures (e.g., cohesive sense of self, good observing ego). Thus, the issue of increasing the development of an integrated sense of self is not addressed in the differential treatment of the dependent behavior of the hysteroid borderline patient (who requires greater therapist involvement, limits, and support) from that of the hysterical neurotic patient (who requires therapeutic abstinence and the promotion of regression while recognizing the patient's real capabilities).

Developmental issues are more clearly addressed in the model of psychotherapy (based on object relations and ego psychology principles) used by Althea Horner (1979, 1991). While Horner does not specifically systematize the particular therapeutic behaviors appropriate for the resolution of specific developmental failures (and their resultant character pathology), she does discuss different treatment implications relevant to patients with differential pathology.

For example, in discussing the tasks of treatment in working with a schizoid patient (whose developmental failure is seen as stemming from the symbiotic stage and the hatching phases of separation-individuation), Horner (1979) states, "One must provide a matrix of relatedness so that, as differentiation proceeds, it is not equated with object loss, with its danger of dissolution of the self" (pp. 92–93). In contrast, Horner discusses a borderline patient with rapprochement issues who expressed a premature wish to leave treatment. Horner believes that the appropriate stance in this case was to support the patient's separation-individuation striving symbolized in the wish to leave rather than confronting the wish as a resistance to treatment.

In her discussion of treatment for these two patients, Horner thus implicitly suggests that different types of corrective interpersonal experiences are needed for personality disorders that have developmental arrests at different stages. For the schizoid patient who received an inadequate symbiotic experience and consequently struggles with painful underattachment, Horner's therapeutic strategy is one of emotional availability. For the borderline patient who wasn't permitted to separate during rapprochement and consequently struggles with painful overattachment, the appropriate therapeutic strategy is one of supporting the patient's attempts at separation. Horner's (1991) most recent book, *Psychoanalytic Object Relations Therapy,* considers the application of object relations theory to the general themes and phases of the treatment process as applied to patients with various developmental deficits. However, she only briefly refers to therapeutic issues that are differentially relevant to patients with various character disorders (e.g., narcissistic, schizoid, depressive, paranoid).

In this chapter, an extended model of object relations therapy is presented. This model (1) gives greater specificity to the concept of providing patients with a new object or corrective interpersonal experience than previously described by Fairbairn, Guntrip, Sullivan, or Alexander and French; (2) takes developmental deficits and structural change into account more than does Benjamin's SASB model; (3) discusses proactive strategies for dealing with particular character disorders more than does Cashdan's model; (4) further expands upon the therapeutic strategies for remediating developmental deficits as articulated by Horner (1979, 1991); and (5) is applicable to a broader range of disorders than Kohut's (1971, 1977) model.

OBJECT RELATIONS THERAPY: AN EXTENDED MODEL

The model of object relations therapy described in this chapter both draws upon and expands some of the previously explicated premises. The basic tenets of this theory of therapy are as follows. Character is seen as shaped by the interaction of the individual with significant others (Fairbairn 1952, Sullivan 1953). Particular importance is given to the interaction with others during critical periods of social and emotional development as described by Erikson (1950) and Mahler and colleagues (1975). As a result of these interpersonal experiences, individuals more or less successfully master major developmental tasks (e.g., basic trust, attachment, autonomy, separation-individuation).

Over the course of the first five years of life, residues from significant developmental and interpersonal experiences become organized into a mental template of a representation of self in relationship to the important early significant others or objects in one's life. This template influences both the individual's phenomenological experience and his or her interpersonal behavior. An individual's mental template also predisposes him or her to assume a particular interpersonal stance such as moving toward, away from, or against others (Horney 1939), or friendly dominance, hostile dominance, friendly submission, or hostile submission (Leary 1957). From this perspective, character disorders are viewed as a manifestation of a dysfunctional mental template of interpersonal relationships resulting from specific developmental deficits causing the individual to assume a rigid and nonadaptive interpersonal stance.

Object relations therapy thus attempts to provide patients with the opportunity for a corrective interpersonal experience geared to help them to modify their mental template of self and objects, better master unresolved developmental issues, assume more varied and flexible interpersonal stances that are more appropriately attuned to their current social reality, and remediate deficient psychic structures. By offering patients opportunities for corrective experiences, these patients are thus given "a developmental second chance" (Greenberg and Mitchell 1983, p. 356). The kind of corrective interpersonal relationship that a given patient requires varies with his or her particular developmental impasse, structural deficits, interpersonal stance, and resulting character disorder. The impact of a corrective experience depends, in part, on a patient's ability to internalize.

For example, hysteroid borderlines tend to have unresolved separation-individuation issues resulting from failures during the rapprochement subphase of development (Masterson 1981). During rapprochement, hysteroids' maternal objects frequently withdrew emotional supplies in response to their children's separation and individuative strivings (Masterson 1981). With regard to their mental templates, hysteroids manifest a weakened psychological boundary or separation between self and object representations, insufficient integration of good and bad aspects of self and object representations, and a preponderance of negative versus positive affects. As a result hysteroid borderlines rely on good/bad splitting, and thus tend to vacillate between clinging to objects perceived as "all good" or raging against objects perceived as "all bad." Therapeutic goals for hysteroid patients would thus involve helping them to learn to psychologically separate self from others, to resolve splitting (Kernberg 1975), to become more genuinely self-activating (Masterson 1981), and to develop stabilized object constancy (Wells and Glickauf-Hughes 1986).

As a general guideline to the type of experience required for mastery of a given developmental stage, therapists are advised to understand the principles used by good-enough parents to help children with particular developmental tasks and to adapt these principles to the therapeutic situation. The therapist must be careful not to infantilize or condescend to the adult patient with this approach. These principles can be very helpful as guides to treatment, however. For example, in the case of the hysteroid borderline patient, the therapist (like the good-enough rapprochement-phase parent) may best function as a secure base from which to explore (Ainsworth et al. 1969), serving as a constant object while supporting self-activation.

A second example illustrating this model is the case of the masochistic patient who struggles with anxious attachment as a result of his parents' inconsistent attunement and general unpredictability (Glickauf-Hughes and Wells 1991b), which interfered with the patient's completion of transmuting internalizations of his parents' realistic selfobject functions such as empathy and soothing (Glickauf-Hughes and Wells 1995b, Horner 1979). This clinical observation is supported by developmental research that suggests that empathic caregivers raise more securely attached children (Egeland and Farber 1985). Thus, the use of empathy in the psychotherapy of masochistic patients may be an important tool for remediation (Renik, personal communication).

The question of the therapist's importance needs to be addressed. For example, why does the therapist matter so much to patients and how can the therapist's person potentially have such an enormous impact in helping patients overcome their development deficits? First, we agree with Fairbairn (1952) and Sullivan (1940) that the primary human motivation is the need to relate to others. Second, character-disordered individuals often are not able to create or internalize a corrective experience outside of therapy with a trained clinician due to their own resistances or the power of their defenses.

We believe that individuals attempt to repair early trauma and correct developmental deficits through their primary relationships. However, due to repetition compulsions (i.e., repeating similar poor object choices), ego structural deficits (i.e., lack of frustration tolerance), transference, and the fact that significant others have their own needs and their own developmental deficits to rectify, new relationships often repeat rather than rectify old psychological wounds.

Because of their commitment to understanding their own countertransference and appropriately meeting patients' developmental needs, therapists are in an ideal position for offering corrective relationship opportunities. Furthermore, "the sheer intimacy and intensity of the relationship from the patient's side, deriving from the frequency, reliability, and isolation of the contacts, and deriving also from the patient's self-exposure through free association in an inherently unequal relationship, guarantees in most instances that the analyst will matter to the patient—immensely" (Pine 1993, p. 190).

A corrective interpersonal experience is seen as additive to rather than substitutive for interpretation. Insight resulting from correct interpretation provides patients with greater clarity and thus better ego-strength, including better reality testing. Insight is thus seen as enhancing psychological structure, including consolidation of the self (Kohut 1977). Thus, while insight is not seen as sufficient for change, it can greatly facilitate the process of mastering developmental deficits. Furthermore, insight helps patients to overcome resistance to internalization and provides a cognitive structure to understanding their past and current relationships.

Table 2–1 offers a summary of this model of object relations therapy with six personality disorders at three levels of ego development. Each personality disorder is examined with regard to stage of developmental arrest, treatment by significant others, resulting developmental failure, structural defects, and interpersonal stance. Based on these deficits, therapeutic goals and corrective interpersonal experiences are formulated. Personality disorders are grouped according to level of ego development due to the commonalities in treatment priorities appropriate for individuals at similar levels of ego development and object relations. For example, with neurotic patients, uncovering of repressed material/memories via therapeutic abstinence and promotion of regression is given priority. Encouraging transmut-

Table 2–1. Object relations therapy of six personality disorders

Borderline Personality Disorders	Schizoid	Hysteroid
Stage of Developmental Arrest	Autistic and early symbiotic (Johnson 1985)	Practicing and rapprochement
Treatment by Object	Rejection, neglect, negation of child's right to be or live (Guntrip 1969)	Withdrawal of attention, support, and approval when child begins to separate and individuate (Masterson 1981)
Developmental Failure	Lack of adequate symbiotic attachment (Johnson 1985)	Insufficient separation and individuation
Resulting Interpersonal Stance	Defensive withdrawal from others	Alternation between rage and clinging
Structural Issues	1. Detached self that fears regressive self-fragmentation 2. Rigidly maintained self–other differentiation	1. Identity diffusion 2. Lack of object constancy 3. Vulnerability to transitory self-fragmentation or brief psychotic episodes in regressive states
Therapeutic Goals	*Interpersonal* 1. Protect client from gross anxiety 2. Establish an attachment from which client can separate *Structural* 1. Develop cohesive sense of core self that is not defensively based (Guntrip 1969) 2. Integration of part self representations (especially or affective and cognitive part self representations)	*Interpersonal* 1. Support separation 2. Foster individuation *Structural* 1. Resolve splitting (Kernberg 1976) 2. Develop object constancy 3. Develop integrated sense of self 4. Increase frustration tolerance

	Narcissistic	Masochistic
Corrective Interpersonal Experience	1. Therapist must be available, contactful, present, and congruent 2. Therapist must establish a safe relationship	1. Therapist must set appropriate limits 2. Therapist must balance need for support and autonomy by being a secure base from which to explore 3. Therapist must support genuine self expression and saying no 4. Therapist must refrain from revenge and retaliation (Wells and Glickauf-Hughes 1986)

Preneurotic Personality Disorders	Narcissistic	Masochistic
Stage of Developmental Arrest	Rapprochement (Johnson 1987)	On the way to object constancy (Horner 1979, Johnson 1985)
Treatment by Object	1. Rejection of true self (Miller 1981) 2. Uses child as selfobject or ideal object 3. Provides admiration rather than love and acceptance	1. Scapegoating and/or parentification 2. Abuse, neglect, and intermittent reinforcement of dependency needs 3. Controlling (but without self-discipline) 4. Squelching the child's will (Johnson 1985)
Developmental Failure	1. Lack of authentic, reality-based sense of self 2. Lack of genuine self-esteem 3. Inability to self-soothe 4. Inability to love	Failure to identify, leading to lack of transmuting internalizations of caregivers' realistic and soothing capacities (Horner 1979), such as empathy and auxiliary ego functions
Resulting Interpersonal Stance	1. Pseudoindependent false self representation 2. Manipulation, idealization, and devaluation of others 3. Relates to others as selfobjects	1. Alternation between anxious attachment and counterdependence 2. Overt compliance (but covert defiance) 3. Compensatory caregiving

(*continued*)

Table 2-1. (*continued*)

Preneurotic Personality Disorders	Narcissistic	Masochistic
Structural Issues	1. Grandiose false self structure 2. Central ego sensitive to slights (resulting in feelings of envy, shame, and rage)	1. Lack of complete integration in self structure 2. Lack of transmuting internalizations (Horner 1979)
Therapeutic Goals	*Interpersonal* 1. Develop ability to love realistically perceived whole objects 2. Develop ability to be authentic with others *Structural* 1. Develop transmuting internalizations for genuine, reality-based self-soothing and self-esteem 2. Integrate grandiose false self representation into nuclear core self (Kohut 1977)	*Interpersonal* 1. Resolve ambivalent attachment 2. Master separation and loss 3. Learn to genuinely depend on others 4. Develop appropriate self assertion *Structural* 1. Develop transmuting internalizations for genuine, reality-based self-soothing and self-esteem 2. Resolve "masochistic splitting" (Meyers 1988)
Corrective Interpersonal Experience	1. Therapist must be nonimpinging, sensitive, accepting, and attuned 2. Therapist must provide an empathic, optimally frustrating environment (Kohut 1977) 3. Therapist must support strengths and empathize with vulnerabilities (Johnson 1987)	1. Therapist must be empathic and have genine positive regard for client 2. Therapist must be constant, dependable, reliable, and nonreactive 3. Therapist must acknowledge relational mistakes 4. Therapist must be emotionally available without being possessive, controlling, or infantalizing

Neurotic Personality Disorders	Obsessive-Compulsive	Hysterical
Stage of Developmental Arrest	Late separation-individuation (anal/early oedipal)	Late oedipal
Treatment by Object	Harsh discipline and overcontrol of child's impulses, affects, and autonomous actions	1. Seductive behavior of opposite-sex parent 2. Alliance of opposite-sex parent with child against same-sex parent 3. Castration of aggressive impulses 4. Fosters "myth of passivity" (Krohn 1978), pseudodependency, and helplessness
Developmental Failure	Insufficient sense of autonomy leading to feelings of shame and doubt (Salzman and Thaler 1981)	1. Difficulty taking initiative 2. Guilt about sexual and aggressive impulses 3. Confusion between sexual and affectional needs
Resulting Interpersonal Stance	1. Pseudoautonomous, self-contained presentation of self 2. Frequent power struggles (Salzman 1985)	Pseudodependent, seductive
Structural Issues	1. Stable sense of self but lack of integration of affective experience into core self 2. Stable object constancy but proclivity to sacrifice relationships to appease harsh superego	1. Has self and object constancy 2. Has but underuses good ego function 3. Has proclivity to act out conflicts rather than reflect

(continued)

Table 2-1. (*continued*)

Neurotic Personality Disorders	Obsessive-Compulsive	Hysterical
Therapeutic Goals	*Interpersonal* 1. Increase value of relationship (over being right or in control) 2. Increase spontaneity, affective expression, and playfulness with others (Wells et al. 1990) *Structural* 1. Further individuation: develop genuine sense of autonomy rather than reactivity and power struggles 2. Soften harsh superego	*Interpersonal* 1. Develop appropriate self-assertion, initiative, and independent actions with others 2. Learn to distinguish between sexual and dependency needs *Structural* 1. Further integration of ego dystonic self experiences 2. Increase frustration tolerance and ability to reflect rather than act out 3. Encourage use of ego functions (e.g., observing ego)
Corrective Interpersonal Experience	1. Therapist must be warm, spontaneous, and emotionally expressive 2. Therapist must model appropriate risk taking (Wells et al. 1990) 3. Therapist must acknowledge mistakes and let clients off the hook when they make mistakes 4. Therapists must be nondirective and nonauthoritarian	1. Therapist must be warm and nondirective 2. Therapist must not dominate, get seduced, or foster too much dependency (Mueller and Aniskiewicz 1986) 3. Therapist must support strength, competence, and appropriate assertion 4. Therapist must clarify emotions and ask for factual details

ing internalization of specific ego functions is recommended with preneurotic clients, and developing self and object constancy is the focus when working with borderline clients. Specific differences in treatment strategies are recommended, however, for clients within similar levels of ego development who have received differential treatment by objects and have developed different defensive and personal styles. For example, as illustrated by Horner (1979), it is recommended that therapists facilitate greater attachment in schizoid borderlines who never experienced an adequate symbiosis, and encourage greater autonomy in hysteroid borderlines whose attempts at separation-individuation were consistently unsupported. Thus, at each stage of ego development, we discuss the diagnosis and treatment issues related to one disorder of underattachment and one disorder of overattachment.

We do not specify all aspects of treatment for these disorders. Nor would this model be appropriate for other personalities. In fact, a third continuum, hostile (i.e., individuals who are primarily abused and move against others), including antisocial, aggressive-sadistic, and paranoid, should be developed. But it is beyond the scope of this book to describe the etiology and treatment of all the major personality disorders. Rather, our goal is to begin to describe and operationalize a model of object relations therapy so that clinicians who subscribe to object relations principles can systematically begin to integrate these formulations into their treatment strategies.

We are not, however, advocating a "cookbook" approach to treatment (e.g., if a patient meets *DSM-IV* criteria for schizoid personality, the therapist should act engaged). Rather, we provide guidelines and explanations about particular relational experiences that tend to be corrective for specific developmental issues (e.g., mirroring and empathy for disorders of the self). Timing, context, and situational variables all need to be taken into consideration by the therapist in devising an appropriate therapeutic treatment plan.

Very few patients clearly fit into one diagnostic category. Most of the patients we see manifest mixed personality or characterological issues. Furthermore, characterological issues are viewed as similar in nature to colors on a palette. Everyone has more of some and less of others. For example, a patient might have a strong masochistic component, some underlying narcissistic issues, and a tendency to use obsessive defenses under stress. However, the patient does not have schizoid features, has few hysterical qualities (e.g., pseudoemotionality, global perceptions, dramatic presentation), has reasonably developed object constancy, and thus infrequently uses splitting as a defense. The therapeutic approach prescribed for such a patient must reflect whatever complicated mix of experiences his or her character requires (e.g., empathy, nonreactivity, insight into use of obsessive defenses, etc.). Chapter 12 contains an instrument that helps clinicians understand the variety and predominance of characterological issues exhibited by a particular patient.

The suggested task is neither simple nor easy. This is particularly true because many patients present in therapy with contradictory issues. For example, patients with strong narcissistic and schizoid issues require the therapist to manage the difficult balancing act of being engaged without being experienced as intrusive or engulfing. Therapists often find such patients most challenging and frequently respond to them by interpreting their conflicting needs (e.g., "When I speak, you feel invaded, and when I'm quiet, you feel abandoned").

While specific corrective behaviors are thus suggested in this book, we are not overly categorical in understanding patient issues, and do not recommend that clinicians follow a simple, step-by-step treatment approach. Rather, the suggested guidelines are intended to inspire a new way for therapists to creatively use developmental theory in the treatment of their patients.

CASE EXAMPLES OF MODEL

Understanding the patient's underlying structural and developmental issues is extremely important with regard to both formulating appropriate treatment goals and ascertaining for each patient what constitutes a corrective interpersonal experience. For example, consider the ramifications of misdiagnosing a schizoid-like borderline client who employs many obsessive defenses as an obsessive-compulsive neurotic. Such a neurotic client maintains the ego strength to manifest a cohesive and integrated sense of self under stress and the experience of intense affect, but presents a personality style that is overconstricted and counterdependent. In one such case, the consequence of this misdiagnosis was that the therapist explored and encouraged the activation and expression of the patient's feelings (including anger) and dependency or relationship needs. When the therapist then went on a two-week vacation, the patient decompensated (e.g., had panic attacks, suicidal ideations, transient psychotic symptoms) and abruptly left the therapeutic relationship out of fear of destruction by the therapist and rage over feeling invited to depend and then rejected by the leaving.

Had the therapist recognized that the patient's obsessive-compulsive defenses and cognitive style masked a borderline ego organization, she would have avoided encouraging the expression of the patient's underlying feelings (e.g., rage) until he had established a relatively stable and positive relationship with the therapist and been able to use that relationship to augment self-soothing and self-validating functions. In addition, the therapist would have focused on the patient's tenuous capacity for object constancy rather than on the expression of his dependency needs per se. As a result of this change in focus, the therapist could have helped the patient to better anticipate his reactions to the therapist's leaving on vacation and could have joined the patient in creating strategies for managing his internal turmoil/separation anxieties during the therapist's absence.

The following cases illustrate different types of corrective interpersonal experiences that are needed by patients who have different developmental deficits and who repeatedly express the wish to leave therapy mid-session. In the case of the schizoid patient (who has experienced chronic rejection and neglect by objects leading to the lack of an adequate symbiotic attachment), a corrective interpersonal experience requires, above all, that the therapist "be there" (Johnson 1985, p. 83). The schizoid must first be helped to establish an attachment (from which he or she can later separate). The therapist facilitates this attachment by being contactful, present, and congruent. Thus, should a schizoid patient request to leave mid-session, the appropriate therapeutic response would be to encourage the patient to remain and to process with the patient the wish to leave the session early. We have observed that schizoid patients often make this request as a means of testing their assumption that they are not wanted.

In contrast to the literal abandonment often experienced by schizoid patients, narcissistic patients have experienced the physical presence of, but insufficient attunement from, the selfobjects in their early lives. Rather than having caregivers who mirrored and empathized with them, they learned to accommodate themselves to parental needs, giving up their true selves to serve as their parents' ideal objects or selfobjects (Miller 1981). As a result, narcissists fail to develop an authentic, reality-based sense of self. Consequently, they greatly fear the engulfment of their own impoverished selves into the needs and demands of others.

For the narcissistic patient, a corrective interpersonal experience involves the therapist's being a nonimpinging, sensitive, highly attuned, "good-enough" (Winnicott 1958b) selfobject who provides the narcissist with the necessary functions that were missed during early development (e.g., mirroring, echoing, admiring, soothing, empathy). Should a narcissistic patient thus express a wish to leave mid-session, the appropriate response would be to comply with the request (without interpreting it) and for the therapist to warmly tell the patient that she would see the patient next week. One narcissistic patient both frequently left therapy mid-session and took a one-year leave of absence from therapy after nine months of treatment. For this patient, simply accepting his need to move away from and to return to the therapist without interpreting it or rejecting him was the most crucial element of treatment during the first phase of therapy. When this patient did return for long-term treatment, he did so with the clear sense that his motivation for doing so was internal rather than an attempt to please the therapist. At this phase in treatment, the patient's absences were interpreted. For narcissistic and borderline patients, the therapists' remaining a secure and emotionally available base as the patients move toward them and away from them to explore the environment helps patients to rework their unresolved issues from the rapprochement subphase of separation-individuation.

In summary, the strengths and weaknesses of the clinical or treatment applications of current object relations theories and interpersonal theory have been described. An alternative model of object relations therapy (including its basic premises and practical applications) has been presented. In this model, therapy is seen as providing opportunities for a corrective interpersonal experience to help patients modify their interpersonal template of self and others, better master unresolved developmental issues, assume more varied and flexible interpersonal stances, and develop more mature psychic structures. Table 2–1 provides an overview of this model, the stage of developmental arrest, environmental treatment and resulting developmental failures, structural issues, and interpersonal style of six personality disorders. Therapeutic goals for resolving these developmental failures, rectifying structural deficits, and modifying interpersonal style are outlined as well as the necessary corrective interpersonal experience for accomplishing these goals. A more detailed approach to the differential diagnosis of these disorders is described in the next chapter and an elaboration of this model of treatment is provided in later chapters.

3

An Ego-Structural/Object Relations Approach to Differential Diagnosis*

For all therapists, and most especially beginning therapists, the process of learning differential diagnosis entails relatively complicated and difficult processes. A number of models have been proposed to help structure this endeavor (APA 1987, 1994, Kernberg 1976, Millon 1985). However, many models, such as the *DSM-IV* (APA 1994), employ a symptom-based, descriptive approach that does not address structural development or psychodynamic (i.e., motivational) theory. Like Kernberg (1975), we believe that the problem with such atheoretical approaches is that they limit connections to salient treatment considerations. In the first section of this chapter we delineate diagnostic criteria (i.e., major defenses, ego identity, reality testing, object constancy) that clinicians need to observe and understand in order to differentiate between the five levels of structural organization. This part of the model expands Kernberg's (1980) ego structural paradigm (i.e., psychotic, borderline, neurotic) to include preneurotic (Horner 1979) and normal ego structures. In addition, interspersed throughout our discussion

---

*Portions of this chapter are reprinted with permission from Wells and Glickauf-Hughes (1993).

of these structural differences, we have highlighted a number of salient treatment issues relevant to different levels of ego-structural organization.

In the second section of this chapter we present a diagnostic schema designed to differentiate six personality disorders that fall within three structural organizations (i.e., borderline, preneurotic, and neurotic). These personality disorders are compared across a number of critical dimensions, including cognitive style, major defenses, primary aim, related entitlements, ego mode, superego mode, and prevailing patient myth. Several treatment considerations relevant to the different character formations are cited.

We realize that even the complexity of this two-part ego-structural/object relations model simplifies human experience. Many patients manifest mixtures of the various character disorders and ego structures described in this book. The purpose of categorization, however, is to ease the clinician into the mind set of this diagnostic model. We present supervisors and clinicians with a point of departure that is elaborated upon more specifically in Chapters 5 through 11, which focus on the conceptualization and treatment of particular disorders. The uniqueness of the patient is attenuated in the forced categorizations, and a number of personality styles (i.e., paranoid, sadistic) are excluded. In part, the relevance of such a model lies in the degree to which it elicits the curiosity, better understanding, and more effective interventions of clinicians striving to make sense of the inner life of their patients.

In this model, structural deficits take therapeutic precedence over characterological conflicts whenever both are presented simultaneously by the patient (Horner 1991). For example, if the patient presents with difficulties in the ability to self-soothe and with conflicts between wanting approval from others and wanting to bluntly self-assert, the therapist would focus on completing the development of object constancy, rather than elucidating unconscious conflicts about a domineering parent through regression in the service of the ego.

MODIFIED KERNBERG MODEL OF
EGO/STRUCTURAL DIAGNOSIS

The diagnosis of a patient's level of ego development is crucial for developing effective treatment strategies (Kernberg 1975, 1980). For example, the use of therapeutic abstinence, the promotion of regression, and the goal of uncovering or making the unconscious conscious are appropriate for the neurotic patient who can sustain such abstinence without decompensating, but inappropriate for the borderline patient who tends to rely on splitting under stress and is prone to temporary decompensations (e.g., loss of reality testing, self fragmentation) when faced with prolonged therapeutic abstinence and/or assaults on higher level defenses (Goldstein 1985, Masterson 1976).

For patients with borderline personality organization (Kernberg 1975), therapeutic goals should center on ego strengthening. The therapist thus serves as the patient's auxiliary ego whenever it is required, providing or modeling ego functions that these patients have only weakly developed (i.e., self-soothing, integration of good and bad aspects of self and others). With borderline patients, the therapist focuses on empathic clarification, confrontation, and interpretation of primitive defenses in the here-and-now relationship with the therapist, such as splitting and projective identification (Kernberg 1975). In addition, the therapist helps the patient to temporarily bolster (or at least not rigorously challenge) more advanced defenses such as intellectualization, repression, rationalization, isolation of affect, and reaction formation.

Early in her career, one of the authors misdiagnosed a high-functioning schizoid-borderline patient who employed many obsessive defenses as an obsessive-compulsive neurotic. The therapist thus believed that the patient had the ego strength to manifest a cohesive and integrated sense of self under stress. She conceptualized his treatment issues as lack of spontaneity, an overcathected intellect, an overrestricted ability to express emotions, and counterdependence. In this case, the consequence of such a misdiagnosis was that the therapist explored and encouraged the activation and expression of the patient's feelings and needs. When the therapist went on a one-week vacation, the patient abruptly decompensated (e.g., had panic attacks, suicidal ideation, severe dissociative reactions) and prematurely left the therapeutic relationship out of fear of abandonment by the therapist and rage over feeling invited to depend on the therapist and then feeling rejected by the therapist's leaving.

Had the therapist recognized that the patient's obsessive-compulsive defenses and cognitive style masked a schizoid personality style with a borderline ego organization, she would have avoided encouraging the expression of the patient's underlying feelings (e.g., rage) until he had established a relatively stable and positive relationship with the therapist and had been able to use that relationship to develop self-soothing and self-validating functions. In addition, the therapist would have focused on the patient's tenuous capacity for object constancy rather than on the expression of his dependency needs per se. As a result of this change in focus, the therapist could have helped the patient to better anticipate his reactions to the therapist's leaving on vacation and could have joined the patient in creating strategies for managing his internal turmoil and separation anxiety during the therapist's absence.

In contrast to treating borderline patients, regression is frequently promoted in the treatment of neurotic patients in order to facilitate the exploration of their unconscious inner life. The purpose of this exploration is to help patients reclaim what has been repressed, providing the opportunity to experience fuller, richer lives with increased awareness and potential conscious control of their feelings, impulses, and behavior. The neurotic patient has sufficient inner resources (e.g., frustration tolerance, object constancy) to regress in service of the ego without unconstructive or harmful regressions (e.g., decompensations). As a result, a degree of therapeutic abstinence or neutrality (particularly early in treatment) can be a helpful therapeutic technique with these patients when they are highly defended. Such techniques generally raise these patients' anxiety and thus increase their awareness of repressed experiences, allowing them to explore with the therapist.

Because neurotic patients have achieved object constancy including full integration of good and bad aspects of self and others, the therapist can rely on the neurotic's access to an observing ego (i.e., friendly observer) to ally with the therapist's efforts at facilitating the patient's self-exploration. Thus, a therapeutic alliance is developed more quickly with neurotic patients who generally sustain the ability to self-reflect with the therapist. In addition, with the therapist's aid (i.e., through the use of clarification and interpretation), the neurotic patient is also able to maintain or reestablish the capacity to differentiate the real person of the therapist from the patient's transferential perception of the therapist. In contrast, the patient with a borderline ego structure often cannot make this distinction, even with the therapist's assistance.

One patient with borderline personality organization experienced the therapist as uninterested in her and self-serving. Despite the therapist's genuine attempts to demonstrate interest, the patient interpreted all silences in terms of the therapist's disengagement and lack of interest. In addition, the therapist's attempts to offer genetic (historical) interpretations (i.e., linking the patient's current feelings toward the therapist with how she had felt as a child with a very self-involved and cold mother) were met by either the patient's general indifference or anger.

The patient once remarked, "What difference does it make that my mother was cold and indifferent to me. The point is you are, too! The whole transference thing just seems very convenient for you so you don't have to admit to doing anything wrong."

Thus, therapeutic efforts with borderline patients most effectively focus on empathic confrontations in the present relationship between the therapist and patient.

Because of borderline patients' structural deficits (i.e., poor differentiation, integration, and reality testing), the therapist more often directly answers patients' questions about what the therapist is actually experiencing in order to help them begin to differentiate their projections from the reality of the therapist. This process also enables these patients to gain more reality-based information about their relationship with the therapist. When one borderline organized patient asked the therapist, "Are you really bored with me?" the therapist replied, "I think, from what you've said before, that you tend to think I'm bored with you when I'm quiet. [Patient nods affirmatively.] It seems like you're not sure whether you have an impact on me or not. Are you important to me? Do you matter? [Patient nods affirmatively.] Actually, when I'm quiet I'm often trying to sort out something in my mind or I'm letting something simmer to see what bubbles up. I experience you as having a considerable impact on me and think of you as intense, not boring."

In contrast, a neurotic patient thought that the therapist was angry with her whenever the therapist was silent for any length of time. At one point the patient asked the therapist, "Are you mad at me?" As neurotic patients are able, with help, to differentiate the therapist from past significant others (even during transference experiences), therapists are advised to understand rather than soothe the patient's feelings. Rather than directly answering the patient's question, the therapist might say, "Let me answer that question after we explore what made you ask me that. That way, we may learn something more about you." Through empathic exploration of the patient's past and current relationships, this patient was eventually able to recognize how his mother had always become very quiet just before she blew up at him. He said, "I can see the warmth in your expression, but when you are quiet, I feel nervous, as I used to feel with my mother when she stopped talking, and I want to appease you."

Another example of the importance of making a correct structural diagnosis demonstrates the hazards of misdiagnosing a neurotic hysteric as a borderline hysteroid or infantile character. Krohn (1978) discusses the

necessity of accurately assessing whether a patient's presentation of helplessness and passivity is (1) due to a neurotic hysteric's interpersonal mode
(e.g., illusion of inadequacy), or (2) reflective of the borderline patient's
genuine lack of resources (e.g., lack of object constancy, self-integration,
and self-esteem). A therapist who misdiagnoses a "good," neurotic hysteric
(Easser and Lesser 1965, Krohn 1978) as a hysteroid borderline (Kernberg
1975, 1992) will tend to excessively respond to or gratify the patient's experiences of helplessness that are both ego-syntonic and not reality based. The
patient will thus continue to over-rely on others, instead of learning to realize or utilize his or her own internal resources.

Table 3–1 outlines an expanded model of Kernberg's ego-structural levels. This model presents a vertical diagnostic paradigm with the normal ego
structured at the more advanced or mature level of organization and the
psychotic ego structured at the most primitive or immature level of organization. Throughout the rest of this book, we describe our model of treatment in relation to three levels of object relations and ego development (i.e.,
borderline, preneurotic, neurotic). However, to help the reader more
broadly understand the range of ego/object relations development, we have
included the extreme levels of normal and psychotic ego development. The
table differentiates the five major ego organizations according to the following categories: (1) identity, (2) orientation of thought processes, (3)
primary anxiety level, (4) manifest object relations, and (5) major defenses.

BRIEF SUMMARY OF THREE EGO STRUCTURAL LEVELS

Borderline Ego or Personality Organization

Kernberg (1975) originally introduced the conceptualization of borderline
personality organization as opposed to borderline personality disorder (APA
1994). As a level of ego/object relations structure, borderline personality
organization was thus intended to describe a level of development more
advanced than the psychotic and less mature than the neurotic ego structure. According to Kernberg, borderline personality organization can be
differentiated from psychotic organization by (1) the patient's ability to
perceive consensual reality (although patients with borderline personality
organization still typically experience feelings of depersonalization and
derealization); and (2) the relative strength of the patient's ego (in comparison with the psychotic patient), which can quickly recover from the transient psychotic episodes they occasionally experience under extreme stress.
Borderline patients are oriented to time, place, and person. For the most

part they do not hallucinate and, if they do (during transient psychotic episodes), they express concern about themselves and are able to recover in a range of minutes to a day.

Borderline personality organization can also be differentiated from neurotic personality organization by (1) the borderline patient's identity diffusion, as opposed to the neurotic patient's core sense of a cohesive and integrated self; (2) the borderline patient's global use of primitive defenses (i.e., splitting, projective identification, primitive idealization, and devaluation), as opposed to the neurotic patient's use of higher level defenses (e.g., repression, intellectualization, suppression, identification); (3) the borderline patient's lack of frustration tolerance and/or use of subliminatory channels, as opposed to the neurotic patient's ability to tolerate and more effectively cope with more frustration and anxiety; (4) the borderline patient's structural deficits (e.g., lack of object constancy and observing ego under stress), as opposed to the neurotic patient's unconscious conflict between well-developed psychic structures (e.g., harsh superego versus id, self versus object); and (5) the borderline patient's focus on dyadic problems (e.g., envy, conflict between wish to and fear of merging with object) related to lack of separation-individuation, as opposed to the neurotic patient's triadic problems (e.g., jealousy, competition).

Preneurotic Ego Organization

Horner (1979) originally introduced the term *preneurotic* to signify a level of ego/object relations development that is more mature than borderline personality organization (Kernberg 1975) and less mature than neurotic ego organization. Like Kernberg's work, Horner's formulations were based upon a "theoretical framework rooted in Margaret Mahler's stages of separation-individuation" (Varga 1985, p. 59). Horner describes the preneurotic ego structure as having sufficiently negotiated separation-individuation to have achieved a cohesive self-concept, a differentiated and fully integrated self and object representations, and good reality testing and object relatedness. For the preneurotic, developmental failures manifest during the late rapprochement phase due to intense ambivalence toward the maternal figure. This results in limited and/or weak internalizations of the maternal object's realistic capabilities. For example, a maternal object's chronic inconsistency in offering comfort (substituting annoyance or rejection) could lead to preneurotic ambivalence that interferes with the child's ability to internalize the maternal object's real, but erratically employed, soothing abilities. These weaknesses in critical internalizations result in the preneurotic's fail-

Table 3–1. Differentiation of five major ego organizations (a modification of Kernberg's ego structures)

Normal ego organization	Neurotic ego organization	Preneurotic ego organization	Borderline ego organization	Psychotic ego organization
[Intrapsychic conflicts are delimited to certain areas, usually reality based]			[Intrapsychic conflicts are global, and affect most areas of life]	
Higher level defenses: Sublimation, altruism, intellectualization, suppression, humor (defense becomes an adaptive coping structure)	Higher level defenses: Frequent use of fantasy, repression, sublimation, intellectualization, identification	Higher level defenses: Intellectualization, rationalization, fantasy	Higher level defenses: Occasional use of intellectualization and rationalization	Higher level defenses
Middle level defenses	Middle level defenses: Rationalization, reaction formation, denial, undoing, isolation, substitution of affect, displacement	Middle level defenses: Frequent use of denial, reaction formation, undoing, substitution of affect, idealization, and devaluation	Middle level defenses: Occasional use of reaction formation and substitution of affect	Middle level defenses
Lower level defenses	Lower level defenses: Occasional acting out	Lower level defenses: Introjection and projection, masochistic splitting; very occasional use of projective identification and acting out	Lower level defenses: Frequent use of splitting, primitive idealization and devaluation, derealization and depersonalization, projection, introjection and projective identification, extreme acting out, derealization and depersonalization	Lower level defenses: Derealization, depersonalization, hallucinations, severe dissociations, delusions

	Normal personality organization	Neurotic personality organization	Preneurotic personality organization	Borderline personality organization	Psychotic personality organization
	Regression: Generally in service of ego and easily reversible; interpretation improves functioning	Regression: Infrequent and temporary Selfobject functions: Improve functioning		Regression: Frequent and reversible Confrontation and clarification improve functioning	Regression: Severe decompensations, not easily reversible Interpretation furthers regression
Orientation of thought process	Secondary process thinking (rational thought as trial action based on reality principle; rational, logical, reality-based thinking intervenes between impulse and behavior (Kernberg 1967)		Secondary process thinking with relatively rare regressive episodes with primary others	Tendency toward primary process (immediate discharge) thinking on unstructured tests or under the influence of alcohol, drugs, or stress (Kernberg 1976)	
Primary anxiety	Fear of superego; personal conscience (appropriate guilt)	Fear of superego (inappropriate guilt), punishment or castration and impotence; fear of loss of object's love; signal anxiety	Upper level: Fear of loss of object's love and approval; fear of abandonment by object Lower level: Fear of loss of self-esteem, fear of impingement	Upper Level: Fear of object loss (total isolation from objects) Lower level: Fear of annihilation, fear of loss of self	
Object relations	Whole object relations; capacity for real object love and lasting relationships of some considerable depth; capable of reciprocity, giving, caring for objects for reasons other than the functions they can provide		Unstable whole object relations; regression to need-satisfying level can occur during threat of loss of security object that provides security or esteem	Need-satisfying level of object relations; need and dependency replace love; intense transient or superficial relations	Extremely impoverished to barely discernible relationships with others; lack of ability to empathize

(continued)

Table 3–1. (*continued*)

	Normal ego organization	Neurotic ego organization	Preneurotic ego organization	Borderline ego organization	Psychotic ego organization
Identity	Integrated identity: A stable, well-integrated (good and bad), realistically based sense of self that remains constant over time; resilient self-esteem; peripheral inconsistencies are ego-dystonic	Stable object constancy: A stable, well-integrated, and primarily good mental representation of internal objects; realistically perceived external objects; the ability to maintain a stable emotional tie with others; the ability to self-soothe when distressed	Cohesive but fragmented identity: Differentiated, cohesive, but somewhat vulnerable sense of self; problems with integrating ego-dystonic self experience; nonresilient self-esteem; contradictions in self experience are ego-dystonic	Identity diffusion: a noncohesive, vague, undefined sense of self; a contradictory set of self representations that are poorly integrated and actively (though unconsciously) kept mutually exclusive; the therapist often can construct only a diffused, chaotic, inconsistent internal image of the client; contradictions in self experience are mainly ego syntonic	
	Basic trust: Able to depend on realistically perceived others, who are viewed as predominantly good until proven otherwise; able to depend on/trust (i.e., one's own perceptions, feelings)		Incomplete object constancy: Overdependent on a somewhat idealized object to maintain sense of security and self-esteem; vulnerable to anxiety and depression; ambivalence toward objects	Object constancy defects: A contradictory, poorly integrated non-reality-based representation of others; the inability to maintain a stable emotional tie to external others; the inability to self-soothe when distressed	
			Weaknesses of basic trust: Underlying lack of basic trust compensated for by defenses such as introjection, rationalization, denial, and idealization	Lack of basic trust: Unable to really depend on others; predominantly negative anticipation of others' behavior and intentions	

ure to achieve well-secured object constancy. Due to having incomplete object constancy, the preneurotic patient is excessively dependent on others to provide security and esteem and thus frequently struggles with depression, shame, and feelings of insecurity.

While finding most of Horner's descriptions of the preneurotic very useful, we have consistently observed specific, limited, integrative weaknesses in this ego structure that, under sufficient stress to security operations, can induce a particular form of splitting. For example, as self and object are differentiated, preneurotic masochistic patients can perceive the self as all bad in order to protect the relationship (Meyers 1988), while narcissistic preneurotics can see the object as all bad to protect the self. The authors also believe preneurotic structures are subject to some degree of defensive grandiosity (usually unconscious) in order to protect the self from feelings of humiliation, shame, depression, and inferiority.

We believe that some preneurotic patients also have minor problems in integration and incomplete object and self constancy. While splitting in the preneurotic is vertical rather than horizontal (like the repression barrier), it is more precise (i.e., an ego-dystonic self aspect is fragmented off from the core self concept rather than the self being experienced as alternately all good or all bad). In addition, recovery of the mostly integrated self and object is typically quick, with splitting being replaced by intense ambivalence.

The strength of the preneurotic ego lies in its cohesion, object relatedness, good reality testing, and considerably developed sense of self or core identity. In addition, preneurotic patients rarely struggle with feelings of unreality caused by depersonalization and derealization like borderline patients do. Maintaining a completely, consistently integrated sense of self and others in a primary relationship remains the foremost challenge for preneurotics who are willing to sacrifice the integration of ego-syntonic aspects of the self in order to maintain approval from or attachment to the security object.

Neurotic Personality Organization

Neurotic patients are differentiated from preneurotic and borderline patients not only by their complete integration of good and bad experiences and their attainment of fully stabilized object constancy, but most especially by their attainment of a firmly established, continuous sense of self or identity. In contrast to borderline patients, neurotic patients have established stabilized secondary process thinking (that is, thinking that is guided by an awareness of external reality). While borderline patients fear abandonment or engulfment, and preneurotic patients fear loss of admiration or security, the neurotic patient fears the loss of the object's love.

The neurotic patient is characterized not by a feeling of something missing (e.g., structural defects), but of something dammed up and needing to be released. What is dammed up is the patient's repressed unacceptable wishes or impulses. Neurotic organization thus represents a relatively benign disorder, characterized by incomplete insight into the nature of the difficulty, mental conflicts, anxiety reactions, and partial impairment of the personality that does not involve any gross falsification of external reality, such as hallucinations, delusions, splitting, and primitive projective identifications. Therapeutic goals often revolve around helping patients to soften their superego and gain insight into what is out of their awareness. The therapeutic focus is on undoing repression (i.e., making the unconscious conscious) and resolving internal conflicts.

Unlike patients with a borderline or preneurotic level of ego development, neurotic patients have adequately developed psychic structures (e.g., self cohesion, self and object constancy, ego, superego). However, due to parental suppression of the child's impulses and strivings (e.g., sex, aggression, autonomy, initiative), the neurotic is conflicted about the use of these structures and thus underuses or overuses them.

For example, while hysterical patients have perfectly good ego functions, they fear that using them will interfere with their obtaining the object's love and approval. While obsessive patients have a cohesive sense of self and a noncorruptible superego, due to their sense of pseudo-autonomy and consequent vigilance about being controlled by others, these structures are rigidified. We agree with Stern (1985) that self development is a lifelong process. Neurotic patients are thus thwarted in the further evolution of their psychic structures through the passages of adult development.

EGO DEVELOPMENT AND PERSONALITY STYLE

Within each level of ego development described in the previous section, there exists a number of typical personality styles. For example, when therapists assess that an individual is functioning at a borderline level of ego development, they must then determine what type of borderline patient they are treating in order to develop the most effective approach to psychotherapy. The same approach is also relevant at the neurotic and preneurotic levels of ego structure.

Millon (1981) postulated that there are two basic continuums along which different personality styles are organized. These include the hysteric continuum, with individuals who tend to overrely on others for rewards and comforts (i.e., are overattached), and the schizoid continuum, with individuals who tend to overrely on themselves for rewards and comforts (i.e., are underattached).

We believe that there is also a third continuum (hostile) that corresponds to Horney's (1939) description of individuals who move against others. This category includes disorders such as sadistic (low-level borderline) and paranoid (high-level borderline). We did not develop this third continuum in this book because we focus on patients who more often seek treatment. However, for the sake of comprehensiveness and completion, we believe that extending the model presented in this book to include the third category of personality styles and disorders is important.

In this model we postulate that the primary environmental treatment that respectively leads to securely attached (toward others), overattached (anxious attachment toward others), detached (away from others), and hostile (against others) styles are respectively (1) a secure base from which to explore; (2) inconsistent, ambivalent treatment (intermittently rewarding attachment behavior interspersed with abuse or neglect); (3) lack of affection and warmth, and chronic neglect and chronic sadistic and abusive treatment (interspersed with neglect). Again, this is an oversimplification that is meant to illustrate a point. We do not mean to imply that primarily detached individuals have never been abused or that aggressive-sadistic individuals have never had a moment of love. Rather, our intention is to emphasize the *preponderant* style of object relations experienced by the individual. Needless to say, as many individuals have mixed personality disorders, patients generally do not correspond perfectly to the model. To demonstrate this point, in Chapter 6, under differential diagnosis, we distinguished between a pure schizoid character and a paranoid-schizoid character.

We now examine the two continuums of this model that are described in this book. Table 3–2 gives an overview of the schizoid (i.e., underattached) and hysterical (i.e., overattached) continuum and the personality styles or disorders that fall on each within each category of ego/object relations development.

The authors propose that the evolution of structure and character development outlined in Table 3–2 can be used as a general guideline to understanding the object relations and ego development as well as basic defensive style of the six personality disorders we examine in detail later in the book.

TABLE 3–2. Personality styles and disorders in ego/object relations development

Primary environmental treatment	Chronic neglect of the child or neglect of the child's true self (conditional love and acceptance for meeting parent's selfobject need)	Inconsistent, ambivalent treatment of the child depending on parents' moods and needs (i.e., parents are capriciously and intermittently rewarding, interspersed with punishment and/or rejection)
	Basic attachment style	
Stage of developmental arrest	Detached self-sufficiency: Exteme introversion or withdrawal of true self from objects	Overattached/dependent: Ambivalent attachment (acting out); anxious attachment (clinging)
1. Autistic and symbiotic (psychotic level)	Schizoid personality	
2. Separation-individuation (borderline level)	Narcissist preneurotic* personality	Hysteroid personality
3. On the way to object constancy (preneurotic level)		Masochist personality
4. Oedipal (neurotic level)	Obsessive-compulsive personality	Hysterical personality

*Table only includes the disorders described in this book. Thus, the narcissist borderline would be placed in the same category as schizoid, and antisocial and paranoid personalities would be under aggressive-sadistic.

BORDERLINE LEVEL OF EGO DEVELOPMENT: SCHIZOID AND HYSTEROID STYLE

At the borderline level of ego development the authors have charted the prototypical schizoid (Guntrip 1979) and hysteroid (Easser and Lesser 1965, Krohn 1978) or infantile (Kernberg 1975, 1976) character organizations along a number of critical dimensions (Table 3–3). At this level of ego development, the hysterical (i.e., attached) style is organized around a clinical picture of emotional lability, overinvolvement, vacillations between desperate clinging to and rage toward others, and a proclivity to aggressively act out these needs and feelings.

In contrast, the schizoid (i.e., detached) style is organized around a clinical picture of emotional withdrawal, isolation, a flat, colorless presentation

Table 3–3. Differentiation of two borderline personality disorders

Personality disorder	Schizoid	Hysteroid/infantile
Cognitive/emotional style	Overcathected intellect; lack of awareness of affects	Intellect often overwhelmed by intense affects; subject to transient affect storms and primary process thinking when regressed
Major defenses	Emotional detachment and isolation: Dissociation, avoidance, depersonalization, derealization	Acting out; splitting, projective identification; projection; externalization; primitive idealization and devaluation
Patient's aims	Validation for the right to exist	Validation for the right to separate and individuate without being abandoned
Related entitlements and strivings	Entitlement to be left alone (i.e., not impinged on or forced into performing ego-dystonic behaviors); if in a relationship, entitled to have a relationship on one's own terms	Entitlement to a symbiotic relationship with an idealized other who can be used exclusively for immediate need gratification
Ego mode	Organization is maintained as long as rigid defense system is upheld; regressions and acting out are rare but can be severe when they occur; consensual reality testing is usually intact; social reality is distorted due to living in a world of internal objects	Tendency to transitory regressions; concomitant non-specific ego immaturity; basic reality testing is intact but feelings of reality can be compromised (e.g., derealization, depersonalization, splitting)
Superego mode	Superego composed of primitive introjects that are punitive, rejecting, and rigid; rigid, idiosyncratic value system unmodifiable by external objects; ego-ideal: "I am very special, autonomous, and unique"	Superego composed of primitive introjects; value system can shift depending on approval of designated good object; ego ideal: "I am a good boy/girl who can get taken care of by others"
Prevailing patient myth	Myth of self-sufficiency	Myth of fusion with the all good maternal object
Major fears/defensive arena	Fear of annihilation, engulfment, and loss of self; fear of the "bad object"	Fear of abandonment, separation, or loss of the good object; fear of experiencing the terrifying emptiness of absolute isolation

of the self, and a preoccupation with inner life including exaggerated reliance on ideas and thought processes. Projective distortions of aggression or destructive love induce emotional withdrawal and/or noninvolvement in the schizoid personality. Relationships, when they exist, manifest an underlying lifelessness. Furthermore, social communications are often irrelevant or tangential (Millon 1981).

Both the hysteroid and the schizoid personalities have different solutions to the need-fear dilemma. Schizoid patients' great need for others is countered by their fear of engulfment (i.e., that the self will be devoured by the object); that their own destructive love (i.e., the schizoid's hunger or neediness) will devour others; and utter and complete neglect. For the hysteroid, the individual's great need for others is countered by a great fear of abandonment or total object loss. Masterson (1976) purports that a primary fear of abandonment represents a higher level of ego development than a primary fear of engulfment.

In terms of ego structure, the schizoid and the hysteroid present distinctively. Self/other differentiation or psychological boundaries are rigidly and vigilantly maintained by the schizoid in order to prevent engulfment or loss of self. The hysteroid, on the other hand, is vulnerable to denying or blurring selfobject differences or psychological boundaries in regressive states in order to prevent abandonment or loss of the object. Both hysteroids and schizoids have difficulty with self cohesion (i.e., having enough psychic glue to keep the self from disintegrating). The schizoid manifests great fear that some violation of their self will lead to disintegration or annihilation, although the degree of self disintegration varies (Meissner 1984). Hysteroids are vulnerable to transient episodes of self-fragmentation (Meissner 1984) and disintegration in severely regressed states.

PRENEUROTIC LEVEL OF EGO DEVELOPMENT: NARCISSISTIC AND MASOCHISTIC STYLES

The narcissistic personality can be conceptualized as an advanced solution along the schizoid continuum (Meissner 1984). The schizoid's central defense of emotional withdrawal is replaced by the narcissist's withdrawal of his or her true self and central reliance upon the grandiose false self structure (Glickauf-Hughes et al. 1987).

At the borderline level of ego development, narcissistic defenses function primarily to restore self cohesion and stability and reduce the feeling of self disintegration. At the preneurotic level of ego development these defenses primarily function to provide positive valence to the self representation (Stolorow 1975) while reducing feelings of inferiority and unworthiness.

At both levels of ego development, the narcissist's authentic self is very sensitive to slights, rejections, and disappointments, and prone to corresponding feelings of inferiority, envy, shame, and rage. The preneurotic narcissistic personality compensates for or tries to defend against these feelings through constant achievements, and attachments to idealizing or idealized objects who sustain the narcissist's self-esteem and provide psychic direction. As a substitute (or when this mechanism fails), narcissists tend to either choose new admiring/admired objects or to rely on the invocation of their grandiose false self structure. Ego-dystonic aspects of the self are fragmented off from the core self.

The masochistic character is organized much like the preneurotic narcissistic character (Horner 1979), but while the grandiosity of the narcissist has to do with personal perfection ("I am the greatest") the grandiosity of the masochist has to do with goodness ("I am the most generous, giving, and loyal of all") (Glickauf-Hughes and Wells 1991b). Both character styles function in many ways as compensations for acute, hidden, or overt feelings of inferiority and worthlessness. In this regard, narcissistic characters feel entitled to admiration and adoring regard because of their compensatory illusion of and efforts to attain personal perfection (e.g., "I am great, talented, and wonderful, and therefore entitled to respect, admiration, and special treatment"). In contrast, masochistic characters feel entitled to a loving, secure relationship because of their myth of fairness and reciprocity (e.g., "I take care of you so I am entitled to have you reciprocate") (Glick and Meyers 1988). Both character styles have one-sided, implicit expectations in their relationships with others.

The preneurotic masochistic character can be conceptualized as an advanced solution along the hysterical continuum. The hysteroid's central defenses of acting out and splitting are replaced by the masochist's central reliance on internalization, denial, rationalization, and reaction formation. The masochistic character is organized around the compelling need to obtain love from an often unloving or erratic love object (Berliner 1947) as a reward or compensation for their great effort, suffering, or submission. The operating directive is, "If only I were good enough, I would earn the love that I desire; but it's very, very difficult to get real and worthwhile love."

An important difference between the preneurotic narcissist and the preneurotic masochist is in their perceptions of objects. While both narcissists and masochists have incomplete object constancy and thus overrely on others for selfobject functions, the narcissist (even at the preneurotic level) does this to a greater degree. While preneurotic narcissists have more capacity than borderline narcissists to relate to others as whole objects, they still relate to others excessively through object usage. In contrast, the preneurotic masochist is more capable of real object relating.

Furthermore, while preneurotic narcissists have a much better sense of their wants, goals, and desires than the borderline narcissist, they are still to a great extent out of touch with their deepest needs (particularly their needs for others). In contrast, preneurotic masochists have a greater awareness of their needs. Their needs, however, are ego dystonic and cause the masochist to feel shame.

Table 3–4 examines a number of critical dimensions that often differ in preneurotic patients who manifest narcissistic versus masochistic styles. These dimensions include cognitive style, defenses, aims, ego mode, superego mode, prevailing myth, and major fears/defensive arenas.

NEUROTIC LEVEL OF EGO DEVELOPMENT: OBSESSIVE AND HYSTERICAL STYLE

At the neurotic level of ego development are the obsessive and hysterical personality disorders. The obsessive tends toward a more microscopic, detailed, precise cognitive style in contrast to the hysteric, who tends more toward a macroscopic, vague, global, impressionistic cognitive style (Shapiro 1965). The obsessive is thus susceptible to missing the forest for the trees—missing the big picture or the overall point because he or she is overinvolved in endless details. Also, the obsessive is subject to excessive rumination, worry, and trial action by thought. In terms of object relations, the obsessive has acquired basic object relatedness but retains a proclivity to sacrifice relationship needs in order to appease the standards and dictates of an excessively harsh superego whenever the two are at odds (Salzman 1980, Wells et al. 1990).

The obsessive is appropriately placed on the schizoid continuum (i.e., underattachment), although more advanced defenses such as intellectualization and isolation of affect have replaced the narcissist's use of grandiosity, idealization, and devaluation or the schizoid's use of dissociation, depersonalization, and derealization. In addition, the rigidity of the narcissist's false self has been replaced by the more integrated but rigid self of the obsessive. The obsessive's unrealistic ego ideal is more integrated into his or her core self and has more to do with doing things perfectly or being right than with the narcissist's desire to be perfect.

Table 3–4. Differentiation of two preneurotic level personality disorders

Personality disorder	Narcissistic	Masochistic
Cognitive style	Denies/distorts reality in order to maintain self-esteem	Negative distortion of self; positive distortion of significant other(s) (Glickauf-Hughes and Wells 1991a)
Major defenses	Omnipotence, grandiosity, idealization and devaluation, sexualization of intimacy needs; rationalization or projection of own flaws	Reaction formation, introjection of object's flaws, denial; idealization and devaluation, rationalization of object's behavior; believes self-deflation accompanies being loved
Patient's aim	Admiration	Love and security
Related entitlements and strivings	Idealization, adoration, mirroring, and empathy for being perfect; avoidance of criticism	To get critical, rejecting objects to give love and approval through giving and self-sacrifice; to avoid fear of abandonment or loss of the object's love through submission
Ego mode	Better impulse control and frustration than borderlines; reality testing compromised by massive denial of imperfections in self	Good impulse control; general difficulty of ego to modulate harsh superego; reality testing compromised by denial and rationalization of negative characteristics of idealized security object and introjection of object's negative projections into the self
Superego mode	Corruptible value system and lack of concern for needs of others; unrealistic ego ideal; ego ideal: "I am above others"	Excessively harsh, punitive conscience; unrealistic ego ideal; ego ideal: "I am good and giving"
Prevailing patient myth	Myth of self perfection; seeks perfect mirroring of his/her grandiosity	Myth of fairness and reciprocity (wants quid pro quo with and control over object love)
Defensive arena	Defends against paranoia, depression, mourning, guilt, shame (Kernberg 1975), and dependency needs	Defends against experiences of object loss (Avery 1977), loss of object love, anger, and negative perceptions of idealized others

95

The obsessive struggles with what Erikson (1950) refers to as autonomy versus shame and doubt (Wells et al. 1990), and has an overdeveloped need for control because of deep-seated, excessive insecurities and a precarious sense of autonomy. Obsessives attempt to gain the illusion of control through an excessive use of their intellect, through pseudomoralistic rules that dictate what is right, and through power struggles with others. What is technically correct is often more important to the obsessive than what is emotionally fair (i.e., the obsessive values justice over mercy). The classic obsessive is exceedingly afraid of making mistakes or being out of control and thus has a very difficult time making decisions and commitments, and being spontaneous, emotional, or enthusiastic. The obsessive patient attempts to secure guarantees in a world that does not give them.

While obsessives are detail oriented, self-contained, and overly intellectual, hysterics are global, relational, and emotional. The hysterical personality replaces the masochistic personality's overreliance on internalization, reaction formation, denial, and rationalization with pseudoemotionality, repression, and cognitive fog. Like obsessives, hysteric patients have attained stable object constancy and integrated object relations and thus are placed on the neurotic level of the hysteric continuum (i.e., overattachment).

However, instead of hysteroid patients' attempt to merge with objects and masochistic patients' overreliance on others for security and self-esteem, hysterical patients "act" dependent because they have been reinforced for doing so and have internalized a self-perception of incompetence. These patients are in reality, however, very capable individuals who simply underestimate themselves. They have good ego functions that they underuse for fear of losing the love and approval of others. After years of underuse, hysterics begin to lose confidence in their capacities. They are similar to other personality disorders on the hysterical continuum in that their primary motivation is to secure some form of love or security from the object.

Hysterics, like masochists, appear highly relational and oriented toward pleasing significant others in order to gain their love and approval. They manifest a much more dependent, childlike, and/or seductive role in order to be appealing and win love and appreciation. In contrast, masochists act industriously counterdependent and take on the role of emotional caregivers in order to earn love and gratitude (Glickauf-Hughes and Wells 1991b).

By abdicating responsibility and competence, the hysteric's manifest behavior is designed to elicit caregiving from the love object. Such abdication, however, also tends to induce controlling behaviors in the significant other, reactivating the hysteric's fears of being dominated by an insensitive

Table 3–5. Differentiation of two neurotic level personality disorders

Personality disorders	Obsessive-compulsive personality	Hysterical personality
Cognitive style	Detailed, ruminating (Shapiro 1965); black and white thinking related to right and wrong dichotomies	Global, impressionistic thinking (Shapiro 1965)
Major defenses	Isolation of affect, intellectualization; rationalization, reaction formation, undoing, and doubting	Repression, displacement, cognitive fog, substitution of affect, and dissociation
Patient's aim	Approval for "doing things right or perfectly" (Wells et al. 1990)	Love from an incestuous, unavailable, or forbidden object or parent substitute (Krohn 1978)
Related entitlements and strivings	Entitled to control of self and objects	Entitled to love and attention from incestuous object
Ego mode	Excessive trial by thought or tendency to "think out" conflicts (Shapiro 1965)	Excessive trial by action or tendency to "act out" conflicts (Shapiro 1965)
Superego mode	Integrated but excessively harsh; endures beyond expectations of the immediate personal or cultural milieu; loyalty to introject	Far more negotiable; reflects what is current and fashionable; aim is more interpersonal; emphasizes what will bring acceptance, praise, and love from others; what is "right" is largely defined by what will bring approval
Ego ideal	Ego ideal: "I am honorable and just"	Ego ideal: "I am attractive, desirable, and lovable"
Prevailing patient myth	Myth of control; believes it is better to be right than liked	Myth of passivity and helplessness (Krohn 1978); believes that it is better to be liked than to be competent
Defensive arena	Defends against feeling out of control, being wrong, or making mistakes	Defends against incestuous sexual desires and competitive feelings

and self-indulgent object on whom they depend. In their significant relationships, hysterics are often caught between their wishes for gratification of their dependency needs and their fears about being dominated (Mueller and Aniskiewicz 1986).

Table 3–5 examines a number of critical dimensions that often differ in neurotic patients who manifest hysterical versus obsessive-compulsive styles. These dimensions include cognitive style, defenses, aims, entitlements, ego mode, superego mode, prevailing myth, and major fears/defensive arenas.

CONCLUSION

This chapter briefly described a two-part object relations model of differential diagnosis based on ego-structural, developmental, and motivational theory. In the first part of the model, we focused on introducing important distinctions among five broad ego-structural organizations (i.e., normal, neurotic, preneurotic, borderline, psychotic). In the second part of the model, we introduced, compared, and contrasted six personality disorders (three overattached and three underattached) falling within neurotic, preneurotic, and borderline levels of ego-structure across a number of critical dimensions. While this model oversimplifies and reduces many aspects and categories relevant to differential diagnosis, we believe it also gives clinicians a clear schema to begin to make discerning hypotheses about client dynamics. Since we believe effective treatment follows from structural and characterological diagnosis, such a model is critical to the therapeutic process. In later chapters this model will guide the application of object relations therapy principles in treating the six different personality disorders outlined in this chapter.

4

Treatment Contracts and Goals

Over the last twenty years, we have supervised many practicum students, interns, and residents in psychology, psychiatry, counseling, and social work. One of the things that we have often observed throughout this process is that beginning therapists seem to have a notably higher frequency of therapy cancellations and dropouts than experienced therapists.

A number of factors may account for this observation. Certainly, less expertise could influence important variables such as a diminished therapeutic alliance, lower patient expectations of receiving help, and less effectiveness in treatment. There may also be a semiconscious selection process in agencies in which experienced therapists intuitively accept into treatment those patients who are more likely to be treatable or are a better fit for them, and unconsciously refer patients with a more guarded prognosis. These patients are then, by default, seen by new staff and trainees who are not yet able to discern which patients that psychotherapy (or they) are more or less likely to help. Retrospectively, remembering our own practicum and internship experiences, we became aware of the number of difficult borderline patients that we were attempting to treat long before we even knew what a borderline personality disorder was.

In addition to these factors, we believe that a major contribution to trainee patient dropout resides in the lack of adequate knowledge about how to negotiate an appropriate therapeutic contract. This lack of knowledge may also be a factor in situations where more experienced therapists find themselves struggling in interminable treatment with patients whose psychotherapy seems to be going nowhere.

THE THERAPEUTIC CONTRACT IN OBJECT RELATIONS THERAPY

Zetzel (1956) introduced the concept of the therapeutic alliance in psychoanalytic treatment. Greenson (1967) expanded this concept, referring to it as the working alliance which he described as "the relatively non-neurotic, rational rapport which the patient has with his analyst" (p. 192). Sterba (1934) believed that this alliance is formed between the patient's reasonable ego and the analyst's analyzing ego. The therapeutic alliance is the part of the patient that wishes to use the therapist as an assistant in the process of maturation.

In a recent conference given on the therapeutic alliance by the American Psychoanalytic Association, noted analysts debated what a therapeutic alliance was and if indeed there was an alliance as a phenomenon existing separately from positive transference. Jacobs (1993) described the "gezundheit factor" as a means of determining whether an alliance is established with a patient (i.e., if when the analyst sneezes the patient says "gezundheit," an alliance is present in treatment). In a discussion group with one of the authors, conference participants defined their own criteria for ascertaining a therapeutic alliance, which the author has termed the "attendance factor" (i.e., if the patient comes regularly to treatment, there is a therapeutic alliance). However, we believe that a patient's regular attendance in therapy sessions does not necessarily indicate the presence of a therapeutic alliance and a realistic treatment contract.

WHY PATIENTS SEEK TREATMENT

"Commonly, analyst and analysand begin their work with different views about the latter's problems" (Weinshel and Renik 1992, p. 96). There are many reasons that patients seek psychotherapy other than a desire for insight about their unconscious conflicts or a desire for characterological change. At times, patients want gratification of the emotional needs that are not adequately being met in their lives as an end in and of itself. At other times, patients desire reparation for injustices from their past. They may, for example, want to act out a self-sabotaging pattern (i.e., to defeat an authority figure) or to repeat a trauma from the past. They may want a good parent or a friend. They may wish for a magic cure. They may simply want to feel better.

None of these motivations are bad. They are just unrealistic and may serve as a resistance or defense against experiencing uncomfortable emotions. Furthermore, all these motivations in some way involve using the therapist as a substitute for, rather than as a bridge to, life. Additionally, all deny the length of time, hard work, and painful affect that Freud (1937) believed accompanies characterological change.

There are many reasons that patients, at some level, do not really wish to change. However dissatisfied they may be with their present lives, they are often more afraid to be different, as making significant changes in one's self can lead to feelings of separation-anxiety and require adapting to an evolving, albeit improved, identity. For example, one patient who was a concentration camp survivor noted how much of his identity had been predicated on that status. Redefining himself in a different way felt unfamiliar, uncomfortable, and confusing.

A second reason that patients may at times have difficulty changing involves an inability to grieve. For example, one 54-year-old patient's husband died when she was 35 years old. She never remarried and thus often struggled with profound feelings of loneliness, isolation, and depression. These feelings, however painful, were preferable to truly acknowledging the permanent loss of her husband. This failure to grieve recapitulated her inability to mourn the death of her father, with whom she had an unusually close relationship.

For this patient, it was better to remain attached to lost objects than to face the terrible sense of grief that would accompany truly acknowledging their absence. Thus, as in the fear of being different, patients often suspect that they will be unable to survive the emotional pain that would need to be encountered in order for real change to occur in their world or in themselves.

Thus, patients often unconsciously seek familiar substitutes for old objects rather than changing their life, despite a significant wish to do so. For this reason, the therapists may unconsciously be used to replace the abusive or rejecting object because this compromise is seen as less traumatic for patients than entirely losing the object.

Patients do not want to change due to their excessive sense of shame. Guntrip describes the antilibidinal ego (i.e., the part of the self that is critical of needs and of the object that promises to, but does not, gratify) as the major resistance to therapy and to the therapist (Sutherland 1989). For patients to change themselves, they must view their problems from a more internal perspective, and many patients experience this process as an extreme narcissistic injury. While patients have less control over external problems, they usually also have less guilt or shame about them. Such patients thus often come to treatment wishing for the therapist to collude against some "bad" object in the patient's life (e.g., employer, spouse, parent), without wanting to take much responsibility for altering the current course of their life.

In addition to differences between therapists and patients about what constitutes a reasonable treatment goal, part of the difficulty in establishing workable treatment contracts with patients is that insufficient attention has been paid to addressing what problems that therapy can and cannot affect. Furthermore, this varies greatly with the theoretical orientation and confidence (or omnipotence) of the therapist.

In addition, some problems are more effectively treated by one type of therapy than another. Other problems (e.g., sociopathy) are fairly resistant to psychotherapeutic intervention altogether. While psychotherapy research has attempted to articulate what treatments help particular patient problems, a great deal of work remains to be done in this area, and the findings that we do have are often not utilized by clinicians, who are generally more influenced by their own theories about how therapy helps people than by empirical research. This occurs in part because empirical research has not had adequate methodologies or resources (e.g., experienced clinicians rather than graduate student therapists) for assessing the complexities of the therapeutic situation. Furthermore, clinicians from differing orientations have very different notions about what constitutes an appropriate treatment goal (e.g., changing behavior, modifying outdated cognitions, resolving transference, reducing symptoms, gaining insight, increasing ego strength).

PROBLEMATIC THERAPEUTIC CONTRACTS

While therapists differ in their notions about which patient problems are treatable and which are not, or how explicit a therapeutic contract needs to be, there are some implicit treatment contracts that all therapists are adviscd to be aware of and cautious about making with patients. These include the therapist as the solution to the patient's problem, impossible contracts, no contracts, and covert contracts.

The Therapist as the Solution to the Patient's Problems

One problematic therapeutic contract, the therapist as the solution to the patient's problems, often comes in the form of the patient requesting support or someone to listen in regard to the problem that brings him or her into treatment. While listening is an important component of the therapeutic process, and support is at times an aspect of the therapeutic alliance, when listening and support are all that a patient wants, it is a mistake for therapists to covertly agree to participating as the end rather than the means of treatment.

Therapy is a process in which we teach patients how to fish rather than provide them with fish. Thus, while we regard the therapeutic relationship as extremely important, we view it as the means to an end, the end being mastery of developmental issues at the intrapsychic or structural as well as interpersonal levels.

This caution may seem like common sense, especially to the experienced psychodynamic psychotherapist. However, it has been our experience in supervising unfruitful or interminable therapies in even seasoned therapists that there is often an implicit contract between the therapist and the patient that the therapist *is* the solution to the patient's difficulties. Indices of such unspoken agreements are a lack of progress in treatment combined with frequent expressions of appreciation by the patient toward the therapist. These include statements such as "I really like coming here," "It helps to have someone to listen to my problems," "I'm glad to have your support," "This is the only place that I can count on receiving support," and "I always feel so much better after I come here." Such statements may in fact indicate the presence of a narcissistic collusion rather than a therapeutic alliance and workable treatment contract.

Impossible Contracts

A second type of problematic treatment contract is the impossible contract (i.e., problems that the therapist cannot directly help the patient with). Some examples of impossible contracts are the patient wishing to lose weight, finish his or her dissertation, or become more organized. These problems usually reflect an internal conflict in the patient rather than a lack of information. In such contracts, helping the patient often means aligning with his or her superego. The implicit message in these contracts is "Make me do _____" or "Stop me from doing _____."

Any perceived covert agreement on the therapist's part to such a contract frequently increases the patient's resistance to change (i.e., "You can't make me do _____ or stop me from doing _____"). This is particularly the case in patients who are struggling with a precarious sense of autonomy or are prone to experiencing negative therapeutic reactions.

A different and more useful contract might be to help patients better understand why they are not losing weight or finishing their dissertation and help them to resolve the underlying issue. Such contracts may result in behaviors such as the patient's accepting his or her normal weight range or leaving graduate school for a more intrinsically motivated pursuit.

No Contract

A third problematic therapeutic contract is accepting a patient for psychotherapy who comes to treatment not knowing what he or she wants to get from it. Such patients often enter treatment in order to have the experience of psychotherapy or to see what psychotherapy is like. We have observed that this seems to be a fairly common request among patients who are mental health professionals-in-training. In fact, university counseling centers often have predictable yearly peaks of intake interviews with graduate students in counseling, psychology, or social work whose professors suggested to the class that personal therapy is important for therapists. While personal therapy is indeed often one of the most instructive experiences for therapists-in-training, the patient must be open for self-exploration and have a genuine, therapeutic need at the time.

We recommend that a contract with a patient that involves a patient's learning about what therapy is like (i.e., an educational psychotherapy contract) be made on a time-limited basis and then be replaced by a more specific contract. Early in treatment, many patients are unable to articulate what they want. Furthermore, they have little or no idea of how therapy might be able to really help them. This includes patients who are therapists-in-training.

In some instances, the lack of an explicit contract or treatment goal may be an indication of the patient's general lack of awareness of his or her needs or the patient's shame about having any form of need or problem. In such cases, issues that impede the patient's articulation of treatment goals may be the very problem around which a treatment contract might be made. For example, the therapist might suggest to such a patient that together they can help the patient understand and resolve why having needs feels so shameful.

Covert Contract

In a covert contract, patients overtly request help in solving a particular problem; however, covertly they want from the therapist something very different from what they have requested. Usually, this is something that the patient knows that the therapist will not want to provide for him or her. For example, a patient may make a contract with a therapist that he or she wishes to feel less depressed but covertly have the agenda "Be my mother." Some other examples of covert contracts are acting out sadistic impulses, defeating authority figures, and proving that people are not trustworthy.

It is important to note when becoming cognizant of problematic patient contracts that therapists should not assume that patients have "bad" motives. Rather, patients are often unaware of their motives and uninformed about what therapy can and cannot do, how it works, and each party's respective role. Thus, a part of the initial phase of treatment is often educational.

IMPORTANCE OF THE FIRST SESSION IN EDUCATING PATIENTS ABOUT THERAPY

An important aspect of educating patients about psychotherapy is the process of making a therapeutic contract. Patients often feel unhappy or anxious and desperately want help but genuinely do not understand what their "real" problem is or how a therapist can help them. In such instances, patients may require the therapist's assistance in articulating reachable treatment goals. Some useful questions that therapists can ask patients in order to facilitate the articulation of workable treatment goals are "What brings you to therapy now?" "What would you like to get from therapy?" and "How would you like to be different as a result of being in treatment with me?" Such questions help patients focus on the precipitating incident leading the patient to seek treatment and direct the patient to make his or her hopes and wishes more overt. Additionally, they emphasize the therapeutic relationship as an agent of change rather than as an end in and of itself. These type of questions also focus on problems in an internal manner. The inability to answer such questions over time may be an indication that psychotherapy may not be an effective intervention for a particular patient.

MAKING A DEVELOPMENTAL-INTERPERSONAL CONTRACT IN OBJECT RELATIONS THERAPY

As object relations therapy utilizes both interpretations and a corrective interpersonal experience as agents of therapeutic change (Glickauf-Hughes and Wells 1995b), it is recommended that therapeutic contracts emphasize both insight and characterological change. Interpersonal and developmental goals may be identified for each patient by examining the issues underlying his or her stated problems.

For example, a patient whose presenting problem is procrastination on his dissertation may be struggling with the developmental issue of autonomy versus shame and doubt and an interpersonal style characterized in large measure by passive-aggressive behavior. A useful therapeutic contract with such a patient might involve helping him or her to feel more in charge of his or her life and understanding why he or she typically doesn't feel that way.

In contrast, a patient whose presenting problem is frequently feeling overwhelmed or depleted as he or she is always taking care of other people may be struggling with unresolved problems of basic trust and an interpersonal style of counterdependency. Some useful therapeutic goals with such a patient might be helping him or her to feel more comfortable having and expressing needs, learning to set better limits with other people, and gaining a better understanding about why both of these processes are so difficult for him or her.

It is thus recommended in doing object relations therapy that therapists make treatment contracts with patients that involve the understanding and resolution of the developmental and interpersonal issues that underlie their presenting problems. This necessitates therapists' having adequate knowledge about developmental theories and character pathology.

Earlier in this chapter it was suggested that therapists ask their patients about what they hope to gain from or how they wish to change as a result of treatment. In our experience, some examples of patient answers that we have found to be good prognostic indicators for a successful therapy include "I want to feel better about myself," "I'd like to get along better with people,"

"I want to be more assertive," "I'd like to know more about who I really am," and "I want to feel closer to people." Each of these answers indicate an awareness in the patient about something internal that needs to change for the patient's life to be more satisfying. Each clearly reflects an underlying interpersonal and developmental problem that requires further resolution (e.g., self development, self-esteem, initiative, basic trust). Furthermore, all of these problems have the potential to be affected by insight in conjunction with a particular type of corrective interpersonal experience. For example, empathy has been postulated (Kohut 1971, 1977) and empirically demonstrated (Rogers 1965) to increase self-esteem. A nondirective approach is recommended in treating patients with a lack of assertiveness or ability to take initiative. Mirroring and empathy can further self development. Tactful confrontation and modeling can improve interpersonal relationships, and providing an authentic connection can increase interpersonal relatedness.

In contrast, an example of a problematic patient answer is a patient who states that what he wants from therapy is "someone to listen." This is an example of the potentially problematic therapeutic contract in which the therapist is the solution to the patient's problems. Instead the therapist might suggest to such a patient that it might be important for them to try to get a better understanding of why the patient is not getting such an important need met in his or her current relationships.

A psychologically sophisticated but still problematic patient request is "I want to understand more about my family." A therapeutic contract based on a request such as this can lead to an overly intellectualized therapy experience that never has emotional impact on the patient in any significant way. In this case, the therapist might inquire of the patient how he or she hopes that this understanding will improve his or her life.

Patients sometimes evade answering such follow-up questions. In such cases, it is often helpful for therapists to postulate the relationship of the patients' evasive behavior to their underlying problems. For example, in the first case the therapist might observe to the patient that when the therapist asks the patient a question, the patient often does not respond to it. The therapist may suggest that this process could be related to the patient's not feeling adequately listened to in his or her life. What is implied here is not that therapists cannot treat patients who are unable to articulate what they need help with, but rather that in such cases presenting problems or requests must first be transformed into a workable treatment contract, preferably one with relevant developmental and interpersonal goals.

TRANSLATING BAD CONTRACTS
INTO GOOD CONTRACTS

An example of translating a bad treatment contract into a potentially workable one is suggesting to patients who ask the therapist for support that it might be helpful for them to understand why they are not currently receiving the emotional support that they need. An alternative strategy would be for the therapist to listen to the patient's reports about his or her interpersonal relationships as well as observing his or her behavior with the therapist.

Based on these observations, the therapist might then make a reasonable hypothesis about why he or she thinks that the patient might not be getting adequate support. A treatment contract could then be made about changing what impedes the patient's obtaining support from others. For example, the therapist might say, "I've noticed both in our sessions and in your descriptions about your relationships how difficult it seems to be for you to take things from other people. We might want to better understand why this is so hard for you in order to help you to get more of the support in your life that you want and need."

Another example of a potentially problematic treatment contract is a patient who told the therapist that what she wanted was someone to listen to how difficult her marriage was. Some statements that a therapist might make to or questions that a therapist might ask such a patient in order to form a more workable contract are "How will that help you?" "Sometimes it feels like the problem is out there. If only your husband would change, things would be fine. Yet, you and I can't make him change, which must leave you feeling impotent and helpless." "My guess is that there is something frightening or uncomfortable about looking at your own contributions to your relationship problems. Perhaps this might be something that we could understand better."

Implicit in this discussion is the assumption that psychotherapy is not appropriate for everyone. There are several approaches that a therapist can take when, after repeated efforts, the therapist is still unable to arrive at a workable treatment contract with a patient.

The therapist can first educate the patient about the process of psychotherapy, in general, and object relations therapy, in particular. This includes informing the patient that therapy can be a long, difficult process that involves taking risks, feeling uncomfortable, and examining frightening issues. The therapist might describe to the patient that as much as he or she would like a "magic cure" (and the therapist would like to provide one), therapy is an active, collaborative process, not a passive one, and since most problems do not begin overnight they do not go away overnight either. We have found that it is often helpful to tell patients that therapy is a bridge to life (i.e., a place to learn to get support from other people rather than to indefinitely get it from the therapist).

Thus, for all these reasons, we do not believe that psychotherapy is a helpful, desirable process for all patients who seek it. Sometimes, a simpler, faster, less expensive solution to the patient's problem is preferable. In such cases, the therapist might recommend alternative procedures such as medication, stress management programs, support groups, learning skills classes, or a talk with an advisor.

Sometimes this process can be clarifying to patients and can thus overcome their initial resistance to treatment. For example, one patient, who was depressed, externalized her problems and requested support, saying, "I wish that you could give me a pill that could fix everything in my life but I know that I have problems getting along with people. My whole family does and I really need help with that." Thus, in confronting a patient's resistance to treatment, the therapist at times encounters the patient's genuine motivations for seeking help, leading to a therapeutic alliance with a workable treatment contract and goals.

5

Differentiating Self and Object in Countertransference Feelings

Two contrasting views of countertransference have been described in the psychoanalytic literature. The first of these, the classical approach to countertransference, is described as the therapist's unconscious, undesirable emotional response to the patient (Freud 1910) or the unconscious reaction of the psychotherapist to the client's transference (Kernberg 1965). Such responses, like transference responses, are viewed as emerging from the history and resulting neurotic conflicts of the therapist.

The classical perspective views countertransference responses as an undesirable hindrance [that] ideally should not occur (Fliess 1953). Reich (1951) argued that the therapist's countertransference was destructive to the process of psychotherapy.

More recently, an approach to understanding countertransference that has been referred to as totalistic provides a less restrictive view of countertransference, emphasizing the idea that a therapist's reaction to a patient stem from both the therapist's objective and idiosyncratic reactions to the patient and from the patient's real and neurotic needs (Kernberg 1965). The totalistic approach views countertransference as the unconscious introjection of the patient's projections and the therapist's conscious reactions to the patient as well as his or her unconscious response emerging from the therapist's own personality and neurosis (Grayer and Sax 1986).

111

The fundamental difference is that the totalistic approach very strongly advocates the importance of understanding and resolving the countertransference, but also acknowledges its indispensable role in a therapist's ability to understand a patient's dynamics experientially. This view is in line with the thinking of Kernberg (1976), Little (1951, 1957), Heimann (1950), Racker (1953), and Winnicott (1949).

Thus, in describing the treatment of severely regressed patients, Kernberg (1976) believes that therapists frequently

experience, rather soon in the treatment, rather intense emotional reactions having more to do with the patient's premature, intense and chaotic transference and with the therapist's capacity to withstand psychological stress and anxiety, than with any specific problem of the therapist's past. Thus, countertransference becomes an important diagnostic tool, giving information on the degree of regression in the patient, his predominant position vis-à-vis the therapist, and the changes occurring in this position. [pp. 179–180]

In such a view, patients are viewed as projecting experiences "into" the therapist as well as "unto" the therapist (Segal 1981).

Within this totalistic view of countertransference, Winnicott (1949) distinguished between objective countertransference (i.e., the feelings that patients induce in the therapist that are central to the patient's conflicts) and subjective countertransference (i.e., the therapist's response to the patient arising from the therapist's historical issues). Needless to say, differentiating between these two responses and refining one's understanding of objective countertransference is crucial for appropriate diagnosis and treatment.

USE OF SELF AS AN INSTRUMENT OF PSYCHOTHERAPY

The totalistic approach to countertransference necessitates that the therapist learn to use his or her feelings as a diagnostic tool for treatment. Miller (1990) discusses a three-stage process to the use of self as an instrument: (1) recognition of the projective identification and countertransference responses to it, (2) processing the meanings of the projective identification, and (3) determining an appropriate therapeutic use for the countertransference material. In this chapter, we describe a four-step model for utilizing countertransference responses: (1) experiencing, (2) observing, (3) judgment, and (4) action (i.e., therapeutic intervention).

An important prerequisite to the therapist's use of this process is the ability to regress in the service of the ego or to alternate between experiencing feelings toward the patient and observing them. It is, thus, important for therapists to be able to have their feelings and then be able to step back and reflect upon them in order to understand their meaning and to make an appropriate treatment decision. For example, one of the authors began to feel bored with a patient. She noticed that her attention continued to drift. She examined why this was occurring and noted that the patient was talking in a monotone and was avoiding eye contact. She then began to attempt to understand the dynamic meaning of this process, which was the patient's fundamental lack of relatedness to others and belief that people were not interested in her. Had the therapist not allowed herself to become bored and to then observe and understand her experience, she would not have homed in on the patient's basic issue as quickly.

The therapist's own personal therapy is crucial to the successful utilization of such a model as it teaches regression in the service of the ego, helps therapists to have a good general understanding of what issues they bring to treatment, and allows for self reflection without undue shame.

EXPERIENCING COMPONENT

Mahrer (1993) addresses the experiencing component of understanding countertransference feelings when he speaks of plugging into the patient. "Plugging into the client means that the therapist situates [him- or] herself so that the words spoken by the client are as if they are coming in and through the therapist" (p. 414). In essence, the therapist allows a temporary symbiosis to occur between he or she and the patient. "It is as if lots of wires connect the therapist to the client so that whatever is occurring in the client is occurring in the therapist" (p. 413). This is the type of attunement that occurs in the mother–infant relationship in which the mother, in part, learns what her child needs by allowing herself to feel the infant's feelings. Mahrer thinks that "plugging into the client" indicates the therapeutic relationship has evolved beyond ordinary empathy (Havens 1978, Margulies 1984, Rothenberg 1987). Rather, Mahrer believes that in this experience, the therapist is "virtually melded into or fused into" (p. 415) the patient's experiencing process.

The importance of the experiencing component of therapy is that in some way the therapist's ability to experience his or her own feelings in response to the patient's feelings and behaviors is clearly in the service of bonding with or helping the patient. For example, in the previous example, in listening to the patient the therapist allowed herself to experience the world with the degree of dissociation with which the patient experienced it.

OBSERVING COMPONENT

In addition to having one's responses to patients, therapists must be cognizant of these responses (i.e., to note that they are having them). Traditional psychoanalytic theory recommends awareness of one's countertransference responses as a type of preventive measure against acting them out.

In contrast, Renik (1993) does not believe that it is always possible or even desirable to prevent countertransference enactment, and that when it is appropriately utilized countertransference enactment can provide patients with corrective experiences.

> One Portuguese patient repeatedly arrived late for treatment. The therapist attributed this behavior to cultural differences and thus did not confront or interpret it until she noted that she, too, had begun to arrive late to sessions. The therapist at that point observed this pattern to the patient (i.e., that she noticed that she came late to sessions, assuming that the patient would not be there) but that she had not explored this pattern with the patient as she had attributed it to different cultural norms about time. The therapist then asked the patient if her lateness was related to this phenomenon. The patient said that it was not and they began to explore the dynamic motivations behind the patient's behavior and its interpersonal consequences.

JUDGING COMPONENT

A major focus of this chapter is on the judging component in learning to use one's countertransference responses as a component of treatment. A similar process has been undertaken by Racker (1960) and Grinberg (1993), who distinguish between the therapist's concordant and homologous identifications, complementary identifications, projective counteridentifications, and concordant countertransference. While some of Racker's concepts will apply here, we use a somewhat different and simpler model. We think that the process of discerning one's various countertransference responses is important and difficult enough to warrant continual clarifying efforts on behalf of this objective.

SUBJECTIVE COUNTERTRANSFERENCE:
COUNTERTRANSFERENCE NEUROSIS

In making cognitive decisions about one's countertransference feelings, the first decision that a therapist must make is whether these feelings are subjective (i.e., idiosyncratic) or objective responses that most individuals would experience in response to the patient's behavior. A positive response to any of the following questions may indicate the presence of a subjective countertransference reaction.

Is This a Very Familiar Feeling or Experience?

One supervisee who believed that her patient was trying to take advantage of her felt chronically used by her mother and quite frequently felt taken advantage of or used by others. Another supervisee felt rejected when her patient canceled sessions for financial reasons. In the latter example, while there may have been some distancing component in regard to the patient's behavior, it was not the patient's primary motive. Furthermore, this therapist had strong abandonment issues and often felt rejected by others.

Most of us have negative feelings and beliefs that are "old friends." Thus, when these beliefs emerge in the countertransference, explaining these responses as subjective countertransference is a viable alternative.

Is it Difficult to Switch from Experiencing the Feeling to Observing It?

Often, a nontemporary regression occurs in which the therapist is unable to get distance from his or her feelings. When this pattern perseveres, it may be an indication of some neurotic struggle occurring in the therapist that makes it difficult for the therapist to detach from his or her experience. For example, the therapist had a patient who refused to leave her office at the end of the session and threatened suicide when the therapist did not gratify her wishes. This tended to leave the therapist with angry and guilty ruminations. While most therapists would respond negatively to such a patient's behavior, the therapist experienced this type of manipulation and boundary violation with her own mother. It thus became more difficult to detach from and objectively examine her responses to the patient's behavior.

Are There Difficult Events Occurring
in Your Life at This Moment?

All therapists go through periods of difficulty during which it is harder to concentrate on their patients' concerns or easier to be more reactive with them. It is crucial to note these times so that responses such as boredom or detachment are not inaccurately attributed to patient dynamics (e.g., schizoid processes or obsessive defenses). This is especially important when the issue that the therapist is struggling with parallels that of the patient. For example, one therapist noted that she experienced difficulties at work similar to those of her patient. She thus attempted to be especially careful that she did not attribute her own feelings to the patient's experience.

Have You Felt This Way with Other People,
Including Patients, That Day?

An important indicator of subjective versus objective countertransference during times of therapists' experiencing their own situational concerns is observing their responses to all their patients throughout the day. When a therapist notes that some response such as detachment cuts across patients, it is probable that the likely origin of the therapist's feeling is within the therapist. If, however, a therapist feels bored with only one patient and not with others, variables related to the patient must be considered, such as the patient's dissociating or relating to the therapist as a selfobject.

OBJECTIVE COUNTERTRANSFERENCE

Objective countertransference is a response to the patient's behavior that would likely be experienced by most people rather than being an idiosyncratic response of the therapist. Objective countertransference responses come in a variety of forms with corresponding meanings and different treatment recommendations. The two general categories include projective identifications and interpersonal reactions.

Projective Identifications

Projective identification is a process originally described by Klein (1935) and further elaborated by Ogden (1979) in which individuals attribute egodystonic aspects of the self to an object, behave toward the object so as to induce the object to experience the projected affect, and identify with the object's experience. As previously described, in contrast to projection in which impulses or affects are projected onto objects, in projective identification they are projected into objects. Projective identification is an unconscious experience for both participants.

There are two important forms of projective identification with relevant treatment implications: (1) an unconscious identification with the patient's self, and (2) an unconscious identification with the patient's internal object. In both cases, the behavior that is responded to by the therapist reflects something that is ego-dystonic for the patient.

In the first type of projective identification, which is the most common, an ego-dystonic or unacceptable aspect of the patient's self is projected onto the therapist. For example, one narcissistic patient continually behaved toward the therapist in a contemptuous and devaluing manner so as to induce shame in the therapist, an ego-dystonic experience for the patient. Another patient, for whom anger was ego-dystonic, continually behaved in passive-aggressive ways toward the therapist (e.g., whining, coming late, help-rejecting, complaining), thus inducing feelings of irritation in the therapist. The unconscious wish is for the therapist to provide a new model of handling this experience with which the patient can identify. Therapists can thus determine if this type of projective identification is occurring by asking themselves if they are feeling what the patient must have felt with significant others such as parents (Glickauf-Hughes and Campbell 1991).

The second and more confusing type of projective identification is when the therapist is unconsciously induced by the patient to behave toward him or her as one of the patient's bad internal objects does. For example, the therapist noted that she often felt like criticizing or behaving sadistically toward a patient. She clarified the interaction that induced these feelings and asked the patient how his parents responded when he behaved in that way toward them. The patient said that his parents were both physically and verbally abusive toward him at those times.

In such instances, the unconscious wish of the patient is for the therapist to understand the patient's early and often misunderstood negative experiences with significant others and to unconsciously test therapists to determine whether they are like the patient's bad objects. Therapists can determine such a dynamic by asking themselves if how they feel like behaving toward the patient (e.g., criticizing or rejecting the patient) is how the patient describes parents or significant objects from the past behaving toward him or her.

Interpersonal Reaction

When the therapist's response to the patient's behavior is more conscious, it may be a here-and-now interpersonal response. An interpersonal reaction is a conscious response of the therapist to some ego-syntonic aspect of the patient's personality. It may be a reaction of the therapist to some habit that the patient acquired late in life that has no deep unconscious motivation. The response may even result from a cultural clash between therapist and patient. For example, a therapist from a southern state may feel uncomfortable with the more straightforward, aggressive style of a patient from a northern state.

While an interpersonal response may not have dynamic meaning in regard to the patient's history, nonetheless it may provide a clue about interpersonal difficulties that the patient currently has with people.

A patient moved to the United States from Italy five years ago. He came from a large, verbal family (with a large, verbal, extended family with which his family had daily contact). This patient, who entered treatment complaining about difficulties in relating to other people, talked nonstop with the therapist and interrupted the therapist during the few times that she spoke. The therapist noted that she often felt relieved when the patient canceled his appointment. As the patient began to speak about people not returning his phone calls, the therapist began to hypothesize that her own response to the patient's controlling, highly verbal behavior was probably an indication of the type of problems that he was experiencing with other people in his life.

Some questions that therapists may ask themselves to determine the presence of an interpersonal response are "Is how I feel what many people would feel in response to this patient's behavior?" and "Is the problem that is occurring between the patient and me what the patient reports as occurring with significant others in his or her life?" (Glickauf-Hughes and Campbell 1992). In the last example, the answers to both questions were affirmative.

CONCORDANT IDENTIFICATION

Sometimes the therapist's response to the patient is both subjective and objective. Racker (1960) refers to this type of response as a concordant identification. "Concordant identifications would be a reproduction of the [therapist's] own past processes that are being relived in response to a stimulus from the patient" (Grinberg 1993, p. 51).

The previous example of the patient who would not leave the therapist's office (in which the therapist's mother frequently pushed her limits) is an example of a concordant identification, as most therapists would respond negatively to a refusal to leave one's office and to threats of suicide. However, this therapist's response to the patient was somewhat stronger due to her own family history.

Another therapist, who one of the authors supervised, had an intense response to the verbally abusive behavior reported by a masochistic patient about her husband. While this was a clear example of masochistic triangulation, the therapist's response was particularly strong due to her own history of observing her mother being abused by her father.

ACTION COMPONENT—THERAPEUTIC INTERVENTION

The importance of determining the origin, type, and meaning of our responses to our patients is the increased potential for therapists to make more optimal treatment decisions. After therapists are able to make reasonable determinations as to whether their countertransference feelings are subjective, objective, or both, and if objective, if they are projective identification (reflecting a deeper dynamic disturbance within the individual) or a more ego-syntonic interpersonal response acquired at a later phase in development, will inform therapists about the best way to proceed in therapy. In this section, we discuss some treatment recommendations that follow the determination that a countertransference reaction is of a particular type.

Subjective Countertransference

When the therapist believes that his or her own countertransference response is subjective or idiosyncratic, the appropriate means of handling such a response is to first determine whether insight prevents acting out. If the subjective countertransference response continues to be an interference to treatment, the therapist should resolve it in his or her own psychotherapy.

It is recommended that the therapist's subjective countertransference response not be shared with the patient unless it has been acted out and noted by the patient. In such instances, we believe that it is detrimental not to acknowledge one's response to the patient. If, for example, a therapist was distracted on a particular day due to occurrences in his or her own life, and the patient observed and reacted to the therapist's behavior, the therapist might acknowledge feeling a bit distracted and ask the patient to talk about the meaning that it had for him or her.

When therapists have negative countertransference reactions that are subjective and continue to interfere with treatment, it is recommended that they do everything that is possible to resolve these issues so that treatment can proceed in a constructive manner. However, if the therapist is unable to do so, and his or her response is subtly injurious to patients, particularly when it is a recapitulation for the patient, it is recommended that the therapist terminate treatment with a brief explanation such as, "Due to some issues of my own, I'm afraid that I am not going to be the most helpful person to you with your problems right now."

It is extremely important that the patient's responses to this intervention be explored and an appropriate referral made. It is, however, the authors' experience that on the rare occurrences that such interventions are necessary, patients are very appreciative.

The preceding problem, however, points to the necessity of personal therapy for the therapist, leading to a high degree of self-awareness. It is the authors' experience that potential unworkable subjective countertransference responses can be detected in the first few interviews by an experienced therapist. The better choice is thus not to treat such a patient in the first place.

Projective Identification with Patients' "Bad" or Fragmented Self Experiences

When the therapist has made a reasonable determination that the feeling that he or she is experiencing is a projected aspect of the patient's self, it is recommended that the therapist express the feeling to the patient in a "metabolized" or mediated form (e.g., hate may be contained and transformed to annoyance), which can then be processed and assimilated by the patient. The patient is, thus, provided with an opportunity to reintroject the ego-dystonic feeling into his or her own core self experience.

One patient for whom anger was extremely ego-dystonic continually behaved in passive-aggressive ways toward other people, including the therapist. On one occasion when the patient was describing his last encounter with his parents (in which they did not listen to him at all) and rationalized his parents' behavior, the therapist observed feeling frustrated with the patient when the patient interrupted everything that she said. On obscrving this pattern and making the connection between her experience with the patient and his experience with his parents, the therapist said, "You described an experience with your parents this weekend in which you didn't feel heard. I'm aware today that you have interrupted me a number of times and that you don't usually do this. I was aware that when I thought you weren't listening to me, I felt a little bit irritated and I was wondering if you might have felt this way with your parents this weekend." The patient admitted that he had indeed felt a bit irritated but that he felt guilty about feeling that way, as his parents were such good, hard-working people.

By the therapist's expressing her own aggressive feelings in a modulated tone of voice and in a euphemized form (i.e., "a little irritated" rather than "angry"), the patient was able to identify with his own feelings of aggression.

Projective Identification with Patients' "Bad" Internal Object

In a previous example, in which the therapist experienced sadistic feelings in response to the behavior of a masochistic patient whose parents had been abusive toward her in such interactions, the therapist then related that experience to other problematic interactions that the patient was having in her current life:

"When you complained to your father, he didn't listen to you. When he tried to solve your problems to get you to stop complaining, you acted stubborn with him as you were angry at him for not being understood. He then started to shout at and to criticize you. You report a similar type of disturbing interaction that occurs with your husband, which is confusing to you. I'm aware that when you discuss your problems with me, you reject anything that I say. For example, when I said you sounded like you were feeling irritated, you said that you weren't feeling irritated—just frustrated. When I stopped responding to you, as I felt my responses had been off base, you became angry with me for being quiet. I became aware of feeling an impulse to act like an impatient parent with you—and you already had one of those and don't need another one.

"My guess is that this is what happens when your husband gets impatient with you. I don't think that you really want either of us to act that way. What I think that you're trying to determine is whether I will be 'mean' to you like your parents were, when you complain and are a little fussy."

This instance is an example of what Weiss (1993) refers to as the patient's putting the therapist through tests in order to repair an early traumatic occurrence.

Interpersonal Reaction

When the therapist has reasonably determined that his or her reaction to a patient reflects a response that most people would have to the patient's behavior, but believes that the response and the behavior do not reflect a deep, unconscious conflict in the patient, it is recommended that the therapist tactfully share his or her response with the patient and relate it to some current area of interpersonal disturbance.

One group member had a rather blunt style of speaking. The therapist believed that this behavior was not a reflection of extreme underlying aggression, ego-dystonic aggression, or severe narcisstic injuries, but rather reflected a lack of interpersonal skills, including lack of awareness of his impact on others. His presenting problem in therapy was an inability to get along with the people that he supervised.

The therapist observed that at times she felt offended by this patient when he had not intended to do so and noted that a number of group members seemed to respond in a similar fashion. After the patient had established a sufficient alliance with the therapist and the group, she encouraged a group member to share his hurt feelings with the patient when the therapist noted that the group member had seemed to be offended. The patient was genuinely surprised by the member's response. The therapist suggested that perhaps such interactions might partially explain the difficulties that the patient was experiencing with his employees at this time.

Concordant Identification

In concordant identification, in which there is a simultaneous occurrence of subjective and objective countertransference, it is recommended that the therapist first clarify and resolve his or her own feelings and experiences in supervision and/or personal psychotherapy. When the therapist is sufficiently able to separate his or her own idiosyncratic responses from those induced by the patient, he or she is then free to contain, metabolize, and understand the patient's projected ego-dystonic self experience. In the previous example of the patient who would not leave the therapist's office, the therapist needed to first clarify and adequately resolve her own feelings toward her mother before appropriately setting limits with the patient and using her feelings to empathize with how the patient's parents continually violated her boundaries as a child.

CONCLUSION

Despite the notable efforts that therapists have made over the years to eliminate emotional responses to patients, many theorists have noted that these responses seem inevitable, and believe that when they are appropriately understood and utilized, they are an important adjunct of treatment. In this chapter, we have systematized and expanded upon the thinking of the totalistic theorists in order to provide a model for therapists to use for their affective responses to patients in the service of therapeutic gain. These efforts will be further delineated in later chapters in response to the countertransference that therapists are most likely to experience with patients that have specific characterological issues.

6

Object Relations Therapy of the Schizoid Personality: Treating Impaired Bonding

Fairbairn (1954) derived his object relations theory from studying schizoid problems. In fact, some contemporary ideologies have a schizoid aspect. Hegel (1967) talked about the world as an idea. Existentialism discusses the schizoid sense of futility, disillusionment, and despair. In fact, Sartre (1943) believed that the only thing that we can affirm is nothingness.

The schizoid personality is popularly described as someone who is absent-minded, difficult to know, lives in a world of ideas, has gone in a shell, or is a cold fish (Guntrip 1969). William Hurt's character in the film *The Big Chill* is a classic example of the schizoid personality. He is remote, cynical, uncommitted, and unattached to anyone.

DESCRIPTIVE CLINICAL OVERVIEW

Preoccupation with Fantasy

The schizoid personality appears extremely introverted, detached, and remote. He or she often has a rich fantasy life with internal objects that substitute for relationships with real people (Guntrip 1969). For example, one schizoid patient, who spent little time outside of work with anyone other than her dog made up stories in her mind that rivaled J. R. R. Tolkien's.

Another Don Quixote–like patient, who had more "apparent" social relationships, spent months "pursuing" women who were not interested in him. While these women repeatedly responded to his advances by telling him that they were busy, they responded politely to him when he called because he was not intrusive. Thus, in his mind, they were dating. He had elaborate fantasies about these women that only ceased when they did something more extreme (e.g., telling him that they were getting married to someone else). Even then, he frequently reminisced about the potential that their relationship would have had. Mental life, thus, replaced real life for this patient. These women were just stimuli for his fantasies.

Difficulty with Self-Reflection

While schizoids have an active fantasy life, genuine introspection is generally avoided through mental machinations and distraction techniques. When relationships with others have been chronically nonresponsive, depersonalizing, or humiliating, self-reflection is often intolerably painful due to intense feelings of shame. One patient complained that he felt "trapped between a rock and a hard place" (i.e., he experienced pain when he was involved with both his internal and external objects). His only recourse was flights of fantasy, excessive daydreaming, dissociative forgetting, denial of all needs, and functioning like an automaton.

Lack of Relationships (or Emotionally Distant Relationships)

Schizoid individuals may be very successful at work, especially when there are few relationship demands and their work focuses on data and things (e.g., computer analyst, librarian, researcher). Schizoids, however, typically have no intimate relationships or their primary relationships are devoid of emotion. For example, one patient, who was a highly respected surgeon, rarely spoke with his family, and when he was forced to attend social gatherings he went off by himself and read. Under closer examination it was noted that he treated his patients as "diseases" or "injuries" and, while very skilled, was known for his remote bedside manner.

Withdrawal and Sense of Detachment from Others

Guntrip (1969) believes that schizoid individuals tend to be removed from the world. As other people were not originally a source of nurturance, the schizoid tends to withdraw from rather than approach others and is often anxious in social situations. He or she thus tends to feel lonely even in the middle of a crowd.

Even when schizoid individuals are superficially engaged with other people, they are usually detached. Their attitude toward the world is one of extreme noninvolvement or observing others from a distance without affect. For example, one patient who attended a World Series baseball game said that he found people's emotional responses at this game "to be somewhat amusing." A group therapy patient, who was an artist, began to live in a fantasy world from early childhood. While this patient spoke frequently during the group, he did so in a manner that was disconnected from the other group members. He looked at other people infrequently, and was rarely aware of anything that they said to him. It was as though he were speaking to himself.

Disconnection from Their Own Needs and Feelings

In general, schizoid individuals are disconnected from life, including other people, their own feelings and sensations, and even food (Johnson 1985). Thus, one schizoid patient became very ill before she sought medical assistance because she was not really aware of how she was feeling. Schizoid individuals often regard eating as a nuisance and eat to live rather than live to eat. One schizoid patient rarely kept food in the house, would go long periods without eating, eventually notice that he was ravenous, and eat large quantities of whatever was convenient.

Illusion of Self-Sufficiency and Self-Containment

The schizoid individuals' apparent capacity for self-sufficiency and self-containment protects them from the potential dangers involved in relying on others. They develop this capacity early in life by prematurely assuming adultlike functions and depersonalizing and detaching from their relationships with others. While schizoid patients appear self-sufficient, their self-sufficiency is an illusion. The schizoid was required to learn to become independent outside of a relational context. The same is true for their self-containment. Rather than having their expression of affects contained (i.e., held, soothed, protected) by parents, the schizoid patients' affects were simply ignored. Thus, as children, schizoid patients learned to deny and dissociate themselves from their emotions and their needs.

Schizoid Position (i.e., Fear of Devouring or Being Devoured by Others)

Fairbairn (1954) describes the depressive position as one in which the self is made angry as the object gives and then hatefully denies love, leaving the individual with a feeling of paradise lost. In the *depressive position*, the object is whole. As depressive individuals understand that the good mother and the bad mother are the same person, they realize that t*heir anger will hurt the object*. However, they are still free to love the object.

In contrast, Fairbairn views the *schizoid position* as one in which the object rejects the self's love, leaving the self hungry and with a sense of having paradise denied to them. The object is seen as a desirable deserter. As the infant is helpless, his or her needs are urgent. If they are not met quickly, feelings of panic and rage develop. As a consequence, the schizoid individual fears devouring the object with his or her hunger. Schizoid individuals are thus in an untenable position as they believe that *both their love and their anger are bad and will hurt the object.*

Schizoid individuals often experience objects as tantalizing. They feel goaded into needing the object, but fear that their needs are bad for people and will wear them out. This is often an accurate perception of the parent's response to the schizoid patient as an infant. Schizoid individuals thus often fear their "hunger" for relationships with others, believing that their love is destructive. They respond by withdrawing from relationships and turning inward, focusing on their internal world.

Furthermore, schizoid patients often project their feelings and needs onto others. They also fear that if they become involved with objects, they will be devoured by them. This is related to their lack of self-cohesion and what will be later discussed as the in-and-out program.

Sense of Superiority About Their Self-Sufficiency

The schizoid individual often develops a sense of superiority about not needing people and things (Guntrip 1969). One schizoid patient felt pleasure and pride in not eating when she was hungry and denied her need for her husband when he was out of town. The schizoid individual wishes to be special in order to compensate for the feeling of being unloved. Furthermore, feeling special enables the individual to rise above the tragedy of his or her existence. Whether through being withdrawn and introverted or through a sense of superiority in self-sufficiency, the schizoid's fundamental aim is to maintain a safe distance from others (Klein 1995b).

Denial of Anger

Schizoid patients also tend to deny their anger and idealize their own loving nature. They are often drawn to philosophies such as New Age religion. As such they attempt to rise above the tragedy of their existence in a spiritual or intellectual manner. For example, one tremendously isolated patient's contact with others was almost exclusively derived from being part of the audience of a spiritual leader who preached about love and compassion. He followed the leader around the country attending as many lectures as he could. He bought his books and tapes and attempted to rigorously subscribe to his philosophy. He never, however, extended this knowledge to dyadic relationships with real people.

The In-and-Out Program

As previously described, the schizoid individual also tends to project his or her needs onto others. As schizoid patients' suppressed needs are so great, when they project these needs onto others, they fear that they will be devoured by other people's needs. One patient expressed a concern that other people would "use me up and suck me dry." Relationships are thus experienced as too dangerous to be in—and also too dangerous to be out of. This conflict constitutes the underlying core need-fear dilemma experienced by the schizoid patient and leads to what Guntrip (1969) describes as the "in-and out program." When schizoid individuals are separated from objects, Guntrip believes they feel isolated and insecure. However, when reunited with objects, schizoids feel swallowed up and break for freedom.

There are several solutions to this dilemma. The schizoid individual may go back and forth in relationships. For example, when one schizoid patient was feeling too close to the therapist, she terminated treatment, only to call the therapist with an emergency the next day. Another patient withdrew to his computer upon moving in with his partner. After she left him, he suggested marriage.

Another solution to this conflict is living with a great amount of interpersonal distance, often literally. For example, one schizoid patient maintained an extended long-distance relationship, while another lived in a separate house from his wife. Still another patient traveled so much that he rarely saw his partner. A fourth stayed home, but spent most of her time in her study writing and thinking.

Attempt to be Inconspicuous

On the surface schizoids appear relatively untroubled, shy, reserved, and indifferent. They stay in the background of life and work quietly. For example, one schizoid patient was employed as the night watchman for a large office building and thus rarely had contact with anyone. He was the "invisible person who kept things safe for people at night."

As a result of staying in the background, they rarely get either the positive or negative attention of others. Often they would remain in tangential inconspicuousness "were it not for the fact that there are persons who expect or wish them to be more vibrant, alive and involved" (Millon 1981, p. 273).

Overcathected Intellect

It is common to find schizoid individuals who have overcathected their intellect. Johnson (1985) believes that schizoid patients live in their heads rather than in their bodies or in the world of people. They thus tend to make contact with the world through their ideas and pursue mental processes and fantasies as a safe haven from life. For example, one schizoid patient taught himself five languages (which he never used with anyone). Another schizoid patient frequently played the game Dungeons and Dragons in which he viewed himself as a knight in the wrong century.

Inability to Express Affect

Schizoid individuals generally express little or no emotion. When they do, they often have a remote or mechanical manner of self-expression and, like William Hurt's character in *The Big Chill*, they can be callous, cruel, and insensitive. However, while there is a conspicuous absence of spontaneous affective expression in these patients, underneath, schizoid individuals are often dominated by feelings of terror and rage (Johnson 1985). Thus, when defenses do become overwhelmed, they feel and express a preponderance of primitive affects.

Concern with Issues of Existence

The schizoid individual is frequently concerned with issues of existence, either philosophically (e.g., "Does life have meaning?") or literally (e.g., "Is there money for rent this month?"). As they were so neglected as children, these patients frequently exhibit difficulties related to adequately caring for themselves. Often they live at a subsistence level (e.g., living in shabby dwellings in impoverished neighborhoods, wearing genuinely old blue jeans with holes, having cars that frequently break down, eating canned beans). Even when they earn sufficient money, they may not think about the continuity of their lives and plan for the future. Schizoids, even wealthy schizoids, thus often appear to live on the edge. For example, one patient who earned over a hundred thousand dollars a year, chronically mismanaged her money while worrying that she did not have enough and eventually went bankrupt. Often, these patients do not know how to keep a budget, nor do they seem to care to learn. There is a way in which they appear to accept what they see as their fate (e.g., to live on the periphery of life and never feel a fundamental sense of comfort and security).

At times, schizoids may avoid their fears about existence by using denial and reaction formation. For example, one patient frequently stated his belief that the universe was a benevolent place that provides people with all that they need. Given how starkly depriving his upbringing had been and how barren his current life was, this statement clearly represented his wish rather than his experience.

Disengagement and "As-If" Relating

The schizoid individual often has a sense of unreality about the world and his or her connection with it. Guntrip (1969) believes that the vital self of the schizoid individual died early in life and that he or she goes through life like an empty shell going through the motions in an "as-if" manner, relating to others through the assumption of roles (i.e., feeling disengaged but saying what they believe people are supposed to say in a particular situation). As a result, schizoid borderlines often have a feeling of artificiality about them. Several of our schizoid patients have talked about experiencing the strange sensation of having "plate glass" between themselves and others. They can see the world, but nothing gets in or out. The patient in the case example at the end of this chapter exemplifies this trait.

Extreme Sensitivity

Schizoid individuals, especially hyperaesthetic schizoids (who will be discussed in the next section), are extremely sensitive to any harshness in life. One patient would not see any films with any form of suffering or violence.

Another patient carried a piece of cloth around campus for opening door-knobs so that other people's "negative energy wouldn't touch me." Part of schizoids' sensitivity is due to feeling overwhelmed by the world due to poor selfobject differentiation. This is exemplified by the patient in the above example who feared that if her hand touched public doorknobs, the other people's "bad energy" would get inside her. The cloth that she carried provided a way "to ensure" a boundary between herself and others.

Withdrawal from the Real World to a World of Internal Objects or to a State of Objectlessness

The schizoid withdraws from a world of bad external objects to a world of internal objects (Fairbairn 1954). Initially, this is a relief. However, Fairbairn believed that schizoids ultimately duplicate their original frustrating objects in their inner world. Unfortunately, the more that people cut themselves off from real relationships with other people, the more they tend to with-draw into their internal object relationships from the past. Guntrip (1969) thinks that, as these internal objects are also experienced as bad, the schiz-oid withdraws from even internal objects to the womb for safety and rebirth. Schizoids can regress and withdraw so completely into themselves that they are often out of touch with the outer world and in danger of total alienation from the self as well as others. The schizoid patient thus often suffers in detachment as well as attachment.

TYPES OF SCHIZOID PATIENTS

Anesthetic and Hyperaesthetic

Kretschmer (1925) originally proposed two polarities within the schizoid temperament, the "anesthetic" and the "hyperaesthetic." He described the anesthetic-schizoid as unresponsive to and uninterested in the world, fla-vorless, boring, and indifferent. "He draws himself back into himself . . . because all that is about him can offer him nothing" (p. 172). An example of the anesthetic schizoid is a patient (described later in this chapter) with whom the therapist almost fell asleep during a session.

In contrast, Kretschmer described the hyperaesthetic schizoid as "timid, shy, sensitive, nervous [and] constantly wounded. . . . They seek as far as possible to avoid and deaden all stimulation from the outside" (pp. 155–161) because such stimulation is experienced as very painful. An example of the hyperaesthetic schizoid is the previously described patient who would not touch doorknobs in public places in order to avoid being invaded by "other people's bad energy."

Thus, anesthetic schizoids' insensitivity and lack of perceptiveness with others is an intrinsic condition or a reflection of their feeling of numbness. Hyperaesthetic schizoids' exquisite sensitivity to the moods and thoughts of other people serves the function of protecting themselves from danger. Kretschmer believed that both sets of characteristics could co-exist within the same schizoid individual.

Types Delineated in *DSM-III* and *DSM-IV*

It has also been suggested that the traditional schizoid category confused two quite separate disorders (e.g., Klein 1970, 1977). As a result, the authors of the *DSM-III* (American Psychiatric Association 1980), in an admittedly confusing move (Millon 1981), subdivided the original schizoid personality disorder (from the psychoanalytic tradition and the *DSM-II*) into three disorders: (1) the schizoid (asocial) personality, (2) the avoidant (fearful) personality, and (3) the schizotypal (eccentric) personality. The *DSM-IV* (APA 1994) description of the avoidant personality disorder resembles Kretschmer's description of the hyperaesthetic schizoid, while the *DSM-IV* redefinition of the schizoid personality disorder resembles Kretschmer's description of the anesthetic personality.

Both the redefined schizoid and the newly formulated avoidant personality disorders represent a detached relationship style characterized by superficial similarities. The crucial discriminating factor between these two disorders is their desire and capacity for social relationships. The schizoid personality has neither, and the avoidant, while having both, is terrified of having his or her self further damaged by more experiences of being rejected or ridiculed by other people. The schizoid personality is thus passively detached from others and relatively content with isolation and solitary activities. In contrast, the avoidant personality is fearfully detached. He or she is caught in the painful struggle between wanting affection from others but fearing rejection and humiliation. He or she thus withdraws to a world of inner humiliating and rejecting objects. The avoidant personality's strategy for coping with this dilemma is to be confused and detached and to dissociate.

Many of the schizoid patients seen in our private practices would best be categorized as avoidant personality disorders in *DSM* language. While they initially appear to be detached, unemotional, and lacking vitality, they are privately very sensitive and afraid of their intense longings for relationships with people.

However, a subgroup of our schizoid patients is predominantly anesthetic (i.e., appear deadened to all desire or interest in having relationships with people) or are a combination of both schizoid types. Predominantly anesthetic patients generally have a poorer prognosis for therapy because they often appear to remain uninfluenced by and uninterested in engaging in a relationship with the therapist. However, it is important to note with these patients that while they appear to be detached and uninvolved in treatment, they express their desire for a relationship with the therapist through behavior rather than words (e.g., they come to sessions regularly and on time). Some of our patients with this behavioral presentation have rarely missed an appointment.

In this book, the term *schizoid* will be used to refer to the traditional schizoid disorder as described by Arieti (1955), Fairbairn (1944), Guntrip (1969), and Kretschmer (1925). It will thus include both hyperaesthetic and anesthetic characteristics.

PRESENTING PROBLEMS IN PSYCHOTHERAPY

Response to Intolerable Stress

Severely damaged, predominantly anesthetic schizoids are unlikely to enter treatment unless they are experiencing some intolerable stress in their lives that has severely compromised their defense system, and they fear that they are on the verge of decompensating. At this point they enter therapy desperately seeking stabilization to help them sustain at least peripheral functioning. Their primary goal is to re-erect their defenses.

Loneliness

Less damaged and avoidant-schizoid patients usually enter treatment complaining about how alienated or lonely they feel. They frequently feel cut off or apart from other people and generally have few, if any, relationships. While they use reaction formation and attempt to convince themselves that they prefer it that way, these defenses are not entirely successful.

Feeling Too Withdrawn and Out of Touch with the World

Many schizoids enter treatment when their defenses have progressed too far. While they are accustomed to a certain degree of withdrawal, at times the amount of detachment that they experience is beyond their comfort zone. Such patients describe this experience as feeling so withdrawn from the world that they "will not be able to come back." In this state, they often feel odd and removed from a world that feels strange and unreal.

The experience of these patients in this state is akin to taking too much of a mind-altering drug. For example, one patient said life sometimes seemed to her like watching a TV program with people assuming the role of different characters in a show. Another patient talked about how the colors of things always seemed off. A third patient complained that the therapist seemed unfamiliar, like a stranger, even though she had been working with the therapist for over a year. In such cases, individuals may be experiencing what Guntrip (1969) referred to as the regressed ego.

Preoccupation with Existential Concerns

Frequently, schizoid patients enter treatment discussing existential concerns. They express a sense of futility and a belief that life is meaningless. They may wonder about life's purpose and turn to the therapist for intellectual answers to these questions. The deeper wish and the source of their cure, however, is in finding, for the first time, a sense of real relatedness with another individual.

Sensitivity to Intrusion

Schizoid patients' fear of intrusion is related to both the projection of their own ravenous needs onto others as well as their lack of self-cohesion, which makes them fear losing themselves in relationships with others. These patients often complain that other people (e.g., family, friends) are intrusive or demanding. For example, one patient wondered how he could get his wife "off my back." She always wanted him to talk more and share his feelings about things. He felt incredibly pushed by her demands, which made him want to "run back inside my cave and never come out." In another example, after her father's death, one patient complained that her older brother left too many messages on her answering machine so that she was thinking of getting rid of her phone. She felt overwhelmed by his pleas and what she experienced as his "demands" for her to respond to him. She knew that he just wanted her to sign some papers so that she could collect her inheritance, but the more he "pushed" her, the more she felt compelled to withdraw.

SCHIZOID DEFENSES

To cope with painful, unmet needs and both an internal and external world of depriving objects, schizoid individuals characteristically utilize particular defenses: denial, dissociation, reaction formation, splitting, projection, intellectualization, digressive ideation, depersonalization, and derealization.

Denial

Johnson (1985) believes that in order to cope with a cold, unresponsive world in which his or her needs are chronically unmet, the schizoid individual learns to deny those needs. For the schizoid character, it is a relief not to have needs rather than to feel chronically frustrated and lonely. For example, one patient, even as a small child, believed that she preferred to be by herself.

Dissociation

It is difficult for a small child to both deny his or her needs and the reality of chronically cold, neglectful, and unresponsive parents. Thus, another defense frequently utilized by the schizoid patient is to dissociate him- or herself from needs and affects and the awareness of a painful, depriving reality. When the world becomes too painful, the schizoid individual learns to "space out." Unfortunately, this response becomes automatic and chronic and extends to situations in which such dramatic defenses are not necessary. This causes the schizoid individual to continually feel apart from both him- or herself and from the world of objects.

Reaction Formation

A third defense used by schizoid individuals is reaction formation. Schizoid patients often believe that they are not needful, but, instead, are extremely self-sufficient. They believe that they are *not* terrified and enraged, and they view themselves as "extremely mellow." Their sense of identity (e.g., self-sufficient) and their ego ideal (e.g., not needful themselves, but good and giving to others, in a spiritual sense, like Buddha) are often based on these reaction formations.

Projection

As schizoid individuals often function at the borderline level of ego development and object relations, self–other differentiation is generally not well established. Thus, defenses such as projection can also be used to cope with ego dystonic aspects of the self such as anger and dependency. Thus, one patient stated her belief that other people were too demanding and would destroy her with their ravenous needs. Another patient avoided people because they were seen as potentially violent.

Intellectualization

Schizoid patients are also prone to use intellectual defenses to shore up their more primitive ones. This is one reason that they often appear to be higher functioning than the hysteroid borderline patient, although they are not. For example, they may espouse philosophies such as Zen Buddhism that value rising above one's needs. Their isolation may appear to be a thought out, philosophical position rather than a child's response to a cold, unresponsive world.

Digressive Ideation

Schizoids can also defensively use irrelevant and digressive ideations to muddle their minds and distract them from intolerably painful thoughts and feelings. This technique is disruptive to effective communication and is experienced by others as confusing and distancing. However, the schizoid often prefers the diffuse disharmony of being muddled to the experience of "a sharp stick in the eye" that can accompany clarity (Millon 1981).

Depersonalization and Derealization

Fairbairn (1940) also stressed the schizoid's reliance on depersonalization, derealization, and other reality disturbances. Schizoid patients typically objectify other people, depersonalizing the object and de-emotionalizing the object relationship (Fairbairn 1940). For example, one patient later in treatment recalled that she had initially perceived the therapist as if she were a piece of furniture. As therapy progressed, she came to see the therapist as a sweet-smelling flower, and later as a favorite pet who provided consistency and unconditional regard. Only late in treatment did this patient see the therapist as a helpful human being.

ETIOLOGY

Lack of an Adequate Symbiotic Attachment

Johnson (1985) believes that the schizoid character develops out of the environment's negation of the child's right to be or to live. Very early in life, the child is met by a world that he or she experiences as cold or un-involved. For example, one schizoid patient's parents were research physicians at the Mayo Clinic. While they attended to the child's physical needs, their primary attachment was to their careers.

Parents of schizoids are often schizoid themselves. They are typically not cruel or abusive to their children. They are merely unresponsive. They are thus frequently physically rejecting toward the child, leaving him or her alone for long periods of time. One patient remembered spending hours as a child being home by herself, looking out the bedroom window. Schizoid individuals like this patient often wonder if anyone is there to care about or join them.

Even when the schizoid's parents are physically present, they are often emotionally detached, preoccupied, and unresponsive to the child. While they may responsibly tend to the child's physical needs, they ignore his or her emotional needs and are rarely, if ever, spontaneously affectionate. The schizoid individual learns early not to cry if he or she is lonely as tears are of no avail. More importantly, the child does not acquire the secure sense of being valued and loved and thus lovable. One schizoid patient remembers observing her mother with her younger brother, who was also schizoid. She recalled that her mother responsibly fed her brother and kept him clean but rarely held or talked with him.

The schizoid individual thus fails to make an adequate symbiotic attachment to the maternal object, causing him or her to be withdrawn, detached, and unresponsive. The schizoid's failure to make an attachment often leads to disruptions in attachment throughout his or her entire life (Johnson 1985). One patient flew into town with his fiancée to surprise his parents. They responded by telling him that they were to busy to see him. Needless to say, he had a proclivity to behave toward his fiancée in a similar manner.

At times, the parents of schizoid individuals are not necessarily cold and rejecting individuals. Rather, due to circumstances, the child was simply not wanted. For example, one patient was the ninth child of Catholic parents who did not wish to have another child. Her older brothers and sisters were adolescent or beyond and were involved in their own lives. As a result, this patient experienced substantial neglect and loneliness.

Guntrip (1969) believes that if maintaining good relationships with others is too difficult, children learn to deny their needs for other people and withdraw into a shell. For example, one patient remembers spending hours as a child painting and drawing and reading books, but remembers spending little time with her mother.

As a result of repeated maternal rejection, the child defensively withdraws. The more extreme the rejection, the more extreme the withdrawal. Eventually, the child learns not to experience his or her needs. Johnson (1985) believes that the schizoid individual has an underlying sense of rage and terror about this abandonment that he or she has also learned to deny as it was so intolerable. This is an important observation for therapists to note in regard to treating schizoid patients.

In the same way that starving individuals wish to devour food but are unable to eat, the schizoid individual wishes for symbiosis, but angrily refuses to merge. It is not uncommon for schizoid individuals to partner with hysteroid borderlines (McCormack 1984) who meet their need for fusion and who they reject so as to induce ego-dystonic needs in the object rather than in the self.

Ostracism or Rejection in Peer Relationships

Millon (1981) has observed that, as children, schizoid patients often have the unfortunate tendency to identify with a grossly inept or socially inadequate parent in their infrequent searches for a connection to other objects. Thus, schizoid patients tend to have relatively few social skills. The social skills that they do develop are often awkward, inappropriate, and not helpful to them in establishing relationships with peers. During latency and adolescence, peers frequently sense these children's weakness and vulnerability and thus often treat them cruelly (e.g., pick on them, ostracize them). In such instances, their uninvolved parents did little to protect them or teach them to protect themselves. This left them feeling humiliated, frightened, alone, and motivated to withdraw even further.

An exception to this scenario is when the schizoid patient's parents also have narcissistic dynamics and force the child to "act social." This is one aspect of the case example at the end of this chapter, in which a schizoid patient who was the daughter of a minister was forced by her father to develop a social false self that she used for "as-if" relating when it was necessary to do so. Such patients are less likely to experience peer ostracism and more likely to have some narcissistic issues (e.g., an even greater lack of awareness of their true self) than do narcissistic patients.

DEVELOPMENTAL FAILURE

As a result of repeated rejection or nonresponsiveness from parents throughout their life, but particularly during the symbiotic period, the schizoid individual fails to make an adequate symbiotic attachment, leading him or her to be chronically withdrawn and detached. As a result of parental rejection, the infant defensively regresses to a state of nonrelatedness. For example, one patient was told that she did not speak as a small child except to statues. No one in her world expressed any interest in hearing what she had to say. Johnson (1985) believes that this developmental failure leads to two core decisions: (1) "There is something wrong with me," and (2) "I have no right to exist." The schizoid individual's life was thus arrested before it truly began.

STRUCTURAL ISSUES

It is in the initial attachment to the maternal object that the organizing principles of the ego develop (Horner 1979). During symbiosis, through identification with the maternal attitude, the individual develops his or her sense of identity and a confident expectation about the world from which he or she can differentiate, practice, and eventually fully separate. When the symbiosis is disrupted, the stage of separation-individuation and the development of the organizing processes of the ego are also affected.

Lack of a Cohesive Sense of Self

Schizoid individuals thus fail to develop a cohesive, separate sense of self. Like other characters structured at the borderline level, they often do not truly know who they are and what they feel and believe. They thus fear losing themselves in relationships with other people. This is a primary contributor to the in-and-out program.

Lack of Object Constancy

Schizoid patients have not developed object constancy. Due to their more reserved and detached stance, this is less apparent than with overattached hysteroid patients, who act out with the object (e.g., clinging, hostile attacks) when their needs are not gratified. However, lack of object constancy continues to be a major issue with schizoid patients being inclined to prematurely terminate or go mute in response to empathic failures. It is thus important for therapists to take structural issues such as object constancy into account when they are treating these patients. These considerations are especially relevant to therapeutic decisions regarding when to avoid the encouragement of regression in favor of focusing on structure building (e.g., object constancy, frustration tolerance).

Undeveloped Ego Functions

As the schizoid's ego functions are developed outside of a secure attachment, they are more precarious. Schizoid patients thus appear more capable than hysteroid patients as they seem more contained and compensate better for their primitive needs and feelings. However, they are less object related so that their underlying ego functions such as integration, differentiation, and frustration tolerance are even more fragile. Thus, until their ego functions are developed within a relational context, schizoids, like hysteroids, remain vulnerable to decompensation and acting out. A more complete description of borderline level structural issues, including treatment methods, is given in Chapter 7.

RESULTING INTERPERSONAL STANCE

The schizoid individual moves away from other people. Like the children in the B group of the Ainsworth and colleagues (1969) observational study (who played by themselves when both mother and stranger entered the room), the schizoid patient primarily relates to things, animals, places, and internal objects rather than to people. Some items on the Psychodynamic Character Inventory (presented in Chapter 12) that reflect the schizoid stance are (1) "I am painfully shy"; (2) "I would like to live somewhere that's remote and beautiful"; (3) "I spend most of my time daydreaming and having fantasies"; and (4) "I live by myself and have few, if any, relationships."

Treatment of the Schizoid Personality

Oedipal problems involve a struggle with life, whereas schizoid problems involve a flight from life (Guntrip 1969). With the schizoid personality, as the developmental damage is early, the interpersonal impact is extreme and the structural damage is considerable. The treatment process is thus often quite lengthy. Short-term psychotherapy is generally unlikely to be very effective and, if it appears to be so, it is often a manifestation of the patient's compensatory false self (e.g., "I don't need anyone"). The impact of managed care on the sense of security that the patient with more severe personality disorders is able to develop within the therapeutic relationship is a major treatment consideration.

Johnson (1985) believes that schizoid patients are often damaged by therapeutic techniques that overwhelm their defensive structures. Because of our culture's bias toward emotional reserve over emotional expressiveness, individuals who appear to be independent and unemotional people are often perceived as psychologically healthier. As a result, schizoid patients may appear to be higher functioning than they actually are.

Thus, techniques that attempt to bypass defenses can at times promote malignant regressions (i.e., unconstructive, not temporary) in schizoid patients. Basic trust must first be established before regression is encouraged rather than contained. Johnson (1987) also believes that mature ego functioning must be developed before encouraging the activation of the patient's more primitive affects (e.g., rage) or the patient will be prone to destructive acting out. For example, when techniques to promote the experience of catharsis were used by a supervisee with a schizoid patient that she misdiagnosed as obsessive, the patient experienced uncontained rage, experienced herself and the therapist as all bad, and went on an alcoholic binge.

While we typically emphasize building structures before other therapeutic goals, in the case of the schizoid patient an object relationship first needs to be established so that structural development occurs within a relational matrix. However, it is important to remember to balance establishing an attachment with structure building.

INTERPERSONAL GOALS

Establish an Attachment from Which the Patient Can Nondefensively Separate

As the schizoid patient's main failure is attachment, the therapist needs to provide a relationship for the patient in which he or she can learn to bond and eventually nondefensively separate. A symbiotic attachment must thus be established with these patients before it is resolved (Johnson 1985).

Guntrip (1969) states that the schizoid patient needs to believe that if his or her needs for passive dependence are met by the therapist, he or she will not collapse. The schizoid must come to understand that regression and illness are not the same thing. However, as much as the schizoid individual may harbor a wish for dependence, he or she is terrified of it. The therapist must thus first deal with what Fairbairn (1954) refers to as the patient's antilibidinal ego (i.e., his or her contempt for needs and distrust of the gratifying object) before the schizoid patient is able to depend on the therapist.

In *The Big Chill*, William Hurt's character, a psychology graduate student who had achieved all but the completion of his dissertation and had a successful call-in radio show, gave it all up because he felt he was a failure. He tells his friends that "it's a cold hard world" and challenges them regarding their feelings of caring for one another. However, underneath his cynicism was a desperate desire for relatedness. At the end of the film, he moves into an abandoned cottage owned by his friends. Not only are corrective relational experiences provided by therapists, but therapy also helps people when ordinary relationships are insufficient.

One of the first issues to be addressed and interpreted with the schizoid patient is what Erikson (1950) refers to as basic trust versus mistrust and Bowlby (1973) describes as attachment. The schizoid patient has several concerns about self and object: (1) that the object will be cold and unresponsive, (2) that his or her needs are contemptible, and (3) that his or her needs are harmful and will destroy the object.

The initial transference to the therapist may be one of anticipating lack of interest, lack of concern, or rejection. A times, this is expressed by the patient directly. For example, when asked why he did not contact the therapist when he was told that his mother died, a schizoid patient responded, "I assumed that you had better things to do than to talk with me." Usually patients express these beliefs more subtly. For example, one schizoid patient unconsciously did not make eye contact with the therapist in order to avoid seeing lack of interest in her eyes.

We have observed that schizoid patients often communicate with the therapist in a manner that promotes lack of interest or lack of involvement on the part of the therapist. While the patient may overtly appear to be engaged in the therapeutic process (e.g., bringing concerns to discuss and understand), the patient often talks to the therapist in a remote manner, which can induce an almost hypnotic experience in the therapist. One of the authors shared with a schizoid patient that she spoke to the therapist as though she did not expect the therapist to be listening. This brought back several memories for the patient of a remote, self-absorbed mother. The patient recalled that as a small child, when she spoke to her mother she sometimes put her mother's face in her hands to direct her mother's attention toward her.

The schizoid patient unconsciously does not expect anyone, including the therapist, to pay attention to him or her and is often concerned that his or her needs will harm others, including the therapist. Thus, the schizoid patient may withhold expressing needs to the therapist for fear of damaging the therapist in some way. For example, one patient vigilantly watched the time in order to ensure that they never ran over time, thus taking too much from the therapist. It is important to clarify this dynamic with the schizoid patient and to interpret its historical antecedents.

> In the last example, the therapist observed this pattern to the patient and asked why he was concerned about taking too much of her time. The patient said that he did not want to make the therapist too tired. The therapist asked the patient if she looked tired. The patient said, "No, but I'm still afraid that I'll make you tired." The therapist asked if there was anyone he thought that he tired out as a child. The patient began to discuss his relationship with his mother who was frequently ill. He described how careful he was not to take too much of her time and deplete her even more. At this point the therapist noted that they had run over the time limit and asked the patient if she looked tired. The patient looked at the therapist intensely, paused, and said, "No. You really don't."

As schizoid patients struggle with what we previously described as the in-and-out program, they are afraid of engulfment as well as rejection by others. In therapy, due to the projection onto the therapist of the patient's own overwhelming needs, the schizoid patient is likely to, at times, see the therapist as engulfing. During this experience, the therapist's usual ways of showing interest in a patient may, at times, be experienced as the therapist's attempting to impose an agenda on the patient (Klein 1995b).

This issue is often enacted in the arena of "whether or not" or "if and when" the patient is going to communicate. In fact, quite often the patient induces activity in the therapist through the patient's muddled communication (i.e., inspiring clarification) and long, protracted silences (inspiring comments on or questions about the silence). When the therapist does respond, the patient often experiences the therapist as intrusive.

For example, in a later phase of treatment, a schizoid patient told the therapist that he believed that his long silences during the first 6 months of treatment were really a test of the therapist's patience and her willingness to set aside her agenda to follow him at his own pace. This had resulted in many sessions in which the patient spoke only three or four sentences.

Thus, understanding the patient's underlying needs and issues can help the therapist maintain a patient and emotionally available interpersonal stance during these silences. In addition, the therapist can periodically join with the patient by offering tentative interpretations that address the patient's underlying issues. These interpretations can thus lay the groundwork for the later integration of the schizoid patient's template of split self and object relations.

It is also helpful to increase schizoid patients' awareness of the great conflict that they have between what Fairbairn (1954) describes as their libidinal ego (i.e., needs for attachment to and gratification by others) and their antilibidinal ego (i.e., hate for the exciting and disappointing object and contempt for the naive needful self). As described earlier, Fairbairn believes that when an object (e.g., the parent) is chronically depriving, the child splits the object into two bad objects (i.e., the exciting and the rejecting object) and one good object (i.e., the ideal object). To feel some sense of control over his or her object world, the child internalizes these objects. However, as Fairbairn believes that the child's self is inextricably tied to the object, the self also splits into three corresponding parts.

The libidinal ego (i.e., needful self) remains attached to and continues to seek gratification from the exciting but disappointing object. The antilibidinal ego identifies with and remains attached to the rejecting object. The antilibidinal ego feels rage toward the exciting object for its continued failures to gratify and contempt for the libidinal ego for its foolish attempts to continue to seek gratification.

Fairbairn believes that schizoid patients have a strong antilibidinal ego. They therefore have a condemning, almost puritanical, attitude about their own needs. Even when they work through their transference with the therapist and come to believe that he or she is not cold and will not be hurt by their needs, they often still feel ashamed of needing other people. For example, one patient did not tell his wife for a week when his doctor told him that he would need to undergo surgery.

It is thus crucial to help these patients become aware of this conflict and its relationship to their simultaneous identification with and hatred toward the rejecting object. The antilibidinal ego, as a resistance to treatment, must be understood and resolved before an attachment is made to the therapist or other people (Sutherland 1989). When the schizoid patient's transferences and resistances with regard to dependency needs are resolved, the patient is then more available for a corrective interpersonal experience with the therapist in which he or she can bond and nondefensively separate for the first time.

The process of forming a safe and genuine attachment with the therapist can take years. However, once accomplished, it is important for therapists to help schizoid patients to separate and individuate from an attached position (i.e., to help them become aware of and support their needs for aloneness and develop acceptance for their differences from others with whom they feel connected). In doing so, therapists provide schizoid patients with a genuine rapprochement experience. For example, one patient initially had no response to either her husband's or the therapist's leaving town. As treatment progressed, she began to feel more dependent on the therapist and moved into a phase of wanting to do things by herself but feared losing the connection with the therapist. During one week, this patient planned a vacation in the mountains (which was only a few hours from the therapist) and thus canceled her appointment. When the patient expressed her anxiety about being apart from the therapist, the therapist suggested that if she needed to, she could come back as she was close enough to return for an appointment with the therapist during the week. In such a manner, the therapist provided the patient with a secure base from which to explore the world.

Containing Patient's Anxiety

Johnson (1985) believes that a major component of the treatment of the schizoid patient is protecting him or her from gross anxiety. The internal experience of the schizoid patient is one of a small, fragile child who cannot cope with what appears to be the frightening and confusing realities of the world.

The world feels too big, overwhelming, and dangerous to the schizoid patient and he or she feels alone in the process of coping with it. Both as a child and as an adult, his or her response is to physically withdraw and emotionally detach. While the schizoid patient still has a residual wish to be attached to safe objects, it is usually directed toward internal fantasies, beautiful places, and animals.

The therapist thus needs to help the schizoid patient learn to cope with the realities of the external world without feeling overwhelmed by them so that he or she is better able to live in the real world of objects where needs can be gratified. This is accomplished by clarifying the patient's anxieties, reality testing about the validity of his or her fears, teaching him or her to manage difficult situations, and, most important, by containing the patient's affects as they are expressed. (The latter process is described in detail in Chapters 7 and 9.)

One patient came to her therapy session behaving in an unusually dissociated way. The therapist commented on this and said, "You seem very far away today. Is something happening in your life that makes you feel like escaping?" The patient agreed that she felt far away and confused and was not sure if something was bothering her or not. As the patient began talking about her week, she mentioned that her employer had transferred her to another unit. The therapist asked the patient how she had interpreted his behavior. The patient took several minutes to think about it and said that, she guessed that "it meant that he thought I wasn't doing a good job." The therapist asked her how that made her feel and she said "hurt and scared about losing my job."

The therapist asked the patient if she had received any indication from her boss that he was displeased with her work. She thought about it and said she had not. The therapist then asked the patient if this felt like it did when she was a little girl (e.g., "that you could be rejected or dismissed at any time for no reason?"). The patient said that it did and began to talk about that period and how scared, isolated, and alone she felt. The therapist empathized with her experience but did not press her to talk further as she had been treating the patient for only five months. The therapist thus thought it was best that the patient experience her anxiety in an amount that could be tolerated by her current ego.

The therapist returned to current reality and asked the patient whether her boss had a reputation of firing people with no warning and the patient said he did not. The therapist told the patient that it sounded like not understanding why her boss changed the unit where she worked elicited childhood feelings of being dismissed by her mother. The therapist said that from the patient's description, it did not sound as though there was any indication that her boss was displeased with her or fired people without warning. She suggested to the patient that if she still felt anxious, she might schedule a brief appointment with her boss to ask for feedback about her performance and/or the reason for transferring her to another unit.

In this example, the therapist used the patient's increased dissociation as an indication that she was defending against an affect and helped the patient to identify that affect. The therapist next helped the patient to distinguish between the real and transferential components of her anxiety. When discussing the childhood origins of her anxiety, the therapist empathized with the patient's experience without encouraging her to feel or express more primitive emotions. The therapist believed that the patient's ego functions were not yet strong enough to manage the experience of intense primitive affects. Rather, she returned to discussing the patient's current situation and helped her figure out how to determine if her childhood fears were true in her current situation.

STRUCTURAL GOALS

Thus, through establishing a secure symbiosis and containing the patient's anxiety, the therapist begins to provide a situation in which structural deficits can be remedied. With the schizoid patient, after a relationship is formed, a cohesive sense of self, object constancy, and ego functions can be established in a relational context rather than in a compensatory manner. The means of developing object constancy to minimize redundancy are described in Chapter 7.

Develop a Cohesive Sense of Core Self
that Is Not Defensively Based

The schizoid patient has substituted the appearance of detached indifference for real separation and individuation because attachment experiences were too painful and infrequent. As a result, the schizoid's self-concept is based on denial and reaction formation (e.g., "I don't feel or need other people"). It is, thus, important to help the schizoid patient become more aware of his or her feelings and needs.

After forming an attachment to the therapist, one schizoid patient began to become aware of how little she knew about what she truly felt or wanted. At this stage in treatment, the therapist's primary focus was in being attuned to, clarifying, and mirroring the patient's feelings and needs. The therapist particularly attended to the patient's nonverbal indications of underlying needs and feelings. Thus, when the patient was fidgeting in her chair as she talked in a flat tone of voice about an upcoming dinner with her mother, the therapist said that she noticed that the patient was fidgeting while she talked about seeing her mother. The patient said that she had not been aware of it. The therapist asked the patient if she knew what she was feeling about having dinner with her mother. The patient said that she really did not know. The therapist asked whether she might be feeling "a little fidgety or nervous" about spending the evening with her mother. The patient was quiet for a few minutes and then began to talk about her fears about having dinner with her mother. The therapist mirrored and empathized with the patient throughout the patient's elaboration of her concerns (e.g., "You really want dinner to go well with your mother but are afraid of being disappointed.").

Therapists can also help schizoid patients become more conscious of their needs by sharing with the patient what the therapist might be needing in a particular situation. Thus, one patient was talking about failing an exam in a course he was doing well in. He said that he did not feel very good that night and tried reading a book to distract himself but that it did not make him feel any better. The therapist said that she imagined that he must have felt surprised, disappointed, and perhaps "a little bit bad" about himself for failing an exam in a subject he generally did well in. She shared with the patient that under similar circumstances she might need to talk to someone and have that person reassure her that she was a smart person and that the course would turn out all right. The patient said that he could see how that might help as it did when the therapist reassured him at times. However, it had never occurred to him.

Of particular importance in helping the schizoid patient develop a cohesive, nondefensive core self, the patient must first experience the therapist as being able to truly empathize with his or her internal world. The therapist can thus offer tentative interpretations that address the enormous fear the patient has of getting too close and thus subjecting him- or herself to the experience of rejection, humiliation, lack of interest from, or domination by another person. The schizoid patient has learned to protect him- or herself from dangerous external objects by retreating inside to a safe place (e.g., "Going to Carolina in my mind").

However, while schizoids attempt to retreat to a good fantasy world, when they withdraw they frequently face the hostile, rejecting objects that they have internalized. If schizoid patients consequently withdraw from even their internal objects, they often begin to feel too detached and/or regressed and fear that they will remain completely and permanently isolated.

The therapist is thus advised to repeatedly interpret and empathize with the terrible dilemma that schizoid patients face. For example, the therapist said to one patient: "It seems as though you feel like there is no safe place for you. You feel hurt and rejected by the people in your life. When you withdraw into your mind, you hear your parents' voices criticizing you. When you dissociate, you feel alienated, frightened, and full of despair."

In sum, being attuned to, mirroring, and empathizing with schizoid patients' needs and feelings can help them develop a cohesive sense of self (i.e., "I am seen and understood. Therefore, I must exist"). This is particularly true when the therapist is able to understand the schizoid patient's internal world. As authentic self development is such an important component in the treating of other disorders, particularly the narcissist patient, this process will be elaborated on in greater detail in Chapter 8.

Create Noncompensatory Ego Functions

In some instances (e.g., with feelings of terror and rage), the patient must first develop better ego functions (e.g., differentiation, integration, reality testing, self-observation, self-soothing) before he or she is helped to develop awareness of affects (Johnson 1985). Thus, self-awareness and ego development are a tandem process for the schizoid patient in psychotherapy. For example, as the schizoid patient becomes aware of angry feelings toward objects (often bordering on rage), it is important for the therapist to simultaneously help him or her integrate these feelings with his or her loving feelings toward the object. As the patient learns to experience needs and affects, the therapist must also help him or her learn to step back and observe them so as not to be overwhelmed by them. Regression in service of the ego is, thus, a primary treatment goal.

One patient was becoming more aware of his feelings. Upon being overwhelmed by an altercation with the woman he had begun dating, he called the therapist for an extra session (which the therapist gave him the next morning). The patient was feeling confused and overwhelmed. He did not have much dating experience and, after feeling somewhat more bonded to the therapist, responded to advances from an attractive, friendly co-worker. They had dated several times. He said that he had fun with her and liked her company, although she seemed a little intense. He had to cancel their fourth date, due to an emergency that occurred at work with the computer system that he needed to attend to immediately. He called and left her a message on her machine, apologizing and telling her that he would call her back to reschedule.

When he returned home, he had received a message from her, crying and telling him that she hated him, that he was mean and sadistic like all men, that she should have never trusted him, and never wanted to see him again. The therapist asked how he felt and he said he felt confused and that he wanted to withdraw as relationships were too much trouble. The therapist empathized with him and briefly compared this situation to his childhood feelings of being rejected by his parents for no reason that he was able to understand. She then talked about how helpless he felt as a child, particularly since his parents' behavior made no sense to him. As he could not predict what upset them or what would make them reject him, he felt powerless to have any impact on them.

The therapist then asked him if he would like to understand the woman that he was dating more objectively. He said he really would because he have never experienced a person like this and did not understand what he did to provoke her. The therapist briefly explained to him that it sounded like the woman that he was dating had difficulty trusting people and was sensitive to being abandoned. When someone disappointed her, even one time, she became very angry and assumed that the person was completely untrustworthy. Her behavior made him uncomfortable (as it would with many people) and that when he was uncomfortable, his tendency was to withdraw from everyone, not just the person who upset him. Understanding this situation helped the patient feel less overwhelmed and less inclined to overgeneralize from his current relationship to relationships with all people. The patient said that he could understand her feeling of not trusting the world as he often felt that way himself. However, he still thought that remaining involved with her was not such a good idea.

One ego function that schizoid patients often need to develop is frustration tolerance. Billie Ables (personal communication) feels that patients have to learn to meet their own needs, express their needs appropriately, and tolerate the frustration of unmet needs. The latter two goals are particularly important with schizoid patients, who must be helped to learn appropriate outlets for their needs and must develop the belief that gratification will eventually come. This can be accomplished by enabling the patient to experience optimal frustration in the therapy session (e.g., the therapist attempts to be attuned, responsive, and empathic enough so that the patient is able to tolerate the times when the therapist is unable to be that way).

Helping the patient internalize the therapist's soothing functions such as empathy and perspective also makes frustration easier to tolerate without detaching. The process of internalizing therapists' selfobject functions is addressed in detail in Chapters 8 and 9 on preneurotic patients.

Another ego function that is important to develop is reality testing. Schizoid individuals generally learned to cope with painful reality by using fantasy. Due to early experiences of chronic deprivation, they tend to believe that the world is more barren and nonresponsive than it really is, attempt to avoid seeing reality as it is, and wish for the world to be different. They need to learn to make peace with the realities of the world and enjoy its benefits. For example, one patient alternated between the belief that she could have a totally loving, fulfilling relationship (as her guru told her) and feeling completely disappointed on the occasions that her partner, a physician, had a long day and came home feeling tired and preoccupied. The previous example of the patient whose job changed illustrates how a therapist might help a schizoid patient with this process.

Part of developing schizoid patients' reality testing coincides with the goal of helping them to develop a more positive and more realistic view of themselves. Schizoids need to learn to recognize and appreciate their strengths in order to combat the severe self-alienation they feel. Once they are less self-alienated they can become less alienated from others. In the beginning of this effort, schizoids may need the direct assistance of the therapist, who can authentically express appreciation of their worthwhile characteristics.

For example, one schizoid patient was surprised to hear that the therapist recognized and appreciated how much willpower and self-discipline the patient had. While these qualities were overdeveloped at the expense of spontaneity, they were, indeed, real strengths worth valuing. Therapists must often first value where the patient is, and what it has taken to get there, before encouraging these patients to move to another destination. Schizoids are survivors who do not realize they have already made it through their history and that they are now, in all likelihood, in a kinder, gentler, and more gratifying object world.

CORRECTIVE INTERPERSONAL EXPERIENCE

To help the schizoid patient learn to bond with other people, manage the anxieties of the real world, and develop a noncompensatory sense of self and ego functions, the therapist must provide the patient with a corrective interpersonal relationship. Some of the important characteristics of this relationship are contact and safety.

The Therapist Must Be Available and Contactful

Johnson (1985) states that in treating schizoid patients, what is most important is that the therapist "be there" (p. 83). Johnson believes that it is crucial for the therapist to be available, contactful, and congruent in order to help the schizoid patient learn to make an attachment, and that this helps to repair the original experience of being unwanted. Unlike treatment of hysteroid and hysterical patients, it is acceptable and even necessary for the therapist to assume a nurturing but nonintrusive parental role with schizoids in order to encourage the development of a somewhat symbiotic attachment. The therapist of the schizoid patient must thus be able to tolerate a great deal of dependency.

Guntrip (1969) discusses a particular manifestation of the in-and-out program that represents an "as-if" manner of interpersonal relating. In essence, the patient "acts" involved with others, including the therapist, but is not. As previously described, this patient often emerges when one parent has narcissistic proclivities.

One way that a therapist may note this dynamic is by observing his or her own feelings of unrelatedness to a patient who appears to have a good social adaptation. For example, the therapist noted that she chronically felt unconnected with a patient who on the surface had excellent social skills. Over time, the therapist observed that while the patient appeared to be maintaining unrelenting eye contact with the therapist, the patient was actually focused on the therapist's forehead, giving the illusion, but not the feeling, of relatedness.

It is thus crucial that the therapist not inadvertently provide the schizoid patient with this type of false self experience of "as-if-relatedness" in return. This is not easy to do as it is difficult to be emotionally available with someone who is not able to do so. While the as-if way of relating does provide a neurotic solution to the schizoid's approach-avoidance dilemma with other people, it does not solve his or her problem with impaired bonding.

Johnson (1985) thus believes that it is important in the treatment of the schizoid patient for the therapist to be authentic with the patient. Guntrip (1969), too, notes that the therapist must be the right kind of person (as well as someone who makes accurate, well-timed interpretations) in order to help the schizoid patient. He believes that patients cannot surrender their bad objects until the therapist is experienced as a sufficiently good object. An aspect of this goodness is authenticity.

As previously stated, authentically being available and dependable with a remote detached, withdrawn person is not always easy to do. The authentic response is often reciprocal withdrawal and detachment. For example, a therapist who is an insomniac noted a proclivity toward sleepiness with one schizoid patient. As hard as she tried to "be there" and to "act there," her "traitorous eyelids" betrayed her. The patient eventually noticed and forced the therapist to discuss the process of reciprocal detachment that was occurring between them. In so doing, genuine engagement was facilitated. This is an example of how countertransference enactment when appropriately processed can be a corrective experience as described by Renik (1993).

Another aspect of providing the schizoid patient with a corrective experience is that if the therapist must, in some way, make a choice between behaving in a way that the patient experiences as impinging and behaving in a way that the patient may experience as abandoning, it is usually preferable to take the former route. Thus, when schizoid patients express a desire to leave treatment prematurely, it is better to process this request with them, since allowing them to leave can be experienced as abandoning. While Guntrip (1969) discusses schizoid patients having both concerns in equal measure, the authors have found abandonment to be a far greater anticipated danger in most schizoid patients, particularly preneurotic and upper level borderline schizoids.

Due to her own countertransference issues, one therapist tended to lean in the direction of avoiding impingement and as such made several therapeutic errors in treating schizoid patients. For example, one group member with schizoid dynamics told the group that she was not ready to speak and deferred to another group member. The therapist allowed that process, which eventuated in the patient feeling rejected and isolated.

In contrast, one schizoid patient habitually responded to the therapist's absences by canceling the next appointment. The therapist noted this process to the patient, discussed the patient's feelings about the therapist's absences, and suggested the importance of their keeping appointments in order to facilitate the patient's sense of continuity and connectedness to the therapist. Such processing, over time, increased the patient's trust of the therapist.

Simple soothing gestures such as bringing the patient a cup of tea, giving him or her an authentic warm smile at the appropriate moment, and having shawls around the office if the patient gets cold are very important. We have also noted that these patients are especially responsive to a warm, comforting office (e.g., with a fireplace, plants, soothing pictures, overstuffed furniture, extra pillows on the couches and chairs). What is particularly important about the latter is that is provides comfort without impingement.

The Therapist Must Establish a Safe Relationship

Guntrip (1969) believes that the therapist of the schizoid patient must be someone with whom the patient can safely regress in order to redevelop his or her true self. The therapist of the schizoid patient must help him or her to have a controlled and constructive regression in which the patient can, for the first time, find him- or herself in an object relationship of understanding acceptance.

Thus, while it is most important for the therapist to be available, contact-ful, and authentic, it is also important for the therapist not to be impinging or to overstimulate the patient. Like an individual who has not had food and water for too long, the schizoid patient, while "starving," can only toler-ate so much contact.

For example, one extremely schizoid patient with paranoid tendencies could not tolerate being seen. This dynamic was initially processed with regard to its meaning. However, the patient continued to feel this way. The therapist began to conduct therapy sessions with the shades closed and very subdued light in the room. Such an environmental change greatly increased the patient's feeling of comfort and trust, and allowed her to share her in-ternal world with the therapist more readily.

This next point may seem like therapeutic common sense: the therapist must also ensure that he or she does not subtly impose his views of psycho-logical health on the schizoid patient. This includes persuading the patient's antilibidinal ego that needs and feelings are good. For example, one schiz-oid-obsessive patient repeatedly discussed his agreement with Zen Buddhist philosophy regarding the value of rising above one's needs. When the thera-pist interpreted this, the patient regarded her interpretations as a subtle form of attempting to persuade him that his views were irrational and not in his best interest (which was, indeed, the case). As a result, the therapist altered her approach, focusing, instead, on understanding the importance of these views to the patient and how he experienced the therapist's interpretations regarding their etiology as attempts to force him to have needs.

Due to the great resistances posed by the antilibidinal ego, it generally takes a long time for the schizoid patient to have needs or feelings with the therapist (i.e., to "be there" him- or herself). It is thus important for the therapist to be patient and to be able to tolerate a great deal of nonrelated-ness as well as being able to eventually tolerate the patient's dependence.

Guntrip (1969) thinks that the schizoid patient must come to believe that if the needs of the regressed ego for passive dependence are met by the therapist the patient will not totally collapse but will be revitalized. Guntrip states that patients must come to learn that regression and illness are not the same thing. Regression is a flight backward toward dependency in search of a new beginning. However, regression becomes illness in the absence of a therapeutic person with whom to regress, as otherwise the schizoid's bad internal objects prevail and unmercifully attack the patient for having de-pendency needs.

Part of providing a safe environment for the schizoid patient involves not promoting regression before developing ego functions in the patient.

Thus, initially, when the patient begins to slowly express feelings of anger and fear, the therapist must provide the patient with auxiliary ego functions with which the patient can identify, rather than promoting catharsis and further regression.

DIFFERENTIAL DIAGNOSIS

Early psychoanalytic writers (e.g., Arieti 1955, Fairbairn 1940, Guntrip 1969, Laing 1960) did not distinguish between schizoid, avoidant, and schizotypal disorders. In fact, the term *schizoid* historically referred to a mix of characteristics that only since the *DSM-III* (APA 1980) has been differentiated into three separate disorders. We have already briefly discussed some of the major differences between the redefined *DSM-IV* schizoid and avoidant disorders. In this section, we continue the discussion, distinguishing between these two disorders and including the differentiation of the more narrowly defined *DSM* schizoid disorder with the schizotypal disorder. We then propose a paradigm that looks at these three disorders as variations of the same disorder along a schizoid continuum. In this model, structural differences account for the variations.

Two other detached character types, the narcissistic and obsessive-compulsive personalities, are compared to the classic or traditional schizoid personality.

The Schizoid Versus the Schizotypal Personality

In *DSM* terms, the schizoid and schizotypal personality disorders share several social deficits and exhibit socially odd behaviors. However, the schizotypal personality is portrayed as exhibiting more bizarre, eccentric social communications and behaviors and reflects an ostensive genetic connection to schizophrenia that, at least some research (e.g., Baron et al. 1985) suggests is not a factor in the etiology of the schizoid. In addition, the *DSM* schizoid personality does not manifest the positive psychotic-like symptoms that distinguish the schizotypal personality disorder.

However, studies have indicated that the highest comorbidity rates with the schizoid personality and the other *DSM* axis II disorders is between schizoid and schizotypal, "perhaps because of the high overlap between the two criteria sets (e.g., social isolation, restricted affect). Avoidant personality disorder also demonstrated high comorbidity with schizoid personality disorder" (Kalus et al. 1995, p. 65). These comorbidity rates suggest that the criteria for distinguishing the three disorders may be insufficient or the three disorders are not really sufficiently different to warrant separate categories. Perhaps one reason for this lack of clarity is that both the schizoid and avoidant disorders are known to be susceptible to rare but severe decompensations under stress. When decompensating, both schizoid and avoidant personalities can regress into more socially inappropriate, bizarre, and psychotic-like symptoms.

The Schizoid Versus the Avoidant Personality Disorder

An initial differential diagnosis between the *DSM* schizoid and avoidant personalities can be difficult because both disorders present as socially hesitant and unresponsive (Millon 1981). As we have previously noted, however, some research (e.g., Trull et al. 1987) suggests that schizoid personalities can be distinguished from the avoidant in terms of their differential subscription of intimacy needs and their sensitivity to rejection. In contrast to the schizoid, who is portrayed as indifferent to normal social reinforcers (e.g., praise and criticism) and to relationships in general, the avoidant is portrayed as extremely sensitive to rejection or criticism, but aware of his or her need for relationships. Recent empirical studies (e.g., Kalus et al. 1995, Overholser 1989) have suggested, however, that anxiety and other symptoms coexist in both the schizoid and avoidant disorders. These findings make the distinction between schizoid and avoidant less clear.

We propose that the schizotypal, schizoid, and avoidant disorders might actually reflect the traditional schizoid disorder at different levels of ego-object relations structure. In this proposed schema, schizotypal would be structured at the lowest level of borderline ego/object relations. The *DSM* schizoid disorder would be structured at a more advanced level of low to mid-range borderline ego/object relations, while the avoidant personality would be structured at the upper borderline or preneurotic level. This schema would reflect what appears to be underlying structural differences in basically the same detached disorder.

Thus, the *schizotypal* patient lacks a sense of identity, the capacity for relationships, and awareness of social reality. While the schizotypal patient manifests bizarre, eccentric behaviors, he or she has no florid hallucinations or delusions (common to the psychotic level of ego object relations). However, both the terms *schizoid* and *schizotypal* were derived from the original term *schizophrenia,* implying that each disorder is related to schizophrenia and perhaps has a genetic component.

The *schizoid* patient struggles with identity diffusion and an incapacity and seeming lack of desire for social relationships (i.e., we believe that this desire exists in all humans and the schizoid patient is thus less aware of his or her need for and fear of relationships). However, the schizoid patient has more apparent ego strength (e.g., a more accurate sense of social reality) and thus appears more normal than the schizotypal patient.

The *avoidant* personality has a sufficient sense of self to have developed a shame-based identity. In addition, avoidant patients have some capacity for and the desire to form social relationships (Millon 1981). They are, however, deeply conflicted about realizing these relationships because of their conscious awareness of their extreme vulnerability to interpersonal rejection. Schizoid patients appear to have more severe ego deficits that result in their seeming to experience a sense of comfort in their detachment. In contrast, the avoidant personality has better-developed ego functions and thus is better able to tolerate remaining engaged in the painful conflict between needs for affection and distrust of others, and needs for others are less ego-dystonic.

The Schizoid Versus the Narcissistic Personality

Both the schizoid and narcissistic personality have an insufficiently developed sense of self and may have a compensatory false self that appears to be highly independent. Furthermore, both personality styles can be sensitive to intrusion from others.

The narcissist, however, is even more sensitive to intrusion than the predominantly anaesthetic schizoid. In contrast, more predominantly hyperaesthetic schizoids (i.e., avoidant personalities) have an even stronger competing need for relatedness. Treatment decisions for both must be made accordingly.

The therapist is likely to experience feeling disconnected or uninvolved with both the schizoid and the narcissistic patient. The reasons behind this experience, however, are somewhat different. The therapist often feels detached from the schizoid patient because he or she tends to be nonrelated (e.g., dissociated, involved with internal objects), whereas the therapist is likely to feel detached from the narcissistic patient because he or she is being related to as a selfobject rather than as a person.

The narcissist thus initially demands selfobject functioning from the therapist, whereas the schizoid patient needs more of an unintrusive but authentic connection. In addition, the narcissist is likely to appear more charming as a means of gaining attention and admiration from the therapist, whereas schizoid patients, although aloof, typically seem more genuine with the little they do share with the therapist than the narcissistic patient does.

In general, narcissists have a more phallic-exhibitionistic quality than the more reserved schizoid patient. Differential diagnosis becomes more difficult with what Willi (1982) refers to as the more reserved, regressive, or schizoid narcissist who gets self-esteem needs met through idealization and identification with others, rather than from obtaining mirroring and admiration.

The Schizoid Versus the Obsessive-Compulsive Personality

A well-constituted schizoid personality shares several surface characteristics with the obsessive-compulsive personality. Both are often intellectual, introverted, and have problems making commitments.

However, the obsessive-compulsive, a neurotic type, has a better developed sense of self and a greater capacity for relationships with other people than the schizoid personality. In addition, while the obsessive can come across as somewhat stilted due to assuming roles, rather than living authentically, the obsessive is still more present and available for relationships than the schizoid who comes across as "not at home." Obsessives can also empathize with others and are generally introspective. While schizoid patients spend a great deal of time in their inner world, they prefer fantasy to reality. They generally avoid introspection at all costs because to become self-aware and expressive is to suffer unbearable pain.

Furthermore, the obsessive-compulsive patient aspires to be right, whereas the schizoid patient wishes to be ideal in a particular way. In addition, one rarely encounters the pervasive problems related to control in schizoid patients that one does with obsessive patients. For example, in an argument the schizoid patient is more likely to detach than to fight to the bitter end as one observes with obsessive-compulsives. Both personalities resist being influenced and tend to use cognitive distracting tactics to interrupt thought processes. However, obsessives wish to avoid the responsibility for and shame over making a mistake, while the schizoid wishes to avoid the pain of experiencing an empty self, unable to relate to others because of its "badness."

Both the schizoid and obsessive-compulsive greatly fear losing control of their emotions, particularly their anger. This fear, however, is generally unfounded in the obsessive-compulsive, who has both object constancy, higher level defenses, and good ego functions. Johnson (1985) believes, and we concur, that this fear is at times legitimate in the schizoid personality who can be overwhelmed by primitive feelings. This is why, like Johnson, we believe that ego development must be emphasized before catharsis.

The Schizoid Versus the Schizoid-Paranoid Patient

A number of our patients were primarily rejected by parents rather than abused. However, the neglect they experienced was what Fairbairn (1940) referred to as hateful neglect rather than mere preoccupation or unresponsiveness. In such cases, the parents' neglectful behavior verged on being shunning. In addition, on occasions their parents treated them in a cruel and shaming manner or failed to protect them from the sadistic behavior of other people.

For example, one paranoid-schizoid patient recalled her parents asking her to try on her new dress. Her two older brothers teased her mercilessly, telling her that she was fat and ugly, and her parents did nothing to stop the behavior. Another patient reported that when he was 5 years old, his mother told him that he caused her depression and that was why she had no energy left for him or anyone else. Another patient had an older brother who regularly beat her up. When she came home crying, her mother (who was reading) would tell her that she was busy and not look up from her book.

One paranoid-schizoid patient brought her mother into the therapy session. The therapist asked her mother what the patient was like during her first three years. She said that the first few months, the patient cried a lot. When she was 3 months old, her father (who was impatient and had a bad temper) was annoyed with her for crying and threw her across the bed. The mother said that as an infant and small toddler, the patient would be running around too much, and her father would hit her with a belt and leave welts on her. The mother said that she did her best to keep her out of the father's way (e.g., she would tell her to go to her room or not to talk to her father). The therapist asked the patient's mother if the patient was affectionate as a child. The mother said that she didn't know as she (the mother) was so reserved. The mother said, "There was never much warmth and affection in my family, so I didn't know how to be that way. Neither did my husband."

Thus, children with primarily unresponsive objects that at times are shaming or cruel, or don't protect the child from being abused by other people tend to develop paranoid as well as schizoid proclivities. Their distrust of others is much more extreme, and they use less reaction formation to deal with it (e.g., the world is a good and loving place if we trust in God). Their rage is closer to the surface and they are much more suspicious of people's motives and more easily use projective identification and splitting. Structurally, however, they are at the same level of ego development and object relations as the schizoid patient. Both groups of patients thus have the same structural issues.

COUNTERTRANSFERENCE ISSUES

As schizoid patients' developmental issues are so early, they are likely to elicit a variety of countertransference responses in therapists. All therapists thus cannot provide corrective experiences for schizoid patients. This is most especially true in regard to therapists who have schizoid proclivities themselves. The primary countertransference issues that therapist may struggle with in treating schizoid patients are fear of abandonment, fear of closeness, and response to the in-and-out program.

Fear of Abandonment

The primary countertransference issue evoked in therapists treating schizoid patients is the fear of abandonment or separation. The schizoid patient is nonrelated. He or she is emotionally disengaged from his or her self and interpersonally distant from others, including the therapist. Schizoid patients require therapists to be related, despite their own nonrelatedness.

As previously stated, it is difficult to "be there" with someone who is not. When the therapist him-or herself has had cold, aloof, or rejecting parents, he or she may experience subjective as well as objective countertransference. In such instances, therapists are likely to respond defensively by being withdrawn or by acting engaged without being truly emotionally present with the patient.

Furthermore, therapists who fear abandonment can foster the initial symbiosis with the schizoid patient, but fail to adequately allow the eventual separation that is required. For example, one therapist supervised by one of the authors discouraged a schizoid patient who had formed an attachment and was beginning to experience genuine autonomous strivings from reducing her scheduled appointments from twice a week to once a week.

Fear of Dependency

Therapists who fear dependency themselves may initially be comfortable with the schizoid patient, as he or she seems to require so little of it. However, reparation for the schizoid patient involves the provision of a symbiotic-like relationship in order for the schizoid patient to learn to make an attachment to people.

If the therapist fears engulfment of close relationships, he or she will be unable to provide such a relationship for a patient. Therapists with this issue may thus collude with the schizoid patient's intellectual defenses. They may also role play nurturance rather than truly offer it. Both behaviors reinflict the original wound upon the schizoid patient. Guntrip (1969) believes that when the schizoid patient senses that the therapist is critical of his or her needs, he or she may become more demanding (e.g., clamor for love refused). We have observed that such patients merely remain disengaged.

Response to the In-and-Out Program

As previously described, due to conflicts between the needs for and fear of relationships, schizoid patients are in a continual in-and-out program with other people, including the therapist. The patient may, thus, begin to attach to the therapist and then defensively withdraw when hope is the highest. For therapists, whose parents were exciting and rejecting objects, this behavior can stimulate feelings of rejection and rage.

We have treated a number of schizoid patients who appeared to be developing an alliance and then terminated treatment abruptly. Often such patients return to treatment (sometimes the next day) only to leave therapy again.

One of the authors supervised a therapist who became hurt and angry when her patient behaved in such a manner with her. She thus responded defensively, and rather than processing the leaving while maintaining the therapeutic relationship with the patient, the therapist told the patient that a vacation from therapy was probably a good idea. While such a response can be useful at times with narcissistic patients, it is usually not advised for schizoid patients. Such suggestions generally are precipitated from either the lack of knowledge or more often from the therapist's countertransference feelings.

EXTENDED CASE EXAMPLE

Jean, a 40-year-old Caucasian woman who had never been married, was the youngest of two siblings with a sister six years older. Her father, now retired, had been a minister. Her mother had been a housewife and was the primary caregiver of the children.

Jean had two casual friends at work and currently had a semi–live-in lover with whom she had been involved for three years (her lover kept a separate apartment). While they were fond of each other and argued infrequently, Jean noted that they spent a lot of time apart. In general, Jean felt isolated, although she did not initially complain about feelings of loneliness. Rather, she frequently felt cut off from her feelings, detached from people, and somewhat bored. She described herself as highly introverted and generally withdrawn, preferring solitary activities. "I'm just not a people person." She reported that she often felt like an alien in her own country. So many things that should be familiar to her felt strange.

Jean derived the majority of her gratification from her job as a computer analyst. "I feel at home in my cubicle." She spent hours troubleshooting computer problems for other people and she was quite competent at it. She did not enjoy talking to the people who called upon her services, however, except to get information. She saw talking to people much the same way she saw food—necessary in order to survive or get the job done. People "took a lot of energy" and often seemed to be talking a foreign language. However, Jean could enact a number of superficial social skills and had learned how to look engaged by putting on her "small talk face," which she had adopted by imitating others in her father's parish when she was a child.

Recently, Jean had been wishing there was more to her life, that she could feel more alive and have a greater sense of purpose. She complained about feeling dead inside and disconnected from the world, in general, and people, in particular (even when she outwardly appeared to be engaged and articulate). She wished there was a safe way to connect with "at least one other person."

Jean had two cats who she adored. She fed them regular food rather than cat food and said that she wished her own mother could have cared as much. She clearly felt attached to her cats more than she did with any people in her life. "Cats are safe. People don't give a damn." Prognostically, Jean's ability to attach to her cats in such a positive manner was critical, indicating above all that she was still in touch with both the desire and ability to attach to objects even though she was terrified to do so with people.

Jean entered treatment with a lack of clarity about what she wished to gain. She said that she felt dissatisfied with her relationship and at a loss as to what she wanted from or with people. When asked how she wanted her life to be different, she responded "I don't know. I'm not really sure what there is to get from life."

During the first phase of treatment, the therapist noted and attempted to understand the contradiction between Jean's engaged persona and her subjective reports of feeling detached and dead inside. Jean complained about experiencing burnout at work because of so many troubleshooting calls, said that she had problems with self-esteem, and was disturbed by the remoteness of her partner (who appeared to be even more schizoid than the patient).

Over time, the therapist observed that Jean did not seem emotionally connected to her feelings, appearing instead to describe them from afar. Thus, even Jean's feelings of depression and shame appeared muted or masked. She did not seem to be in pain as much as she seemed distant or remote, appearing engaged through as-if behaviors that over time begin to seem superficial. Furthermore, Jean's relationships with people did not seem to hold much valence for her. She had an unusual semi-bond with a partner who was characterologically much like herself. She acted as though she could take or leave this relationship and eventually did the latter with little angst. Most importantly, the therapist noted her own great difficulty in feeling connected to her.

The therapist, thus, found herself "acting" related to someone who was "acting" related to her. Unfortunately (or fortunately), the therapist frequently became sleepy with Jean and was unable to entirely hide it from her.

When Jean inquired about the therapist's obvious sleepiness, the therapist initially asked what meaning it had for her. Jean talked about how unresponsive her mother was and how, as a child, she frequently found her asleep on the couch, engrossed in television, or sequestered in her bedroom. She remembered initially being angry, lonely, and frightened. Eventually, she "somehow gave up."

When the therapist continued to get sleepy with Jean, she apologized to her and explained it in regard to the therapist's schedule (after which she processed the impact on Jean). Jean initially said, in a totally monotone voice, that she "certainly understood that the therapist was busy." The therapist responded by noting that, in a similar situation, she might feel at least a little annoyed. After a long silence, Jean replied that she would not allow herself to get annoyed because she was afraid her anger might get out of control and destroy their relationship. Upon further exploration, Jean was able to explain how she "killed off" people inside her by making them dead or totally irrelevant once she became too angry at them. She talked about this mechanism like a switch inside her, noting that she had "killed off" all her significant relationships in this manner. Once this switch was pulled, there had never been any turning back. Remaining detached was thus Jean's way of saving the relationship (or the possibility of a relationship in the future).

The therapist empathized with Jean's need-fear dilemma, acknowledging with the patient how lonely she was and yet how dangerous relationships seemed to be for her. The therapist also noted that she understood that while a part of Jean wanted to feel more enlivened and connected to herself (as well as others), that being connected with her real feelings felt very dangerous as they could lead to more loss and alienation. Detachment appeared to be the patient's main recourse. Over time, as the therapist repeated these interpretations and Jean felt safely joined by the therapist in understanding the nature of her inner world, she was slowly able to talk a little more about her experience of detachment.

For example, at one point when the therapist continued to feel sleepy with Jean but with no other patient, even on the same day, she decided to share with Jean that she wondered if they were mirroring each other. The therapist noted that, despite her wish to feel otherwise, she was aware of a tendency to "space out" and to get tired when she was with Jean. Jean shared that she felt that way most of the time. She said that as a child, her mother and her father were cold and withdrawn. Jean remembered feeling chronically lonely and scared as a young child. She learned to daydream and read books voraciously. Eventually, she learned to detach herself from her feelings and needs and found that it was a great relief. Her father, however, was a town minister and required her to be social, so she had learned to "go through the motions" of relating to people while she really felt withdrawn from them.

Jean expressed a mixed reaction to talking about the process of mutual detachment that was occurring between herself and the therapist. The very act of discussing this problem increased the degree of authentic relatedness between therapist and patient. Jean both felt relieved and appreciative of the connection with the therapist and then afraid that she had said too much, gotten too close, and wanted to hide away in her cave again. The therapist acknowledged that in order to feel safe the patient needed to be in control of moving in and out of the relationship with the therapist. Jean talked about how she wanted to be able to retreat into the cave when she felt like the "whole relationship thing was too much," but she also wanted to be able to count on the therapist to wait for her, to remain interested in her, and not retaliate. The therapist noted that she thought that Jean needed someone who was genuinely interested in, emotionally available, and patient with Jean while she determined the pace of their contact with each other. Jean's eyes welled up for the first time as she slowly nodded her agreement.

After processing the issue of mutual detachment over a number of sessions, the therapist made a treatment decision geared toward decreasing her own proclivity to detach and become tired with this patient. She suggested to Jean that they meet during the first hour in the morning when the therapist was more alert and thus available for a connection if Jean wanted one. Jean was very appreciative of the therapist's concern. On the first day of the new appointment time, as the therapist had just made coffee, she spontaneously asked Jean if she would like a cup. Jean said that she would. The therapist asked her how she liked her coffee and then prepared it for her in the preferred manner. The patient commented on how much she liked the warmth of the coffee cup.

On future sessions, the therapist greeted the patient with this ritual. While nothing else had changed (other than processing the reciprocal detachment, changing the appointment time, and serving the patient coffee), the character of the therapy was subtly altered. The coffee exchange had initiated a process in which the therapist became more attuned to the patient's subtle needs and feelings. The patient, in turn, began to be more aware of and express her needs. The therapist also noticed that both she and the patient seemed more engaged, and that this was even the case on mornings in which the therapist felt tired. One might argue that with the introduction of a social ritual, such as drinking coffee, that the patient was again acting social as she had learned to do as part of her father's ministry. However, the patient was slowly becoming more genuinely enlivened and thus appearing less inauthentic. She reported feeling less artificial to herself and talked about spending more time outside of the cave when she was with the therapist. While it is still a possibility that she was acting, it seems much more likely that this was what had been previously occurring, whereas the patient was now genuinely more involved with and beginning to form a real attachment to the therapist. Furthermore, the therapist rarely felt tired with her.

Therapy proceeded in this vein until the patient experienced a crisis (i.e., her mother's death) during which she canceled her appointment by leaving a message with the therapist's answering service. When the patient returned from the funeral, she felt depressed and talked about how isolated that she had felt during the two weeks in which she had been gone. The therapist asked the patient why she had not called the therapist and the patient responded that she didn't want to burden the therapist with her needs, that she felt so desperate that she was afraid that she would be too much for the therapist (reflecting Guntrip's notion that the schizoid believes that his or her needs are destructive to others).

As Jean began to increasingly accept her needs (due in part to her increased attachment to the therapist), the therapist began to process in more depth Jean's great fear of and shame about her needs. Jean talked about how she believed that her needs were overwhelming and destructive to other people. She began to discuss how, as a child, when she continually saw her mother asleep on the couch, she concluded that it was her needs and demands that were tiring her mother out. Even when her mother was awake, she seemed preoccupied or emotionally unresponsive. As a result, Jean learned to play by herself. Jean had frequent memories as a child of being alone in her second-floor bedroom and staring out the window.

As she continued to discuss her mother, Jean began to realize that her mother was probably chronically depressed and unhappy with her father due to his frequent absences and remote behavior when he was home. She also noted that her mother was still depressed, tired, and withdrawn (even though the patient was no longer there to tire her out with infantile needs). Jean began to realize that her mother's behavior, however painful, had little to do with her. Jean also began to realize how angry she was at her mother and that, in reality, her mother had mostly abandoned her because of her mother's inadequacy and marital problems (not because of Jean's needs).

As Jean began to feel more conscious and accepting of her needs, she began to demand more of her partner and the therapist. Most of her requests/demands were appropriate. However, on those occasions when the therapist disappointed her, Jean became enraged and threatened to terminate treatment. The therapist processed these eruptions in terms of the progress Jean was making in being aware of her needs and how she felt horribly rejected and shamed when she allowed herself to be vulnerable enough to ask for something, only to be disappointed by the other person. Wanting to terminate the treatment represented a regression back to the safety of detachment. The therapist noted that if, together, they could help Jean work through these kind of disappointments and the horrible feelings of rejection and shame they evoked, Jean would be able to enjoy a lot more of what relationships had to offer without being so afraid.

At this stage of treatment, much time was spent on processing Jean's feelings of shame and rejection. Jean tended to globalize her disappointments, feeling that if someone declined one of her requests that they felt total contempt for her as a person or were "never really there for me anyway." Helping Jean learn how to recognize projections of her own self-hate and contempt, her proclivities to view other people and herself as all bad when they disappointed her (even one time), and her tendency to globalize and transform disappointments into despair was crucial. She was then more able to truly see and acknowledge what was available to her in the world (which while not ideal was usually not chronically barren, empty, and unresponsive as it was for her as a child).

After a long period of consolidating the therapeutic relationship and increasing object constancy, the patient decided to pursue couples' treatment with another therapist. This therapy was unsuccessful due to the emotional unavailability, rigidity, and lack of identity of her partner, who refused any kind of therapy for himself. As a result, they decided to separate. However, Jean decided to resist her urge to respond with detachment as she would have previously, and instead allowed herself to share her feelings of grief with the therapist and a friend.

While treatment is not complete, Jean has made significant progress in her ability to bond with other people. She is more aware of and less frightened by and ashamed of her needs. Treatment consisted of helping the patient to become aware of her difficulty becoming attached to people, its etiology, and its consequences. It also helped her gain a different perspective about her belief that her needs overwhelmed her mother and would thus continue to overwhelm other people. Finally, Jean learned to feel, and through increased ego development mediate her feelings or rage, shame, and terror rather than detach. She thus learned to tolerate feeling more vulnerable with others and became more enlivened as she learned how to remain connected with her own needs and feelings.

This patient was not a typical schizoid patient at the lower borderline level of object relations and ego development. While she used primitive defenses such as splitting, she recovered more quickly than is typical. Furthermore, while her feelings of basic trust were compromised, she had already developed a strong attachment to her cats and was able to develop trust in the therapeutic relationship somewhat more easily than many schizoids. Treatment thus progressed somewhat more quickly and smoothly than it might have with a more severely damaged schizoid patient. Furthermore, due to the patient's false self, which developed in response to pressures from her father to behave more sociably, she did not initially give the appearance of a schizoid patient. To some extent, the first important clue to diagnosis was the therapist's objective countertransference response of disengagement (including tiredness) with this seemingly engaged patient. This kind of patient thus illustrates best what Klein (1995a) refers to as the secret schizoid who looks engaged on the outside but who subscribes to the three essential characteristics of withdrawnness, introversion, and lack of affect.

7

Object Relations Therapy of the Hysteroid-Borderline Personality: Facilitating Separation-Individuation

The hysteroid personality (Easser and Lesser 1965, Meissner 1984) has variously been referred to by such terms as the *primitive hysteric* (Meissner 1984), the *infantile personality* (Kernberg 1975, Klein 1929), and the *histrionic personality* (APA 1987, 1994). The description of the hysteroid personality actually has its origins in the literature on primitively organized hysterical patients in which the role of infantile factors such as demandingness and dependency are emphasized (Marmor 1953). In many ways the hysteroid represents the quintessential borderline personality disorder that is most readily identified and diagnosed.

The hysteroid-borderline personality was recently portrayed in the movie *Fatal Attraction* with Glenn Close's characterization of Alex. Alex initially appears to be an engaging, intelligent career woman who is also an attractive and enticing seductress. However, after a one night stand with a married man, Alex assumes that she has a more intimate relationship with him than has actually developed. When he tries to leave, she experiences severe separation anxiety and alternates between manipulative clinging and rageful acting out against both herself and him (e.g., suicide attempts, threatening his family). Like Alex, hysteroids lead crisis-ridden lives reflecting poor social judgment (Meissner 1984). While most hysteroid patients are not homicidal, they often manage their separation anxiety through self-destructive behaviors experienced by others as coercive (Kernberg 1975).

Hysteroid patients have a hysterical personality style and a borderline level of ego organization (Klein 1965, Meissner 1989). Hysteroid patients use primitive defenses when stressed. They have the capacity, however, to rely on more neurotic-level hysterical defenses such as repression, cognitive fog, and displacement when they are not regressed (Meissner 1984). While able to maintain appropriate social skills during structured situations, hysteroids tend to regress to more primitive behavior in unstructured or more intimate situations.

DESCRIPTIVE CLINICAL OVERVIEW

Caricature of the Hysterical Patient

Easser and Lesser (1965) believe the hysteroid patient's fixation at the preoedipal level produced a caricature of the hysteric, marked by extremes of emotional instability, irresponsibility, turbulent love relationships, and markedly disturbed sexuality. Meissner (1988) has observed that the hysteroid manifests a "floridly" histrionic style (e.g., seductiveness, demandingness, hyperemotionality, and flagrant flamboyance). However, unlike the delightful, theatrical presentation of the hysterical personality, the hysteroid patient often behaves in an inappropriately intrusive and disturbingly provocative manner that would be ego-dystonic for a neurotic-level hysteric.

Ego-Syntonic, Inappropriate, Provocative Behavior

One hysteroid patient typically "flounced "into therapy. As she sat down, she fanned her skirt in such a way that the therapist could not avoid seeing her undergarments. This patient would distractedly complain about how hot she was, then look coquettishly at the therapist and say, "I'll be done in a minute. I do this all the time when I'm hot." She would then dramatically describe the crises of her day.

The therapist noted this ritualized pattern of fanning herself and asked the patient what she thought about this. The patient replied, in a lowered, husky voice, "I'm just hot. I don't know why people get so excited about the fanning thing. I just figure, why suffer. You don't want me to suffer, do you? You should try it . . . you look pretty hot yourself."

This vignette illustrates the ego-syntonic nature of the hysteroid's provocative, inappropriate acting out while denying any intent to discomfort or excite the object.

Search for the Ideal Maternal Object

Of particular importance, hysteroid patients are involved in a lifelong search for an idealized maternal object with whom they can merge and be restored. Through this relationship they hope to reclaim the security of being one with the all-good maternal object of earliest childhood.

In their desperate search for a maternal object, hysteroids misperceive others' intentions and distort ordinary social interactions. As these patients do not perceive others realistically, they project their image of the ideal maternal object somewhat indiscriminately. Furthermore, due to their desire for instant intimacy, they tend to be drawn to exciting and rejecting individuals who rather quickly self disclose, become passionately involved, feel engulfed, and then withdraw. This type of attraction lays the groundwork for intense, but short-lived, relationships.

> One hysteroid patient reported that she had fallen in love with her tennis instructor. His warmth, support, and undivided attention during their lessons made her feel very special. After lessons they began to talk to each other. He told her that his wife was pregnant with their third child and that he was somewhat anxious about this. Although she knew that he was married and had two children, she began to have serious fantasies about him. She told the therapist that she could tell that he was truly her soulmate.
>
> During their tennis lessons, the patient frequently flattered and flirted with the instructor, who, feeling a bit rejected by his wife, eventually flirted back with her. She told the therapist that he would not be responding to her if he were not feeling the same way that she was. After seducing him on one occasion, she shared her fantasies about their future with him. When he set limits, she refused to take no for an answer and "became hysterical." The tennis instructor refused to give her any more lessons. The patient experienced abandonment panic and vacillated between hating the instructor and hating herself.

Aggressive Acting Out

Excessive frustration coupled with lack of object constancy leads to rage and aggressive acting out (both hallmarks of the hysteroid borderline). When hysteroids split "bad," they expel positive internal images of the object from their mind and feel hate and distrust toward others. Furthermore, due to their low frustration tolerance and poor impulse control, they often act out their rageful feelings toward the "bad" object. For example, one patient's date was going to be late for their second date (he had also arrived late for their first date). Before she entered his car, she scratched the door with her key as she knew that his car was important to him.

Excessive Needfulness and Poor Object Choices

Due to their feelings of emptiness and lack of ability to self-soothe, when hysteroids feel alone, they feel terrifyingly alone. When they feel needful, like a small child with no concept of time, they are unable to tolerate not getting their needs gratified immediately. Consequently, hysteroid patients often feel desperate. They do not take mature responsibility for getting their needs met, like people who don't plan meals and suddenly become aware of being ravenously hungry, who then end up eating their food from vending machines. Thus, one patient reported feeling overcome at times by a sense of yearning. At those times, she went to her favorite bar in her most seductive dress and flirted outrageously with men until someone went home with her and she consciously had unprotected sex. When the therapist asked her if she felt concerned about the latter behavior, she said that she did not as compared with the compelling feeling of having no barriers between herself and another person, the danger involved felt unimportant. "Flesh to flesh is so compelling."

As in the example of the patient and the tennis instructor, bad object choices, demandingness, and splitting inevitably cause the hysteroid patient's relationships to fail. The end of the relationship is followed by abandonment depression, rage, despair, and another search for an all-good maternal object. When their relationships fail, they typically experience themselves as the victim and have difficulty acknowledging their contribution to their chronic relationship failures.

Lack of Ability for Authentic Self-Expression

A major problem for hysteroid patients is their lack of awareness of, and their inability to express, their authentic self. Masterson (1976) notes that, due to their early experiences of being abandoned for individuative strivings, the urge for authentic self expression is associated with feelings of separation anxiety. As hysteroid patients lack object constancy and are thus excessively dependent on others for self-cohesion and security, the awareness of having opinions that differ from those held by others evokes intense fears of rejection.

For example, one hysteroid patient would stop in the middle of express-ing herself, look down and say, "I'm sorry," and then resume her train of thought. Upon exploration, the therapist and patient came to understand that she apologized without thinking whenever she had an unspoken hos-tile or contradictory thought toward the therapist. Her apology represented a semiconscious effort toward achieving restitution with the symbiotic object.

Intense Separation Anxiety

Because of their experiences with mothers who discourage separation and may even reject the child for independent actions, these patients are very sensitive to situations that potentially elicit feelings of separation anxiety and abandonment. They usually have a long history of difficulty with normal life events that involve separation experiences (e.g., going to day care or elemen-tary school, high school, and college; moving to another house or city). In fact, chronic and intense feelings of separation anxiety are one of the most common complaints presented by hysteroid patients.

Excessive Demandingness

The need-fear dilemma (i.e., need for objects and fear of being abandoned by them) is another hallmark of the hysteroid condition. The longer and more significant the relationship, the more likely hysteroids are to behave in a petulant, demanding manner where they aggressively insist on the im-mediate gratification of their needs (e.g., "Where's my hug? Why are you leaving now? Do you have to go back to work?"). When the object or impor-tant other is unavailable or frustrating, hysteroid patients feel abandoned and vacillate between (1) defending against their needs (i.e., raging against or devaluing the object) and (2) defending against their fears of being aban-doned (i.e., clinging to the object). The hysteroid's "struggle in relation-ships always reflects how they are attempting to deal with, defend against, and resolve this underlying and central dilemma" (Meissner 1988, p. 14).

Summary

Hysteroid patients tend to be highly emotional, reactive, dramatic, attention seeking, and dependent on external attention to stabilize their object con-stancy and their sense of self continuity. Hysteroids sacrifice authentic self expression in order to maintain a symbiotic relationship with a maternal ob-ject who provides needed self-cohesion and self-soothing functions. Because of this excessive dependency on others, they often feel like, and are experienced by others as if they were, children demanding the immediate gratification of their needs as though they were not able to emotionally, or even physically, care for themselves. Moreover, their insistence on their needs being immediately gratified is ego syntonic. As a result, many adult hysteroids resent having to work to earn a living, openly wishing for someone to step in and take over for them and becoming outraged when disappointed.

HYSTEROID DEFENSES

The hysteroid's primary defensive motivation is to avoid separation anxiety and abandonment depression by merging with the all-good preoedipal object. Each of the hysteroid's more primitive defenses support this aim. These defenses include (1) splitting, (2) primitive idealization and devaluation, (3) projective identification, and (4) dissociation (Kernberg 1976, van der Kolk 1994). When not regressed, the hysteroid is able to mobilize more mature hysterical defenses.

Hysterical Defenses

As previously noted, in more nonregressed states the hysteroid can mobilize neurotic-level hysterical defenses, which include repression, cognitive fog, dramatization, denial, and pseudoemotionality. The hysteroid, like the hysterical patient, can appear to be both "spacey" and intensely seductive. Like hysterics, hysteroids are often genuinely surprised when the object of their provocation responds to their blatant innuendos. These defenses will be described further in Chapter 11.

Globalized Splitting

Defensive, globalized splitting is another hallmark of the hysteroid character. When regressed the hysteroid often experiences objects as all bad or all good in order to manage the overwhelming anxieties associated with the ambiguities, complexities, and ambivalence of relationships. Splitting simplifies the hysteroid's perspective. These patients often seem the clearest and most confident when interacting either from the position of experiencing the internalized selfobject as all good (i.e., gratifying object merged with good, compliant self) or from the position of projecting the all-bad selfobject experience onto the external object (rejecting object merged with a bad self) (Masterson 1976).

Splitting thus functions as a protective mechanism that actively separates conflicting experiences with objects. This is especially important when one lives in a psychic world composed of three quarts of sour milk to every one quart of sweet milk (John Nardo, personal communication). When mixing one's experiences can only ruin one's very limited "sweet milk experience," actively keeping one's good and bad experiences separated wards off intense anxiety, albeit at the price of identity diffusion and compromised social reality testing (Kernberg 1975).

Thus, to protect the limited good selfobject experiences that they have introjected, hysteroids utilize defensive splitting as a means of keeping their good and bad, satisfying and frustrating experiences from influencing one another. Unfortunately, the problem with splitting is that it interferes with the further internalizing of comforting, reality-based objects as well as the integration of good and bad aspects of their self. Without this integration, hysteroids continue to lack a realistic and consistent perception of themselves and other people. This deficit contributes enormously to their extreme insecurity, emotional lability, and consequent acting out.

Primitive Idealization and Devaluation

Primitive idealization and devaluation are often used to support the splitting defense. When the external object is frustrating and not gratifying the hysteroid's needs, the hysteroid patient vacillates from idealizing to devaluing the object. Devaluation minimizes the object's power and serves the protective aim of preventing the frustrating object from being transformed into a dangerous and feared persecutor (Kernberg 1975) or keeping the object from becoming too important.

For example, when the therapist failed to return a patient's phone call because the answering service gave the message to a different therapist, the patient, who previously experienced the therapist as very intelligent and dependable, now thought that the therapist was completely incompetent for not having a more dependable answering service. She said that she had discussed this with her friends (who were therapists) and they were all in total agreement with her.

Projective Identification

Both projection and projective identification are common hysteroid defenses. In particular, projective identifications serve to "externalize the all-bad, aggressive self and object images" (Kernberg 1975, p. 30). In projective identification, the hysteroid unconsciously projects an ego-dystonic aspect of the self *onto* the object and then behaves in a manner that induces the experience *in* the object. The patient then unconsciously identifies with the object's experience (Ogden 1979).

For example, one hysteroid patient visited his elderly mother before going to his therapy session. His mother looked, and complained about being, very ill, but rejected all the patient's efforts to try to help her. In the session, the patient was critical, argumentative, and rejecting of all the therapist's interventions, causing the therapist to feel depressed, angry, and helpless (the feelings that the patient was likely experiencing as a result of being with his mother). We believe hysteroids unconsciously use projective identifications to help the therapist empathize with the patient's visceral experience. The patient then watches to see how the therapist handles these feelings in the hopes of internalizing more effective coping strategies.

Aggressive Acting Out

Hysteroids manage intolerable feelings of anxiety through various kinds of aggressive acting out, including intense transference acting out (e.g., a patient throwing and breaking the therapist's cup because he thought that the therapist had misunderstood him). Mentation is quickly transformed into action that allows for the immediate gratification or discharge of impulses and feelings. Self-destructive acting out can include suicidal gestures, superficial self-cutting, or involvement in dangerous relationships (e.g., going to a raunchy bar, picking someone up, and having unprotected sex). It also involves minimally provoked, grossly inappropriate hostile behavior toward others. For example, one patient who was angry at her boyfriend for forgetting to call her sent him roses in a florist box filled with feces.

Dissociation

Dissociation is a common defense mechanism for hysterical characters, trauma survivors, and borderline-level personality disorders, both schizoid and hysteroid (van der Kolk 1994, van der Kolk et al. 1994). In general, dissociation is "a way of coping with inescapably stressful situations that consist of a general constriction of consciousness, which allows the person to detach from the reality of psychological and somatic distress" (van der Kolk et al. 1994, p. 719). When dissociating, the patient tends to minimize the pain of the traumatic experience by denying its meaning and importance (Basch 1981, 1983, Brende and Parson 1985, Cohen 1980, 1981, Ulman and Brothers 1988).

This defense is often accompanied by "spacing out" and memory loss for the stressful event. In treatment, hysteroids often evidence dissociation by appearing glassy-eyed, losing their train of thought, becoming disoriented, and in severe forms losing time or having memory gaps. The more that patients use extreme dissociation, the more fragmented their sense of self is and the poorer their reality testing is.

Hysteroid patients with histories of severe trauma or abuse often experience derealization and depersonalization as defenses against retraumatization. As one hysteroid patient noted, "When the experience feels unreal, it distances me from what happened or from what is happening. I can make it feel like it's happening on TV to someone else and so isn't even true." The problem is that this defensive structure promotes misperceptions of other's intentions and prevents a more balanced and accurate assessment of self and others. Reality testing is thus diminished.

PRESENTING PROBLEMS IN THERAPY

Another hallmark trait of hysteroid patients is their polysymptomatic profile. Hysteroids typically enter therapy with a multiplicity of complaints (e.g., multiple phobias, obsessive-compulsive symptoms, hypochondriacal tendencies, dissociative reactions, polymorphous perverse sexual behavior, and primitive self-destructive acting out). Common presenting problems include (1) severe depression, (2) catastrophic problems, (3) extreme acting out following a loss, (4) intense feelings of emptiness, (5) unclear goals, and (6) the implicit or indirectly expressed wish for the therapist to be an all-good mother.

Severe Depression

Many borderline patients enter treatment with a history of severe depression, including frequent suicidal ideation. This is due in part to the hysteroid patient's lack of object constancy, overreliance on the splitting defense, and lack of capacity for self observation. These constructs are elaborated on in the following sections on structural issues and hysteroid defenses. Simply speaking, the hysteroid patient has little or no ability to self-soothe and maintain any sort of perspective during difficult times.

Thus, one hysteroid patient presented in the initial interview with severe depression. She had recently terminated with her therapist of twelve years (who was moving to another city) and was defending against feelings of separation-anxiety and loss. However, while she liked and felt helped by her therapist, she reported that she began therapy feeling depressed and that she remained so for the entire twelve years. The therapist told the patient that she thought that this phenomenon would be important to understand (i.e., why she remained constantly depressed for so long while working with a therapist that she liked and respected). The therapist was given permission to speak to her former therapist who reported that when this patient was depressed, she was unable to remember depression-free periods. This tendency, coupled with her proclivity to catastrophize when she was unhappy and her discouragement about not being able to be helped by anyone, exacerbated her depression.

Catastrophic Problems

Due to their borderline-level difficulties in reality testing and self-soothing and their hysterical tendencies toward overdramatization, the hysteroid patient tends to present in treatment with a variety of rather extreme past and present problems with other people. For example, one patient said that she explicitly remembered her father's having intercourse with her during the first year of her life. Another described feeling "permanently broken" by the behavior of a boyfriend (she had broken up with two years before) who she believed was chronically unfaithful to her ("at least sixty times") during a relationship that lasted five months. Many of these patients report such things as being multiple personalities, being repeatedly raped throughout their life, being severely mistreated by many therapists (e.g., verbally and/or sexually abused, abandoned, used, and betrayed), and/or repeatedly and unfairly failing at school or being fired from jobs by sadistic bosses or teachers, through no fault of their own.

There is a strong correlation in the literature between trauma and borderline personality disorder (Herman 1992, Stone 1987). Although hysteroid patients commonly present exaggerated and distorted descriptions of their lives, all patient reports of traumatic abuse need to be respected and explored with the understanding that, without objective confirmation or disconfirmation, the truth may remain unknowable. For example, one patient reported remembering her father having intercourse with her a number of times when she was 6 months old. Research has shown that human memory does not extend much before 2 years of age. What does such a memory mean then? Is it a bid for attention or a way to make sense of the feelings the patient has? Is it a confabulation or a screen memory of sorts for something else?

This patient's sister (who was six years older than the patient) eventually confirmed that she had witnessed the patient being molested and then spanked by an uncle when the patient was 14 months old. The sister had told the patient what she had witnessed when the patient was five and the patient had then constructed an elaborate memory of her father having repeatedly raped her before she was 1 year old. The patient had had practically no contact with the uncle after she turned 2, but she had known and hated her father who grossly mistreated her, not through sexual intercourse, but interpersonally (e.g., calling her names such as "stupid slut" and cutting up her new dress when he got mad at her for bothering him at breakfast).

Extreme Acting Out Following a Loss

As previously described, a hallmark of hysteroid pathology is extreme sensitivity to separations and loss. Feelings of rage and terror over being abandoned often accompany separations and loss. In reaction, hysteroids tend to dramatically act out, often through self-injurious behaviors (e.g., superficial self-cutting, suicidal gestures). These symptoms often provide them with their ticket into therapy. One patient "freaked out" when her regular therapist went on vacation, and she immediately entered treatment with another therapist. A second patient was referred to therapy by the hospital that treated him after he made a somewhat serious suicide attempt when his partner of four months broke off the relationship. Another hysteroid patient entered treatment after punching his fist through the wall of his house after his wife suggested a separation.

Intense Feelings of Emptiness

Kernberg (1975) believes that when hysteroid patients experience their self as abandoned by their internal objects, they experience intense loneliness, emptiness, and futility. This experience of emptiness is common in both narcissistic and hysteroid patients. Kernberg thinks that the subjective experience of emptiness assumes many forms. These include feeling mechanical, distant from others, confused about what is meaningful and important and hopeless about getting it, and devoid of love. For example, one hysteroid patient said that she felt hollow and the world felt like a void. She wondered why she even got up in the morning.

Unclear Goals

Many hysteroid patients present in treatment without it being clear to the therapist or the patient what he or she hopes to gain from the experience. Often, hysteroid patients are so unaware of who they are and what they want and need that they are truly unable to describe why they are coming to therapy—except "to get some kind of help with something" or "to feel better." Even when hysteroid patients have a fledgling idea about what they want, their global, impressionistic cognitive style makes it difficult for them to explain it to the therapist.

Many hysteroid patients want to feel better but do not necessarily want therapy. They do not really want to change anything about themselves. What they truly want is for the world to change. In particular, they consciously or unconsciously hope that the therapist will be the all-good maternal object who gratifies their needs without their having to articulate what they want.

Seeking an All-Good Mother

One of the reasons that hysteroid patients have unclear goals when they enter treatment is that, as described in Chapter 3, their desire is often not really to change (e.g., become more mature, self-activating, effective, higher functioning individuals), but to experience the good childhood that they never had and to which they feel entitled.

One hysteroid patient's presenting problem was that all four of her previous therapists were too cold and unfeeling toward her. She wanted to know if the current therapist did body therapy or holding, as she thought that she needed to be physically held. The therapist processed the question, empathized with how deprived the patient felt, and then told the patient that her hunch was that this type of treatment was not in the patient's best interest.

The therapist acknowledged that physical holding might feel comforting temporarily, but it would mean treating the patient as if she were really still a small child rather than an adult. The therapist explained that gratifying those needs would interfere with her learning to make the comforting things that other people told her a part of herself so that when someone disappointed her, it would be a less devastating experience for her.

The patient decided to continue in treatment with the therapist and began relentless efforts to transform the therapist into a preoedipal mother. She wrote the therapist childlike love notes that she left in the therapist's mailbox, continued to ask for hugs, stroked the therapist's hair as she was leaving the office, and eventually refused to leave the office. She once explained how it wasn't right that she had such a bad childhood and that she thought it was only fair for her to get some needs met now. She believed that the therapist, like her mother, was "just mean" not to give her a little love.

In therapy with hysteroids, the therapist and patient often have competing goals. Occasionally, the hysteroid patient does find a therapist who is willing to try to enact the patient's wish for the re-creation of a good childhood (because the therapist feels omnipotent or has the same wish). Unfortunately, the hysteroid's wished-for goal is ultimately unattainable as the therapist, even one trying to reparent by being an all-good, gratifying object, will eventually reach limits and/or make empathic errors that disappoint the patient.

ETIOLOGY

Controversy still reigns over the etiology of the hysteroid-borderline. In our own treatment of these patients, we have found their retrospective histories to include insufficient attunement to early needs and extreme maternal interference for the promotion of separation-individuation (Masterson 1976).

We believe the major factors that influence the development of this disorder are (1) a mother who is grossly unattuned to the child's needs, providing enough attention to the infant so that an attachment is established, albeit an insecure one; (2) maternal withdrawal in response to the child's attempts to separate and individuate; (3) maternal reinforcement of the child's regressive clinging (Masterson 1976); (4) inadequate containment and limit setting of the child's anxiety, rage, and acting out; and (5) excessive frustration, pain, and abandonment, which sometimes includes traumatic incidents.

The Taste of Symbiosis

As previously described, schizoid patients were never responded to by the maternal object and consequently withdrew during the symbiotic stage before an attachment was even formed. In contrast, due to the intensity of hysteroids' mothers' own needs, they are sufficiently involved with the infant to begin a budding attachment. However, gratification of the infant's needs is inconsistent, leaving the infant feeling excited but unfulfilled. As the child does not receive sufficient soothing, affection, and empathy, he or she fails to internalize a comforting, soothing object (Kohut 1977). Hysteroid patients' symbiotic experience with exciting but ungratifying maternal objects predisposes them to endlessly yearn for an idealized, all-gratifying, preoedipal mother.

General Unattunement

Many mothers of hysteroid patients appear to be hysteroid themselves (Masterson 1976) or have other psychiatric disturbances, chronic illnesses, or extreme marital discord. Due to their own problems, mothers of hysteroids are profoundly unattuned to the child's needs. Due to the continued lack of maternal attunement, these children eventually lose awareness of their feelings and needs. Chronic severe unattunement thus inteferes with the development of children's sense of self and their sense of basic trust in the world to reliably gratify their needs. Furthermore, these children have not received sufficient affection, soothing, and empathy to internalize a comforting object (Kohut 1977).

In such cases, in addition to the maternal object's failure to respond to the child's needs when he or she is having them, the maternal object frequently impinges on the child when he or she is in a nonneedful state. This is due to the mother's use of the child to gratify her own unmet preoedipal needs for attunement, comforting, and soothing. Giovacchini (1989) believes that due to her own lack of soothing internalizations, the hysteroid's mother frequently uses her child as a transitional object. In lieu of an alternative object who can help the child through this developmental period, this pattern facilitates the tragic intergenerational problem of hysteroid mothers raising hysteroid children.

Withdrawal for Separation-Individuation

During the normal separation-individuation stage of ego–object relations development, the child is propelled by unfolding autonomous functions (e.g., learning to walk and talk) and the discovery of other interesting objects (particularly involved fathers) in order to move out of the symbiotic orbit with the mother. When this process is successful, the child establishes an autonomous sense of self. Success depends, however, on the mother's ability to be used as a secure base from which the child can explore the world.

Parents who delight in their child's evolving autonomy and individuality while still providing an emotional refueling station when needed enable the child to master separation anxiety. Through optimal frustration, parents help children integrate the good and bad aspects of themselves and others (as bad experiences are not overwhelming). As a result, object constancy begins to develop.

The hysteroid's parents are poorly equipped to help the child negotiate this stage. As the hysteroid's mother's own needs for the child to serve as a security object for herself competes with her child's need to separate from her, the mother unconsciously withdraws her love, attention, and approval when the child attempts to separate from her. If the mother herself has a borderline ego organization, she experiences the child's natural impulses to separate as an act of intentional abandonment. What the hysteroid's mother unconsciously or consciously supports is the child's regressive cling-ing (Masterson 1976, 1993, Rinsley 1977, 1982).

As one hysteroid patient reported, "My mother had me when she was 16 years old. She said she got pregnant because she wanted to have some-one just for herself who would always love her. It's just that then I grew up feeling I could never leave her. I had to remain her 'little darling' forever."

Another hysteroid patient noted that when she wanted to go out and play as a child, she learned to check out her mother's mood. If her mother looked unhappy, she knew she needed to "stand by so that if Mommy needed me I would be available. When she needed me she would say 'Come give mommy a hug,' and then I knew I was supposed to comfort her. If I had been outside playing when she needed me, she would have felt I had betrayed her. When I was 4 years old, she came out after me yelling at the top of her lungs: 'What are you doing? Are you trying to kill your Mommy? You know I need you inside. Now get in this instant.'"

In both of these examples, the mother actively seeks to keep the child within the symbiotic orbit as an extension of the mother's self. The child's developmental needs are thus subjugated to the mother's needs.

Maternal withdrawal for individuative strivings is believed to have the greatest impact during the rapprochement subphase of separation-individu-ation (16 to 27 months). At this time, toddlers alternately feel compelled by their developing physical (e.g., walking) and language abilities to prac-tice independent self-expression and a need to reconnect with their mother for security and reassurance (Masterson 1976, 1996). As object constancy is not yet established, the child experiences maternal withdrawal for individuative strivings as terrifying and feels totally abandoned and alone.

If this pattern is chronic during this critical stage of separation-individuation, children begin to abdicate their natural individuative strivings. When the mother rewards the child for regressive clinging, the child's development is truncated and excessive dependence on others, including symbiotic longings, persists.

A second opportunity for separation-individuation lies in the child's relationship to the father. The father's normal role is one of encouraging independence (i.e., inviting the child out of the symbiotic orbit to participate in the larger world of people and things) (Masterson 1976). Fathers of hysteroids have typically opted out of the parenting process, implicitly contracting with the mother that she care for the children (and herself) while he attends to life outside of the home (Slipp 1984).

Under optimal conditions, the father also provides the mother with additional support to help her with the difficult task of raising a child. John Nardo (personal communication) believes that one of the father's primary roles is to be the "mother's mother." Fathers of hysteroids, however, are not generally very supportive of their wives. At times, the father and mother are involved in an ongoing marital struggle. Usually, the father is merely absent. The hysteroid's father can also be punitive, rigid, or even physically or sexually abusive. This leaves the child with no parent to turn to for help.

Thus, when hysteroids reach adulthood, their desperate search for security through a symbiotic relationship continues because their self-development and achievement of object constancy was aborted in order to obtain the minimal gratifications provided by the maternal object. Their longing for symbiotic attachment is then transferred to other designated security objects (e.g., friends, partners, teachers, or therapists). In a typical pattern these substitute security objects are at first loved and idealized as the fantasied good object and then hated when they inevitably disappoint and frustrate the patient. The desperate search for another maternal object is then reactivated.

Inadequate Containment of the Child's Anxiety, Anger, and Acting Out

As described earlier in this book, Bion (1962, 1967) believes that it is extremely important for the mother to bear or tolerate her child's anxiety and anger without becoming damaged or retaliating, so that the child feels contained and secure. However, mothers of hysteroids are not good containers, either in terms of their own or their child's feelings and impulses. For example, one hysteroid said that whenever she had a tantrum as a child, her mother just "had a worse tantrum right back" (e.g., one time her mother even bit her). When her mother was in a bad mood or the child was irritable, her mother would drag her into a closet and leave her there for hours. This patient became aware that what she had needed from her mother as a child was to be scooped up and physically held or contained. She loved to have her head stroked and she thought if her mother had only stroked her head or held her at those times, it would have made a great difference for her.

Children need to be emotionally as well as physically held and soothed. Parents must be able to set aside their own needs (e.g., being tired, annoyed, hassled, preoccupied), at times, to attend to the child's feelings, problems, and anxieties. For example, another hysteroid patient recounted that when she had sobbing fits because she was so distressed, her parents would dismiss her by saying, "What's wrong with you again?" Had they quietly talked to her about what was frustrating her instead of blaming and shaming her, the patient may have learned how to talk her feelings through rather than blurting them out.

Unassisted Trauma Experiences

Some hysteroid patients report early traumatic experiences, including parental loss, intense parental discord (Bradley 1979, Soloff and Millward 1983), and physical and sexual abuse (Herman 1992, Stone 1987). Herman and colleagues (1989) believe that early and severe traumas disrupt developing ego organization and can become a contributing factor in the development of the hysteroid-borderline personality. They suggest that the finding that 80 percent of borderline personality disorders are female may be accounted for by the fact that 80 percent of child abuse victims are girls. Gunderson and colleagues (1995) believe that severe trauma may account for a number of classic hysteroid-borderline symptoms, including (1) needy dependency, (2) disoriented and unstable self identity, (3) self-destructiveness, and (4) frequent use of dissociation.

We do not believe that all hysteroid pathology is due to specific trauma situations, such as sexual abuse. However, hysteroid patients report experiencing chronic and extreme frustrations from early childhood without the aid of an adult to help them work these through. When this history includes severe abuse, development is further disrupted, and the hysteroid is predisposed to use dissociation even more extensively.

DEVELOPMENTAL ARREST

The hysteroid's developmental arrest occurs at the symbiotic and separation-individuation stages of development. Due to maternal preoccupation during the symbiotic stage leading to insufficient attunement to and gratification of the hysteroid's needs, the hysteroid forms an insecure attachment to the maternal object. Having received a taste of maternal attunement and symbiotic gratification, the hysteroid perpetually longs for a symbiotic relationship with an idealized maternal object (Masterson 1975).

A striking parallel often exists between the hysteroid's struggles and the rapprochement subphase of separation-individuation (Mahler et al. 1975, Masterson 1975, 1996). The hallmark of the rapprochement subphase is children's ambitendency between their strivings for separation and individuation (e.g., independence and authentic self expression) and their need for emotional refueling (e.g., clinging to the maternal object to obtain reassurance). It is this ambitendency that underlies the hysteroid's repeated interactions with others.

For many hysteroid patients, life appears to be one long rapprochement crisis (Masterson 1976). When development is derailed at this juncture by inadequate attunement and rejection of the child's efforts to separate and individuate, object constancy never solidifies, and the synthetic or integrating function of the ego is compromised. As a result, the ego never fully separates self and object representations or integrates good and bad experiences of the self and objects. This developmental arrest explains many of hysteroid patients' most salient characteristics, especially their vacillation between idealized clinging and devaluing rage as they urgently search for symbiotic reunion.

STRUCTURAL ISSUES

The hysteroid's developmental arrest at the separation-individuation stage results in a number of structural issues, including (1) split ego and object relations units (Kernberg 1975, Masterson 1996); (2) lack of object constancy; (3) identity diffusion; (4) tendency toward primary process thinking and vulnerability to transient psychotic episodes; (5) poor social reality testing; and (6) ego weaknesses (e.g., poor impulse control, low frustration tolerance, weak observing ego functions). Primitive defenses described in the previous section could also be included here as a structural issue.

Split Ego

The hysteroid's intrapsychic map consists of a split ego and split object relations units (Kernberg 1975, Masterson 1993). As with the schizoid patient,
understanding the hysteroid's intrapsychic map furthers therapists' understanding of the dynamics behind the patient's behavior.

According to Masterson (1993), the hysteroid's *split ego structure* consists
of the *reality ego* (which functions according to the reality principle) and the
pathological ego (which functions according to the pleasure principle), and
has weaknesses in ego functioning such as poor reality perception, defective
impulse control, frustration tolerance, and poor ego boundaries. The concept of the split ego explains why hysteroids do not act borderline all the time
(i.e., when they act from their reality ego, their behaviors are not remark-
ably different than those of neurotic patients). Hysteroids are, however, much
more vulnerable to stress (especially separation anxiety) and experience
subsequent ego regressions to the pathologic ego (Masterson 1993).

These ego regressions differ from the regressions in service of the ego
that are common in neurotic patients who typically operate according to
the reality principle. Even when regressed, the neurotic patient is able, with
the therapist's help, to objectively observe the therapeutic interaction, differentiate the therapist from his or her projections, understand and appreciate the limits of social reality, and maintain object constancy. When regressed, hysteroids lose these abilities, believe their distorted perceptions,
and are primarily motivated by their desire to reduce internal tensions.

Split Object Relations

The hysteroid's split object relations consists of an all-good selfobject unit
(i.e., the good, compliant self feeling gratified by the good object) and an
all-bad selfobject unit (i.e., the bad self feeling enraged with the rejecting
object). Masterson (1993) believes that the patient defends against painful
affects, such as abandonment depression, by one of two means. The patient
can defensively assume a regressive, clinging stance toward the projected
image of a good self-object. The comforting feeling of oneness with an
omnipotent protector wards off the patient's bad feelings. On the other
hand, the patient can defensively assume a righteously hostile stance toward
the projected image of a rejecting, bad self-object. In this defensive split, by
acting out gratifying aggressive impulses, the patient usually is able to stave
off abandonment depression.

Lack of Object Constancy

Object constancy is the ability of individuals to soothe themselves with a good-enough, comforting internal object when the real object is unavailable or disappointing. Failures in object constancy result in an overreliance on others for soothing, validation, approval, and auxiliary ego functions. As hysteroids have not established object constancy, they are unable to maintain a predominantly positive emotional memory of the object when the object is frustrating or unavailable, and thus have great difficulty tolerating being alone.

Identity Diffusion

As hysteroids' developing sense of self was not encouraged in the first place and their enfeebled self representation is subject to splitting, their sense of self is generally experienced as discontinuous, vague, and confused. The hysteroid patient thus has not developed a sense of self-cohesion or self-constancy. Hysteroids may express strong opinions about themselves or other people. However, upon further questioning their descriptions are vague, contradictory, and shallow. The therapist may feel like he or she has bits and pieces of different puzzles rather than a continuous, integrated portrait of the patient (Kernberg 1975).

Tendency Toward Primary Process Thinking and Transient Psychotic or Severe Dissociative Tendencies

Kernberg (1976) believes that hysteroids have a strong tendency to regress toward primary process thinking (e.g., immediate gratification and discharge of impulses without reflection or reality testing). One patient in this state drew graphic part-object images (e.g., genitals) having sex of every kind. Another patient described how she would get enraged at her husband and just say everything that came to her mind, including things that she would never ordinarily say. This susceptibility to primary process thinking is closely related to (1) the hysteroid's vulnerability to transient psychotic or severe dissociative episodes; (2) ego weaknesses, such as lack of impulse control and frustration tolerance; and (3) poor social reality testing.

When hysteroid patients experience brief psychotic or severe dissociative episodes, it may reflect (1) a temporary breakdown in ego functioning or (2) posttraumatic flashbacks (van der Kolk 1994). For hysteroid patients who experienced early, repeated traumas during childhood, these episodes represent intrusive affective and sensory memories (e.g., partial recollections of traumatic conditions that were stored on a somatosensory level but never synthesized into the individual's personal narrative) (van der Kolk 1994).

Poor Social Reality Testing

When regressed, hysteroids have difficulty differentiating self from nonself and determining the origins of their perceptions (i.e., internal versus external). As mentioned earlier, hysteroids tend to distort the intentions of others to conform with their own projected split object relations. As a result, reality distinctions between self and objects become emotionally blurred. These patients frequently become unsure what their needs and feelings are separate from those of significant others.

For example, during a difficult divorce, one hysteroid patient, a nurse, described a dream whereby she was cut open from neck to foot with the pipes of her lymphatic system exposed. The pipes were leaking milky white fluid onto the floor, leaving her feeling weakened. A doctor stood over her, looking concerned with a surgical knife in hand. She looked again and the doctor wore her face. The patient's association with the lymphatic system was, "It identifies self from nonself and protects the individual." When asked what she thought the dream meant to her, the patient replied, "These days I feel so raw and confused about everything. In the dream I couldn't tell if the doctor had cut me open to hurt me or if she was there to help sew me up. And then I couldn't tell if I was the patient or if I was the doctor. It's hard for me to know who is dangerous and who is safe, and who I am and who others are."

Hysteroids' vulnerability to primary process thinking further distorts their ability to see reality accurately. In fact, the initial purpose of the hysteroid's defenses (e.g., splitting, dissociation, derealization, projection, projective identification) was to provide global protection from reality that was too painful for the child to acknowledge or endure. Unfortunately, self-protection is achieved at the price of losing important information about the self and the world.

Ego Weaknesses

In addition to poor reality testing, hysteroids manifests ego weaknesses such as poor frustration tolerance, lack of impulse control, and poorly developed subliminatory channels (i.e., ways to channel feelings into prosocial activites such as art, vocations, or athletics). Hysteroid patients are often sensitive to abandonment. When they feel rejected, they do not have adequate ego functions to evaluate whether their feelings are realistic and to then mediate between feelings and actions. Thus, one hysteroid patient's favorite teacher looked preoccupied when she saw the patient at school. The patient felt completely abandoned and suicidally depressed, and spent the next 24 hours calling the teacher's house and hanging up. He was unable to contain his impulses, reassure himself, or attempt to get an objective perspective on the situation before acting out.

Hysteroids generally have a poorly developed observing ego. It is difficult for them to evaluate themselves and others objectively (rather than splitting and making themselves or others all bad). It is nearly impossible for hysteroids to realistically assess their impact on others, much less to understand how their behavior creates a self-fulfilling prophecy (i.e., how it provokes people to behave toward them in the very manner that they fearfully expect). For example, the patient who felt rejected by his teacher was initially quite well liked by her. However, after repeated, desperate attempts to discuss with his teacher why she did not like him and then revengefully acting out toward the teacher, she eventually withdrew from him. This patient was completely unaware of how his behavior created this situation. Rather, he perceived the teacher's withdrawal as just one more disappointing parent figure.

RESULTING INTERPERSONAL STANCE

The hysteroid's attachment style best fits the category of anxious-ambivalent. His or her overriding interpersonal stance is best described as hostile-dependent. While the patient exhibits occasionally appropriate, superficial social skills, he or she often presumes that there is more mutual involvement in a relationship than there really is. The patient thus behaves in an intrusive, needy, insistently demanding manner, resulting from his or her anger toward, and lack of trust in, significant relationships, including the relationship with the therapist. The hysteroid patient vacillates between clinging and rageful acting out. One of the authors told a hysteroid patient, "It's difficult when you want to suck and bite at the same time."

Hysteroid patients' clinging behavior can be inappropriately seductive, hostile, or demanding (Goldstein 1985). The patient's aim is to coerce an object into being more involved than is the object's proclivity. In addition, hysteroids often use fantasy about the new idealized object as a replacement for object constancy.

As the hysteroid's intense demands on the new object increase, the object's failures to satisfy the patient's needs begin to mount. The hysteroid begins to devalue, hate, and eventually act out against the object. Because hysteroids are so dependent on others for self-cohesion, soothing, and feelings of security, their interpersonal stance often borders on hypervigilance. When coupled with frequent use of primitive defenses, the hysteroid's hostile-dependent interpersonal stance can become intensely unnerving for the current designated object.

For example, one patient told the therapist stories of repeated, unprotected sexual encounters, vigilantly monitoring the therapist's face for expressions that might indicate any negative reaction. If the patient interpreted any nonverbal reaction from the therapist as critical, she burst into tears and told the therapist, "No one wants me to get any love in the world. You know how much I need your support, yet you always look so disapproving no matter who I see and you don't care that I'm so lonely. You want me to stay unhappy so I'll have to come here forever and keep paying you and never stop."

Some items on the Psychodynamic Character Inventory (PCI-2) that reflect the hysteroid patient's interpersonal stance include (1) "My relationships generally tend to be short and intense." (2) "Things feel black and white to me. When I like and feel supported by someone, I think that they're absolutely perfect. When they disappoint and I get angry at them, it's difficult for me to remember anything good about them." (3) "I often have the experience of being 'one' with important people in my life. When I do, I both like it and feel frightened by it." and (4) "Separations from people that I'm attached to are almost unbearable for me."

TREATMENT OF THE HYSTEROID PERSONALITY

Therapy with hysteroid patients contains two phases. In the first phase, the primary goal is dealing with preoedipal issues such as establishing self and object constancy. During this phase, the therapist helps the patient with both interpersonal objectives (e.g., developing a working alliance) and structural objectives (e.g., developing object constancy). In the second phase of treatment, with the working alliance better developed and object constancy more stabilized, the therapist can focus on resolving higher-order hysterical defenses and transferences (Kernberg et. al. 1989). Idealized internalizations of the therapist can be gradually modified through optimal frustration. Fostering the hysteroid's individuative strivings continues to be important.

The interpersonal and structural goals of the first phase of therapy are now discussed.

INTERPERSONAL GOALS

Foster a Therapeutic or Working Alliance

While fostering the therapeutic alliance is a critical therapeutic goal for the treatment of all disorders, it carries special significance when working with the hysteroid (Adler 1974). The therapeutic alliance refers to the collaborative relationship between therapist and patient (Greenson 1967). It is evidenced by the patient's feelings of liking, respect, and trust for the therapist and the patient's commitment to the process of therapy. Zetzel (1956) thinks that alliance is a necessary precondition for exploring the patient's unconscious and interpreting transference. Greenson (1967), Meissner (1992), and Zetzel (1956) regard the alliance as the stable context that enables patients to allow themselves to experience and understand the regressive pulls and painful affects that occur in psychotherapy. Sterba (1934) also considers the therapeutic alliance to be the bond that is forged between patient and therapist to enable the patient to observe and understand the defensive and maladaptive aspects of his or her behavior. Zetzel, however, maintains that the alliance depends on the patient's mature and integrated ego functions. Levy (1990) concurs and believes that the alliance is dominated by the patient's conscious, secondary-process, reality-oriented thinking.

Thus, patients who have difficulty with basic trust, reality-oriented thinking, and neutral self-observing are likely to have concomitant problems in establishing an alliance with the therapist. With these patients, development of an alliance and strengthening the observing ego are interwoven goals in which incremental accomplishments in one area affect therapeutic gain in the other.

As a result of their primitive defenses, their lack of basic trust, and their weak observing ego, hysteroid patients have great difficulty establishing a therapeutic alliance. Therapists can promote this goal by (1) maintaining appropriate therapeutic boundaries, (2) empathically confronting the avoidance of individuating to maintain symbiosis, and (3) reducing or containing affect storms. While fostering the patient's observing ego is important in accomplishing this objective, this process is addressed under structural goals.

In the early phases of treatment, the hysteroid typically challenges the therapist's boundaries (e.g., with repeated derisive comments, acting out with self-destructive behaviors, raising a crisis at the end of a session, demanding to be held or hugged). At this stage, the hysteroid patient is often testing the therapist's ability to contain the patient by maintaining appropriate limits without retaliation or becoming overwhelmed. For example, one patient began to discuss a crisis at the end of the session, becoming very emotional in the process. The therapist said, "I know that it's very difficult to leave, especially when you're feeling bad, but we need to stop now and we'll finish talking about your feelings on Thursday."

Without the development of the working alliance with the hysteroid's real self, the therapeutic options are limited to a transference cure, whereby the patient improves in order to please the therapist. This option does a disservice to the hysteroid even if improvement is noted because the improvement is generally temporary and the gains are incurred at the expense of further solidifying the hysteroid's assumption that having a relationship requires a regressive giving up of one's individuative strivings and real self-assertion.

One patient had been in treatment several times before. The patient was an intelligent, charming articulate physician. The patient told the young therapist that he was the first therapist he had worked with who truly understood him. The patient frequently asked the therapist for advice, which he always followed. Afterward, the patient told the therapist how helpful he was. The patient also shared with the therapist that he had never been able to cry with anyone before and that he felt that he could really trust the therapist to be there for him when he needed him.

The therapist was very flattered and truly wanted to be an all-good rescuing object for this patient. Gradually, the patient began to call the therapist's answering service with emergencies. The therapist really wanted to respond to this patient and not be neglectful like the patient's parents were. The patient began to feel happier and described feeling much better about things in his life.

However, emergency phone calls from the patient (e.g., "The woman that I'm dating hasn't returned my call") increased. The volume of phone calls, which were initially occasional, became as often as three times a night, every night. The therapist told the patient that they were going to have to limit the number of times per week that he could call the therapist and that he would have to bill him for all phone calls that were over ten minutes. Needless to say, the patient split on the therapist and became enraged. Thus, while the therapist and patient appeared to have a good relationship and the patient reported that he was improving, an alliance between the rational, observing, mature part of the patient and the therapist had never really been formed through which disappointments and frustrations could be tolerated and understood.

Affect storms, acting out, and self-destructive behavior can be reduced and the working alliance strengthened by endorsing the following guidelines: (1) immediately interpret anger, hate, and destructiveness when appropriate (Druck 1989, Kernberg 1984, Masterson 1976); (2) focus on resolving primitive defenses while respecting the patient's need to maintain his or her higher level defenses (Wells and Glickauf-Hughes 1986); (3) focus on building object constancy and observing ego rather than regressive uncovering (Wells et al. 1995); (4) refrain from using confrontation at times of stress in the patient's life outside of therapy (Buie and Adler 1982); and (5) avoid overstimulating hysteroid patients' wish for closeness as well as their rage (Buie and Adler 1982). Several of these objectives are described in greater detail later in this chapter.

Support Separation

The most important component of supporting the process of separation in hysteroid patients is for the therapist to be a secure base from which these patients can explore. Should patients undertake appropriate adventures or cancel sessions in advance to do something on their own, the therapist is advised to genuinely support these actions (without being a "cheerleader"). It is also useful to discuss patients' fears beforehand and offer a welcoming environment when they return. In particular, the therapist needs to appreciate hysteroid patients' autonomous accomplishments and empathize with any separation-anxiety that they have experienced.

One patient had always wanted to travel to Paris. However, she was mildly agoraphobic (i.e., she was frightened to leave the city that she lived in as it was her secure object). After several years of treatment, when she had internalized some of the therapist's empathy, soothing, and containing, and had begun to develop more mature ego functions (e.g., integration, reality testing), she decided that she was ready to take this trip. After her initial period of excitement, she began to experience feelings of separation-anxiety. As she did not speak the language, she was afraid that she would feel utterly alone. The therapist empathized with her feelings of anxiety and suggested that together they would find what would help her feel safer there. The therapist told her about a novel and film entitled *The*

Accidental Tourist, in which the main character, a writer of travel books, tells people how to keep everything the same as it was in the United States when they traveled out of the country. She laughed and said that some of that might be good but she "also wanted to explore the differences in Paris or what would be the point of going?" Over the next several sessions, she reported that she was teaching herself French and was reading a travel book. She said that the book talked about the different customs in France, where to go if you needed help with different things, and also described a number of very exciting things to do. The therapist mirrored the patient's pride and exhuberance. When the patient returned home, she talked about the wonderful experiences she had on her trip. She also discussed one occasion when she had a panic attack. The therapist helped her to understand what had elicited her anxiety and empathized with how frightened she had felt. The patient said that she really had felt frightened but that she hadn't let it ruin her trip. The therapist gave her a congratulatory gesture and asked her what helped to turn things around for her after her panic attack. She laughed and said that she read her travel book. She said, "I guess it was sort of my teddy bear while I was over there."

The primary goal in enabling hysteroid patients to master separation and loss is to develop object constancy (i.e., the ability to maintain a good-enough, comforting internal object that can be used for self-soothing and security in the object's absence). This goal is addressed in detail later in the chapter.

Foster Individuation

To foster individuative strivings in hysteroid patients, the therapist needs to (1) support their efforts at authentic self expression (Masterson 1976) and their autonomous pursuits of intrinsically gratifying activities, and (2) help them learn to appropriately say "no" and set good-enough limits for themselves. When the hysteroid expresses an authentic but controversial opinion, it is important for the therapist to be interested in and understand the patient's unique point of view. Additionally, when the patient begins to discuss a real interest or goal (e.g., applying for a long-desired job or academic program), the therapist is advised to express genuine interest and curiosity, but not subtly take over or become overly involved in the patient's following through on this goal.

The therapist may also facilitate individuative strivings in these patients by (1) observing with the patient how saying "no" indicates having a mind of one's own, and that honoring one's own limits is self-respecting; (2) discussing the dilemma that hysteroid patients experience between their individuative strivings and their fears that being their own person will lead to abandonment; and (3) balancing the patient's need for support with his or her need for autonomy.

> One hysteroid patient reported to the therapist that he was afraid to come to this session as he had done something that he thought would invite the therapist's disapproval. The therapist encouraged the patient to discuss what he had done and asked the patient what he feared would happen if the therapist did not approve. The patient feared that the therapist would punish him by withdrawing from him. The therapist asked the patient if this occurred in the patient's family of origin. At the end of the session, the patient asked the therapist if she did disapprove of what he did. The therapist replied, "More important than whether I do or don't approve of what you did, have you felt in any way rejected by me today?" The patient said that he did not. The therapist said that she thought that while he sought approval from others, what he truly wanted was to be accepted by them whether or not they approved of what he did.

STRUCTURAL GOALS

Develop a Cohesive Sense of Self

Due to a severe lack of parental attunement to the child's needs and feelings, parental impingement on the child when he or she is not needful, a lack of mirroring and empathy, and interference with the process of individuation, the hysteroid patient fails to develop a cohesive, integrated, and constant sense of self. A therapist can enhance the hysteroid's self-development by providing the parental functions that the patient missed as a child.

Thus, the therapist is attuned to and mirrors the patient's nonverbal expressions of feelings and needs. The therapist does not impinge on the patient in a nonneedful state and supports the patient's individuative efforts (e.g., saying no to the therapist, articulating differences from the therapist). The therapist must help the patient's nascent experiences of authentic feelings and needs to be seen, heard, and understood, and, if appropriate, responded to. Differentiation must be encouraged, accepted, and acknowledged. A more detailed discussion of self-development is described in Chapter 8.

Resolve Splitting

To resolve splitting the therapist needs to (1) contain the patient's rage (Adler 1985), (2) observe when the patient is using this defense, (3) state confusion over the discrepancy or extreme views presented by the patient, and (4) invite the patient to share the meaning that he or she makes of these extremely disparate views of the therapist (Wells and Glickauf-Hughes 1986).

The therapist thus serves a holding function for the patient who splits. Through the therapist's empathic understanding, tolerance of, and lack of reactivity to the patient's intense affects, the patient is able to develop the capacity to integrate his or her feelings (Druck 1989, Wells and Glickauf-Hughes 1986). The therapist must maintain good-enough boundaries to sustain a viable relationship that protects both therapist and patient, listen empathically to the patient without introjecting his or her hostility, and help the patient become aware of his or her distortions of the therapist.

An example of working with the hysteroid's splitting defense is illustrated by the following: "I feel confused. When we started this session you commented that you were really glad to be with someone who truly listens and you just wished that you knew more about what I thought regarding your problems, but all during the session you have been rolling your eyes and dismissing my comments and questions as if they were worthless to you. I wonder how you put together those two sentiments about me."

This type of intervention needs to be repeated many times, as initially the patient often denies the implications or is unable to integrate the discrepant part selfobject representations. At this point, it does not matter to the patient that he or she felt differently at another point in time. As hysteroid patients are functioning on "child time," they believe that their momentary experience is how they have always felt and will always feel.

We also recommend using the seventy percent rule as a replacement for the hysteroid's all-or-nothing tendencies. That is, the therapist is advised to tell the patient that one cannot realistically expect another person to be present, responsive, and understanding much more than seventy percent of the time (Wells and Glickauf-Hughes 1986). The patient also does not need to settle for much less. The seventy percent standard is a more realistic way of evaluating others as well as oneself.

The therapist's integrative interventions are intended to model and encourage the development of the patient's observing and synthesizing ego functions. As hysteroid patients join in the therapeutic effort, they become better able to pull together their discrepant experiences. As splitting is resolved, these patients begin to manifest (1) realistic ambivalence toward the object; (2) appreciation of other people as separate, whole objects (with needs of their own); (3) more integrated and thus more benign superego functions; and (4) appropriate guilt about harming others.

The therapist needs to be particularly alert for the patient's developing ambivalence toward the therapist. In the beginning of this shift from splitting to ambivalence, the positive side of the patient's feelings toward the therapist are often expressed behaviorally, rather than put into words. For example, one hysteroid patient who had always been late to sessions, started coming on time while still complaining about how the therapist was too withholding.

Resolve Projective Identifications

Ogden (1982) discusses the important process of projective identification in which "bad" or ego-dystonic aspects of the self (e.g., anger, dependency needs, sexuality) or internal objects (e.g., rejecting, critical, abusive parents) become projected *onto* another person. This process is then unconsciously buttressed by behaving toward the object in such a manner that the ego-dystonic experience is induced *into* the object, causing the object to feel or enact the patient's projected experience.

In treatment of hysteroids who commonly utilize this defense, the unconscious wish of patients is that therapists will somehow manage the experience appropriately so that they provide patients with a new model with which to identify.

A hysteroid patient with sadistic tendencies was being treated at a university counseling center that emphasized long-term treatment. At the beginning of the session, she told the therapist that she was feeling sad and scared that she might have to terminate treatment with the therapist. When the therapist asked her why she was scared, the patient said that she had overheard the therapist's colleagues saying bad things about the therapist, like how she worked with her patients too long. The therapist found herself feeling concerned for her patient, hurt that her colleagues were gossiping about her, and angry at the patient for telling her this.

After reflecting on her feelings, the therapist said to the patient: "I'm aware of having a number of feelings—being concerned about your feelings, feeling hurt by my colleagues, and feeling a bit annoyed at you for telling me this. Then, I tell myself, Jan's motivations in telling me this were innocent, so I shouldn't feel upset. Do you remember ever having these type of feelings?"

The patient free associated to two memories. The first memory was of her mother making a special birthday cake for her sixth birthday party with a doll on top of the cake in a dress that her mother had hand sewn. When her mother brought the cake out with the candles lit, the doll caught on fire. The patient reported how sad that she felt about her mother's disappointment. "She tried so hard to make my birthday extra special and it didn't work out that way." The second memory was going as a child to San Juan Capistrano with her mother. The two of them were sitting outside and having a good time feeding the swallows. Her mother then put birdseed in the patient's hair and the birds came down and pecked her head. Her mother laughed about how much fun that they were having.

The therapist asked the patient if she and her mother ever got angry at one another and the patient said "never." The therapist said that she thought that it would be "hard to grow up in a family where no one ever directly expressed anger, since we all get angry sometimes." The therapist said that if she had been in the situations that the patient described, she might have felt at least a little annoyed with her mother for bringing out a cake with a burning doll or causing her to get pecked by birds. However, she might also be thinking something like "My mother wouldn't want to hurt me so I shouldn't be mad." The patient said that she did not know if she felt that way toward her mother or not.

The therapist said that this was how she (the therapist) was feeling toward the patient and asked this patient if there might have been even a "little teeny part of her" that wanted to hurt the therapist. The patient thought about it and said that maybe she was feeling a little annoyed or jealous because it seemed like the therapist had everything, including lots of people who liked her, whereas she always felt lonely and thought that no one liked her. She did not, however, think it was right for her to feel that way.

The therapist said, "It sounds like a small part of you wanted me to feel the type of sad, hurt feelings that you feel when you believe that people don't like you, but that you don't feel like it would be okay to tell me that. It also sounds like in your family, since it wasn't acceptable to feel or act angry, mean, or jealous, that people acted that way subtly while pretending that they had good motives. It must have been very confusing for you, trying to figure out what was really happening and whether or not your feelings were acceptable."

The patient responded that she did feel confused in her family and even now did not always know when her feelings were "right." The therapist said to the patient, "Maybe, in here, we can try to pay attention to some of the things that you are doing that might tell us something about how you are feeling so that we can learn more about your feelings."

In this case, the therapist became aware of experiencing the patient's projected feelings, shared her experience with the patient in a metabolized form (e.g., "a little annoyed" rather than "angry"), learned from the experience about the patient's self and object experiences, and made a contract with the patient to understand the ego-dystonic feelings that the patient defended herself from experiencing.

Resolve Aggressive Acting Out

Techniques aimed at resolving the hysteroid's aggressive acting out include (1) developing frustration tolerance, (2) establishing object constancy, (3) developing observing ego functions, and (4) empathically but firmly setting appropriate limits. This latter technique is particularly important because the patient's emotional ventilation (e.g., shouting insults) without feeling a relational connection to the therapist may be instinctually gratifying, but results in the patient feeling further shame over his or her authentic self expression. It is also important for the patient to know that the therapist can protect him- or herself without retaliating toward the patient. These goals are discussed throughout the remainder of the chapter.

An especially difficult area of acting out involves the hysteroid's use of self-injurious behaviors (e.g., superficial self-cutting, suicidal gestures). The ongoing assessment of suicidality is especially crucial as treatment proceeds, with suicidal impulses serving as one piece of information that can help the therapist and patient pace the treatment. For example, escalating symptoms may indicate that the therapy is moving too fast and the patient is experiencing too much anxiety.

Self-injurious symptoms may also indicate the need for strengthening the patient's coping mechanisms through the judicious use of prescription drugs (e.g., antidepressants, antianxiety medication), regulation of phone contacts, journaling, transition objects, and comforting rituals. In addition, maintaining structure by setting up clear expectations, sustaining viable boundaries, and giving five-minute warnings before terminating a session (but ending on time) are important.

It is particularly important for the therapist to help the hysteroid patient to understand the meaning behind their self-injurious behaviors (i.e., the underlying issues that propel their behavior). In self-mutilation, patients can become both the attacker and the victim. They may feel empowered by identifying with the aggressor and feeling like the strong, active punisher instead of the weak, helpless child. Patients can also fantasize that parents or parent substitutes can be coerced into providing the long wished for response if the patient can only dramatize his or her sorrowful state sufficiently. For example, after one hysteroid patient's boyfriend broke up with her, she took a bottle of antidepressant medication after which she called him and told him what she did. Finally, self-injurious behaviors can also be a defense against homicidal urges toward the "bad" object. Understanding the underlying motivation of the patient's self-injurious behavior helps the therapist to direct the focus of treatment.

Finally, self-injurious behaviors need to be replaced by more constructive behaviors that address the patient's need to (1) relieve intolerable states of numbness, pain, or tension; (2) calm or neutralize states of hyperarousal; (3) learn to become more conscious of dissociative processes; (4) feel greater self-control (e.g., "I can do something"); (5) reenact the original trauma; (6) repair self-cohesion in the face of overwhelming anxiety; (7) identify with the aggressor (i.e., replacing fear and helplessness with a sense of control); and (8) overcome separation anxiety by reexperiencing the pain associated with parental care (e.g., Bach-y-Rita 1974, van der Kolk 1989).

For example, one hysteroid patient had a history of superficial self-cutting and suicidal threats when her love object disappointed her. As a substitute, the therapist helped her to learn to discharge her feelings by talking them out rather than acting them out. Thus, after a recent altercation with the man that she was dating, she told the therapist about what had occurred and how hurt and angry that she felt. After listening to and understanding the patient as she expressed her feelings, as a means of helping the patient to modulate her feelings and gain perspective, the therapist told the patient that she thought that her revenge plans were not vicious enough and suggested a few ideas herself. The patient thought of some new revenge fantasies that were even worse. As the revenge plans became more and more exaggerated, the patient and the therapist began to laugh. Afterward, the patient said that she was still angry at him but that she had better things to do with her time. She also reported feeling "a lot better."

Develop Object Constancy

The most important treatment goal for hysteroid patients is to provide these patients with a therapeutic relationship that will help them to develop the capacity for object constancy. This involves helping the patient to gradually internalize (via introjection and selective identification) the therapist's good-enough maternal functions of recognition, containment, validation, soothing, empathy, and limit setting, as well as fundamental support for the processes of separation and individuation (Wells and Glickauf-Hughes 1986).

In general, the therapist enables hysteroid patients to accomplish this objective by three developmental steps: (1) the ability to develop and maintain a constant, predominantly positive, and object-related attachment to a specific other; (2) the capacity for firmly established affective, evocative memory; and (3) the resolution of primitive defenses that interfere with the functional use of memory (Adler 1985). Wells and Glickauf-Hughes (1986) have compiled a list of techniques that can facilitate each of these developmental steps.

Helping the Patient Form a Predominantly Positive Attachment to the Therapist

The major focus in the first phase of treatment is to develop and sustain holding introjects (i.e., soothing and containing internal objects) and to interpret threats to such introjects caused by the patient's rage and fears of abandonment (Buie and Adler 1982, Druck 1989, Wells and Glickauf-Hughes 1986). To accomplish this goal, the therapist needs to offer good-enough maternal functions (e.g., empathy, attunement, containing, holding, limit setting) so that the patient can build positive identifications with the therapist that support separation and individuation (e.g., development and expression of the hysteroid patient's true self).

Techniques designed to help foster a holding (i.e., secure, protected) relationship with the patient include (1) consistency and reliability (e.g., being on time, maintaining regular appointments, returning patient's phone calls in the manner agreed upon); (2) being sufficiently attuned and responsive to the patient's affects and needs; (3) containing the patient's negative affects such as primitive rage (e.g., not allowing the patient to hurt the therapist or violate the therapist's limits); (4) generally accepting the patient's authentic self, including tolerating and understanding the patient's initial use of the therapist as a need gratifying object; (5) empathizing with the patient's unrealistic and inappropriate needs rather than attempting to gratify them (some highly intelligent hysteroid patients can make convincing cases for doing the latter that are difficult for beginning therapists to resist); (6) refraining from revenge or retaliation; (7) setting good limits to protect the patient, the therapist, and the viability of the therapeutic relationship (e.g., "I understand how much that you wish that you could see and talk to me whenever you want; however, if I did that I'd be too tired to be useful to you and you'd fail to learn how to comfort yourself"); (8) serving as the patient's auxiliary ego when the patient cannot do this for him- or herself (this is further explained later in this section); (9) being knowledgeably empathic (e.g., "It seems as though right now you believe that your husband is a bad, withholding person who reviles your dependency on him that you, too, are ashamed of" rather than "You feel bad about your fight with your husband"); and (10) mediating the patient's experience of abandonment, terrifying aloneness, and subsequent decompensation (Wells and Glickauf-Hughes 1986).

In addition to establishing conditions in which a holding relationship can develop, the therapist also needs to actively address the patient's resistances to using the therapist as a sustaining selfobject. The hysteroid's typical resistances include (1) basic mistrust of others (e.g., "It sounds like you're afraid to trust me as I may let you down or hurt you as your family did"); (2) intense self-hatred that leaves them feeling undeserving (e.g., "I have the sense that while you desperately want me to care about you, you believe that you are so bad that you don't deserve it"); (3) intense shame associated with what they experience as their inner badness; (4) fear of abandonment (e.g., "You're afraid that if you begin to count on me, I'll leave you"); (5) fear of intrusion (e.g., "It's hard to believe that you could experience us as allies without me taking over in a way that feels invasive or bad"); (6) disappointment over the reality of separateness and having to give up the illusion of fusion (e.g., "The reality of our being, at some level, alone in the world or in our own skins feels painful and frightening"); and (7) distancing and/or clinging defenses (Wells and Glickauf-Hughes 1986).

Establishing Evocative Memory

In addition to establishing a holding relationship that can be internalized, the therapist needs to help the hysteroid patient bolster his or her evocative memory (i.e., the ability to emotionally remember positive experiences with others). We have previously articulated a number of techniques designed to foster this ego function: (1) ascertaining the optimal number of appointments per week to both sufficiently modulate separation anxiety and allow internalization of the therapist's functions; (2) offer "occasional" extra appointments and/or telephone contacts after hours at times of crisis, in order to help the patient reaffirm that the therapist still exists (if the patient is using this privilege excessively, preset the number and length of extra appointments or phone calls per week so that the patient can save them for those times that they are most needed); (3) use of transitional objects such as books, postcards, or objects made important by the patient (e.g., shells or stones in the therapist's office), geared to make use of recognition memory in order to allay separation anxieties and help the patient control destructive acting out between sessions; (4) when appropriate, directly answering patient's questions about the therapist (e.g., about where the therapist is going on vacation) in order to give the patient a point of reference (i.e., the therapist still exists in the world; however, she is in New Mexico); (5) recommend the use of a journal in order to practice an internalized dialogue with the therapist in the therapist's absence, as well as to chronicle and concretize the patient's thoughts and feelings (see use of distancing techniques for an elaboration); and (6) work with patient in the use and development of guided fantasies or imagery to develop the ability to visualize calm, safe places and comforting, sustaining relationships with other people.

Resolving Primitive Defenses

To facilitate the development of object constancy, the therapy must help the patient resolve factors that can interfere with the functional use of evocative memory. These factors include aggressive acting out, splitting, dissociation, projective identification, and other primitive defenses, which have been discussed in previous treatment sections.

Increase Frustration and Anxiety Tolerance and Decrease Impulsivity

One of the salient therapeutic goals in treating hysteroid patients includes decreasing their impulsivity and increasing their frustration and anxiety tolerance by developing object constancy, and reducing patients' reliance on splitting and projective identification. In addition, once the patient and the therapist agree on the definition of the problem, therapists can work on decreasing impulsivity through a number of different means: (1) attempting to create optimal frustration through the amount of therapeutic contact; (2) encouraging the patient to call a friend for soothing or help in gaining greater perspective before acting out; (3) having the patient use a journal and write down thoughts and feelings before taking action; (4) teaching the patient self soothing techniques, such as going for a walk, taking a hot bath, listening to calming music, and having a cup of tea; (5) learning what's realistic to expect from self and others; and (6) learning to become aware when they are beginning to become frustrated and to stop what they are doing at that point before their feelings overwhelm them.

For example, while one patient was cooking an elaborate meal, she noticed that she was missing a few important ingredients. While she was cooking, she received several frustrating phone calls, during which the bread that she was baking almost burned. Shortly after, her children returned home from school and were quarreling with each other. She noticed that she was beginning to feel very agitated and decided to finish cooking the meal another day rather than continue to cook the meal until she exploded with her children and did something like throw the meal down the toilet, as she would have done in the past. She told the children that she had had a frustrating day and that she needed a "time out" to take a bath, drink a cup of hot tea, and calm herself down, but she would come back down in a half hour. She suggested that they might want to take a time out to calm down too, and there were some freshly baked cookies on the counter that they could have with a glass of milk.

Use of soothing rituals are important at these times. Some of them (e.g., drinking tea) can acquire extra meaning if done in the presence of the therapist or another soothing object. Furthermore, as a small child learns frustration tolerance by being contained and soothed by the parent, this goal can be accomplished in the therapy session by the therapist containing the hysteroid patient's affects and verbally soothing him or her.

Increasing Observing Ego Functions

The development of observing ego functions is a crucial component in the treatment of hysteroids. For example, one method for helping hysteroid patients increase frustration tolerance is for them to learn to observe when they are just beginning to feel frustrated rather than allowing the experience of frustration to escalate until they feel overwhelmed and unable to control their expression of feelings in an appropriate manner. However, accomplishing this goal is contingent upon the patient having some ability to self-observe.

Glickauf-Hughes and colleagues (1997) describe several techniques for increasing observing ego functions in patients: (1) the use of clarification, particularly following catharsis; (2) serving as an auxiliary ego; and (3) use of distancing techniques. Some of the methods that they describe will be applied to hysteroid patients. Glickauf-Hughes and colleagues believe that a strong observing ego is one of the hallmarks of mental health.

Clarification Following Catharsis

The first method described by Glickauf-Hughes and colleagues (1997) is catharsis followed by clarification. There is much confusion in the literature about the meaning (i.e., are feelings entities that must be discharged or actions?), use, and importance of catharsis. Unlike interpretation, catharsis is not a technique but a process occurring in a patient that can occur naturally or be induced by therapeutic techniques. Critics of catharsis believe that catharsis implies one's losing control (Lawy 1970). However, Nichols and Kolb (1986) believe that catharsis combined with clarification entails not losing control but giving it up both purposefully and temporarily. Thus, encouraging affective expression in hysteroid patients at about the same time that they intellectually understand their feelings enhances hysteroids' ability to self-observe as they are able to alternately experience and reflect upon their feelings. Appropriate timing is very important (e.g., not encouraging expression of affect near the end of the session).

Rogers (1942) introduced the term *clarification* and described it as a process of restating a patient's problems in a somewhat clearer form. He believed that the therapist "serves as a companion for the patient as the latter searches through a tangled forest in the dead of night" (pp. 112–113). This quotation is an apt description of the hysteroid's experience. In clarification, the therapist makes connections for the hysteroid patient between his or her behavior and ways of thinking. This, at times, includes sharing the therapist's perspective with the patient (e.g., "I know that right now it feels as though your pain will go on forever and that this belief terrifies you. When we feel regressed as adults time can feel as it did when we were children. Children often feel as though how ever they are feeling right now is how they are going to feel forever. It will be important for us to remember at these times how your feelings have changed in the past and to hold on to the notion that they will change again in the future."

Serving as Their Auxiliary Ego

Another method for increasing the observing ego in hysteroid patients is serving as their auxiliary ego, which Edward and colleagues (1991) describe as the object's taking over for the ego when the infant or regressed individual is unable to protect him or herself. Some ways that therapists can do this with hysteroid patients are clarification, being objective, and breaking interpersonal problems down in order to understand them.

The therapist can also model objectivity with the patient by helping him or her examine, step by step, how an interpersonal problem developed

(Glickauf-Hughes and Wells 1995b). Over time the hysteroid patient begins to internalize this approach and becomes more able to observe as well as experience his or her relational problems.

Use of Distancing Techniques

Scialli (1982) notes the relationship between dissociation (especially the conscious use of dissociation) and the observing ego. Some techniques for helping patients gain distance from and consequently feel more separate from their problems include conscious projection of the problem; journal writing; use of humor, stories, and metaphors; and identification with the therapist's observing ego functions.

> One hysteroid patient said that her boyfriend of three weeks had not called for a few nights and that she was sure that he hated her. She was considering going to his house that night "to have it out with him." The therapist asked the patient how her best friend might interpret the situation and what she might advise her to do. She reflected on this and then said, "I think she would tell me to chill out—that he's probably busy working or something and that going over to his house feeling angry could be a really bad move." The therapist asked her what she was thinking and feeling, and she laughed and said, "I get the point!"

While the use of journaling has been previously mentioned, it can specifically be used to increase observing ego functions. Therapists may advise hysteroid patients that when they are feeling emotionally overwhelmed and need to gain perspective about their feelings and situation, they should write down in their journal whatever comes to their mind. It is then suggested that patients put the problem on hold for a few hours during which they engage in a soothing activity. When patients are feeling less emotionally overwhelmed, it is recommended that they read their journal entry and attempt to view it from the therapist's perspective. We have found that this exercise also facilitates the patient's internalization of the therapist's self-object functions.

Facilitate the Development of Reality Testing

Several methods are recommended for facilitating better reality testing. One technique is the empathic confrontation of the patient's use of avoidance and denial in potentially dangerous relationships, particularly their denial of danger related to impulsive, need-gratifying behavior. For example, the patient who picked up men in bars and had unprotected sex needed to be confronted about how this pattern of behavior put her at risk for physical illness as well as emotional disappointment.

Providing auxiliary ego functions as needed is also useful (e.g., it lends perspective and reframes possibilities when the patient catastrophizes and overgeneralizes). These functions include helping the patient to "cognitively bind" impulses and affects through contemplation, fantasy, reflection, and symbol formation, so as to structure the delay of action and detour their impulses and affects.

Another means of increasing reality testing is validating the patient's perceptions or aspects of these perceptions that the therapist believes to be true (Glickauf-Hughes and Wells 1995b, Seltzer 1983) and discussing the realistic aspects of the situation. Therapists are advised to initially empathize with the patient's feelings before confronting reality distortions. For example, one extremely paranoid hysteroid patient, who projected her neediness onto others, told the therapist that she felt outraged that people thought that they could come up to you and ask you for the time any time that they wanted to. The therapist told the patient that she thought that it was true that many people were a little self-absorbed, and thus more concerned about their own needs. The therapist empathized with the patient about how this tendency in others was very distressing to her as it made her feel very impinged upon and used by people. After the patient felt acknowledged and understood, the therapist began to discuss with her the realistic components of the situation (e.g., asking for the time is an acceptable social custom in our culture) and the transferential components (e.g., how unresponsive her mother was to her needs while simultaneously using her to meet her own).

Another means of helping hysteroid patients develop better reality testing is by working through their transference with the therapist. This, in addition to confronting primitive defenses, helps to change the hysteroid's object relations template so that it more accurately represents the real world. For example, this same patient interpreted the therapist's questions as attempts to control (rather than understand) her. The therapist empathized with her experience, which the patient continued to discuss. As the patient had previously discussed her mother's controlling behavior, the therapist said, "It sounds like you experience me as wanting to control you as your mother did." The patient began to talk in detail about her mother's intrusive, controlling behavior, including frequently looking through all the patient's drawers and reading her diary. The therapist said, "Perhaps when I ask you questions to try to understand you better, it feels like your mother prying into your secret world without permission." The patient reflected for a minute and said, "I guess I was feeling that way, but it's really not the same because you're not really sneaky like my mother and when I say 'no', you stop."

As the hysteroid, like the hysteric (Shapiro 1965), has a global, impressionistic cognitive style, therapists are encouraged to help these patients attend to the factual details of emotionally charged situations. For example, when one hysteroid patient said that she had the worst day in her whole life, the therapist said, "Exactly what happened?" She then said, "Well first of all my boss was a complete jerk." The therapist asked, "What did he do?"

Resolving Previous Traumas

At times, the treatment of hysteroid patients involves the resolution of early trauma. Wells and colleagues (1995) have discussed the importance of the therapist's respecting the hysteroid patient's underlying structural deficits, and thus avoiding cathartic uncovering of the patient's memories before a full working alliance and object constancy have been established. For "patients who manifest severe structural impairment or ego deficits, techniques aimed at retelling and reliving the experience can eventuate in temporary ego regression and lead to decompensation, transient psychotic episodes, and destructive acting out" (Wells et al. 1995, p. 420).

In other words, the intense affects associated with reexperiencing past childhood traumas can regress and/or fragment hysteroid patients' fragile egos and retraumatize patients by inducing them to actually relive rather than remember the trauma without the benefit of object constancy, an observing ego, and a stable working alliance with the therapist. In addition, regressive techniques designed to help patients recall trauma experiences are also likely to induce splitting, suicidal ideology, and destructive acting out (Wells et al. 1995). Repairing structural deficits of hysteroid patients with abuse histories thus takes therapeutic precedence over cathartic reworking of childhood trauma experiences. We do not minimize the importance of childhood trauma in derailing the patient's ego organizing processes and inducing the patient's symptomatology. Understanding the common effects of repeated childhood abuse can, in fact, help the patient to understand his or her symptomatology in terms of survival skills. This often helps the patient to feel "less crazy" and less self-hatred.

In addition to developing object constancy, an observing ego, and a working alliance, the first phase in the treatment of trauma with hysteroid patients involves helping the patient develop a sense of internal and external safety (Herman 1992), and replacing self-injurious behavior patterns with more adaptive alternatives. In addition, when unresolved trauma pervades the history of the patient, therapists need to interpret and work through particular transference-like reactions to the therapist's activity level (e.g., patients with trauma histories often experience the more active therapist as intrusive or exploitative and the more passive therapist as unwilling or unable to protect the patient).

The recommended sequence of treatment for these patients includes an initial stabilization stage similar to the initial phase of treatment already described in this chapter. Once object constancy, synthetic ego functioning, and a stable working alliance are developed, the hysteroid is ready to remember and resolve childhood traumas. At the conclusion of treatment, Herman (1992) recommends a period of reintegrating the patient into the real world (e.g., helping them to differentiate past from present dangers).

Resolution of Hysterical Character Traits in Hysteroid Patients

In the second phase of treatment, once a working alliance and object constancy have been established, the therapist can begin working with hysteroid patients on increasing their capacity for insight into their hysterical character dynamics, resolving their hysterical defenses, and softening their harsh superego. In particular, therapists are encouraged to help hysteroid patients to gain insight into their (1) use of cognitive fog; (2) use of sexual provocativeness to secure power, get physical affection, and feel desired (rather than a true desire for sexuality); (3) use of dramatic acting out to command the attention of others; and (4) secondary gains from acting helpless (e.g., presenting themselves as nonthreatening and inducing other people into behaving in a protective maternal way toward them). A more elaborate discussion on how to accomplish these goals will be presented in Chapter 12.

CORRECTIVE INTERPERSONAL EXPERIENCE

While the components of what constitutes a corrective interpersonal experience have been implied throughout this chapter, they will be summarized here. These include (1) good-enough attunement to the patient's needs, (2) balancing the hysteroid's needs for being dependent and autonomous by being a secure base from which to explore the world, (3) supporting genuine self expression and saying "no," and (4) setting appropriate limits and refraining from being revengeful when experiencing countertransference hate.

The good-enough therapist, like the good-enough mother, must be at-tuned to and aware of the patient's authentic needs and feelings. These may not, in fact, be those that the hysteroid patient is expressing. For example, a therapist told one hysteroid patient, "I know that you say that you feel very angry right now but when I look at how you are sitting and imagine how I might feel in your situation, I wonder if you are really feeling scared."

Furthermore, the therapist must be nonpossessive, nondemanding, and nonintrusive. Like a parent of the rapprochement child, the therapist must support the patient's efforts at self-activation, whether this involves starting a new project, taking two weeks off from treatment, or arguing with the ther-apist's interpretations. When the patient becomes insecure and contacts the therapist, for example, during the patient's two-week leave of absence or during the opening night of his or her play, it is important for the therapist, if at all possible, to empathize with and contain the patient's anxiety so that the patient is able to return back to the world with a greater sense of security.

While attunement is important, it is also necessary for the therapist to set good limits. Hysteroid patients are very demanding. They push thera-pists' limits to discover whether their therapists are strong enough to take care of themselves (as these patients were unable to do with their mothers). They also push the therapist to determine whether they can make the thera-pist hate (and thus reject) the patient as their parents and current objects have done. We believe that the process of empathic but firm limit setting must begin immediately.

On the first interview with a hysteroid patient with narcissistic features, the patient told the therapist that he hit his wife before his wife left him. He was a recovering drug addict and used to superficially cut himself. He answered yes to the question, "When people do something that angers you, do you have a hard time remembering anything good about them?" (i.e., indicating the use of splitting). However, he had several strengths (e.g., he was not currently blaming his wife for their problems and had some capacity to self-observe). When asked if he had ever made suicide attempts, he said that he had threatened to do it on several occasions, and once made an attempt, but did not think that he would really do it.

He also reported that he recently terminated a five-year relationship with another therapist. He said that he liked her very much and that she had helped him to learn to trust people more than he used to. However, he thought that she was unable to help him further. The therapist asked what he wanted help with now. He said, "I want to be really understood. I felt like there was some way that she didn't understand me. When I read your article, I thought that you would know why I act this way. Also, I couldn't express my feelings in there and I know I need to learn to do that." When the therapist asked him if he could express his feelings with his wife, he said that he could, "but then things got out of control."

The patient asked the therapist if she could help him. The therapist said that she was reasonably sure that she could understand and support his authentic self expression. However, her goal would be to help him express his feelings in a way that neither he nor the therapist would get hurt. He agreed that this was important as he had once attended a workshop on anger that encouraged catharsis and "ended up breaking the windows in the room." He asked the therapist if she was willing to work with him.

The therapist said that she was willing to treat him under certain conditions: (1) during therapy, he never did anything to physically hurt himself or other people (particularly making suicide attempts because he was angry at someone); and (2) both his and her boundaries would need to be respected (i.e., he could "occasionally" run over the ending time in sessions for five minutes, but not refuse to leave her office; he could call her answering service to talk to her on the phone for ten minutes up to twice a week, but not call her at home many times a night).

The patient asked the therapist why she believed that he might do those sort of things as he never hurt his last therapist or called her even once. The therapist responded that she thought that he had a lot of very strong feelings inside him (e.g., he hit his wife last week, broke windows at a workshop, and made suicide threats to people who did not give him what he wanted). The patient said, "Oh, I see what you mean. But I never did that with my last therapist."

The therapist told him that she believed that he did not do those things with his last therapist because he needed to keep the therapist and his relationship with her good. She said that she wondered if the patient was being "the good compliant child" with his last therapist, and thus did not express his feelings (especially his angry feelings) with her for fear of damaging their relationship. Rather, he acted these feelings out in his other relationships.

The therapist asked him what he was feeling now about what she had told him, and he said that he felt ashamed. The therapist empathized with why he might be feeling that way. He began to talk about his mother never setting any limits with him but getting angry and rejecting when he did something that she did not like (e.g., lose his temper).

The therapist said that it sounded like his mother had not been able to help him when he became overly frustrated, scared, or hurt (e.g., showing him how to talk about his feelings and feel comforted and contained by someone rather than acting his feelings out). The therapist told him that she was sorry that what she had said had shamed him. Her intention was to let him know what the conditions were under which she could or could not be helpful so that he could make a choice based on realistic information. If he thought that these behaviors were something that he could not or would not control, she would not be a good therapist for him and would refer him to another therapist who could work with him under these conditions. The session was over, and both therapist and patient agreed that they would think about these things, set up another appointment, and talk about these issues again at that time.

When the patient returned the next week, he decided that he wished to continue treatment with the current therapist. This case is an example of both making a contract (as described in Chapter 4), setting clear limits from the beginning of treatment that both patient and therapist can live with, and using one's countertransference to understand and make treatment decisions with the patient.

It is not implied here that this contract will prevent the patient from acting out but that parameters are set around these behaviors before they occur. It is thus important that therapists carefully monitor their own feelings as the hysteroid patient's limit testing escalates, so that they can set limits in a benign way before becoming overly frustrated with (or even beginning to hate) the patient. Furthermore, if the latter does begin to happen, therapists must acknowledge their feelings of countertransference hate but then observe them in order to understand them rather than to express them or act them out with the patient. Thus, in treating hysteroid borderlines, therapists must be very self aware and be adept at regressing in the service of the ego so that they are able to go back and forth between feeling and thinking.

The hysteroid patient frequently has the belief that a corrective experience in therapy would involve gratification of his or her primitive needs for an all-good preoedipal mother. However, while the hysteroid may need a type of reparenting experience, it is one in which the therapist helps the patient to mature into a separate, individuated person. In contrast to the hysteroid's early objects, the therapist does not use the patient to meet his or her own symbiotic needs and rather than discouraging or ignoring the patient's autonomous strivings, the therapist provides the patient with empathy, guidance, and support for separating and individuating.

DIFFERENTIAL DIAGNOSIS

Both Kernberg (1970) and Meissner (1984, 1988) noted that hysteroid borderlines may at times appear indistinguishable from the narcissistic or hysterical personality. They believe that an accurate diagnosis may be made only when the patient is in a regressive phase or begins to develop transference. Two other personalities that hysteroids can be confused with (particularly under specific conditions) are the masochistic and schizoid personalities.

Hysteroid and Hysterical

Differentiating the hysteroid borderline from the neurotic hysterical character is important in regard to treatment. For example, while the hysterical character can easily recognize and tolerate internal conflicts, distinguish between internal and external reality, and distinguish between the therapeutic alliance and a transference neurosis, the hysteroid has difficulty establishing a therapeutic alliance and may have a flight into health or a regressive transference neurosis before an alliance is established (Meissner 1984).

Kernberg (1975, 1992) noted that the hysteroid is hallmarked by more generalized and diffuse emotional lability, fewer conflict-free areas, a higher degree of social inappropriateness, a generalized lack of impulse control, and overinvolvement with objects characterized by regressed, inappropriate demandingness. The hysteric's sexual provocativeness and need for love and attention is transformed in the hysteroid into sexual provocativeness that is often crude, exhibitionistic, and demanding. The hysteroid also has more primitive, polymorphous perverse sexual fantasies and behaviors.

Although the hysterical patient can be provocative, he or she maintains good feelings about the object. In contrast, the hysteroid's behavior often feels adversarial and even mean spirited. However, while hysterical patients are generally less aggressive than hysteroid patients, the hysteroid is usually less competitive than the hysteric (Meissner 1984).

While the hysteric frequently behaves in a seductive and childlike manner, he or she generally has consistently good social skills and is quite competent. While the hysteric has the myth of passivity (Krohn 1978) and the illusion of inadequacy, these beliefs are not true. In contrast, the hysteroid patient has genuine ego deficits. For example, one somewhat intellectually insecure, attractive 23-year-old hysterical patient, who spoke in a manner reminiscent of a "Valley girl," was a highly successful junior executive in her company. Thus, while she appeared and believed that she was incompetent, her behavior was exceptionally competent. This contrasts with the initial impression of Glenn Close in *Fatal Attraction*, who appears competent but quickly deteriorates.

Hysteroid and Narcissistic

Another particularly important differential diagnosis is between the hysteroid and phallic-exhibitionistic narcissists. Kernberg (1992) notes that these two disorders are often confused because both "entail attention-seeking and exhibitionistic behavior" (p. 62). The primary differences between them are structural and defensive. The exhibitionistic narcissist's grandiose selfobject defensive functioning is continuously activated (Masterson 1993), allowing a less labile, more continuously confident, expansive, charming, or dismissive attitude in contrast to the hysteroid's frequent emotional lability.

Furthermore, the disengaged coldness underneath the superficial charm of the exhibitionistic narcissist can be contrasted with the hysteroid's desperate, hostile, clinging demandingness. At bottom, the hysteroid's goal is to fuse with a good maternal object, whereas the phallic-narcissist wants to be admired by a selfobject.

The narcissist lacks the self-destructiveness, impulsivity, and abandonment concerns of the hysteroid-borderline (APA 1994). This is related in part to the narcissist's more dismissive, in contrast to the hysteroid's more anxious, attachment style. When a selfobject fails the narcissist (e.g., stops admiring, commits an empathic error), he or she is "fired" and the narcissist finds a new admiring or idealized object. In the meantime, the narcissist relies on the continuous activation of the grandiose self representation to maintain narcissistic equilibrium. In contrast, when a selfobject fails the hysteroid, he or she typically becomes desperate, splits, and acts out with the hated, and yet vitally needed, disappointing object.

Hysteroid and Masochistic

The hysteroid also shares several characteristics with the masochistic personality. Both disorders have anxious attachments to objects, are overinvolved in their relationships with others, and tend to be controlling with them in order to gain security. Both the masochist and the hysteroid can behave in a self-defeating manner in their efforts to control and maintain a relationship with the object.

The differences between the two personalities can be observed, however, at many different levels. For example, the hysteroid's interpersonal style is designed to induce being cared for or attended to through inappropriate sexual provocativeness, hyperemotionality, and self-injurious behavior. In contrast, the masochist's style is designed to induce being needed or indispensable through caregiving and self-sacrifice.

Hysteroids and masochists can also be differentiated at the structural level. Masochists are organized at the preneurotic level of ego development and thus have a cohesive sense of self and better, if not complete, object constancy. They are thus able to establish more stable and intimate relationships with others than are hysteroid patients (who are noted for brief, intense but shallow relationships).

Hysteroid-borderline patients, who function at the need gratifying level of object relations, primarily relate to others in terms of the functions that others can provide for them. While masochists defensively focus on taking care of others as a means of geting their own needs met without being vulnerable, they are also able to appreciate others as separate individuals who are valuable beyond what they are able to do for them.

Hysteroid and Schizoid

Hysteroid and schizoid patients are similar in that both are structured at the borderline level of ego development and object relations. Both lack object constancy, self-cohesion, and self-other differentiation. Both schizoid and hysteroid patients struggle with similar deficits in ego functioning (e.g., low frustration tolerance, poor reality testing). However, each tends to overuse somewhat different defenses when overly frustrated (e.g., the hysteroid acts out more whereas the schizoid dissociates more). Hysteroids act dramatic, provocative, and demanding, creating their family's chaotic emotional environment in their current relationships. In contrast, schizoids act detached from their affects and others, re-creating the sterility of their impoverished family environment in their current relationships. However, despite the fact that both are structured at the borderline level, because of their different surface presentation these two personalities are rarely confused (e.g., when the schizoid is more decompensated and ravenous needs and rage erupt, or when the hysteroid is severely dissociated and cut off from his or her experiences).

Masterson (1976) believes that, although schizoid patients appear to have a higher level of functioning than the hysteroid due to their use of compensatory defenses, the hysteroid patient has actually achieved a higher level of object relations development because the hysteroid patient is more object related. While the hysteroid's primary fear is that of abandonment by the object, the schizoid primarily fears annihilation or loss of his or her self through engulfment by the object (a more primitive fear).

The Hysteroid Personality and the *DSM*'s Description of the Borderline Personality Disorder

We have described hysteroids as primitive hysterics with an underlying borderline ego organization. The issue of differentially diagnosing the hysteroid from the borderline personality disorder thus seems moot. However, in terms of *DSM* (APA 1987, 1994) nomenclature, it is relevant to speak to how the conceptualization of the hysteroid-borderline relates to the *DSM*'s histrionic and borderline criteria.

In this book, we have proposed that the developmental arrest and psychostructural issues of the hysteroid are basically the same as what is commonly called the borderline personality disorder. The *DSM-III-R* (APA 1987) appeared to reflect this conceptualization since the histrionic and borderline personality disorders presented in axis II shared so many structural criteria, including identity disturbance, tendency toward developing brief psychotic episodes, ego weaknesses, impulsivity, unstable and intense interpersonal relations, inappropriate and intense anger, affective instability, proneness to suicidal gestures, and incessant attempts to attract attention and reassurance. As Kernberg (1992, p. 64) notes, "In practice, therefore, the histrionic and the borderline personality disorders in *DSM-III-R* largely overlap or coincide."

The *DSM-IV* (APA 1994) modified the criteria of these two disorders so that clinicians would be able to more easily make a differential diagnosis between them. Thus, the manual states, "Although Borderline Personality Disorder can also be characterized by attention seeking, manipulative behavior, and rapidly shifting emotions, it is distinguished by self-destructiveness, angry disruptions in close relationships, and chronic feelings of deep emptiness and identity disturbance" (APA 1994, p. 657). The histrionic personality described in the *DSM-IV* eliminated criterion characteristics such as identity disturbance and tendencies toward transient psychotic episodes, making the histrionic personality seem structured at the neurotic level, thus sharing more similarities with the hysterical character (described in Chapter 11) than the hysteroid-borderline.

COUNTERTRANSFERENCE ISSUES

The literature has frequently commented on the intensity of countertransference reactions that therapists have in treating hysteroid patients (Adler 1985, Briggs 1979, Masterson 1972, 1996). These include the therapist's response to the hysteroid patient's (1) intense and frequent use of splitting and projective identification, (2) excessive demandingness, and (3) disregard of the therapist's limits.

Response to the Hysteroid's Intense and Frequent Use of Splitting and Projective Identification

Despite a therapist's attempt to remain neutral, the prolonged experience of being treated like a bad object and being provoked to experience and enact aspects of the hysteroid's self, such as shame, rage, and separation anxiety, eventually wears down the most experienced and self-aware therapist. In such instances, therapists may respond to the patient in a variety of ways, including internalizing the patient's bad feelings, subtly blaming the hysteroid, and developing countertransference hate.

We believe that therapists tend to have what Klein (1935) refers to as the depressive position (i.e., protecting the relationship at the expense of the self). As they have a propensity to be internalizers, their first response is often to blame themselves for the problem and experience feelings of guilt and shame. For example, when a hysteroid patient told the therapist that she was the coldest person that she had ever met, the therapist felt guilty and concerned because she knew that she was a little reserved.

However, even the most avid internalizers eventually reach their limit of introjecting the bad self and object experiences of others and feel the pull to subtly blame the patient in return. In the last example the therapist might have said, "You seem to blame my coldness for your problems, which you had before entering treatment. Do you often see other people's behavior as the source of your problems? How do they react when you blame them?"

When therapists become overwhelmed by their feelings, they may begin to experience what is referred to in the literature as "countertransference hate" (Carpy 1989, Winnicott 1958a). Sullivan (1987) believes that during countertransference hate, the patient and the therapist become so intertwined that they "interact like elements in a chemical combination" (p. 56). Hysteroid borderline patients have been described as frequently evoking these types of feelings in therapists (Epstein 1977, Poggi and Ganzarain 1983, Reiser and Levenson 1984).

Groves (1978) describes four groups of patients who commonly engender hateful feelings in therapists: (1) dependent clingers, (2) entitled demanders, (3) manipulative help-rejecters, and (4) self-destructive deniers. These behavioral tendencies are manifested in most hysteroid patients, creating feelings of aversion, criticism, and frustration bordering on extreme dislike and even malice. However, while Poggi and Ganzarain (1983) notice the tendency among therapists to hate such patients, Sullivan (1987) believes that it is so distressing to therapists to feel hatred toward their patients that they often deny the feeling. The therapist's hatred is thus expressed through subtle contempt, rationalized terminations, and passive-aggressive behavior.

Response to the Hysteroid's Excessive Demandingness

Hysteroid patients' excessively demanding behavior manifests in a multitude of ways. They may respond to normal disruptions or separations in therapy as though they were being abandoned by a cold, heartless parent. They may attempt to coerce the therapist into an intense, all-consuming relationship. They may find the therapist's phone number and frequently call his or her house with urgent crises. They may incessantly push limits (e.g., putting feet on the furniture, asking provocative questions, dropping ashes on the carpet, demanding more time). They may threaten to act out self-destructively or induce guilt if the therapist fails to meet their demands.

Such behaviors provoke a number of responses in therapists. These include aversion or repulsion (when the therapist's antilibidinal ego is activated), feeling engulfed (especially if the therapist has subjective countertransference as well), feeling guilty, and feeling enraged about being blackmailed.

Response to the Hysteroid's Continuous Disregard
of the Therapist's Limits

As previously described, for hysteroid patients the setting of a limit by the therapist is considered the ultimate challenge. They may respond by talking to the therapist by the door when the session is over, following the therapist around the grocery store discussing their last session, or asking the therapist to hold them and relentlessly repeating this request every session if the therapist says no.

When she was 2 years old, one of the author's nieces asked her mother if she could have a lollipop. Her mother said that she could not have one before dinner. The child then asked her mother "if it would be okay to just hold and shake the lollipop." The mother, trying to be reasonable, thought, What harm would there be in that? The child next asked her mother if she could put it in her mouth with the paper on it. While this sounded strange, her mother rationalized that this would not really spoil her child's dinner and said yes as long as she washed the paper. The child then asked if she could take a corner of the paper off before putting it in her mouth and her mother, in exasperation, told her to go to her room.

The hysteroid's limit pushing is often quite similar to this child's behavior and may have similar developmental origins. Like the child's mother, if therapists pride themselves on being flexible, they may initially attempt to compromise until they feel completely frustrated and impinged upon. At that point, they often set harsh and rigid limits. In either case, an important indication of the therapist's countertransference is his or her simply acting without processing the transaction with the patient. We have found that when processing limit pushing with hysteroid patients, telling them "the hold it and shake it story" can be a useful intervention.

EXTENDED CASE EXAMPLE

Katherine, a 35-year-old, single Caucasian woman, was the youngest of three siblings. Her family had an extensive psychiatric history. Her mother and older sister had been diagnosed with major depression and her older brother committed suicide. When Katherine was 10 years old, her mother died of cancer and her father quickly remarried. Katherine lived alone and attended a master's program in nursing during her two years in treatment.

Katherine had seen five other therapists before entering treatment with the current therapist. She said that for one reason or another, each of them failed or disappointed her. She described her last therapy as being particularly difficult. She sought out a Gestalt therapist who used body work and experiential techniques. He held her, at her request. After she told him that she experienced his holding as erotic, the therapist consulted with a colleague and subsequently told Katherine that he thought that it was in her best interest to discontinue their use of touch in treatment. She became rageful and suicidal and began to frequently call his home and to leave notes on his car. The therapist told her that if she was not able to stop these behaviors, he would need to terminate treatment and refer her to another therapist. She called his home thirty times that night. He sent her a letter telling her that he resigned as her therapist, following which she made a suicide attempt and called 911.

On her initial appointment with the current therapist, Katherine dressed in a seductive, funky style, and gestured dramatically as she spoke. When she thought that she was losing the therapist's attention, she would introduce a provocative topic (e.g., suicidal ideation) or behave provocatively (e.g., put her feet on the therapist's desk).

Katherine's behavior during the therapy hour varied widely. When she was not regressed, she maintained good eye contact and was articulate, socially charming, dramatic, and intense. When she wanted maternal attention, she behaved like a shy, young child, huddled in the corner of the couch, spoke like a little girl, and averted her gaze.

Early in treatment, Katherine began each session describing a crisis. When she experienced rejection, she felt like a victim of objects who were malicious, mean, and hurtful to her. She then behaved like the persecutor (e.g., becoming enraged, describing revenge fantasies, and being verbally abusive).

When Katherine initially entered treatment, her presenting problem was that everyone in her life left, hurt, or disappointed her. She felt depressed, despairing, and rageful about the recent breakup of a three-month relationship. She frequently experienced insomnia and had a compelling urge to hurt herself. Katherine presented herself as overwhelmed, profoundly insecure, desperate for instant intimacy, and afraid that she would never find someone that she could depend on. Despite their repeated occurrences, Katherine had no awareness of her contribution to relational problems.

Katherine was furious at people for not meeting her needs. She felt "dropped and betrayed" by her last boyfriend. When he told her that he no longer wanted to have a relationship with her, she felt so dead inside that she superficially cut herself in order to "feel again." She, then, took a nonlethal dose of barbiturates and called the emergency mental health service to talk things out. Upon further exploration, it became apparent that Katherine told this story to the therapist (as well as the story about her last therapist) to warn the therapist that she was someone whose demands must be taken seriously or she could do something quite awful.

After telling the therapist about her rage, acting out, and self-destructive behavior, Katherine was concerned that the therapist would not want to treat her because she was a difficult patient. The therapist asked Katherine if she felt this way before (i.e., that she had to do something very dramatic to get a response and that if she was assertive or difficult rather than compliant, she would be rejected). She said that she felt that way with both her mother and father.

Katherine reported having multiple caregivers during her first three years of life because of her mother's repeated illnesses and chronic depression. She was told that her first nanny resigned when Katherine was 18 months old because the nanny liked babies but that she didn't like children once they started walking and talking. Katherine said that she thought that her mother was very ambivalent about her. She told Katherine that she had not wanted a third child (i.e., she was a "diaphragm baby") and that she would have had an abortion if there had been abortions in the 1950s—"but we love you anyway."

Katherine desperately wanted her mother's love and attention. However, her mother only paid attention to Katherine when her mother was feeling depressed and needy. At those times, she would track Katherine down, even in the bathroom, in order to get her hug. Other than when her mother needed her, Katherine felt like she was only noticed or comforted when she was sick or acted like a "crybaby."

Katherine remembered feeling desperate as a child when her mother was about to leave for work. She used to follow her mother around the house persistently asking her, "Do you love me?" Her mother became annoyed with Katherine, telling her that she was in a hurry. Katherine also recalled that when her mother was angry at her she threatened to hit her. Her mother then left, ignoring Katherine for hours and even days. Katherine knew that she would have to work very hard to win her mother back (e.g., by apologizing, entertaining her, or making her laugh).

Katherine described her father as a self-absorbed but charming playboy who was also critical, cold, preoccupied, and frequently absent. When he was drunk, he used Katherine as a confidante to discuss his problems with Katherine's mother. Katherine felt special during these occasions and then totally rejected when he withdrew again, especially when he was having another affair. As a teenager, she discovered that she was able to get his attention by doing things like dyeing her hair purple, coming home with an African-American boyfriend, or having an automobile accident while driving when intoxicated.

Katherine described her brother as both her "protector" and her "abuser." While he was her only ally in the family he also sometimes bullied her. Furthermore, when Katherine was 10 years old, her brother began to act sexually inappropriate with her. Her history of self-injurious behavior began at this time (i.e., she began to bite her nails until they bled).

Katherine entered her last therapy with a history of two suicide attempts by drug overdose (one occurred after she felt abandoned again by her father). Her parents became worried, reactive, and exasperated with her for doing this. However, they never attempted to understand the reason for Katherine's behavior.

Katherine also had an erratic history of superficial self-cutting. Katherine said that cutting herself helped her to feel more alive and more in control.

She also understood that it was a way to punish herself when she felt guilty or other people when she felt angry. This behavior could also be used by Katherine as a way of attempting to coerce people into being more involved with her than they wanted to be.

Katherine bordered on being promiscuous as an adult. She confused her needs for affection with her needs for sex. Thus, when she felt lonely (as she had sex and affection confused), she dressed provocatively, went to a bar, and "flirted wildly" with someone until they went home with her. These relationships tended to be turbulent and lasted between two and six months.

Katherine's social relationships were typically fairly shallow. She sustained several superficial friendships in which she tended to be reserved due to her fear of both rejection and engulfment. Katherine had difficulty saying no to people and thus tended to overcomply with friends' requests until she began to feel resentful and then acted out (e.g., showing up late for a dinner date, picking a fight over what movie to see).

Because relationships with others induced painful tendencies to split, Katherine lived alone. However, she also found being alone difficult. She said that sometimes at night she felt scared "like a baby alone in space." When she felt intense loneliness and yearnings to connect with someone, she began to call 900 numbers until late at night.

Katherine thus manifested many of the dynamics and structural issues of the hysteroid personality with an arrest at the separation-individuation stage of development. When experiencing conflicts or separations in primary relationships, Katherine's ego was vulnerable to regression. At these times she defended against feelings of separation and loss by using splitting (which interfered with her ability to separate and individuate and develop object constancy).

In addition to Katherine's tenuous sense of object constancy, Katherine's deficit synthesizing or integrating function, poor frustration and anxiety tolerance, and weak impulse controls reflected her infantile level of object relations and ego development. Her strengths were in her strong intellect, which increased her capacity for insight and helped her to recover more quickly from temporary regressions. Her more primitive defenses included splitting, projective identification, and self-destructive acting out, while her higher level defenses included cognitive fog, denial, and avoidance.

Having multiple caregivers (including one who only liked babies and left Katherine during the rapprochement phase), and an intensely ambivalent mother who usually ignored her, capriciously used her as an object during the mother's periods of depression and used punishing withdrawal with her for minor misbehavior, led Katherine to develop a sense of anxious attachment. These conditions coupled with her father's exciting and rejecting presence and poor boundaries interfered with Katherine's developing both self and object constancy.

Katherine's painful feelings of separation and loss remained unresolved and interfered with her ability to maintain stable, good-enough relationships with people. While Katherine was afraid of abandonment, she tended to behave in ways that induced people to abandon her. For example, her cling-ing demandingness, rage reactions, and self-injurious behavior often pushed people away.

Katherine never really gave up her wish for a symbiotic relationship in order to become autonomous. This was influenced by her mother's procliv-ity to withdraw from Katherine when she asserted herself, her mother's inter-mittent affection (when her mother was needful), and her mother's tacit approval of her passive compliance (e.g., not causing mother any trouble). This resulted in her lack of self development and continued yearning for a symbiotic maternal object.

The goals in Katherine's treatment were to develop a therapeutic alliance with Katherine to help her (1) integrate her split object relations units; (2) increase her capacity for object and self constancy; (3) support separation-individuation; (4) strengthen her observing ego; and (5) improve ego func-tions (e.g., frustration and anxiety tolerance, impulse control, improved reality testing). Secondary goals included insight into and resolution of her character defenses and conflicts.

To accomplish these goals, the therapist functioned as an auxiliary ego that facilitated Katherine's gradual internalization of selfobject functions such as recognition, validation, soothing, comfort, and empathy so that she could more autonomously self comfort during times when objects were unresponsive or absent. Particular emphasis was spent on confronting primi-tive defenses such as splitting and projective identification.

During the initial phase of Katherine's treatment, the therapist focused on developing a sufficient working alliance with Katherine in order to con-front her primitive defenses and attenuate the severity of her depression and acting out. At the beginning of treatment Katherine frequently used de-fensive splitting to manage her abandonment panic following self-activation. For example, Katherine decided that she wanted to take a trip to India (some-thing her mother would have highly disapproved of). When she told the therapist about her decision and the therapist asked about her plan, she experienced the therapist as disapproving and said, "You never want me to have any fun and you treat me like some kind of imbecile who can't take care of herself." At other times, she was overly compliant in order to retain the symbiotic connection. For example, she thought that the therapist wanted her to develop new friendships. She thus began to make weekly reports to the therapist about her progress in this area. On both occasions, these behaviors were processed with the patient (e.g., "You seem to believe that I don't want you to take this trip. Are you afraid that I'll abandon you like your mother did when you were adventurous?" "I've noticed how you seem to report your efforts to develop friendships to me. Sometimes I have the feeling that you are doing this to please me because you think that this is something that I want you to do, rather than from a genuine desire for friends in your life. Is this true?").

The initial phase of treatment was devoted to helping Katherine understand how these behaviors both hurt and served her as well as teaching her more adaptive ways of coping. These coping techniques included the use of transitional objects and keeping a journal to help her manage her anxieties between sessions.

During the initial sessions, Katherine repeatedly tested the therapist's limits and boundaries in order to ascertain whether this was a relationship that she could trust to contain her. Consistent, firm but empathic limit setting was often difficult. Katherine continually attempted to coerce more intimacy and attention from the therapist (e.g., crises, after hours calls, suicide threats, acting out) rather than letting a relationship between the two of them develop. These behaviors were immediately confronted as they occurred. For example, on one occasion, the therapist told her, "Sometimes it seems as though you feel like a baby crying in the night for mother who won't come or like a child who believes that if she bangs her head on the floor enough times, her mother will eventually respond. It seems like you have difficulty believing that I will be responsive enough to your needs. It also appears that it is hard for you to understand that when I say no to you that I really mean it, even if you bang your head on the floor."

Katherine entered therapy at the need-gratifying level of object relations and thus treated the therapist as if she were a set of functions rather than a separate person. For the therapist, accepting Katherine at her current level of object relations meant containing the discomfort of being misrepresented and objectified. The therapist used that feeling to help her to better understand Katherine's internal world.

Over time, Katherine began to understand the link between her individuative strivings, separation anxiety, and self-destructive acting out. This enabled her to better understand how these behaviors kept her from learning about herself or having a truly intimate relationship. As a result of Katherine's new insight and her beginning internalization of the therapist's soothing functions, her self-cutting diminished. On one occasion, she stopped herself in the middle of a suicide gesture and instead talked about her painful feelings with a friend (but did not talk about suicide with her). This was the first time that behaving self-destructively seemed ego-dystonic to her.

In the middle phase of treatment, Katherine and the therapist continued to resolve her use of splitting and projective identification. Katherine now had more perspective on the process underlying these feelings and behaviors and would tell the therapist, "I'm doing that black and white thing again, aren't I?" For example, when the therapist went on a two-week vacation, Katherine said, "I'm a little scared and mad at you for going, but I know you need time to relax, too." While trust remained an issue, acting out diminished.

The therapist loaned Katherine a transitional object (a glass egg) that Katherine kept in her coat pocket during the day and on her nightstand in the evening. She no longer felt intense "baby in space" feelings when she was alone. Katherine began to trust the therapist and to look at her during sessions in order to experience and internalize her caring, her strength, and her nonreactive approach to dealing with life's difficulties. Katherine still occasionally used five-minute "touching base" calls to the therapist when her best efforts to self-soothe failed. However, as her object constancy increased, the phone calls diminished, as she now carried the therapist around in her mind.

In the second year of treatment, Katherine's histrionic tendencies were addressed more directly, including Katherine's desire to get special attention from people with whom she became infatuated by behaving in an overly dramatic, seductive manner. She became more aware that she solicited male attention through sexual provocation and that beginning relationships in this manner did not eventuate in her developing an intimate, committed relationship. Over time she began to understand the origins of these behaviors in the dynamics between she and her parents.

In the last phase of treatment, termination issues were addressed including Katherine's anger toward the therapist (even though it was Katherine who chose to move for a good job opportunity). Katherine noticed her proclivity to want to turn the therapist into a disappointing person so that she would not have to miss her. Therapy thus focused on helping Katherine maintain a positive relationship with the therapist as a good-enough internal object. The therapist's empathy with Katherine's grief helped Katherine to better accept her sadness rather than transform it into depression. Katherine's anxieties about the future were explored and practical plans made when appropriate. The therapist offered to let Katherine keep the glass egg. Katherine thought about it for a while and told the therapist that she didn't think that she needed it any more.

8

Object Relations Therapy of the Narcissistic Personality: Developing the Authentic Self

The narcissistic personality disorder, especially as it is manifested in more subtle forms, is one of the most commonly misunderstood disorders. The popular notion regarding narcissism is that it is a disorder that involves an excess of self love. In reality, narcissism involves an excess of hate for the true self and an absorption with the opinion of others (Lasch 1979). The narcissistic individual is willing to give up his or her true self to become the type of person that receives approval from significant objects in his or her life (Miller 1981).

The narcissistic personality is thus often a study in contrasts. The false, compensatory self of the narcissist is grandiose, entitled, and omnipotent (Bach 1985, Chessick 1985, Kernberg 1975). Narcissists often think that they can be or accomplish anything they want if they put their mind to it. Like the practicing-age child, they believe that the world is their oyster. They often have a deal that is just around the corner and a mental entourage of important people that they associate with in order to sustain self-esteem. They also have a tendency to remember their lives in ways that hypertrophy their accomplishments.

One exhibitionistic narcissistic patient, in attempting to seduce a man, sent him a picture of herself with a movie star. The man, in playful competition, sent her back a picture of himself with an important politician. She sent him back a tape of herself on television. He did not respond and she did not understand why.

DESCRIPTIVE CLINICAL OVERVIEW

Perfectionism

Narcissists believe that they must be brilliant, beautiful, or extremely accomplished in order to get attention and respect (i.e., their substitute for love) (Miller 1981). They also tend to be highly perfectionistic. For example, one patient worked out for two hours each day and had ten forms of cosmetic surgery in order to achieve physical perfection. When she had cosmetic surgery on her nose, she had it redone a year later to make it slightly narrower. Another patient was studying for his third advanced degree. A third patient reported that she began lifting weights to build her muscles when she was 9 years old.

Narcissists believe that they will not be admired unless they are perfect. Due to structural deficits, described later in this chapter, narcissists require constant adulation from others in order to maintain self-esteem (Kernberg 1975, Kohut 1977, Miller 1981). Being narcissistic is a full-time job.

Sensitivity to Slights

The narcissist is a proud person and is easily injured. He or she is extremely sensitive to slights or insults from others (Morrison 1989). This includes not being fully appreciated or admired, not being recognized, and not being understood. As a result, these patients respond to criticism very poorly. For example, when a professor suggested to one narcissistic student that she needed to clarify her dissertation proposal and add one more instrument to her study, the student was outraged. Typically, narcissists react to criticism with contempt and cool indifference. They tend to deny any reality that compromises their grandiose self fantasies, or become enraged (i.e., to defend against underlying feelings of inferiority, shame, and emptiness). They generally deny any reality that deflates their grandiose self-image. They also tend to dismiss the criticism or rejection of others, viewing it as a reflection of the other person's envy over the narcissist's great gifts and achievements (Masterson 1993, Morrison 1987).

Entitlement

Narcissists generally have a great sense of entitlement (Kernberg 1975, Masterson 1993). Although they are very ambitious and hardworking, they also believe that the world owes them a promotion, a living, success, fame, and fortune because they are so obviously superior. For example, one patient, who was a journalist, accurately believed that she was hardworking and exceptional at her work. She was thus outraged when she did not get promoted because she was "honest with the peons" around her about their substandard work.

Furthermore, narcissists often believe that they should be able to achieve their goals and fulfill their fantasies without making a direct effort to achieve or obtain them. One very brilliant narcissistic graduate student's master's thesis was not passed because he had done a halfhearted job. He was very surprised. He had thought that it was possible for him to excel without devoting much time and effort to the project (as this strategy had worked in high school). Another narcissistic patient had his home foreclosed because he had not paid his mortgage. He felt enraged when this occurred. The patient fundamentally believed that he should not have to pay for his home. At the very least, he felt entitled to leniency on the payment schedule. In fact, he was angry that he did not have a more luxurious home that was more worthy of him.

Underlying Feelings of Shame

Underneath their prideful arrogance and entitlement, narcissistic patients struggle with intense feelings of shame (Lowen 1985, Morrison 1989). Their expressions of outrage are usually compensatory. Thus, the patient who was angry about losing his home was defending against feelings of shame and inadequacy. The student who was enraged at her professor's implied criticism (and failure to admire her initial attempts at self-expression) felt that her flaws had been publicly exposed. The contemptuous patient who felt entitled to a promotion despite her rude behavior toward employees was adamant about getting accolades as a compensation for her fear that she would never get love because she was fundamentally unlovable. Shame and a deep underlying feeling that their true self is unworthy thus represent narcissistic patients' core affective experience. The narcissist mightily defends against this feeling with substitute affects (e.g., contempt rather than shame), compensatory structures (e.g., grandiose versus real self), and other defenses that will be discussed later in this chapter.

Manipulative and Exploitative Behavior

Narcissists also tend to be manipulative (Chessick 1985) and exploitative (Masterson 1993), using other people for their idealizing and mirroring functions rather than relating to them as whole persons (Kohut 1971). Because they need other people so much, they are often very skilled at knowing what motivates them. For example, one narcissistic patient gave a woman that he was newly dating a coupon book for her birthday that included a massage, a trip to Bermuda, and a dinner at her favorite restaurant. This patient thus used his knowledge about his partner's romantic fantasies in order to seduce her. As a consequence, the woman initially experienced him as sensitive and generous (i.e., "almost too good to be true").

However, narcissists often use their understanding of other people's needs in service of their own needs. Once the patient had seduced this woman, he resented her expectations that he continue to be romantic with her and began to experience her as demanding. He wanted her undivided attention, admiration, and understanding (i.e., for her to now serve as his selfobject) or, at the very least, to leave him alone.

Self-Absorption

Narcissistic patients, especially the progressive (i.e., exhibitionistic) subtype described later in this chapter, frequently appear to be very self-involved (Chessick 1985). They spend a great deal of time thinking about their appearance, their health, their achievements, and their more superficial needs. For example, one patient asked her sister to fly down to the city where she lived for the day to give her feedback about which new dress she looked better in (despite the fact that her sister had three children and a part-time job). However, while narcissists devote much time and care to their false, grandiose self-image, they rarely attend to their underlying emotional needs (e.g., for love, affection, meaning, the pursuit of activities for their intrinsic satisfactions).

Extreme Need for Attention and Admiration from Others

Because the opinions of other people are so crucial, the narcissist, like Billy Crystal's character, Fernando Lamaz, on "Saturday Night Live," believes that "it is better to look good than to feel good." One patient had approximately fifteen forms of cosmetic surgery. When she had her teeth bonded (for the second time), she had elective periodontal surgery to recess her gum line in order to make her teeth larger. She also had undergone three breast implantations. This patient was 40 years old, had been married for 16 years, and had three children. Her need was thus not to improve her appearance to attract a love object, but to attract the attention of others and to become her ego ideal, to appease her harsh maternal introject and get the attention and admiration of others.

Feelings of Emptiness

Underneath their compensatory false selves, narcissists often feel very empty (Chessick 1985, Kernberg 1975). Narcissistic patients frequently do not know who they really are, what they want in life, and what is truly important. One patient wrote:

> Am I?
> Beneath paper lace, plastic smiles
> and reusable words in disposable bags,
> am I?

Life often feels meaningless to narcissistic patients (Chessick 1985, Miller 1981). They resent having to constantly please other people or, as one patient described, "always playing to an audience." We believe that this monumental effort to get admiration contributes, in part, to narcissists' feelings of entitlement. For example, the patient who had undergone so much plastic surgery felt entitled to receive unlimited attention from other people. Indeed, she believed that she had worked very hard to earn it.

Shame and Rage About Empathic Failures and
Lack of Recognition for Their True Self

As previously mentioned, the narcissist hates his or her true self. Because the child's evolving true self (Winnicott 1965b) received little or no acknowledgment from parents, the narcissist believes that it is of no real worth. For example, the previous patient was fundamentally ignored by her narcissistic mother and workaholic father. She only received attention for "acting and looking good."

Narcissists thus struggle with feelings of shame and rage about repeated empathic failures (Morrison 1989). For example, every time that the previous patient called her mother to tell her about a problem or a special accomplishment, the mother changed the topic to herself. This patient compensated by talking nonstop with the therapist and became very angry with the therapist at times when the therapist seemed at all tired or distracted or had not understood what she was trying to express.

Underlying Search for Recognition and Validation of True Self

While narcissists are preoccupied with getting admiration for their false, grandiose self, at a deeper level they are in search for their true self, including becoming aware of their real feelings, needs, and goals (Miller 1981). While narcissists overtly pursue fame, fortune, and the power to seduce and manipulate others, what they truly need is love and acceptance for their authentic, albeit flawed, self. While they seek others to function as the selfobjects that they missed during their early years (e.g., mirroring selfobjects, idealized selfobjects, and twinship or soulmate) (Detrick 1985, 1986, Kohut 1971), they unfortunately use them in service of shoring up their grandiose self rather than redeveloping their true self. The latter thus becomes the main task of treatment.

TWO NARCISSIST STYLES OR SUBTYPES

Part of the confusion about narcissism is that there are two narcissist styles with very different self presentations (Kohut 1971, Willi 1982). These two narcissistic styles correspond to (1) the narcissist's parents' selfobject needs for the child (i.e., whether the child was used to being the parent's ideal or to understand and soothe the parent), and (2) the narcissist's current preferred compensatory selfobject experience. In essence, is the narcissistic patient primarily seeking an idealizing or mirroring transference relationship with objects?

Progressive/Exhibitionistic Narcissist

The first type, the progressive (Willi 1982) or exhibitionistic narcissist (Masterson 1993, Morrison 1989), is what we popularly think of as narcissistic. This patient presents in a grandiose, self-absorbed manner, seeking relationships with others who bestow admiration and approval. To acquire this admiration, the narcissist attempts to be the object's ideal self. For example, one patient impressed his partner (who yearned for fame and fortune) by presenting himself as a successful investor who knew many important people on Wall Street. He told her that he was considering moving his business to Los Angeles (where he was friends with a number of movie stars). He was just waiting for the right deal to come up.

Particularly when the grandiose false self is activated and functioning well, the narcissist with this type of self presentation appears to be impervious to external objects. When external objects (because of needs of their own) stop providing the narcissist with constant admiration and empathy, the exhibitionistic narcissist may simply devalue them and find a new audience. Despite their own intense need for understanding and approval, the exhibitionistic, preneurotic narcissist sometimes lacks the ability to empathize with others.

Regressive/Closet Narcissist

The second type of narcissistic style, described by Willi (1982) as a regressive narcissist and by Masterson (1993) as a closet narcissist, has the same underlying structural and developmental issues as the exhibitionistic or progressive narcissist. However, he or she has a somewhat different etiology and a very different self presentation and interpersonal style. These patients were used by parents (and thus reinforced or conditionally loved) for performing selfobject functions (e.g., mirroring, admiration, attunement, and empathy). For example, one patient was thought of by her mother as her best friend who, from an early age, listened to and soothed her mother when she had arguments with her husband.

Regressive narcissists have the same underlying self deficits as progressive narcissists. However, rather than seeking mirroring and admiration from objects, they attempt to gain self-esteem and meet their needs for grandiosity by seeking an idealized object to identify with. To obtain this object and rectify their self deficits, they utilize the skills that they developed in their relationships with their parents (e.g., mirroring, admiring, soothing, understanding).

Thus, since the regressive narcissist does not present as overtly grandiose, self-centered, exhibitionistic, and demanding, they are often not initially perceived as narcissistic. Rather, they are subtly charming, soulful, and intensely attuned to others' unstated feelings; look deeply into other people's eyes, laugh wholeheartedly at their jokes, and look sad when others are troubled. The regressive narcissist is very skilled at behaving in a way that others perceive as extraordinarily comforting and seductive.

For the regressive narcissist, empathy is an art form. They are able to make other people quickly feel seen, known, and cherished. One regressive narcissist, who was a physician, had heard from a friend that a woman that he was casually dating (along with other women) had been diagnosed with a tumor. He called her immediately to see how she was feeling, and offer moral support. He told her that he understood how frightened that she must be and that she could call him any time, day or night. Furthermore, when they made love and she had an orgasm, he told her to look in his eyes.

Regressive narcissists are also masters at self-esteem enhancement. They may express admiration for the subtle talents and charms in the idealized object that they are pursuing or appreciate his or her areas of insecurity (e.g., "I hate thin women. I love women who are round and soft and don't look like boys"). The initial idealization is also not entirely pretense because the perception of admired qualities in the object is necessary for the regressive narcissist's enhancement of his or her self-esteem. It is particularly important that the object be idealized for qualities reflecting the regressive narcissist's ego ideal.

Furthermore, regressive narcissists know how to make their partner feel like a "king" or "queen" (e.g., desirable, brilliant, talented, and thus unable to be understood by ordinary people). On the surface, the regressive narcissist may appear to be more submissive and dependent than the progressive narcissist. In reality, however, a very talented regressive narcissist has the power in the relationship. The regressive narcissist is like a drug that the object comes to depend on for maintaining his or her narcissistic equilibrium. The only exception is when the object is a progressive narcissist who is so successful that he or she has an endless supply of fans.

Finally, the regressive narcissist can be somewhat of a chameleon, changing him- or herself to meet the deepest emotional needs of the pursued ideal object. This is aptly described in a song, "I'm Your Man," by Leonard Cohen:

> If you want a father for your child
> or only want to walk with me awhile,
> across the sand,
> I'm your man.

The regressive narcissist thus truly knows how to temporarily change him- or herself to become the mother, father, and/or lover that the ideal object has always yearned for. Furthermore, a skilled regressive narcissist generally makes accurate guesses about the object's needs and performs the role with an astonishing amount of finesse and apparent authenticity.

PRENEUROTIC VERSUS BORDERLINE NARCISSISM

In addition to two types of narcissistic styles (i.e., progressive and regressive), we believe that there are two other subcategories of the narcissistic personality related to the patient's level of ego development and object relations. We think that this may account for some of the disagreements in the literature, particularly between Kohut (1971, 1977) and Kernberg (1975) regarding the diagnosis and treatment of narcissism. These two theorists treated two very different groups of patients. Kohut treated other psychoanalysts who were more likely to be preneurotic, whereas Kernberg treated inpatients at the Menninger Clinic who were more likely to be narcissistic borderlines. It is understandable that they would develop different approaches to treatment (e.g., empathy versus confrontation).

In general, preneurotic narcissists have much higher levels of ego development and object relations than borderline narcissists. The developmental damage to the borderline narcissist occurred earlier. While borderline narcissists struggle with both separation and individuation issues, preneurotic narcissists primarily struggle with a lack of individuation. Furthermore, both borderline and preneurotic narcissists may manifest progressive and/or regressive narcissistic styles.

Preneurotic narcissists have primarily separated self from object. They thus have a greater ability to identify with their real self than borderline narcissists. With the therapist's help, they are more able to identify their needs, feelings, and goals as separate from those that significant others wish them to have. Preneurotic narcissists are not entirely out of touch with themselves. They are merely ready to become who the significant other wants them to be as they believe that it is a requirement for obtaining the object's love and admiration. Furthermore, in contrast to borderline narcissists, they have a sufficiently cohesive sense of self, and thus have developed more productive work, study, and leisure patterns that reward singularized effort (Patton and Robins 1982).

Preneurotic narcissists have greater ego strength than borderline narcissists. Their reality testing is less compromised. They have a fragile, but workable observing ego and utilize primitive defenses far less frequently. Preneurotic narcissists have a greater tendency to idealize and devalue than to use defensive splitting, have more access to higher level defenses (e.g. intellectualization, sublimation) than do narcissistic borderlines, and use less distorted projective identifications.

While borderline narcissists have a lack of object constancy, preneurotic narcissists have incomplete object constancy. As previously described, they have more extensively separated self from objects and infrequently use splitting. However, due to ambivalence toward the maternal object, they fail to completely identify with the mother's realistic selfobject or psychological functioning. Without these internalizations, they remain excessively dependent on others for soothing and self-esteem maintenance. In the absence of success experiences or others to fulfill these functions, they are prone to experience depression.

The difference between these two groups may account for why Kernberg (1975) believes that narcissists need confrontation whereas Kohut (1977) believes that they need empathy. The borderline narcissist would need confrontation (particularly of splitting) as a prerequisite for the beginning of object constancy. In contrast, the preneurotic narcissist who has incomplete object constancy due to a failure to internalize the object's realistic functions needs these functions from the therapist (e.g., empathy, mirroring, idealizing).

However, while preneurotic narcissists do not have complete object constancy, they are better able to relate to others (including the therapist), at times, as whole objects. These patients are generally more able to empathize with and love other people. While they frequently require others for selfobject functions, they do so less than narcissistic borderlines (who feel psychically merged with others and entitled to use them exclusively and completely).

Preneurotic narcissists are also better defended against painful emotions than borderline narcissists. They are much less likely to exhibit rage and it takes many more failures to elicit their ego-dystonic emotions. While their expression of affect is more subtle than the narcissistic borderline's, when they do regress and experience fragmented-off, ego-dystonic aspects of themselves, it is important to appreciate the depths of their painful feelings (Johnson 1987). As a result of their greater ego strength, preneurotic narcissists are easier for therapists to manage in treatment.

This book does not cover all character disorders, but rather two disorders at each of three levels of ego development. Thus, this chapter addresses the treatment of the preneurotic narcissist rather than the borderline narcissist. For readers interested in the latter, we recommend reading Kernberg (1975) or Masterson (1993).

NARCISSISTIC DEFENSES

To avoid experiencing their depleted or empty true selves (Winnicott 1958a), shame (Morrison 1989), and ego-dystonic parts of themselves that are fragmented off, preneurotic narcissists employ a variety of defenses: grandiosity, idealization, devaluation, projection, projective identification, reaction formation, rationalization, somaticization, and denial (Chessick 1985, Kohut 1984, Masterson 1993).

Grandiosity

As previously noted, the narcissist's reliance on the grandiose false self defends the patient against feelings of fragmentation, depression, shame, and enfeeblement (Kernberg 1975, Kohut 1971, 1977). Kernberg proposed that the grandiose self represented the defensive fusion of the patient's ideal self, the ideal object projected on the patient by the parent, and the patient's real talents and gifts. The activation of this defensive structure allows (1) the borderline patient to perpetuate a cycle of self-admiration and spiteful devaluation of others, and (2) the preneurotic patient to ward off depression. Most important, it helps narcissistic patients defend against truly experiencing a sense of dependency on another, despite the reality that they depend enormously on others' selfobject functions.

Idealization

The narcissistic tendency to idealize others comes from an early unresolved developmental phase described by Kohut (1984) as the idealizing transference. During this phase, the child attempts to gain a sense of power and esteem in the world by idealizing objects and identifying with them. Through identifying with idealized others, narcissists feel strong, regulate their self-esteem, and defend against feelings of inadequacy and inferiority. Narcissists often identify with objects that possess valued family traits and abilities in which they felt deficient (e.g., beauty, intelligence, athletic prowess, musical ability).

Devaluation

In contrast, devaluation protects the narcissist's precarious self-esteem by externalizing bad self feelings. By criticizing others, the narcissist feels superior to them (Chessick 1985, Miller 1981). For example, one narcissistic professor who was very unpopular among her students was frequently contemptuous of the faculty that she envied. She was critical of them at faculty meetings, gossiped behind their back, and occasionally found someone who would collude with her against them. She believed that students did not like her because none of the other faculty had high-enough standards and allowed lazy, undisciplined students to get by doing mediocre work.

Projection

In some ways devaluation serves a similar function to projection for the narcissist. However, in projection, a particular ego-dystonic aspect of the self is attributed to an object. Thus, criticism is not general but about something the narcissist does not accept in his or her self. For example, one patient who was ashamed of her body frequently made critical remarks about other people, including movie stars, for being "too fat." One time, she went to a funeral and told the beautiful daughter of a friend who had just died that she looked like she put on weight.

Projective Identification

In projective identification, the process of projection is bolstered by the narcissist actually behaving toward the object in such a manner that the object is induced to experience the narcissist's ego-dystonic aspects of self-experience (Ogden 1979). These undesirable, fragmented-off feelings (e.g., depression, fear, guilt, and shame) and needs (e.g, dependency) typically cause the patient to feel vulnerable when they are experienced.

For example, the patient cited above often commented to her husband about his eating and exercise habits, told him when his clothes were getting tight, and openly admired other men for looking fit. However, unlike borderline narcissists, preneurotic narcissists use this defense less frequently, and when the ego-dystonic experience that is being projected is addressed by the therapist, it is more accessible to the patient.

Reaction Formation

We have also observed a tendency of narcissistic patients to use reaction formation against the parts of the self that are ego-dystonic. For example, one narcissistic patient who felt ashamed of his needs perceived himself and behaved as a very self-sufficient person. He would not allow anyone to help him, even when he needed it, and would spend hours working on something so that he could say that he did it by himself. He never turned to others for comfort when he was upset. He could, however, use alcohol and drugs by himself.

Rationalization

Narcissists frequently rationalize their own failures, which can lead to a cognitive distortion of the world (Shapiro 1965). For example, one patient frequently came to work late. She did not like to operate according to other people's schedules, did not follow instructions in doing her work (e.g., she did not want her exceptional creativity suppressed), and frequently behaved in a critical way toward her colleagues (e.g., thinking they were only peons). However, she attributed her failure to be promoted to her employer's feelings of competition with and envy toward her.

Somaticization

Johnson (1987) has observed a propensity toward somaticization among narcissistic patients. He believes that this defense serves several functions, including a defense against the feeling of psychological enfeeblement and a socially acceptable way of getting dependency needs met by others. Chessick (1985) cites coronary disease and eating disorders as two common psychosomatic complaints associated with narcissistic disturbances.

For example, one middle-aged narcissistic patient presented as a grandiose, aggressive go-getter whose self-esteem was primarily tied to receiving accolades and financial reimbursement for his work achievements. He characterized himself as a type A personality, who always put out extra effort to excel, but got little intrinsic satisfaction from his work. He went from one project to the next, never feeling like his accomplishments completely met his high expectations. He had his first bypass operation at age 46. This patient, who had never been able to relax, could finally allow himself, at least temporarily, to be taken care of, first by the hospital and then by his wife. He quickly began to run everyone ragged with demands to wait on him hand and foot. However, this patient soon became restless and returned to work against medical advice.

Denial

Chessick (1985) notes that narcissistic personalities, in their unceasing efforts to achieve their ambitions, are not affected by facts and feedback from others. The above patient was thus able to repudiate the meaning of the event (i.e., they caught the problem early and he was feeling fine, now; in fact, he had "more energy than ever").

Another patient who had his first heart attack at 40 argued with the doctors when they told him that he could not eat a diet of hot dogs, hamburgers, french fries, and candy bars. He told the doctors that research constantly contradicted itself about what people were and were not supposed to eat (e.g., "First caffeine is bad and then it's okay. Now you're even 'supposed to' drink alcohol."). He died from his third heart attack at the age of 48.

PRESENTING PROBLEMS IN TREATMENT

Responses to Failure

The narcissist does not enter treatment when the compensatory grandiose self structure is working. The exception to this is when he or she is reluctantly brought into marital therapy by an unhappy spouse. However, since the false self is false and the grandiose self is compensatory, they are generally doomed for failure. And they eventually do fail, leading to feelings of worthlessness, self-depreciation, and vulnerability to shame (Morrison 1989). The narcissist often enters treatment after a failure that cannot be entirely rationalized or projected. One patient entered therapy after being fired from his third job. Another entered treatment after his wife, to whom he felt very attached, left him for another man.

Depression

Preneurotic narcissists often enter treatment with a sense of depression (Johnson 1987, Miller 1981). The depression is usually related to some type of narcissistic injury. Sometimes, as will be later described, it is due to a dawning awareness of the great emptiness and lack of fulfillment that they experience in their lives. However, feeling and expressing their feelings of depression to another person is often humiliating to these patients. It is thus very difficult for them to seek treatment.

Psychosomatic Complaints

When narcissists' defenses are not fully challenged, they may present in psychotherapy with a variety of psychosomatic complaints. As alluded to previously, hypochondriasis serves a number of functions for the narcissist, including releasing patients from grandiose self demands, and providing a way to get taken care of without having to acknowledge dependency needs (Johnson 1987). For example, one narcissistic patient who would not acknowledge her limits or her needs frequently ended up in the hospital for doing something like refusing to take penicillin, so that her body could heal itself naturally. These patients are often referred to therapy by physicians.

Life's Inevitable Confrontation of the Patient's Grandiose Self

Sometimes, treatment is inspired by the aging process, which confronts the narcissist with his or her own inevitable limits. One patient entered treatment because of the changes in her appearance, which her lifelong experiences with cosmetic surgery could no longer entirely correct. Another patient had ideal aspirations that he never accomplished but believed that he eventually would. When he turned 50, he realized that he would never be able to succeed in meeting his career goals and gain the fame and fortune that he so desperately desired. A third patient could not tolerate the notion of her own mortality. She had spent the last ten years going to various New Age healers who told her that if she followed their advice that she would not have to die. However, she continued to notice signs of aging in herself and became despondent. As a result of these narcissistic injuries, successful narcissists often enter treatment at midlife.

Realization of Missing Life's Intrinsic Gratifications

During midlife, in addition to facing their inevitable limitations, narcissists begin to have a dawning awareness of something missing in their lives. They become aware that they have played by the rules all their lives and have acquired some degree of fame and fortune. However, they still feel that there must be more to life. They observe that other people seem to experience intrinsic rewards in activities, get pleasure from simple things, and experience satisfaction from having loving relationships and just being a decent human being. Narcissistic patients realize that such satisfactions seem to have eluded them.

Such individuals begin to become dissatisfied with achieving things that are not of real importance to them, being admired and constantly doing what others (including internal objects) expect from them. They often become aware of how they have spent their entire lives doing what others wanted and begin to be aware of how little that they know about what they really need and want. "This is often accompanied by an amazement at the extent to which they had no interests or the extent that their interests were determined by what others wanted them to be" (Johnson 1987, p. 160). Thus, one successful attorney who had been on Law Review in an Ivy League school and had an upstanding family life entered treatment due to her dawning awareness of her feelings of intense boredom and lack of awareness about what gave her lasting meaning and satisfaction in life.

At this juncture, narcissists begin to notice painful feelings of loneliness and isolation. Having pursued admiration rather than love, their relationships often lack depth and meaning. For example, the previous patient felt detached from her husband and had no close friends. The only relationship that gave her pleasure was with her daughter.

The narcissist may now begin to realize "that he has sacrificed himself for the booby prize, and that . . . there is a nagging awareness . . . that there is more to life than this" (Johnson 1987, p. 49). Johnson believes that in this realization are the seeds for the patient's transformation. For example, the patient previously described who had multiple plastic surgeries realized (after her children left home) that although her husband admired her beauty, they had a distant relationship. She began to notice that while the women she spent time with admired her, they also envied her and were thus frequently critical and rejecting of her. She slowly became aware of how lonely she was and how much time she spent maintaining her beauty and what little reward she actually reaped from these efforts.

ETIOLOGY

The narcissistic personality emerges from a chronic way of being treated throughout his or her early life and from a particular mishandling of the rapprochement subphase of separation-individuation (Johnson 1987, Morrison 1989). In general, parents of narcissists chronically reject or ignore those aspects of the child's self that do not meet their parents' narcissistic needs. The child may be used to mirror, understand, and admire the parent or to become the parent's projected ego ideal (Kohut 1971). In return, the child receives conditional love and admiration but never receives acceptance for his or her true self (Miller 1981).

An example of the latter is a mother who begrudgingly gave up her aspirations to be a dancer when she married and had children. When her daughter was born (who even as a baby had precocious psychomotor development), the mother projected her ego ideal of being a great ballerina on her daughter and intensely reinforced her daughter's dancing. By the age of 4, this little girl was showing off her pirouettes for her mother's friends. The mother felt immense pride about having such a talented daughter and frequently told her daughter so. However, to obtain her mother's conditional love, the daughter had to forgo her own natural inclinations and intrinsic ability for such sports as tennis. Thus, her own ideals and goals were sacrificed for her mother's dream and her true self was neither known nor accepted.

Another example is a mother who dressed up her physically beautiful daughter so that she could show off "what a beautiful baby I made" to her friends and family. Another family dubbed their only child "the brain," requiring him to deny other important aspects of himself in order to play the role of "child genius."

Symbiosis

This pattern of the parents' overabsorption with their own needs and lack of awareness of the child's needs begins in the symbiotic phase of development. During this period, Winnicott (1965a) believes that children need the maternal object to be attuned to their needs when they are having a need. Winnicott believes that for a brief period of time, children need the mother to respond to their needs at the precise moment that they are having it. He refers to this as the "moment of illusion."

When the mother is sufficiently attuned to the child's needs, the child both becomes aware of these needs and feels a sense of impact on the world (i.e., "When I have needs, they are seen and responded to"). When the mother is able to do this in a good-enough fashion, Winnicott believes that the child begins to develop a true sense of self with an awareness of authentic feelings and needs.

Kohut (1971) states that it is important during this period for the child's true self to be mirrored by the parent (i.e., "I am seen, therefore, I exist"). The difference in etiology between the borderline and the preneurotic narcissist at this phase is that while parents of the preneurotic narcissist were not fully adequate at attunement, mirroring, soothing, and empathy, the absence of these parental provisions in the narcissistic borderline was profound due to the lower level of ego development and self-other differentiation of the parent.

Winnicott also believes that in addition to having the child's needs responded to, the child requires the mother not to intrude when he or she is feeling contented (i.e., in a state of "going on being"). For example, when contentedly playing with his or her toys, it is important for mothers not to pick the child up and hold the child because they feel needy. Winnicott believes that when the mother is nonimpinging, the child develops the important developmental capacity to be alone. However, when the mother frequently impinges on the contented child, the child prematurely learns to become attuned to the needs of others. Winnicott believes that this is the beginning of the development of the false self.

Thus, when parents are unattuned and impinging, the child develops a false compensatory self that is geared to please them. In narcissistic families, rather than meeting children's needs for a selfobject (i.e., mirroring, idealizing), parents require children to meet their selfobject needs (Miller 1981). For example, one patient remembered hours of listening to her mother and trying to calm her down. Another patient believed that if he did not get all A's in school, his mother would get depressed and withdraw from him.

Practicing

Narcissism also develops from failures at later developmental phases. During the practicing phase of separation-individuation (Mahler et al. 1975), the child develops upright locomotion and begins to feel that the world is his or her oyster. At this point in time, the child develops what is referred to as "a love affair with the world." This is a less conflictual stage for the narcissistic individual, who often feels relieved to leave the relatively unattuned symbiotic period to enter the elated experience of practicing.

During this time, as the child develops autonomous functions (e.g., walking, talking) and discovers the wonders of the world, he or she is impervious to knocks and spills, feeling captivated and insulated by the experience of blossoming mastery. He or she thus requires less parental nurturance than in the previous period. The child now feels grandiose and omnipotent due, in part, to still feeling merged with the magical powers of the mother. The defense of grandiosity is appealing as it protects the child from the depression associated with the neglect of his or her true self.

Rapprochement

The etiology of the borderline narcissist begins in the symbiotic stage. In contrast, for the preneurotic narcissist, maternal functioning during this period, while somewhat insufficient, was not disastrous. Rather, the child's major difficulties begin during rapprochement. Mahler and colleagues (1975) believe that it is during the rapprochement subphase (15 to 24 months) that the child begins to confront the difficult realities of life (e.g., his or her limits, vulnerabilities, and separateness). The once-omnipotent, grandiose child begins to realize that the world is not always his or her oyster and that, in reality, he or she is just a small child. During this period, the child retreats back to the mother for comfort.

Children need several things from the mother during the rapprochement phase. The first is that they need the mother to act as a secure base from which to explore the world (Bowlby 1969). Children need to alternatively cling to the mother and be autonomous. As toddlers begin to realize that they are separate beings in the world, they return to their mother for symbiotic refueling. Children now need the mother's acceptance of their renewed neediness. When she is able to do this, the child is able to master feelings of separation and aloneness.

The rapprochement subphase is the height of the child's independence-dependence struggle and is thus a difficult stage for the parent to be a good-enough parent. This aspect of rapprochement also differentiates the etiology of the borderline and preneurotic narcissist. Like the hysteroid, when the borderline narcissist separated from the mother and then returned for comfort, the mother responded to the child with rejection. In contrast, while mothers of preneurotic narcissists did not provide completely adequate supplies for refueling the child, neither did they angrily abandon the child. Thus, the borderline narcissist struggles far more with feelings of separation anxiety than does the preneurotic narcissist.

During the rapprochement period, children also need to have their grandiosity gradually deflated and ambitions brought into accord with reality through phase-appropriate disappointments and optimal frustrations. Children need their achievements mirrored and admired and their failures understood (Kohut 1971). When the parent is narcissistically injured and requires the child to be more or less than he or she is, the parent is unable to provide the necessary selfobject functions for the child such as mirroring, admiring, and empathizing (Johnson 1987, Miller 1981). In such cases, instead of providing the child with these functions, parents require the child to meet these needs for them. Generally, when children have parents who require them to be ideal objects, these children develop progressive narcissistic styles (e.g., grandiosity, attention-seeking behavior), and children of parents who require the children to be mirroring selfobjects develop a regressive narcissistic style. In many cases, children are required to do both functions.

Children in such families are never seen or accepted for the unique individuals (with accompanying needs, feelings, and interests) that they are. Instead, children are required to be the kind of people who will, in some important way, meet the parents' needs. The child's true self is either insufficiently developed or developed but unexpressed, and his or her self-esteem remains dependent on the admiration of others and thus unstable. For example, one patient whose athletic ability was not recognized by his intellectual parents (who stressed academics), overachieved in school by working hard all the time but felt like an imposter underneath. He constantly needed reassurance from teachers and friends that he was not stupid and considered his athletic ability, which came naturally to him and gave him great enjoyment, to be of no value.

During rapprochement, children also need adequate fathering. In normal development, the father (the new and exciting object outside the symbiotic orbit) invites the child into the larger world. When maternal supplies have been limited during earlier phases, the child often turns to the father for mirroring and idealizing functions.

Kohut (1971) believes that identifying with an ideal object provides a second opportunity to develop healthy narcissism. Children often turn to their father with this need (i.e., to merge with an omnipotent, tension regulating object). Morrison (1989) believes that if the father provides this function, over time the child identifies with the father. Through this process the child better consolidates his or her self. Idealization thus represents a naturally occurring defensive posture during this subphase, protecting the child from overwhelming feelings of inadequacy, inferiority, and shame.

The child's narcissistic injuries resulting from lack of mirroring are thus exacerbated if one of the parents does not provide an adequate ideal object with which the child can identify. For example, one patient, whose father was mostly absent and inept, felt extremely ashamed of his mother who never learned to speak English and seemed to go out of her way to look unattractive. If later twinship experiences with peers are also unsatisfactory, the final opportunity for self development is impeded. The result of a relative failure in idealization leads to a sense of self-depletion by not making up for the child's sense of inadequacy "through merger with the power of the idealized selfobject" (Morrison 1989, p. 278).

Summary

Masterson (1993) notes that mothers of narcissists tend to be narcissistic themselves. In such families, mothers as well as fathers are narcissistically injured and thus require their children to serve as selfobjects to them, rather than allowing themselves to be used as selfobjects. Generally, when parents require the child to become their ego ideal, the child's real self is neglected as the child identifies with parents' idealizing projections. This both preserves and distorts the grandiose self in order to please the parent. Often, the child chosen for this role possesses some natural talent, gifts, or beauty that inspires admiration in others (Kernberg 1975, Masterson 1993). In such cases, the child develops a progressive narcissistic style as an adult. When narcissistic parents require a child to be a mirroring selfobject for them, the child is more likely to develop a regressive narcissistic style as an adult. In many cases, children are required to function in both ways for parents. In either case, they fail to develop an authentic, fully integrated sense of self. Due to a failure to complete the internalization of parental functions, the preneurotic narcissistic individual remains excessively dependent on others for self-esteem regulation.

RESULTING DEVELOPMENTAL FAILURE

As a result of receiving insufficient attunement to their needs and impingement during contented periods, preneurotic narcissists learn to suppress their real needs and become prematurely attuned to the needs of others. Failing to receive adequate mirroring and empathy, they never feel fully seen and thus lack some clarity about their true versus false self. As a result, these patients have insufficiently learned what type of person they really are and what they need and want, separate from the expectations of others (i.e., what they think that they should need and want).

Furthermore, during rapprochement their sense of self is not adequately repaired by identifying with an ideal object (although preneurotic narcissists have more of these opportunities than borderline narcissists and more capacity for imagining ideal objects or relying on books and television to find an ideal object to emulate). Additionally, when parents are envious of their children, the children's successes are not adequately applauded, and when the parents require their children to reflect their own ideal selves, the children's failures are not sufficiently understood. These children are thus constantly required by parents to be more or less than who they are (Johnson 1987).

In general, narcissists are used children (Johnson 1987). As parents relate to them as extensions of themselves, they attempt to mold their children to fit their needs rather than rejoicing in the discovery of the child's emerging self. Thus, the primary developmental failure of the preneurotic narcissist is the failure to individuate. Narcissists thus continually struggle between the desire to please others and gain their admiration, and feeling impinged on or engulfed by them. As Leonard Cohen expresses it in his song "I'm Your Man,"

> The moon's too bright.
> The chain's too tight.
> I could not fall asleep at night.

For example, one patient attempted to be the perfect husband to his wife. He tried to anticipate what she needed, was a good provider, frequently brought her flowers and other thoughtful presents, worked out regularly at the gym to remain attractive to her, and would at times listen for hours to her complaints about her day. However, when this behavior became excessive, he began to experience his wife as smothering, and felt engulfed by her (i.e., he believed that he could not be his true self around her). His excessive, solicitous, false self behavior toward his wife would thus often be followed by long periods of withdrawal from her that she did not understand.

STRUCTURAL ISSUES

As a result of a failure to completely individuate, and to internalize mirroring and idealized selfobject functions, the preneurotic narcissist develops a disorder of the self and an incomplete sense of object constancy with several structural problems: (1) the lack of an authentic, fully integrated sense of self; (2) a compensatory grandiose self structure; (3) an unrealistic ego ideal; and (4) unstable self-esteem.

Lack of an Authentic, Fully Integrated Sense of Self

Since the preneurotic narcissist has not experienced the severe lack of attunement and the impingement experienced by the borderline narcissist, he or she develops an adequate nuclear self (the early beginning of a nascent self structure). Furthermore, as autonomous behavior was not consistently met with punishing withdrawal, these patients have less difficulty with separation. However, due to a lack of sufficient mirroring and/or idealizing functions provided by parents, and being loved conditionally for providing these functions for the parent, the preneurotic narcissist overrelies on his or her false self. As a consequence of not having one's true self accepted and rejoiced in, he or she struggles with an inability to soothe oneself and with fragmentation of those aspects of the self that were rejected by parents (e.g., dependency, fear, shame). These fragmented self experiences are thus not usually experienced by the patient as part of his or her self concept. Rather, they are viewed by the narcissist as what Sullivan (1940) refers to as the "not-me" part of the personality. When they are experienced, they feel ego-dystonic and shameful.

A Compensatory, False, Grandiose Self

When children receive insufficient mirroring of their true self coupled with conditional approval and admiration for their beauty or talents, then they excessively yearn for mirroring and begin to utilize the grandiose self to obtain it. Kernberg (1975) proposes that the false or compensatory grandiose self structure represents a composite of the parent's projected ego ideals, the child's distorted grandiose self, and the child's innate, special talents and skills that have been selectively admired by significant others.

We believe that the preneurotic narcissist activates this distorted grandiose self for compensatory reasons to defend against painful feelings of rejection, humiliation, and depression. However, unlike the borderline narcissist, we believe that the preneurotic narcissist's grandiose self structure is somewhat ego-dystonic and more modifiable by appropriate treatment. In our own clinical observations, our preneurotic narcissistic patients have a much greater degree of awareness of their underlying wish for the acceptance of their true selves. For example, one patient was frequently told as a child how cute or handsome he was. One day, his mother found him looking in the mirror and crying. When she asked him what was wrong, he said, "I don't want to be handsome."

An Unrealistic Ego Ideal

Narcissistic patients have an unrealistic ego ideal (i.e., aspirations for the ideal version of themselves) for a variety of reasons. First, their ego ideal may not even be their own but rather the parent's projected ego ideal or ideal object image that the child internalized in order to maintain a relationship with the parent. Second, the narcissist's ego ideal is typically extreme or perfect, creating impossible standards for the individual. The perfectionism of the narcissist's ego ideal is intended to prevent the individual from experiencing shame. Paradoxically, as such perfectionistic standards are impossible to achieve, they actually lead to greater self-disillusionment and shame in the patient.

Unstable Self-Esteem

As previously described, due to (1) a lack of appropriate mirroring and idealizing selfobjects, (2) conditional acceptance for their compliant false self, (3) parental failure to gradually and empathically deflate the child's grandiosity, and (4) failure to complete internalizations of the parents' mirroring and idealizing functions, the preneurotic narcissist has not developed resilient self-esteem. This leaves patients excessively dependent on others for maintaining their positive feelings about themselves. As dependency is often ego-dystonic for the preneurotic narcissist, when the patient recognizes the need for reassurance, he or she often feels an accompanying sense of shame. Thus, preneurotic narcissists attempt to get this need met by others in a much more subtle and appropriate manner than the borderline narcissist, which is why they are more difficult to diagnose as narcissistic.

RESULTING INTERPERSONAL STANCE

The narcissistic personality has a pseudo-independent false self presentation. Even regressive or closet narcissists, who present as very sensitive to other people, behave as though they need little for themselves. While narcissists act like they do not need other people, they are in actuality highly dependent on them for shoring up their self-esteem (Kohut 1984). Thus, one narcissistic patient, who was a research assistant for his professor, behaved quite independently, but privately felt enormously injured when the professor did not provide him with the attention and admiration that he secretly wished for.

While preneurotic narcissists have a greater capacity for whole object relations (i.e., relationships with separate people with needs of their own) than do borderline narcissists, they still frequently relate to others like part-objects or selfobjects. They tend to use others for mirroring and idealizing functions and can feel abandoned or impinged upon when objects have needs of their own. For example, when the therapist attempted to empathize with a patient by sharing a brief example of a similar experience, the patient was afraid that the therapist would begin to use her to get her own needs met.

As a result of their strong ego-dystonic dependency and exquisite sensitivity to the responses of others, preneurotic narcissists tend to be quite manipulative (Chessick 1985, Morrison 1989). Others are seen as an indispensable source of narcissistic supplies. For example, one patient called the therapist on a referral from a friend and asked the therapist if she would reduce her fee (the patient earned $70,000 a year). When she told the patient that she would not, he then asked her if she would consider billing him twice for each session.

Furthermore, as previously described, due to narcissists' defensive structure, they also have a tendency to idealize and devalue other people as a means of repairing faulty self-esteem. Thus, one patient, who was a psychiatrist, admired the therapist for "writing books and being famous." When the therapist moved into a group practice, he expressed surprise and disappointment that the therapist wasn't practicing with "other famous people."

Depending on whether narcissists have a progressive or regressive narcissistic style, their initial interpersonal presentation is quite different. The progressive narcissist appears more confident, dominant, and self-absorbed, and more apparently invites others to serve in the role of admiring audience. What may not be apparent to the other, who is initially charmed by the narcissist, is that attention is not reciprocal. In contrast, regressive narcissists' initial presentation is more warm and submissive. They appear to be volunteering to be the object's audience. What is generally not apparent to the other is that this is often a false self presentation, intended to seduce the object. It is thus very expensive and has no warranty.

Some items on the Psychodynamic Character Inventory (PCI-2) (Chapter 12) that illustrate the preneurotic narcissistic's interpersonal stance are (1) "I expect a great deal from people, have difficulty taking no for an answer, and persist in my attempts to get what I want. If people don't eventually go along with what I want, they can be replaced." (2) "It is important to me that my partner is intelligent, attractive, appreciative of me, and a good listener." (3) "I tend to adore and admire people at first, and then get disillusioned with them." (4) "People tend to like me because I know how to make them feel really important and special."

TREATMENT OF THE NARCISSISTIC PERSONALITY

Psychotherapy of the preneurotic narcissistic patient is based largely on the theories of Winnicott (1958a,b) and Kohut (1971, 1977). As a result, treatment is focused predominantly on self restoration. Winnicott emphasizes the importance of providing patients with maternal functions absent in the patients' development (e.g., attunement, optimal frustration, nonimpingement). Kohut believes that what is curative in treating narcissistic patients is recognizing, empathizing with, and providing the missing selfobject experiences that patients did not receive as children. He believes that narcissistic patients need therapists to accurately mirror and understand them often enough so that these patients can internalize these functions and self-affirm when the therapist fails to do so. Additionally, the therapist needs to allow for a certain amount of idealization to provide a new object of strength and competence for the patient to identify with.

In the case of the narcissistic personality, structural goals are discussed before interpersonal goals, as we believe that they are primary. In essence, when patients do not have a sufficiently integrated and authentic sense of self, resilient self-esteem, and fully developed object constancy, it is difficult to relate to other people in a more mature, reciprocal fashion.

STRUCTURAL GOALS

To summarize from earlier in the chapter, structural deficits in the borderline narcissist are much more severe than those of the preneurotic narcissist and thus require a somewhat different approach to treatment. In the preneurotic narcissist, there is greater self cohesion and self-other differentiation and incomplete (rather than no) object constancy. However, while the true self is more accessible, there is still an overreliance on the false self and the grandiose self. While self is primarily differentiated from others, due to incomplete transmuting internalizations, the self is overly reliant on objects and thus susceptible to voluntarily giving up on true feelings and needs with objects, resulting in the feeling of engulfment. Furthermore, fragmentation (i.e., nonintegration) of ego-dystonic parts of the self is still a problem and one that at times can cause relational problems. Thus, the structural goals for the preneurotic narcissistic patient that are discussed in this section include (1) facilitating a sustained, integrated, authentic sense of self; (2) fostering individuation; (3) integrating the grandiose self into the nuclear core self; (4) increasing frustration tolerance; and (5) helping patients to complete object constancy by internalizing the therapist's empathy, soothing, and esteem.

Facilitate the Development of a Sustained, Integrated, and Authentic Sense of Self

While preneurotic narcissists have developed a nuclear self, because they are so attuned to the opinions of others, they can at times lose touch with their own authentic self experience, including an awareness of their feelings, needs, and goals. Thus, helping these patients sustain an awareness of their true self experience (particularly under pressure from significant others to be or feel different) is an important component of treatment. A number of approaches can be used for this purpose. The primary ones include what Winnicott (1958a) refers to as attunement, what Kohut (1977) describes as mirroring, and what Kohut (1977) and Rogers (1965) refer to as empathy.

The first step that the therapist may take to promote authentic self expression is to be highly attuned to what the patient feels and needs (particularly to nonverbal cues, which are frequently different from their words). As with an infant, the therapist initially has to make educated guesses. However, because the patient is verbal the process is less difficult. For example, if a patient is talking about how much she likes her new job (but is fidgeting and moving around in her chair while she is doing it), the therapist has a number of potential interventions that he or she might use: (1) "I'm wondering how you are feeling right now as you are talking to me." (2) "While you speak enthusiastically about your work, you seem anxious. Are you also feeling some anxiety about either your work or something else in your life?" (3) "Last week you told me that your mother wouldn't approve of this job and that you were concerned that I would have the same attitude. While you said that you are feeling good about the job, you also seem anxious. I was wondering if you were concerned that I might be feeling disapproving of your choice."

The range of questions varies (e.g., asking patients about their perceptions about their own feelings, empathizing with a feeling that the therapist believes that the patient is experiencing, interpreting why the patient might be experiencing that feeling). The level of difficulty of the question depends on the patient's relative awareness of his or her feelings, the length of time of treatment, the degree to which there is a therapeutic alliance, and the patient's sensitivity to intrusion or criticism. In the case of the client who talked about how much she liked her job while fidgeting in her chair, the patient was reasonably unaware of her feelings, had a relatively good alliance with the therapist, and was very sensitive to intrusion. The therapist decided to ask the second type of question because (1) the patient still had difficulty identifying feelings on his own; (2) the therapist thought that anxiety was a reasonable guess about his feeling; (3) anxiety was not a highly ego-dystonic feeling for this patient; and (4) interpreting it for this patient, rather than helping him do it for himself, may have been experienced as intrusive. Regardless of which intervention the therapist chooses, they are all designed to help move patients from their happy false self that has no problems (because they were not allowed to have problems) to an invitation for them to explore their authentic self experience with the therapist.

In the above case, the intervention was successful in that the patient began talking about the parts of the job that made him anxious. At some point, he appeared to be more relaxed, and while there were areas that the therapist considered further exploring with the patient, she sensed that the patient preferred to end the discussion. The therapist thus remained silent until the patient initiated the next comment, which was "I feel relieved to understand what I'm feeling. (Pause) You have such nice trees outside your window. Sometimes, it's nice to just look at them." The latter comment was both a message to the therapist that he was finished as well as what Winnicott (1958a) would describe as a state of "going on being," which Winnicott believes is particularly important in the prevention of false self relating. The appropriate therapeutic response is to comfortably participate in the quiet with the patient.

A child whose real self is not accepted loses the sense that he or she is of value outside of other people's needs for and perceptions of him or her. Thus, the next stage of treatment focuses on helping narcissistic patients be aware of this problem and the price they pay for it. Through carefully attending to the patient, particularly the material that they unconsciously "leak" (e.g., taking frequent fishing trips), the therapist can mirror back to the patient his or her observations of the patient's natural interests (e.g., behaviors done for intrinsic gratification rather than for gaining approval and admiration).

At times, patients' false selves are extremely overdeveloped. This issue must first be confronted and understood before the needs and feelings of their true self (e.g., fragmented-off or ego-dystonic aspects of the self) can be accessed. However, while the patient's authentic feelings are at times difficult to reach, they are not entirely unavailable.

The therapist can help patients become more aware of their ego-dystonic feelings by tentatively expressing what the therapist might be feeling or needing in a similar situation.

One patient was talking about what a concerned and responsible parent her husband was with their new daughter. The example that she gave was how he read many books about babies and frequently gave her advice, as the baby was so important to him. The therapist asked her how frequently he gave her advice, and whether he gave her different advice each time or the same advice over and over. The patient said that when she thought about it, she guessed that he did seem to give her the same advice over and over. She did not entirely understand why he did that as she read all those parenting books too and did everything that they and he said. The therapist said that she could understand how it must feel very good to have a husband who was a real co-parent with her rather than an absent father (as the patient's father had been). However, she (the therapist) thought that in a similar situation with her own husband she "might feel just a bit annoyed, too." The patient reflected for a minute and said, "I guess that I do." In this case, the experience of anger was fragmented off and not a part of her core self experience. By the therapist transforming anger into a mediated emotion (e.g., annoyance) and acknowledging it as her own experience, the patient was able to identify with the therapist and make a fledgling beginning at reintegrating the experience of anger into her core self.

This is similar to the process of handling patients' projective identifications that is described in Chapter 7. For the integration to be complete, however, the process must be repeated and insight about shame over angry feelings understood until the patient naturally begins to identify those feelings in him- or herself.

Thus, an important part of the process of self integration is confronting and empathizing with the patient's shame about having needs and feelings. In the last example, the therapist said that it seemed hard for the patient to allow herself to feel, let alone say, that she was frustrated with her husband. The therapist further inquired whether the patient felt that being angry was shameful or bad. The patient said that it did feel that way and began to talk about how her family never had fights, and when her mother and father had a rare disagreement they went to their bedroom to discuss it.

When the patient begins to spontaneously talk about ego-dystonic feelings, it is important for these expressions to be mirrored, understood, and accepted by the therapist (Kohut 1977). For example, "You really sound mad at your husband. It sounds like you get mad because you don't believe that he has any confidence in you and it's hard enough having confidence in yourself without someone else repeatedly questioning your judgment. I can understand why this feels like such a struggle to you."

Fostering Individuation

The first step in fostering individuation in preneurotic narcissistic patients is to help them better differentiate themselves from significant others. Preneurotic narcissists generally do not have self and other merged (particularly with nonsignificant others). They still, however, have the wish to merge or identify with ideal selfobjects to increase self-esteem.

One way of fostering individuation in treatment is underscoring differences between the patient and other people (including the therapist). It is best initially for the discussion of differences to be introduced by the patient. When they are brought up, it is useful for the therapist to process the meaning to the patient of being different from someone important to him or her.

One patient (who was in somewhat of a twinship merger with the therapist) learned from a friend that the therapist was not Jewish; the patient had assumed that she was. The patient shared this information with the therapist and the therapist asked the patient how she felt about this discovery. The patient said that she had thought that as the therapist was Jewish, like her, that the therapist would be able to understand her better.

The patient also wondered if the therapist would accept her if she was different from the therapist. She recalled early experiences of anti-Semitism while living in a small southern town in which she experienced both prejudice and feeling like an "other." This repeated her family experiences in which she was criticized for being temperamentally different from the rest of the family and having different interests. For example, she was told that she was too sensitive, not outgoing enough, and would not be able to earn a living playing the violin. Rather, she was admired and encouraged for using her great intellect to pursue a secure professional career (especially one where she would meet stable, professional men).

The therapist asked the patient if she had felt understood and accepted by the therapist. The patient said that she had, but was afraid that it was an illusion or would change now that the therapist knew they weren't the same. She told the therapist that she didn't expect people who were too different to accept her. She said that she tried at times to pretend that she was like other people when she was not. She found that this was usually successful in making them like her. However, this was starting to feel too hard on her. She said that the best solution was to just be involved with people who were exactly like her and then no one had to change.

The therapist said that it sounded like she assumed that she was not unique and that there were people who were exactly like her. It also sounded like she was unable to even conceive of the possibility of people liking and appreciating her for her differences. The patient concurred, describing multiple rejections that she had experienced. The therapist said, "I know that this may sound kind of scary to you but I think that it would be important in our relationship to acknowledge our differences and find out whether it's possible to value each other, either because of or in spite of them."

Needless to say, the therapist's acceptance (or at least nonrejection) of patients for their uniqueness is crucial to treatment.

Another means of helping narcissistic patients to individuate (particularly patients with compliant false selves) is to affirm the patient's saying no to others, especially the therapist. Like children going through what is popularly referred to as "the terrible twos," it is important for narcissists to say no as a means of communicating that they are different from the object.

Thus, one regressive narcissistic patient reported that her boss asked her to be a "good sport" and help him out by teaching one more course the following semester. The patient told him that while she would genuinely like to help him out, she really didn't have time to teach an extra course next semester. The therapist acknowledged how hard it was for her to do this and supported the patient's self-assertion, noting that the patient's setting limits for herself meant taking a chance that her boss would be disappointed with her, which brought up her fears of losing his respect.

The process of saying no is particularly useful when the patient is able to do it thoughtfully rather than automatically. For example, another regressive narcissistic patient, who had always complied with his parents' demands, went through a reactionary period of saying no to nearly all of his new wife's requests. Eventually, he began to distinguish between those requests that were very important to his wife and not excessively costly to him (i.e., did not engender strong feelings of giving himself up) and those requests that felt intensely ego-dystonic to him and were of less importance to his wife. He gradually began to accommodate some of the former requests and continued to assert himself with the latter.

Integrate Grandiose False Self into Nuclear Core Self

Because this goal is potentially narcissistically injuring, the therapist must help the narcissistic patient to gradually deflate his or her grandiosity, much as the good-enough parent does with the rapprochement child. It is recommended that the therapist discuss with the patient what is realistic for him or her, empathizing with failures, discussing what is good enough, accepting the patient's real self, and when necessary confronting the patient's grandiosity. The latter is usually done later in treatment when softer approaches have not been successful because of overly rigid defenses (often due to a significant amount of obsessive features in the patient).

Part of accomplishing this goal involves helping the narcissistic patient to transform his or her grandiosity into realistic ambitions and to accept fragmented ego-dystonic aspects of the patient's self (e.g., dependency needs, fear). Both must then be integrated into the nuclear core of the personality.

A patient's mother derived narcissistic gratification from seeing her son as a genius. The patient found it difficult to accept his ordinary ambition to be a teacher. In treatment he slowly began to recognize how he dismissed his own desires to teach as he kept hearing his mother's voice telling him that teaching was beneath her genius son. He gradually developed the ability to differentiate his real ambitions and goals from his mother's grandiose expectations for him.

In addition, he was eventually able to recognize and appreciate his love of children and desire to help them to discover their natural interests. This aspect of himself had been particularly ego-dystonic because it challenged his mother's desire for him to be a prominent attorney, maybe even a judge. The patient also began to internalize the therapist's acceptance of the patient's true ambitions and real interests. He eventually made peace with the fact that, although his mother would be disappointed, he was better suited to be a teacher than an attorney. He was no longer disappointed in himself.

With some patients, who do not progress in treatment with a Kohutian approach because their defenses are ingrained and their grandiosity is ego-syntonic, it is necessary to gradually confront these patients about the discrepancy between their ideals and accomplishments. The therapist also needs to repeatedly underline their proclivity to distort feedback from the world.

A 39-year-old narcissistic patient was expected to marry into an aristocratic family and be a socialite and the mother to perfect children. However, what she liked to do was to paint. After years of neither marrying nor finding a career (her parents supported her), she went back to school to get her master's degree in fine arts. She had fantasies of being a great artist (or at least a professor at a prestigious university) and marrying a loving, handsome, down-to-earth man. When she had art exhibitions, she described them as highly successful, although they were mostly attended by friends and she did not sell a single painting ("My friends gave me very positive feedback"). Most of the time, while she thought of herself as an artist, she did not paint.

Furthermore, despite her expressed interest, she never had a long-term relationship. She chose idealized objects and immediately assumed that there was a very good connection between them. With several men that she had gone out with a few times, she continued to call them and when they told her repeatedly that they were busy, she took them literally and kept calling. Furthermore, she considered herself a "good potential part- ner for someone and a giving person." In her self-evaluation, she did not address the fact that she earned no money, barely cared for herself, let alone someone else, and had little ability to listen to and empathize with others. She also rejected men who liked her when she found them unattractive or uncharismatic.

After an initial period of mirroring and empathizing with her, which had no impact as she dissociated from the therapist or interrupted her whenever the therapist spoke, the therapist slowly began to confront both (1) how despite the patient's expressed wish for the therapist's help, she prevented the therapist from talking and didn't seem able to "eat the therapist's food" (e.g., empathy, clarification, soothing); and (2) how the patient's desired goals, her efforts to attain these goals, and reality did not match up.

For example, the patient still considered herself to be dating the man who refused all her invitations because he was busy. The therapist asked the patient that if she were experiencing a very busy period in her life but really liked someone she had met, did she think that she would be able to find one hour in two months to have a cup of coffee with him. The therapist said that she thought that it was important for them to understand why the patient persisted in perceiving reality the way that she wished that it were, despite repeated evidence that her wish was not true. The therapist also asked the patient what she would lose if she did not date a handsome man and where her idea of the extreme importance of physical beauty came from.

The patient talked about her parents' concern with beauty and wealth as the measures of an individual's worth. Because she did not feel beautiful, she thought that she could somehow indirectly be beautiful by having a handsome partner. She also said that her parents would not consider her worthy unless she accomplished something great. She recognized that being an upper-class social hostess just was not who she was and that she was genuinely attracted to art. However, she feared that she was only a "pretty good" artist rather than a great artist, so would never be able to attain her parents' (or her own) approval. As long as she did not really put her full effort into it, she could still pretend that she could be a great artist if she really tried. It was better to be an unemployed, single, potentially great artist than to have an ordinary person love her and have meaningful activities. With repeated confrontation about the patient's distortion of reality and empathy for her underlying feelings, this patient slowly began to realize what an enormous price she had paid for allowing the grandiose ideals that she had internalized from her parents to rule her life. It took a great deal of time, however, to help her give up her parents' ideals and discover and pursue her own, as her fear of not being her ego ideal was enormous.

Johnson (1987) believes, and we concur, that it is important for the therapist to help narcissistic patients believe that they can be loved for their ordinariness, not just their gifts. In the earlier example of the patient who wanted to teach children rather than become a surgeon, the patient needed to learn to appreciate his own uniqueness (e.g., his ability to turn old furniture into whimsical works of art, his freckles, his simultaneous collection of Batman comic books and the complete works of Shakespeare, his sweet and loving nature, and authentic concern for others). The therapist told him that he seemed to have difficulty believing that these qualities were as important as fame and fortune in gaining people's love and respect. In trying to help a patient to understand this principle, she told him that one of the things that she really loved about her dog was how one ear stood up and the other hung down. She told the patient, "While our achievements may get us admired, it is our idiosyncrasies and our own ability to love that brings us love."

Increase Frustration Tolerance

Parents of narcissists did not sufficiently gratify their children's real needs (e.g., needs for love, nurturance, acceptance, understanding). Instead, they compensated by overgratifying their children's nonessential needs (e.g., giving money or material possessions, allowing themselves to be manipulated into changing a limit, allowing tantrums, providing conditional love and admiration.) It is thus extremely important for therapists to help narcissistic patients learn to tolerate the realistic frustrations and limitations in life.

One way to accomplish learning to tolerate frustration involves meeting some of the patient's essential needs that were not met by parents (e.g., doing a good-enough job of empathizing with the patient and helping him or her to internalize empathy during the therapist's empathic failures) (Kohut 1977). If patients are optimally frustrated, it will not overwhelm them when the therapist inevitably disappoints them. This contrasts with their childhood experiences of too many emotional disappointments (compensated for by too many material gratifications or nonessential overindulgences). Furthermore, when the therapist is sufficiently empathic and the patient is able to internalize this function, the patient will be more able to soothe him- or herself during frustrating experiences such as empathic failures.

During one group therapy session held on Rosh Hashanah (the Jewish New Year), a patient shared with the group how sad he felt. He said that on this holiday he became truly aware that his parents were dead and that there was now no one to make his mother's chicken soup for him. Several members of the group offered to make it for him and he rejected their offers saying, "It wouldn't be the same."

Since this patient had a chronic pattern of rejecting help because of shame about dependency needs and concerns that other people wouldn't be able to do things for him in a way that met his standards, the therapist confronted the patient about his refusal of the group members' offers. The patient said that they did not know his mother's recipe. A group member said that he could give it to her.

The patient appeared to be frustrated and resistant and said that he felt misunderstood. He took a few minutes to reflect on his feelings and told the group, "It's not that I think that other people won't do this perfectly or I don't want their help. It's that I feel like if I make the soup, I will somehow have a part of my mother with me today. But I'd be glad for any of you to come join me in cooking or eating it with me."

This case thus provides two examples of increased frustration tolerance. First, since the patient had experienced sufficient empathy from the therapist and the group in the past, he was able to empathize with himself in the face of the group's and the therapist's failure to understand him, communicate it to the group, and reduce his frustration. Secondly, his increased ability to internalize the realistic good features of his mother made the pain and frustration of feeling like an orphan more bearable.

Another way to help narcissistic patients learn to increase frustration tolerance is by setting and keeping reasonable limits. There are many important reasons for setting and keeping limits with children, patients, and narcissistic patients in particular, despite their protests. The first and perhaps most important is that it demonstrates to them a sense of the object's indestructibility in the face of the child or patient's angry feelings (Winnicott 1965a). Thus, the therapist lets narcissistic patients know that while they are free to express themselves authentically, they are not free to do so in a way that is damaging to either themselves or the therapist. This may involve what Bion (1962, 1967, 1970) refers to as containment of the patient's affects and impulses (which is discussed in Chapter 9) or making clear behavioral contracts with the narcissistic patient and sticking to them.

Thus, the narcissistic patient learns in therapy that the good-enough therapist attempts to be reasonably responsible and available but is not available every minute (due to the therapist's own competing needs) and that as adult relationships are reciprocal, patients do have to pay their bills.

One 33-year-old narcissistic patient with obsessive defenses had been in treatment for two years during which the therapist primarily used a Kohutian approach to promote the patient's self development. After two years, the therapist observed that her approach to treatment seemed to have very little impact on the patient. The patient, who had always been supported by his parents, was told by his parents that they would only be able to support him for one more year because his father was retiring. After six months of not looking for a job, the therapist told him that if in six months, he did not have a job and thus was not able to pay his therapy bill, she would need to terminate treatment with him. She said that while she would regret doing this, she did not want to infantalize him as his parents did.

Three months before the end of the year, the patient continued to report that there weren't any suitable jobs or that he didn't have time to make phone calls to inquire about them. The therapist confronted him, saying, "My guess is that at some level you know that you can make your parents feel guilty so that they will still send you money. I think you feel entitled to an important, interesting job without having to make significant efforts toward getting it. Also, this may be your way of making your parents pay their debt for not accepting you or paying sufficient attention to you. It seems like you subtly and perhaps unconsciously punish them for this so that they won't stick to their limits with you."

While setting limits is a difficult process for parents and children and therapists and patients, there is no alternative since limits are an inevitable truth about the world that individuals must learn to accept and cope with. However, setting limits works best and creates less of a power struggle between therapist and patient when they are set clearly, tactfully, empathically, and firmly. Furthermore, it is important to process the patient's feelings about the therapist's limits.

For example, the therapist told the previous patient, "You may also need to test my limits. I, too, will probably feel a bit guilty if we need to terminate because you still have not found a job and are, therefore, unable to be financially responsible for yourself and with me. However, I will stick to my limit because I believe that I will not help you by doing otherwise. How do you feel about what I am saying?"

Narcissists can learn to tolerate frustration better if the therapist helps the patient to learn what is realistic to expect in life and what isn't. Continually pursuing the impossible dream leads these patients to chronic disappointments unless their defenses are working exceptionally well. Thus, the narcissistic personality needs to know that no matter how accomplished we are, we are not entitled to get all of our needs met on demand, and that while we deserved a happy childhood, it is too late now to have one, regardless of how perfect we are now. What we can have now are good-enough relationships with others who can usually understand and appreciate our situations, and realistic and meaningful ways to obtain fulfillment.

Develop Transmuting Internalizations
for Genuine Reality Based Self-Soothing and Self-Esteem

As previously described, while preneurotic narcissists have a reasonably cohesive sense of self, have primarily differentiated self from other, and have some capacity for object constancy, they do not have completely developed object constancy because, due to their ambivalent feelings about their parents, they failed to internalize their realistic functions (e.g., empathy, soothing, admiration) into their self. Thus, a very important treatment goal on which many other goals (e.g., whole object relations, giving up grandiosity) depend is internalizing the therapist's realistic selfobject or auxiliary ego functions.

To help narcissistic patients internalize the therapist's selfobject or auxiliary ego functions, the therapist must first deal with the patients' resistance about doing so. The primary resistance is patients' underlying ambivalence toward the therapist due to transference of their ambivalent feelings about their early objects. Thus, the therapist must be initially alert to when the patient is acting like he or she is listening and responding but is really sidestepping the therapist. For example, after the therapist empathized with one patient about the loneliness that he felt, the patient changed the subject. Another patient would give an artificial smile and say, "Thank you. That was very helpful. I feel really supported by you. I always feel better after coming here." These patients learned to dissociate, change topics, or do false self compliance as an indirect way to keep the therapist from giving them exactly what they truly want and need, because they fundamentally do not trust the therapist.

Generally, when the therapist confronts the patient about this, the patient denies that this is occurring (e.g., "I feel hurt that you don't believe me." "Did I do that?") Repeated confrontations are often required to enable the patient to become conscious of this behavior. At that point, it is important for the therapist and patient to mutually understand the meaning of this behavior. Thus, the therapist might ask, "You have described being hurt by your parents' unwillingness or inability to understand you and your great wish for understanding and comfort from both me and other people. Yet, you seem unable to truly accept it, which keeps you feeling frustrated and anxious."

When this question is thoroughly processed with preneurotic patients, they usually become aware of their underlying resistance as being due to their fear of the therapist's inauthenticity (e.g., "You get paid for saying understanding things") or their fear of criticism. It is difficult for these patients to believe that anyone would genuinely accept and wish to understand their true self. This differs from narcissistic borderlines' refusal to internalize due to fears of losing themselves in their relationship with the therapist or obsessive patients' fear of being controlled.

Usually having these underlying concerns understood and accepted by the therapist strengthens the working alliance, increases trust, and makes the patient more open to listening to, believing, and internalizing the therapist's empathy and acceptance. At this point, Kohut's previously described principles of treatment begin to be useful, again. Over time, as narcissistic patients are generally understood, accepted, appreciated, and soothed, they receive the developmental experience with objects that they missed as a child. Eventually, the self assumes the object's functions, providing narcissists with more resilient self-esteem. They become less dependent on others, including the therapist, for selfobject functions. They are thus more forgiving of their own mistakes and more able to be genuinely concerned about the needs of others. At this stage, object constancy is established.

INTERPERSONAL GOALS

Narcissists' primary interpersonal difficulty is based on their belief that being authentic will lead to criticism and rejection rather than loving, accepting reciprocal relationships. Interpersonal goals with narcissistic patients thus focus on providing these patients with corrective experiences that help them to clarify these issues and provide them with models for new ways of relating. Interpersonal goals include developing the ability to behave authentically with others, and to love and feel loved by realistically perceived good-enough objects. However, each of these goals is contingent on successfully accomplishing the structural goals described in the previous section. For example, an individual needs to be aware and somewhat accepting of his or her true self in order to share it with others and believe that the other person will accept it. Also, the narcissistic patient must first be able to internalize the therapist's selfobject or auxiliary ego functions before he or she is able to love others as whole objects rather than use them for their selfobject or auxiliary ego functions.

Develop Ability to Be Authentic with Others

Before learning to be authentic with others, preneurotic narcissists must be cognizant of the difference between their true and false self and become aware of and integrate the ego-dystonic, fragmented-off aspects of their self into their nuclear or core self (goals discussed earlier in this chapter). However, while these patients deeply wish for authentic relating, they have experienced a lifetime of having their true selves criticized or rejected and their false selves rewarded with attention, admiration, and conditional love. Thus, encouraging these patients to relate to others authentically is a bit like asking someone who believes that the world is flat to sail his or her boat over the edge of the earth. Alice Miller (1981, p. 15), in her book, *The Drama of the Gifted Child*, succinctly describes a case of a narcissistic individual struggling with this problem who asks, "'What would have happened if I had appeared before you, bad, ugly, angry, jealous, lazy, dirty, smelly: Where would your love have been then? And I was all these things as well. Does this mean that it was not really me whom you loved, but only what I pretended to be: The well-behaved, reliable, empathic, understanding and convenient child, who in fact was never a child at all.'"

There are several steps in helping preneurotic narcissistic patients gradually learn to express their true selves with (i.e., relate authentically to) others. These include the therapist's (1) relating to the patient's true self and not responding to the patient's false self; (2) being appropriately authentic with the patient; (3) helping patients to distinguish authentic, accepting people from critical, inauthentic people; and (4) taking small risks. As is perhaps implied by the necessity of first accomplishing structural goals, these goals are to be initiated in the middle to later phases of treatment when the patient has more resilient self-esteem and the therapeutic alliance is stronger.

Relating to the Patient's True Self and Not Responding to the Patient's False Self

For one narcissistic patient, early therapy sessions consisted of frequent cheerful hours. After several months of listening, the therapist expressed confusion over the patient's seeking treatment during a time in which she seemed to be so happy. The patient initially appeared perplexed and then began to describe her mother, who frequently commented on her beautiful smile and told her to be "a happy girl." The therapist commented that this seemed like a tall order given the inevitable frustrations of life. The patient teared up but did not understand why.

Slowly, the patient began to describe serious problems in her life but continued to do so with a big smile on her face. As she more often "talked at" rather than "with" the therapist, it was thus quite difficult to feel empathic or connected with her. The therapist found herself torn between noticing her attention wandering and having the inclination to inauthentically say something empathic. The therapist attempted to reach a compromise of sorts where she did her best to truly listen to and understand the patient, but did not smile and did not verbally respond to the patient unless the patient invited it.

This is a very difficult position for therapists (other than psychoanalysts who are rigorously trained to use therapeutic abstinence and retain a neutral stance) to maintain for fear of being impolite or rejecting. Rather, therapists have a proclivity when treating this sort of patient to join them in a narcissistic collusion (i.e., an "as if" good therapist relating to an "as if" good patient). However, doing this perpetuates inauthentic relationships with other people. Furthermore, in some instances (i.e., when the patient is more self-aware), the therapist's behavior may actually inspire contempt in the patient toward the therapist for buying his or her polished package (Johnson 1987).

While it is important not to collude with the patient by behaving inauthentically, therapists must also be careful not to narcissistically injure the patient. For example, in the case just cited, the therapist first empathized with the patient's problems and ignored her incongruent affect. When she began to discuss the discrepancy between the patient's verbal and nonverbal expressions, the patient talked over her, appearing to ignore her intervention and related to her as an audience. The therapist thus remained silent. After a long period of time, the patient said that she had noticed that the therapist had been quiet and wondered what she was thinking. The therapist said that it seemed like the patient had stopped trying to involve the therapist in this process and asked the patient if she was aware of what she wanted from the therapist at this point. The patient said that she was not really sure. The therapist said that she thought that it would be important to clarify what the patient felt underneath her cheerfulness, what she really needed from the therapist, and what her fears might be about getting it.

Without injuring the patient, it is important for the therapist to be authentic with him or her. This can be difficult because it is hard at times to relate authentically to someone who is not also behaving this way. Furthermore, it is important not to allow one's countertransference issues to emerge so that one's authenticity is expressed harshly. For those therapists who grew up in families where everyone colluded that "the emperor was wearing gorgeous new clothes," it is tempting to unconsciously want to "shove the truth in the patient's face," as the therapist wanted to do with his or her parents. It is important for the therapist to carefully monitor his or her genuine feelings toward the patient and to express them with supreme tact.

For example, one patient, who was a therapist, kept talking about how perceptive and insightful she was. She noted that she had resisted going into therapy because she thought that no one would be able to tell her anything about herself that she did not already know and, anyway, why pay all that money when she could just as well analyze herself. The therapist began to feel subtly devalued by the patient's use of the therapist as an audience for her self-inflated presentations. The therapist used her own countertransference feelings to intervene by sharing with the patient that she felt somewhat distant from her and wondered if the patient was aware of any part of her that might feel threatened by coming to therapy and relying on another person's insight and guidance.

One of the reasons that it is so difficult for narcissistic patients to relate authentically to others is that until they have resolved their transference and begin to use their ego to make choices about who it is safe to be vulnerable with, they have difficulty distinguishing between critical, inauthentic people and accepting, authentic people. They both transfer criticism and insincerity onto objects who are not, in reality, that way, and have an uncanny tendency to choose critical, inauthentic objects. In fact, they are a magnet for these types of people. When one attempts to be perfect because they believe that objects require it, he or she attracts people with narcissistic tendencies who do, in fact, want a perfect partner. One patient, near the end of treatment, said that what she "really trusted was a man who flirts with you at the pool, when you're not in shape and aren't wearing makeup."

The narcissistic patient needs to genuinely make distinctions between who is and is not a good person to take a risk of being authentic with. Some general guidelines are (1) people who do not gossip about other people, (2) people who seem to be able to acknowledge and accept their own imperfections, (3) people who listen (but not people who listen perfectly), (4) people who are able to be appropriately vulnerable, and (5) people who are able to apologize (i.e., love is being able to say you're sorry).

It is important to help the narcissist learn to be authentic with others in small steps. He or she must be able to distinguish who are good people to take a risk with and begin with them. These patients are advised to begin to share something that is only a little bit embarrassing. At that point, it is important for the patient to notice whether the other person listens, is understanding and accepting, and begins to be more authentic in return. If they do not and it does not seem to be a transference reaction, the patient is advised not to continue to pursue an authentic relationship with this person. In general, the best person for the patient to begin to be authentic with is the therapist.

Develop the Ability to Love Realistically Perceived Good-Enough Objects

While not as extreme as in borderline narcissists, one of the salient characteristics of preneurotic narcissists is their tendency to excessively use others for their selfobject functions and their compromised ability to perceive and love others as whole objects with their own needs, feelings, and imperfections. Even with preneurotic narcissists, accomplishing this goal comes in the later stages of treatment after other goals have been resolved. These include (1) resolving idealization and devaluation; (2) being a good-enough selfobject to the patient; (3) helping the patient to internalize the therapist's selfobject functions (e.g., soothing, admiring, accepting, empathizing), so that the patient is less dependent on the therapist and other people for these functions; (4) helping the patient accept and express his or her true self; and (5) the therapist's slowly beginning to relate to the patient in a more authentic, object-related manner (e.g., tactfully confronting the patient when he or she is not relating authentically).

These steps have been described earlier in the chapter. At this point the patient is more available for a real object relationship with the therapist based on knowing one another, appreciating each other, and caring for each other, rather than idealizing or being idealized by the other. The therapist may begin to observe the patient noticing the therapist for the first time, taking a genuine interest in discovering who the therapist is, and asking questions. It is as if the patient has woken up. Common types of questions that patients may ask the therapist at this point are "Have you always had that painting?" "Where did you go on your vacation?" "Have you ever felt the way that I do?" and "You look tired today."

While the patient may have made similar comments at the beginning of treatment, the patient is now generally curious about the therapist (rather than making polite, false-self comments). For the first time the patient becomes aware that he or she does not really know who the therapist is (e.g., what the therapist feels, values, etc.). The patient also begins to see, accept, and develop a sense of humor about the therapist's flaws (e.g., "I can't believe that you actually got the date right on this receipt!"). Patients often begin to relate differently to other people, too. They are more interested in them and less critical, and they more often become involved with people who have the capacity to be intimate or kind rather than for their selfobject functions.

Accomplishing this goal also generally involves providing the patient with a corrective interpersonal experience with the therapist. This includes behaving toward the patient to some extent the way that a good-enough parent does with his or her child to help him or her have a secure sense of self and secure mutual relationships with others. This includes what Rogers (1965) refers to as the three core conditions of therapy (i.e., empathy, acceptance, and unconditional positive regard). However, crucial to this process is that the therapist is not play acting. While it is difficult at times to care for someone so self-involved and inauthentic, the therapist must have the ability to see and care for the person underneath who is doing the best that he or she can in the world. While it is a difficult balancing act, the therapist must be genuine with the patient (in the most tactful and respectful way that is possible), even though the patient is easily injured. Preneurotic narcissists uncannily detect false-self behavior in others. Thus, if the therapist is not authentically caring, the relationship will not be healing. Furthermore, the patient must truly come to believe that the therapist is, in real life, a good-enough object who is genuinely kind and concerned for the well-being of other people.

CORRECTIVE INTERPERSONAL EXPERIENCE

As previously discussed, what is corrective varies with each patient. We believe that the corrective interpersonal experience for the preneurotic narcissistic patient is one that maximally creates conditions that foster individuation, self development, realistic goals and ideals, resilient self-esteem, and reciprocal loving relationships. This includes the therapist being attuned, empathic, tactfully authentic, and optimally frustrating with the patient, supporting his or her strengths, and empathizing with his or her vulnerabilities. While we believe that confrontation is occasionally necessary with preneurotic narcissists, particularly when they have very ingrained defenses or obsessive features, we do not believe that it is a common or essential component of treatment with these patients as it is with narcissistic borderlines (Kernberg 1975). Thus, what follows is a brief synopsis of the general principles utilized in the former two sections.

The Therapist Must be Nonimpinging, Sensitive, and Attuned (Winnicott 1958b)

Relating to an individual with a compromised awareness of his or her true self (e.g., wants, needs, feelings, goals) is a bit like relating to an infant or small child who cannot yet tell his mother what he or she needs. In such cases, a good-enough mother attentively watches her child and notices nonverbal indications of what the child needs, and through trial and error learns to understand the child. The therapist's attunement to patients' nonverbal manifestations of feelings and needs, and when appropriate, understanding or gratifying them, helps the patient feel seen and responded to. As previously discussed, Winnicott (1958b) describes an initial period between mother and child where the mother is almost perfectly attuned to the child, creating in the child the sense that what he or she needs matters and will be responded to in the world. In such cases, children do not repress their needs and feelings because even during periods of frustration they are never too painful.

Furthermore, even preneurotic narcissists are very sensitive to impingement or engulfment. As previously stated, Winnicott (1958b) believes that it is as important that the mother does not disturb the child when the child is not needful as that she respond to the child when the child is needful. Winnicott believes that chronic impingement on a child in a nonneedful state causes the child to overaccommodate to the needs of others, contributing to false-self development.

Thus, therapists must be moderate in their initiation of interventions, if possible waiting for a cue from the patient (e.g., looking up and pausing after talking). Furthermore, as with the rapprochement-age child, the therapist must allow the patient to move toward and away from the therapist on the patient's initiative. Earlier in this book, a case example was given of a preneurotic narcissistic patient who left in the middle of each session, terminated treatment after 9 months, and returned two years later to remain in treatment for 4 years (during which he stayed the entire session and made a great deal of progress). The coming and going was not processed until his second bout in treatment, since the therapist believed that processing or interpreting this behavior would subtly force him to stay. This patient, who spent his entire life pleasing his mother, needed to know that he was in therapy because he genuinely wanted to be, not to please the therapist.

The Therapist Must Provide an Empathic, Optimally Frustrating Environment (Kohut 1977)

As described in the previous section, the therapist must be sufficiently empathic with the narcissistic patient so that when the therapist makes empathic failures, the patient is able to internalize the therapist's function. For example, one narcissistic patient came in and told the therapist, "You know, last week when you told me that you thought that _____, you were wrong. I think that what was really going on with me was _____." The patient thus proceeded to discuss this issue. The therapist listened and understood. When the patient was finished, the therapist commented on how the patient was beginning to develop the capacity to understand himself in a sympathetic rather than critical way.

Making empathic failures is not something to be planned (i.e., a manipulation). Rather, the good-enough therapist does his or her best to understand the patient, but, being a fallible human being, makes mistakes at times. When the hits are greater than the misses, the patient learns to tolerate them without becoming overly frustrated, and begins to utilize his or her newly developing skills in this area.

The Therapist Must Support Strengths and Empathize with Vulnerabilities (Johnson 1987)

As with a rapprochement-age child, it is important for the therapist to support the patient's strengths and empathize with his or her weaknesses or failures when they occur (Johnson 1987). This can be complicated because it is not intended that the therapist admire the patient's achievements to reinforce the patient's grandiose false self. Rather, what is recommended is that the therapist provide support and encouragement for the patient's pursuing and succeeding at activities toward which he or she has genuine intrinsic interests.

For example, earlier in the chapter a patient was described whose mother had molded her athletic daughter into becoming a ballerina (the dream that her mother gave up to have children). The patient had really wanted to become a tennis player, which was discouraged by both parents. During therapy, the patient became aware of a genuine interest in winter-skiing. She had a difficult time being a beginner and going through the frustration of the learning process. The therapist supported the expression of her genuine enthusiasm, and empathized with her difficulty overcoming feelings of shame about "not already being perfect at it." The therapist also celebrated her success when she first mastered the skill of snowplowing and stopping as well as remaining a consistent source of encouragement and comfort during the ups and downs of the learning process involved in mastering a new skill.

Furthermore, the support provided does not need to be stated in a way that reinforces dependency on others for feelings of pride. Rather, the therapist can say something like: "I know that you really wanted to try_____, but felt insecure about your ability and anticipated receiving disapproval from your family. I would imagine that you must be feeling proud of yourself for your courage." Also, like the rapprochement parent, the therapist is advised to empathize with the patient's failures and disappointments. Doing so helps the patient to cushion the blow, forgive him- or herself for failing, and develop both realistic standards for success and less fear of failure. In the example just cited of the patient who discovered her interest in skiing, the therapist helped the patient to cope with her failures and disappointments by listening to her accompanying feelings and thoughts, and recognizing when the patient began to devalue herself for not performing perfectly or for looking foolish in front of others. Opening up these issues for discussion helped the patient learn how to recognize and intervene when the patient was experiencing shame.

DIFFERENTIAL DIAGNOSIS

There are three personality disorders with which the preneurotic narcissistic personality can be confused: the masochistic personality, the obsessive-compulsive personality, and the neurotic hysteric. While the narcissistic borderline is often confused with the hysteroid, this mistake is less likely with the preneurotic narcissist.

The Narcissistic Versus the Masochistic Personality

The masochistic personality and the narcissistic personality described in this chapter are both generally structured at the preneurotic level of object relations and ego development. They thus have a number of similar structural issues, such as problems in self-soothing and self-esteem regulation and incomplete object constancy.

Due to intense ambivalence toward parents, masochistic and narcissistic patients have not sufficiently internalized parents' selfobject functions. Object constancy is thus not fully complete. As a result, both personality types remain excessively dependent on others for selfobject functions. In particular, masochists overrely on others for security, and narcissists overrely on others for self-esteem.

While the masochist and the narcissist both have a history of narcissistic parents and narcissistic injuries, they often assumed different roles in their families (Glickauf-Hughes, in press, a, Glickauf-Hughes and Wells 1995b). The masochist was often used as the family scapegoat or caregiver, whereas the narcissist served as the parent's ideal object. This accounts for a number of differences in defenses and in interpersonal style.

The masochist is more of a caregiver than the narcissist. The masochist's life revolves around solving crises for the people around them. Even when narcissists use caregiving as a means of accomplishing their ego ideal, it has a different flavor. For example, narcissists who have a caregiving style much more obviously give to others with strings attached, expecting appreciation and quid pro quo from people. One patient recalled a narcissistic grandmother who always took pictures of herself giving the patient gifts. In these photographs, the patient was forced to kiss the grandmother as a display of her gratitude and admiration for her generosity. Furthermore, the gifts were quite often not things that the patient wanted, as her grandmother never took time to know her well enough to know her preferences.

Furthermore, masochists generally have more access to their true self experiences and have less developed false selves than the preneurotic narcissist. However, while they are more aware of their true self, they are less defended against the belief that their true self is bad. On those occasions when masochists relate to others with their false selves, it is a much more conscious and ego-dystonic process for them than it is for the preneurotic narcissist.

Masochists also have a greater tendency to relate to others as whole objects. The narcissist, even at the preneurotic level, relates at least to selective others as selfobjects. For example, they are highly dependent on others to shore up their fragile self-esteem. While masochists need this, too, it is not to the same extent. While both types are reliant on others for selfobject functions and have difficulty with separations from them (including the therapist), they respond differently to the temporary loss of that person. The masochist is more likely to forgive the therapist for taking a vacation or not immediately returning an important phone call, whereas the preneurotic narcissist is more likely to become contemptuous or to distance him- or herself from the therapist.

In part, this is related to the masochist's propensity to be an introjector and the narcissist's propensity to be a projector. As the masochist is primarily searching for security and love, he or she tends to assume the depressive position, protecting the relationship with the object at the expense of the self (Glickauf-Hughes 1996). In contrast, narcissists are primarily searching for self-esteem. In fact, narcissists protect their self-esteem at the expense of the relationship with the object. The narcissist is thus more likely to be blaming and less likely to apologize than the masochist during interpersonal conflicts (Glickauf-Hughes 1994).

While both character types wish to be perfect, their goals are different. The narcissist wants to be perfect in order to be admired, whereas the masochist wishes to be perfect in order to gain the object's love (Glickauf-Hughes and Wells 1995b).

The most difficult distinction to make is between the masochist and the regressive narcissist, whose surface presentations can appear quite similar. While both are empathic and appear to be focused on the needs of others, masochists have a tendency to do things for other people (e.g., pick them up at the airport, bring food to them when they are ill) and to take responsibility for them (e.g., lend them money). In contrast, regressive narcissists are not merely empathic. They are *sublimely* empathic, and attuned to the needs of others. However, once they seduce them, they can become uninterested in them, particularly when they fail to live up to the narcissist's ideals. In contrast, the masochist genuinely feels attached to the object. Thus, their caregiving of the object is not entirely an expression of their false self. Furthermore, masochists tend to be "the seduced" rather than "the seducer" and once attached, stick to the object like glue.

The Narcissistic Versus the Obsessive-Compulsive Personality

Both narcissists and obsessive-compulsives tend to be perfectionistic. However, as in the last example, the nature of their perfectionism is different.

Narcissists want their self to be perfect (e.g., beautiful, intelligent, talented), whereas obsessive-compulsives want the things around them to be perfect (e.g., neat, clean, organized, orderly, in control).

In general, narcissists have less control issues than obsessive-compulsives. While they are sensitive to impingement, one rarely observes the chronic pervasive power struggles and nitpicking with narcissistic patients that one does with obsessive-compulsive patients. In particular, this is due to the fact that narcissists are less preoccupied with details than obsessives. Narcissists can manifest needs for control over the behavior of others that impacts their self-esteem. They thus devalue and reject others when they frustrate, injure, or disappoint them. In contrast, obsessives seek control for its own sake as being in control makes them feel more autonomous.

Structurally, the obsessive-compulsive has more of an authentic sense of self than the narcissist. Obsessive-compulsives are more attuned to their thoughts, less attuned to the needs of others (in order to manipulate them), and do less impression management than narcissistic patients. They are thus usually less charming than narcissistic patients in the initial stages of treatment. However, while obsessives appear to be more self-preoccupied, they are more able to genuinely love and make commitments to others than are narcissistic patients, even though they are frequently in conflict with people. The obsessive's difficulty is in expressing rather than having loving feelings. For the narcissist, the problem is often reversed.

Obsessives also tend to have a less corruptible superego than narcissists do. Obsessives tend to have rigid value systems, whereas narcissists may change their values to fit current trends. Narcissists have a greater tendency to follow the rules to avoid being caught and suffering negative consequences. In contrast, obsessives follow rules for the sake of honoring their superegos (i.e., because it is the right thing to do).

Narcissistic and obsessive traits can coexist in the same person. Thus, therapists may at times have a patient who is a narcissistic-obsessive character whose most salient feature is a strong need to be perfectly understood. A more extensive discussion of this type of character is discussed by Glickauf-Hughes and Wells (1995a).

The Narcissistic Versus the Hysterical Personality

Both narcissists and neurotic hysterics can have a similar clinical presentation. They can be charming, seductive, interpersonally skilled, and attention seeking. However, the hysteric has a much more developed sense of self. Hysterical patients may at times consciously hide their real feelings from others in order to gain the object's love and approval. In contrast, narcissists are so invested in impression management that they are often not conscious of their feelings in the first place. For example, one hysterical patient was aware of feeling angry at her husband but chose not to express it for fear that he would stop loving her. In contrast, a narcissistic patient who had been treated unfairly by an employer that he wanted to impress denied his feelings of anger and instead made a greater attempt to impress his employer.

The hysteric is more object related than the narcissist. Both the hysteric and the narcissist are described as manipulative, but narcissists (even preneurotic narcissists) often relate to others as selfobjects, whereas hysterics generally relate to others as whole objects, although it may not initially appear that way due to their dramatic, pseudoemotional, and obviously manipulative presentation (e.g., "You're so strong. Will you help me carry my packages?"). However, while hysterics may initially present in a demanding fashion with others, they are more able to take the object's needs into account. The hysteric thus tends to be warmer than the narcissist and more able to love other people.

The narcissist and the hysteric also have different cognitive styles (Shapiro 1965). Hysterics have a more global cognitive style, whereas narcissists are more cognitively focused but tend to slide meanings in order to put themselves in a better light (Horowitz 1992). Narcissists tend to distort self-perceptions to protect self-esteem, whereas hysterics have a greater capacity for realistic self-appraisal and, if anything, undervalue their capabilities. For example, a narcissistic patient was surprised when she *was not* promoted at work, believing that she was entitled to the job because of her overestimation of her intelligence and special talents. In contrast, a hysterical patient was surprised when she *was* promoted, and feared that she might not be intelligent enough, thus underestimating her ability to do an adequate job.

Hysterics and narcissists reflect the distinction between what Kohut (1971) refers to as vertical and horizontal splitting. Hysterics literally forget traumatic experiences or repress them from their conscious awareness into their unconscious (i.e., *horizontal splitting*). In contrast, narcissists can sustain two contradictory experiences that exist in consciousness at different times (i.e., *vertical splitting*). For example, narcissists generally feel very independent. However, they have a fragmented-off, ego-dystonic, dependent part of the self that they occasionally experience. When narcissists do experience their split-off part, they experience shame.

The narcissist has more dyadic issues (e.g., fear of engulfment, identification with an ideal object) and the hysteric has more triadic issues (e.g., competition with one person for the love and attention of another). Thus, narcissistic patients tend to envy other people (i.e., want to be them), whereas hysterical patients tend to be jealous of others (i.e., want to be more loved by them).

COUNTERTRANSFERENCE ISSUES

In working with narcissistic patients, who are idealizing, devaluing, and frequently relate to the therapist as an object, therapists are likely to experience a number of both objective and subjective countertransference experiences. Schultz and Glickauf-Hughes (1995) describe four common countertransference responses that therapists experience in treating narcissistic patients: (1) response to being used as a mirroring selfobject, (2) response to being idealized (i.e., the narcissistic collusion), (3) response to the twinship transference (i.e., the kindred spirit experience), and (4) response to the negative transference (i.e., becoming the patient's "bad self").

Response to Being Used as a Mirroring Selfobject by Patients

The preneurotic narcissist often has a grandiose self structure invested in its own omnipotence and perfection, which requires being seen, confirmed, and admired. These patients often use the therapist as a mirroring self object (i.e., a person who does not exist in his or her own right but is used for his or her functions such as mirroring, admiring, and empathy). During this mirror transference described by Kohut (1968), the patient views the therapist as an extension of him- or herself. The therapist often has the experience with the narcissistic patient of not being acknowledged as a separate being. Kernberg (1974) believes that this is a very difficult experience for therapists to tolerate.

For example, one narcissistic patient talked "at" the therapist nonstop and interrupted all the therapist's attempts to make an intervention. Another patient told the therapist that when the patient was talking, unless the therapist was supportive, the patient didn't really feel like she was getting her money's worth. Hearst (1988) believes that such an experience is narcissistically injuring to the therapist. This is particularly the case when therapists have narcissistic issues, which Miller (1981) and Glickauf-Hughes and Mehlman (1995) suggest is commonly the case. In such instances, the therapist is likely to experience feelings of anger and resentment toward the patient for being used.

Schultz and Glickauf-Hughes (1995) note a second important cue to the existence of a countertransference response to a prolonged mirror transference. In such cases, therapists may notice themselves feeling bored or having drifting attention. "The unconscious dynamic which often occurs at those moments translates as: You don't listen to what I say so I won't listen to what you say" (p. 602).

Furthermore, an extremely successful, boastful, and self-aggrandizing patient can at times elicit feelings of competition or envy in the therapist. This is especially true if the therapist has frustrated ambitions in the area in which the patient is "displaying" him- or herself. However, as previously described, the preneurotic narcissist is better able to relate to others as whole objects than the borderline narcissist. Thus, countertransference responses to this type of transference are usually much less extreme than with the borderline narcissist.

Response to the Idealizing Transference:
The Narcissistic Collusion

In 1968 Kohut described the second pole of the narcissistic transference, which he referred to as the idealized parent imago. During the idealizing phase of transference, the patient experiences the therapist as omnipotent and perfect, and identifies with him or her. Kernberg (1974) suggests that one of two countertransference reactions may emerge during this phase: (1) rejection of the patient's idealization, and (2) collusion with the patient's idealization.

There are several reasons that a therapist may reject a patient's idealization of him or her. The therapist may have been used by his or her own parents as an ideal object and not seen for his or her true self. In such a case, the therapist may have a subjective countertransference response and experience anger toward the patient for using the therapist and not seeing the therapist as a separate person. This is a similar response to that which occurs in the mirroring transference. Furthermore, Kernberg (1978) believes that the "on-off" quality of the idealizing transference may make a therapist feel uncomfortable and insecure. For example, a patient may put the therapist on a pedestal one week and knock him or her off the next week.

Also, a therapist's own narcissistic needs may lead to the formation of a narcissistic collusion with the patient. In a narcissistic collusion, the therapist accepts rather than understands the patient's idealization. In such instances, therapist and patient may view each other as perfect and avoid criticizing or disappointing each other.

For example, a student therapist, who was feeling very insecure about her competence, began to report how happy she felt whenever she saw this wonderful new patient. In general, therapists may be alerted to the possibility of a narcissistic collusion when they notice themselves frequently discussing their "favorite patient" with colleagues. Johnson (1987) believes that while it is at times necessary "to allow some of the client's idealization of the therapist . . . it is important for the therapist to have a realistic perception of himself, his abilities and limitations" (p. 80).

In conclusion, therapists who have not sufficiently resolved their own narcissistic issues may make one of two countertransference-based errors. They may either reject the patient's idealization or blindly accept it, rather than tolerating it, understanding it, and, if appropriate, interpreting it.

Response to the Twinship Transference: The Kindred-Spirit Experience

The twinship transference (i.e., the search for a perfect twin or soulmate) was Kohut's last major contribution to self psychology (Detrick 1985, 1986). During a twinship transference, narcissistic patients may consciously choose therapists with a sexual preference, religious or political idealogy, or physical appearance that is similar to their own. They may also focus on real commonalities between therapist and patient or project important ego-syntonic traits onto the therapist. The experience of being the same as another person is reassuring to some narcissistic patients and provides them with the important sense of belonging in the world.

When therapists have similar needs, they may err in overconceptualizing the patient's dynamics as similar to their own and fail to sufficiently investigate or acknowledge the differences between them. For example, one therapist who was treating a narcissistic patient during a twinship transference (and countertransference), failed to understand how much more ego-dystonic the patient's dependency needs were than the therapist's. The patient thus consistently rejected the therapist's interpretations in that area, not due to resistance but because they were wrong.

Furthermore, when therapists' parents fail to acknowledge their uniqueness, therapists may unconsciously distance themselves from patients during twinship transferences and overemphasize their differences due to therapists' own individuative strivings. Thus, rather than understanding or interpreting the patient's expressions regarding their commonalities, the therapist may emphatically disagree with the patient. For example, one patient (knowing that the therapist had a cat) commented on their similar love for animals. The therapist unconsciously responded that he didn't love animals, just cats—and mostly his own cat.

Response to the Narcissistic Patient's Negative Transference or Projections: Becoming the Patient's Bad Object or Bad Self

As narcissistic patients have been commonly described as being used by their parents as selfobjects (Kohut 1971, Miller 1981), they frequently perceive the therapist as impinging and requiring them to behave in a particular manner in order to gain the therapist's acceptance. For example, one patient told the therapist that he thought that the therapist did not want him to talk at all so that the therapist could just use him as an audience, as his mother had done and continued to do. When the therapist asked this patient questions, he perceived the therapist as attempting to control the session, forcing him to reveal private things that he didn't want to tell the therapist.

Furthermore, a number of authors (Glickauf-Hughes and Mehlman 1995, McClure and McClendon 1989, Miller 1981) have noticed the prevalence of narcissistic abuse by parents of psychotherapists (e.g., making the child responsible for the parent's needs), not meeting the child's normal needs (e.g., for mirroring, dependency, empathy, and self-confirmation), and criticizing the child's true self. Glickauf-Hughes and Mehlman (1995) believe that this often leads to what Fairbairn (1952) refers to as an excessively harsh antilibidinal ego (i.e., severe contempt for one's own needs).

Schultz and Glickauf-Hughes (1995) have noted that therapists with this family history frequently respond to the narcissistic patient's accusations of impingement with feelings of shame that interfere with the therapist's ability to understand and interpret the transference. For example, when one narcissistic patient told the therapist that he interrupted her too much, the therapist became subtly defensive and rejecting rather than asking the patient if this was a familiar feeling for her.

In addition to having a particular type of negative transference with the therapist, preneurotic narcissistic patients at times use defense mechanisms such as devaluation, projection, and occasionally projective identification as mechanisms for coping with ego-dystonic aspects of the self. Working with patients who at times use primitive defenses can be painful for the therapist (Segal 1981). Feelings of self-blame, impotence, worthlessness, and frustration may result from treating patients who are at times contemptuous of the therapist (Finell 1987).

A common defense used by narcissistic borderlines that is occasionally used in times of intense distress by preneurotic narcissistic patients is projective identification. In this process, the patient attributes an unwanted aspect of the self to the therapist and then induces the therapist to behave in a manner that is congruent with the projection (Ogden 1979). For narcissistic patients, ego-dystonic self experiences commonly include depression, guilt (Kernberg 1975), fear, dependency, and shame (Glickauf-Hughes 1994). When therapists are unaware of their countertransference in these types of situations, they are likely to feel shame and rage toward the patient and consequently withdraw from or subtly criticize him or her rather than observe and process the patient's ego-dystonic feeling.

For example, one therapist found herself thinking about terminating with a narcissistic patient (who projected her feelings of shame and worthlessness on the therapist) and observed herself asking prematurely confrontive questions. Once the therapist observed and analyzed her reactions to the patient, she used her response in a more conscious and helpful manner (e.g., "I've noticed that you've been frequently contemptuous toward me lately which makes me feel a bit insecure at times. Is this what happened between you and your mother?").

In conclusion, rather extreme countertransference responses are common in treating narcissistic patients. Four types of narcissistic transference and related countertransference responses are explored: (1) the mirroring transference, (2) the idealizing transference, (3) the twinship transference, and (4) the patient's negative transference and projective identifications. Subjective as well as objective countertransference responses are more prevalent and intense with narcissistic patients when therapists have had narcissistic parents (and thus have unresolved narcissistic issues) themselves. A number of authors believe that this is frequently the case.

EXTENDED CASE EXAMPLE

Karen is a bright, attractive, 22-year-old single Caucasian woman. She is the only child of two attorneys who labeled her their "little star" from infancy on, focusing intently on their pride in her intelligence and precocious achievements.

Karen entered therapy complaining of intense feelings of low self-esteem and loneliness (which she felt ashamed of feeling) due to moving to a new city for law school. She had attended a small undergraduate school where she was considered one of the best students in the program and an important person on campus. In her new graduate program she was only one of many bright students and she acutely felt the loss of her former status. This experience was exacerbated by her tendency to be subtly contemptuous when she felt unappreciated and insecure, which further alienated her professors. Furthermore, while Karen had been very successful as an undergraduate student in political science, after feeling initially elated because of a particularly successful endeavor, she was unable to derive sustained satisfaction in her studies.

Karen's childhood home was featured in *Architectural Digest.* The living room (with plastic covers on the furniture) was never used because her parents wanted to keep it looking perfect for company. She initially described her father as a very successful, talented genius in his field, who was respected by everyone. She eventually began to also express her experience of him as demanding, self-absorbed, and requiring her to be an admiring audience to him.

Karen reported feeling adored by her mother who treated her like a little doll. Unfortunately, this meant that her mother always wanted her to look pretty. The main argument that she remembered having with her mother was over her getting a dog (which her mother eventually let her have as long as it was a small, attractive one) and getting dirty when playing with the dog.

Karen also talked about feeling a bit abandoned by her mother when she was 8 years old and her mother returned to work. Her mother loved and thrived on her work as an attorney, worked 60 hours a week, and was significantly more preoccupied and less attentive to Karen. Karen talked to her favorite aunt about how much she missed her mother, stating that she thought that her mother did not like being a mother. Her aunt said that her mother happily gave up her career to have Karen because she really wanted a child. Her aunt also told her that her mother genuinely wanted her and was a loving, attentive, more flexible mother when she was a baby and small child (e.g., she even let Karen make big messes finger painting even though she was a neat freak). However, her aunt said that she could understand why Karen might think that as her mother was extremely ambitious.

Karen remembers being frequently told by her mother that she was the smartest little girl in the world and could be anything that she wanted to be. She was acutely aware, however, of both parents' desires for her to follow in their footsteps by becoming an attorney. She feared that they would withdraw their emotional and financial support if she dropped out of law school. The therapist asked her if this had happened before. Karen said that when she wanted to go to a YWCA camp (where she knew people) instead of the fashionable camp where her parents wanted her to go, they refused to pay for the YWCA camp, saying that she "would not meet the right kind of people there." Karen said that her parents always thought they knew what was best for her and discounted her opinion. In fact, they still did.

In Karen's peer relations, she presented an initial facade of a pseudo-humble, attentive, appreciative good listener, which attracted other people to her. However, she eventually leaked her underlying feelings of grandiosity, contempt, and self-absorption. For example, she said that friends invited her to eat at "some Mexican dive," but she didn't like to "eat that shit." She also had a tendency not to answer her phone calls (or even listen to her phone messages), as she found people's needs to be overwhelming.

Furthermore, while desperately wanting a man who she admired to love and "adore" her, none of the men she dated were handsome, bright, or accomplished enough to qualify as a partner. While she enjoyed the early infatuation stage of relationships, she quickly became disillusioned and uninterested and moved on to another relationship. However, unlike borderline narcissists, she was aware that this was a problem that interfered with her genuine interest in having a relationship.

Although Karen was aware at some level that she was a very attractive woman, she was very critical of her appearance and considered having cosmetic surgery. Her father frequently encouraged Karen's mother to undergo a number of such surgeries. However, Karen never pursued this process as she had a "weird feeling" about it and thought that her father had somehow coerced her mother into too many surgeries in order to "keep her looking like she was a young woman."

Karen's underlying problem could be described as an inability to express her true self, with consequent problems in developing intimate relationships with others and a lack of resilient self-esteem. She often felt depleted and yearned for an attachment to someone that she could idealize and identify with. She had conflictual feelings about getting admiration from her parents and the world by getting cosmetic surgery and completing law school versus pursuing her own ambitions and generally being herself.

In the beginning of treatment, Karen tended to alternately idealize the therapist and to keep herself distant from him. She was afraid that if she allowed herself to be close to him, she would want him to be her partner and be filled with feelings of longing and unrequited love that she greatly feared. As the therapist processed the transferential origins of these feelings, Karen became aware of both her feelings of longing and rejection by her preoccupied but admired father and the yearning that she felt for her mother when she initially went back to work and somewhat abandoned Karen.

The therapist and Karen frequently discussed her ambivalence about being an attorney and her lack of awareness of what she really wanted to do with her life. The therapist attentively focused on Karen's affects as he discussed various things in her life and mirrored them back to her. He particularly noticed her enthusiasm for her part time job at the zoo. Karen talked about how much she always loved animals and her fights with her mother about getting a dog.

Although Karen generally idealized the therapist, she did occasionally get angry or contemptuous with him. She did not, however, ever become rageful or lose all of her positive feelings toward him at those times. Furthermore, when she was contemptuous toward the therapist and her contempt was processed, she was able to identify underlying feelings of shame.

Additionally, although she became somewhat insecure and angry when the therapist went on vacations or didn't meet her needs, she never regressed during those times. Rather, she felt a little embarrassed about needing him so much and tended to want to make him unimportant to her. Often, when the therapist returned from vacation, Karen described how well she was doing. Once, she even suggested terminating treatment because she was feeling so good. The therapist noted this pattern and Karen's fear of becoming too attached to him. They again discussed her fears in this area.

Throughout therapy, Karen became more aware of how she used contempt to cover up her insecurities and was more able to deal with them directly. For example, on one occasion Karen told the therapist that she discussed her therapy with her friends who were psychology students. She said that compared to her friends' professors, the therapist did not do very deep work with Karen. The therapist commented (from an observing perspective) that what Karen said sounded contemptuous. He asked Karen if there was something that she was experiencing that made Karen behave contemptuously toward the therapist. Karen thought about it and said, "I guess when you ask me what I'm feeling and I don't know, I feel like a bad patient and that makes me feel ashamed. When my friends told me about all the techniques that they are learning to help people become aware of their feelings, I thought, 'Well, maybe he's not a good therapist.' That made me feel better." The therapist then explored Karen's shame and discussed the connection between having feelings and feeling ashamed.

She eventually began to see the therapist in a more realistic, less idealized way, and realized that she felt closer to him now than she had in the beginning when she had him "up on a pedestal." She also developed more realistic standards for herself and became more accepting and respectful of her needs. This prompted her to make life decisions based on intrinsic interests that she did not sabotage or need to excel in to gain satisfaction. She decided to drop out of law school and work toward owning her own pet store. While she wished her parents would support her decision and give her a loan to open a store, she realized that she could do this on her own if she needed to. Finally, as she began to believe that feeling good was as important as looking good, she begin to date men who she enjoyed and treated her well, rather than men who were merely successful and attractive.

9

Object Relations Therapy of the Masochistic Personality: Creating a Secure Attachment

Due, in part, to criticism from feminist scholars (Caplan 1984), masochism has, over time, become one of the most controversial of diagnostic categories. Franklin (1987) especially expressed concern that this category could become a "dangerous weapon that could frequently be misused to blame women, particularly abused women, for societal failures" (p. 53). Partly because of this concern, the term *masochism* was replaced in the *DSM-III-R* (APA 1987) by the less inflammatory term *self-defeating personality* in the appendix as a personality disorder to be further studied. Despite the fact that the *DSM III-R* described the prevalence of this disorder as frequent, the decision was made to exclude it entirely from the *DSM-IV* (APA 1994).

We believe that eliminating this disorder does not eliminate the problem of relational masochism, frequently discussed in the popular psychology literature (Glickauf-Hughes and Wells 1995b). Rather, efforts need to be made to clarify this important concept and reduce its gender-biased and pejorative associations.

Futhermore, we believe that there are a number of holes in the criticisms against usage of the term. For example, studies demonstrate that only a very small proportion of abused women have a masochistic personality (Grinspoon 1990). Furthermore, while the term *masochistic* is pejorative and may be used more frequently to diagnose women, a stronger case could be made about the term *histrionic*. We believe that American culture reinforces attachment behaviors more in females and separation and aggression more in males. Consequently, most of the disorders on the overattached continuum are likely to have a greater proportion of women and most of the disorders on the underattached continuum and the aggressive/sadistic continuum (e.g., paranoid, sadistic, antisocial) are likely to have a greater proportion of men. Thus, many diagnostic categories would be eliminated on the basis of sex bias.

The masochistic personality as described in this chapter does not refer to the deriving of pleasure from pain and is not seen as a primarily sexual phenomenon as was originally described in the psychoanalytic literature (Freud 1905, 1919, 1924, Krafft-Ebing 1895). Rather, it is seen as a self-defeating way of loving and individuating. Pathological ways of loving include loving an object who primarily gives nonlove in return; associating suffering with loving; rationalizing and denying the object's sadistic or aggressive tendencies; and choosing critical and rejecting, but admired, love objects, and attempting to win their approval through pleasing and self-sacrifice. A pathological way of individuating involves anticipating that the object will force one to submit and to resist compliance through passive-aggressive behavior, overdetermined caregiving, and subtle provocation of power struggles.

DESCRIPTIVE CLINICAL OVERVIEW

Self-Sacrificing

The masochistic personality is commonly seen as self-sacrificing, self-depreciating, and overtly pleasing and compliant (Glickauf-Hughes and Wells 1991a,b). Masochists have a reputation for being giving and compromising, to the point of being martyrs. They often give up their own needs in order to meet the needs of others (e.g., one patient would make sure that everyone else in the family had enough good clothes but herself). Masochists also frequently go out of the way to help others, even when it is not in their best interest to do so. For example, one patient stayed on the phone with a troubled friend (who frequently had crises in her life) for five hours on the night before she had a difficult and important examination at school the next day. Another masochistic patient worked 70 hours a week so that she became indispensable to her boss. She was, however, chronically exhausted.

Desire to Surrender to an Idealized Object

Gordon (1990) believes that individuals have a universal desire to surrender to or worship something beyond one's own being. Thus, an aspect of the masochistic individual's self-sacrificial behavior is related to what Ghent (1983) believes is the masochist's deep desire to surrender to an object. By surrendering, he means letting down one's defensive barriers and facades and expressing one's true self. For example, one patient had repetitive dreams about meeting a man, seeing love in his eyes, letting her guard down, and feeling love and acceptance wash over her.

Ghent believes that the "ultimate direction [of surrender] is the discovery of one's identity" (p. 111). Thus, what the masochist truly longs for is to be reached and known in a safe environment and see the other and be seen by the other correctly. However, as the parents of masochists were critical of the child's true self and suppressed his or her expression of will, masochists believe that expressing their true self will be unacceptable to others. While they wish to be loved and accepted and to surrender themselves to an idealized object, they fear that if they are vulnerable with others, they will inevitably be hurt, humiliated, impinged upon, or abandoned (Glickauf-Hughes, in press, b).

Problems with Basic Trust

Despite their wish to do so, masochists have great difficulty trusting others and voluntarily giving up control. Due to their history of being chronically rejected, verbally abused, and controlled, while they long for a relationship with another and "act" trusting, they are inwardly frightened, angry, and ambivalent (Glickauf-Hughes and Wells 1991a,b, 1995b). Thus, while masochists want love, they view love as a potential Trojan horse, and are afraid of being tricked or gullible.

For example, one patient became seriously involved with a man who, after six months of dating, seemed to be a responsible, reliable, and loving individual. She still, however, believed that he would break her heart, as her last three relationships began on a very positive note and ended badly. Thus, when her partner,who had a solid work history, began his own business, she feared that he was really a "fraud" who she would eventually have to financially support as she did in her previous relationships. Nonetheless, she spent every available moment with him.

Compliance-Defiance Conflicts

Due to their competing need to surrender to the object, their fear of trusting the object, and their suppressed individuative strivings, masochistic individuals frequently become involved in compliance-defiance conflicts in which their desire for surrender inevitably becomes transformed into covert rebellion or gets perverted into submission or unwilling compliance (Ghent 1983). Ghent believes that one may surrender in the presence of another but not to another.

One masochistic patient had a critical, dominating father who insisted that she do everything his way. In contrast, her mother was more submissive. This patient desperately wanted her father's love, approval, and acceptance. However, to get it she had to give up her own position (e.g., ideas, values, and perceptions) and submit to or accept his. Her style of relating to him was to approach him with a problem and ask for his help. He was always willing to help her but did so on his terms (i.e., she had to follow his advice completely, listen to his criticism of her for not managing the situation competently and collude with him that he was right about what she should do and about his negative evaluation of her). He usually gave her a large sum of money as a means of helping her solve her problem.

Having a relationship with her father was very important to this patient (particularly one where she could depend on a good father). She thus remained engaged in this pattern with him, submitting herself to his criticism and dominance (while feeling that her integrity was being compromised). Her neurotic resolution to this conflict was to appear to be submitting while sabotaging something that her father wanted to do.

For example, she needed a new car and asked her father for help. He agreed to buy her a car but insisted that he select it for her (as she "didn't have good common sense about those things"). She resentfully agreed to his conditions but had an accident while driving the new car home from the dealership. Thus, while this patient behaved in a polite, submissive manner, she was extraordinarily willful and unable to express it directly. Furthermore, she recapitulated the pattern that she had established with her father in most of her relationships.

Kainer (1977) thus noted that "nowhere is phenomena of will more perplexing than with masochist[s]" who behave at times as though they are the "seemingly most will-less of people" (pp. 21–22). However, as illustrated in the last example, while on the surface masochists may seem submissive, we concur with Johnson (1985) that due to the parents' attempt to break the child's will, masochists are really very willful individuals. However, as their parents had the power and they have a competing need for maintaining the relationship, their will is generally expressed indirectly.

This leads to a pattern of overt compliance and covert defiance. Thus, while masochists frequently solicit help and advice from others, they tend to be help-rejecting complainers. While they may appear to be doing something considerate for someone (e.g., buying a present for a friend that they feel frustrated with), they buy something that the friend does not really like and is not returnable. Under many circumstances, they behave in ways that make it appear that they cannot (rather than will not) follow the rules (e.g., fail to get their report in on time because they were ill).

This confusing pattern may be due, in part, to Cooper and Fischer's (1981) observation that the masochist's underlying aim is not really a reunion with a loving parent but the fantasized control over a cruel one. For example, one masochistic patient's husband was rejecting toward her to the point of living in a completely separate apartment in their home. She did not, however, want to leave him and did not become interested in other men. Rather, what she most wanted, and persisted in attempting to accomplish, was getting him to change. When he finally entered treatment and began to change, she became angry toward him and uncertain whether or not she wanted to remain married to him.

Difficulty Receiving from Others

Masochists have great difficulty receiving from others and experiencing pleasure. As a result of being raised in a predominantly hostile and unpredictable family, they often become rigidly defended. As a result, when the previous patient described very painful interactions with her husband, she often smiled and was out of touch with her feelings. This patient eventually described herself as having a "big wall" up that she did not know how to let down.

Paradoxically, painful experiences are often more intense than pleasurable ones and are thus more likely to get past the masochist's defensive barriers (Glickauf-Hughes and Wells 1991a,b, 1995b). For example, one patient who was receiving a massage from her partner, told him not to be afraid to really dig his fingers in because if it did not hurt, she could not feel it. The same pattern was manifested by a very guarded masochistic patient with obsessional tendencies who remained preoccupied with a very confrontational ex-lover with whom he ended a relationship. While he experienced her as critical and frequently felt hurt by her, in contrast to the more placid women that he had dated, he said that she really got under his skin.

Painful experiences can thus overcome the masochist's defensive barriers, resulting, at times, in their feeling more alive and less isolated. One masochistic group member, for example, expressed a desire for other group members to confront him and make him cry so that at least he would feel something. The patient whose husband lived in a separate apartment was not able to be vulnerable or authentic with the members of her therapy group until the entire group confronted her about feeling distant from her. This confrontation both hurt her and penetrated her "wall," allowing her to feel more involved with the other people in the group.

In addition to a general difficulty receiving from other people and allowing themselves to have pleasurable experiences, masochists also have great difficulty receiving compliments from other people (Glickauf-Hughes and Wells 1995b). When other people praise them, they frequently discount their positive opinions and interpret the other person's motives as either politeness or a manipulation. For example, one patient's best friend told her how beautiful she thought she was. She discounted the compliment by saying, "She was just trying to cheer me up." Masochistic patients also frequently discount the positive regard they receive from the therapist (i.e., they believe that the therapist is paid to "act" that way or is a nice person who likes everyone). Masochists often have the experience of one critical parent and one parent that "tries" to be supportive of the child. The latter is accurately experienced by the patient as periodically giving him or her a pep talk to boost the patient's self-confidence, rather than an authentic expression of the parent's respect and appreciation of the child.

Overdetermined Caregiving

In addition to having great difficulty allowing themselves to be cared for by others, masochists also tend to be overdetermined caregivers (Gear et al. 1983, Glickauf-Hughes and Wells 1991a,b, 1995b). For example, one psychiatrist with masochistic proclivities had so many patients calling her in a crisis that she said her professional license number should be 911. One patient committed herself to helping other people with things with such regularity that she often became ill from exhaustion. Another patient who was the single mother of four children would volunteer to be in charge of the church bazaar during the one week that her children were at camp. She rarely got babysitters for her children as she thought that it was best for the children to be with her. However, she frequently volunteered to care for other people's children.

One reason that masochists spend so much time and energy helping other people is that they are highly relational individuals. More than anything else, they wish to love and be loved in a secure relationship (Glickauf-Hughes 1996, Glickauf-Hughes and Wells 1995b, Wells and Glickauf-Hughes 1993). However, due to their extreme distrust of others, they arrive at a neurotic solution to this need-fear dilemma by connecting with others in a friendly but dominant and nonvulnerable manner. This is reinforced by masochists' belief that they are loved for what they do, rather than for who they are. Giving becomes a way of earning the affection of others. However, vicarious gratification of dependency needs does not really work on a permanent basis and typically leaves the masochist feeling exhausted and unfulfilled.

The Depressive Position

Furthermore, as relational individuals, masochists typically assume what Klein (1935) describes as the depressive (rather than the paranoid) position (Glickauf-Hughes 1996). As their main goal is to maintain the relationship with the love object, defenses are utilized that facilitate their denial of the objects' sadistic behavior including internalization of the object's aggression. Masochists thus have a great propensity to use introjection. When in conflict with significant others, they generally internalize (i.e., self-attribute) relational difficulties (Glickauf-Hughes and Wells 1991a,b, 1995b). For example, one patient said that if she had been more sensitive and understanding toward her husband when he came home from work, he might not have been so verbally abusive toward her during the evening. Self-attribution of relational problems also gives the masochist the illusion of greater control (i.e., if the problem is their fault, if they behave differently, they may be able to repair the relationship).

Fear of Loss and Separation

Masochists' propensity to internalize relational problems is related to what Avery (1977) describes as their great fear of loss and separation. As previously described, while masochism was originally thought of as pleasure derived from pain, submission, and cruelty, we believe that rather than being pain seeking that masochists are pain avoiding. Masochists believe that the loss of the significant other would cause them such enormous pain that their egos would be totally overwhelmed (Glickauf-Hughes and Wells 1991a,b). Masochists thus believe that the pain in the relationship is far less than and thus preferable to the devastating pain of ending it. They think that if they left their partners their egos would be completely overwhelmed (Glickauf-Hughes and Wells 1991a,b, 1995b). This belief is related to masochist's anxious attachments to others; their structural deficits (described later in this chapter), which make it difficult for them to internally soothe themselves; and their confusion between affective memories and current reality.

One highly defended masochistic patient came into treatment seeking help for her very depressed husband. The therapist told the patient that she would be unable to help the patient to treat her husband; however, she would be glad to hear the patient's concerns and provide her with a referral for her husband.

The patient described her husband as a wonderful, loving, brilliant person, and she said that they had a good relationship until the last year because he was going through a midlife crisis. He was now very withdrawn, hopeless, and occasionally suicidal. She described her life as otherwise very satisfying and described her family of origin as very close and loving (e.g., every summer, the whole family and their spouses and children spent a month together at the beach).

Two months later, she called the therapist for another appointment. She said that her husband refused to see a therapist and she reported that his behavior was deteriorating (e.g., he was more withdrawn, drinking excessively, and verbally abusive). She said that she needed help coping with this situation.

As therapy progressed, she described his extremely hostile and rejecting behavior toward her and began to acknowledge that it had always been there. It had just become so much worse over the last few years that she was no longer able to deny or rationalize it. He was unwilling to either get psychotherapy or stop drinking (which was now up to about seven drinks per night). She was ready to leave for her monthly vacation with her family. She decided that if he did not change his position about getting help with his emotional problems and his alcoholism, she was going to ask him to leave. Unlike most masochistic patients, she seemed sad, but not emotionally overwhelmed by this prospect. Her major concerns were economic and the impact of a separation on her daughter.

When she returned home, the situation had further deteriorated (e.g., her husband frequently did not get dressed, stayed in bed all day, and made covert and hostile suicidal threats). Nonetheless, she did not ask him to leave. He now began to behave abusively toward her daughter at times (she asserted, however, that it was not very often). As she described all the reasons why she did not think that she should separate from him (e.g., she would not be able to get a job, it would be harmful to her daughter not to have her father around, she was being unfair to her husband and a bad wife by not sticking it out for better and for worse), the therapist confronted her about the validity of her reasons for remaining in the marriage under the current conditions.

The therapist shared with the patient, that most of the patients that she had treated who were in similar situations had difficulty separating from their partners because they were very frightened by the prospect of loss and separation. The therapist asked the patient if she felt that way. The patient started to cry and said that she did, but that she did not understand why she felt this way.

The therapist said that this was also confusing to her, as the patient discussed her family in such idyllic terms. The therapist noted that the patient initially spoke about her husband in a similar manner. She wondered if it might be possible that there were some problems in the patient's own family (as there had been with her husband) that were too painful to acknowledge.

The patient began to talk about how she had always felt like an outsider in her family (e.g., everyone but the patient had blond hair and blue eyes). She felt particularly left out by her three sisters, who were similar to each other and to her father temperamentally (i.e., high strung, intelligent, artistic types). She was more similar to her mother (i.e., practical, steady) and became her mother's helper in the family. She said that her father preferred her sisters and did not really know how to relate to her. The therapist asked if she felt like she was her mother's favorite child as they were more similar. The patient began to cry and said that her mother preferred her youngest and oldest sisters as they needed her more.

She said that she had not thought about it for a long time, but she remembered that when she was in the third grade, she told her parents that she would like to spend a year living with her aunt and uncle in Missouri and they said that she could. She said that she really loved her aunt and uncle. The therapist asked her if she felt loved by them and part of their family. The patient teared up and said that she did. She described how painful it was to come home at the end of the year and to once again feel like an outsider. She said that when she first met her husband and they had a child, it was the first time that she felt like she had a family that she belonged in and would not have to leave. Thus, when

she thought about breaking up the family now, the sense of loss and isolation she felt was devastating.

Anxious Attachment

Anxious attachment to significant others is a hallmark characteristic of the
masochistic patient. Ainsworth and colleagues (1969) define anxious attachment as the persistent and urgent clinging to of a preferred person without
there being any obvious conditions to account for it. Individuals who are
anxiously attached have "no confidence that their attachment figures will
be accessible and responsive to them when they want them to be" and have
thus "adopted a strategy of remaining in close proximity to them in order,
so far as possible, for them to be available" (Bowlby 1973, p. 213).

Bowlby believes that anxious attachment is caused by experiences with
others that shake an individual's confidence in the dependability of the
attachment figure. He believes that while early losses and separation affect
this phenomenon, the most influential precipitants are parental threats to
abandon the child.

The phenomenon of anxious attachment is expressed very differently in
masochistic patients than in hysteroid patients. While the latter group deals
with their internal feelings by intrusive, demanding, impinging behavior with
the attachment object, masochists have less tendency to act out this feeling.
Rather, when important objects behave toward them in a manner that could
be interpreted as critical or rejecting (e.g., a friend not calling for a week
when previously contact had been more frequent), they become insecure
and believe that they have done something wrong. When they do act out
this feeling, it is done using projection and reaction formation. In this last
example of the friend not calling, the masochist may call the friend to offer
support as she knows that the friend must be feeling lonely because her
daughter is spending the week with her ex-husband.

Masochistic Defenses

The example of the patient with the depressed husband provides a vivid
illustration of the most common defenses used by masochistic patients. As
previously noted, as masochistic patients' main motivation is maintaining
their love relationships, the defense mechanisms they tend to utilize are
those that foster this objective. They include internalization, denial, rationalization, and masochistic splitting, all of which were used by the patient
who came into treatment because her husband was depressed.

Internalization

As mentioned in the preceding section, masochists tend to internalize relational problems. They thus tend to use mechanisms such as introjection and identification to accomplish this goal. In introjection, the external object becomes an internal object. For example, a masochistic patient introjected his critical and rejecting wife. In his mind, the patient heard her tell him that it was he, not she, who was a mean person or she would not stay out all night.

Thus, it was easier for the patient who felt isolated from her family to internalize her family's view that she did not belong because she was somehow different rather than to consider that her family was critical, rejecting, and self-centered. It was less threatening for her to internalize her husband's view that she was the source of his misery than to admit that he was chronically rejecting, cruel to her, and very impaired.

Denial

Masochists frequently grew up in families with a preponderance of abuse and neglect that was too difficult for them to acknowledge. To cope with this painful reality, they often denied that it was happening. One masochistic patient whose mother was alcoholic, borderline, and verbally abusive, and whose father was manic, narcissistic, and physically abusive, thought that she grew up in a "good family" until she brought her best friend home from college and listened to her friend's observations.

In their adult lives, masochists continue to utilize this defense and consequently often make poor relational choices as they ignore early warning signs (e.g., "I've left every man that I've ever been with, but you're so different from them"). Furthermore, they continue to use denial after they have become attached to another person who hurts or disappoints them so that they will not have to leave the relationship.

Denial was a prominent defense used by the patient whose family and husband were critical and rejecting. At some level, the patient believed that if she did not see the problem, it was not there and then she did not have to feel bad. She said that as a small child, when someone threw something at her, she would put her hand in front of her eyes rather than get out of the way.

However, denial does not work forever. Thus, when this patient's husband's behavior escalated to the point where it was difficult to deny, she began to rationalize his behavior (e.g., he was going through a mid-life crisis).

Rationalization

As illustrated in the last case, when interpersonal situations become so intolerable (e.g., child or spouse abuse) that they are too hard to deny without losing a grip on reality, the defense of denial needs to be buttressed. A useful and common defense for accomplishing this goal is rationalization, the motivated, pseudological explanation of an event. Particularly as an adult, when it is impossible to deny a love object's grossly disturbing behavior (e.g., physical abuse, repeated infidelities, severe alcoholism), the masochist attempts to explain the bad behavior in such a way that the love object remains good. One masochistic patient said that her husband drank so much because he was unemployed. Another patient said that his wife had affairs because she was turning 40 and was feeling insecure about her appearance. A third patient explained her husband's physical and verbal abuse by saying that she had not been sensitive enough to him that night when she knew he had a very difficult day at work.

Masochistic Splitting

In masochistic splitting (Meyers 1988), while the object is not denigrated, the self is perceived as "all bad," protecting the viability of the relationship. Thus, in the previous case example, the patient saw her husband as a kind, loving person and herself as extremely deficient. This process is further described below (see Structural Goals).

PRESENTING PROBLEMS IN PSYCHOTHERAPY

Masochistic patients present in psychotherapy with some common complaints. These include having a difficult relationship with a love object that they feel unable to leave, depression, low self-esteem, and feeling exhausted from excessive caregiving to others.

Difficulty Leaving a Painful Relationship

Difficulty leaving a painful love relationship is the most common presenting problem in therapy for masochistic patients and has been addressed profusely in the popular psychology literature. When masochists enter treatment, they often describe relationships with others (usually love relationships but occasionally relationships with friends and mentors) that began euphorically and currently cause them great pain, including depression and lowered self-esteem. One patient described her mentor as the most brilliant person she ever met. She said that he initially took great interest in her and told her that he thought she was very gifted. Eventually, he became critical and contemptuous of her. The patient however, felt unable to stop working with him as she felt dependent on him for both security and self-esteem. This pattern becomes intensified in romantic relationships.

Depression

While depression is common in many character disorders, it is particularly intense for masochists (Friedman 1991). This may be caused by a biological propensity for depression, repeated trauma, a proclivity for masochists to turn their anger against themselves, lack of adequate ability to self-soothe, and a tendency for parents of masochists to accept the child's sad feelings more than his or her anger. Whatever the cause, the symptom is a frequent one and may be in the form of major depression as well as dysthymia.

Low Self-Esteem

Horner (1979) believes that due to inadequate soothing and empathy from parental figures, masochists (and other character styles with preneurotic ego organizations) are prone to experiencing dependency, depression, and low self-esteem. Masochists' self-esteem is further injured by their propensity to internalize the negative evaluation of the love objects that they choose (who often have narcissistic, paranoid, and sadistic proclivities). Masochists frequently present in treatment with extreme feelings of insecurity about their physical appearance or intellect, overall feelings of inadequacy, or a general sense of being a "bad person who no one will ever love."

Depletion from Excessive Caregiving

As previously described, masochists tend to be caregivers who feel loved when needed and get their own needs met vicariously by meeting the needs of others. Masochists have difficulty getting their own needs met directly and setting limits on what they will and won't do for other people. This frequently leads to a sense of exhaustion or burnout. The therapist metaphorically told one masochistic patient that she drove her car too often without getting tuneups, changing the oil, or even making sure the gas tank was full.

Thus, many masochistic patients present in treatment complaining about feeling overworked, overwhelmed, exhausted, and unable to say no to other people. One finds many masochistic patients in the helping professions or in positions of great responsibility (e.g., administrative assistant). In these positions they often become indispensable to other people so that these people will never abandon them.

One patient entered treatment complaining about feeling exhausted. She recently had a blood test to determine if she was anemic (she was not). So many people called her for help that she needed call waiting. This ensured that she would not miss any of their calls (and let them down). The telephone was kept by her bed (with the ringer on) so that people would be able to reach her during the night in case they needed her.

She was a high school teacher. She frequently stayed after school to help students with their work and listen to their problems. In addition to working full time, she took care of all household responsibilities (including picking up her husband's laundry). She told the therapist that she read an article about chronic fatigue syndrome and wondered if she had it.

ETIOLOGY

The masochistic personality emerges as a result of specific developmental arrests and from chronic treatment of a particular nature by objects throughout their lives. The stage of developmental arrest primarily associated with the masochistic personality is the later stage of separation-individuation referred to by Mahler and colleagues (1975) as "on the way to object constancy" (Glickauf-Hughes and Wells 1995b, Horner 1979, Johnson 1985).

Symbiosis

Unlike the remote parents of schizoid patients, parents of masochistic patients were generally more engaged and loving with the child. Often these parents were more adequate at parenting an infant than a toddler or older child. Sometimes, the child also had loving, dependable alternative caregivers (e.g., grandparents or older siblings). In such cases, the child made an attachment to the alternative caregiver, which accounts in part for their less severe pathology given their history of chronic abuse and neglect.

However, while parents of masochists have some capacity to bond with infants, they are generally quite impaired. Many are alcoholic, depressed, or have narcissistic or borderline traits. Due to their self-preoccupation, their response to the child is generally based on their own (rather than the child's) need state. As nurturing is unattuned and erratic, the child's dependency needs are not adequately met.

Children who have had an undependable symbiosis often develop an anxious attachment to their parents and tend to remain chronically needy. Eventually they learn to deny their needs or use other defenses to avoid feeling painfully deprived. As adults masochistic patients manifest a number of oral traits (e.g., excessive dependencies, trust issues, difficulty receiving).

Separation-Individuation

While the separation-individuation process is fostered to a greater extent in masochists than in borderline and narcissistic personality disorders, it is not completed (Johnson 1985). In contrast to borderlines and narcissists, the parents of masochists permit greater separation-individuation during the practicing and rapprochement periods. The child is thus allowed more self expression than is the narcissist and greater separateness than the borderline (e.g., the child is not punished through parental rejection for engaging in independent activities and relationships with other people). However, while masochists attach and to some extent separate and individuate, their parents do not provide them with adequate selfobject or auxiliary ego functions with which to identify (e.g., mirroring, empathy, soothing, admiring). Furthermore, due to their ambivalent feelings toward their loving and abusive parents, they refuse to identify with the realistic functions that the parents do provide. They thus remain excessively dependent on others for providing them with these functions. This process will be elaborated on later in this chapter.

Masochists thus establish a reasonably cohesive sense of self and primarily have self-other differentiation. However, their self-concept and self-esteem have been severely damaged by relationships with early objects such as parents, siblings, and peers, in which they were criticized, shamed, and verbally abused.

General Childhood Experiences

Scapegoating and Parental Projection

Both in early development and throughout their lives, individuals who later develop masochistic character traits have prototypical types of relationship experiences with significant objects. One of the important features of this relational constellation is the scapegoating of the child. Parents of masochists tend to have severe problems with self-esteem that they defend against avidly. One method for doing this is projecting ego dystonic aspects of themselves onto the child. For example, one very repressed mother told her daughter that she was "born wild." Whatever it is that the parent cannot tolerate about him- or herself is attributed to the child (e.g., aggression, sexuality, insecurity). One counterphobic "macho" father continually berated his son for being a "sissy" whenever the child manifested any sign of anxiety. As projection of the parents' "bad" self experiences is crucial for maintaining the parents' narcissistic equilibrium, the scapegoated child is frequently the older child (Glickauf-Hughes, in press, b).

Children may also be scapegoated, and thus more prone to develop masochistic pathology, when they resemble a grandparent who has in some way hurt the parent. In this situation, a parent who is not conscious of this dynamic has a proclivity to develop a negative transference reaction to the child (Glickauf-Hughes, in press, b). For example, one masochistic patient's mother was adored by her father but rejected by her mother (who preferred males to females). The patient's mother thus strongly favored the patient's brothers over her.

Bromberg (1955) observed that mothers of masochists frequently accuse their children of being ungrateful or inconsiderate in an unconscious attempt to lower the child's self esteem. Furthermore, mothers of masochists are frequently very ambivalent about their child. For example, a mother who feels guilty that she may not truly love the child occasionally overindulges the child to relieve her feelings of guilt.

Internalization of Parental Criticism

Whatever the cause of scapegoating, it leaves the masochist with the underlying sense that he or she is somehow bad or deficient. Thus, the conclusion that the child draws is that the lack of the mother's love is due to the child's "badness."

Intermittent Loving Behavior Interspersed with Abusive Behavior

Part of the puzzle of masochism is that despite the frequent blaming, abuse, and rejection of the child, the child develops a strong bond with the parent (rather than an antisocial or withdrawn interpersonal stance). We believe that the child's intense attachment is because, interspersed with their abusive and rejecting behavior, parents of masochists are sometimes loving toward the child (Glickauf-Hughes and Wells 1991, 1995b). As is found in animal research (Azrin and Holz 1966), intermittent reinforcement interspersed with punishment is a powerful reinforcer of behavior, especially attachment behavior (Fisher 1955).

Positive Regard of Parents Toward a Sibling

Masochists develop strong attachments to parental objects and come to believe that the parent's love is available but withheld because the child is bad (Glickauf-Hughes and Wells 1991). This is exacerbated when the parent favors and is thus less critical toward another sibling. For example, one patient's mother frequently told her that she was "as stubborn as a mule." Her mother favored her younger brother who was more compliant. The mother liked the patient's brother better than her and frequently told the patient that she should be more like her brother.

However, while scapegoating in the family takes a toll on the masochist's self-esteem, it ironically enables these children to achieve greater differentiation and individuation than the favored sibling (who is often more impaired as an adult). By being unable to please their parents or gain their approval because they are female, have gender-nonconforming behavior, are not intelligent enough, or are too beautiful and arouse envy, scapegoated children are more able to be their true selves than their idealized siblings, as there is no reinforcement for being otherwise.

Parental Overcontrol and Immaturity

In addition to being blaming toward the child, parents of masochists also tend to be very controlling. However, in contrast to parents of obsessive-compulsives, who are more rigid and overcontained, parents of masochists tend to be highly un-self-disciplined, themselves. Parents of masochists tend to be like big children with power who have double standards for the child and for themselves (Glickauf-Hughes and Wells 1991, 1995b). They may force the child to eat nutritious, but unappealing food when they have poor eating habits. They punish the child for swearing when they themselves swear (e.g., one masochistic patient's father told him that he "didn't want to hear one more goddamn swear word out of his goddamn mouth").

Furthermore, parents of masochists tend to become engaged in enormous power struggles with the child. These struggles are reenactments of parents' struggles with their own parents. Rather than calmly setting limits based on rational principles with the child, parents of masochists merely want to win the struggle (as they were unable to do with their own parents). Needless to say, parents of masochists have great difficulty setting appropriate limits and containing their own (let alone their child's) overwhelming affects.

Squelching the Child's Will

One patient's father, in a rage, told her that if she said one more word, he would hit her with a belt. This type of attempt to squelch the child's will often produces extreme willfulness in the child. In this case, the patient responded to the father by saying, "One more word." When asked about this incident, the patient said, "I didn't care if he killed me. I wouldn't let him take my spirit away." On some occasions, the parent and the child engage in battles of the will that last for hours. One patient recalled that when she was 7 years old her father told her that she could not leave the kitchen table until she finished her dinner. She fell asleep at the kitchen table.

However, as parents have more power and punish the child's defiant behavior, the child often learns to rebel covertly (e.g., forgetting, whining, not listening, changing the subject). For example, one patient said that she drove her mother crazy. Her mother insisted that she wear types of clothes that the patient disliked. She overtly complied with her mother, and thanked her for the pretty clothes. However, as the patient was very clumsy, she often had accidents as she walked home from school and arrived home with her new dress muddy or torn. As an adolescent, she stopped at her friend's house on the way to school to change into her friend's clothes.

Parentification

In addition to being scapegoated and overly controlled, masochists are frequently parentified (i.e., inappropriately used to fulfill adult roles and obligations) in their families (Glickauf-Hughes and Wells 1995b, Jones and Wells 1996). Bromberg (1955) believes that "because the child represents a parental figure in the mother's unconscious, the demands upon him for all types of gratification seem appropriate to her or at least so tempting that she succumbs to them" (p. 802). For example, one masochistic patient began to care for her baby sister when she herself was only 2 years old. Another patient at age 5 helped her mother clean up her father's vomit when he was drunk. A third patient remembers that when she was 7 years old and her brother was 5, they talked her mother out of a suicide attempt during a serious depression. In this fashion, masochists learn to get their dependency needs met vicariously and come to believe that they are most "loved" when they are needed.

Identification with a Masochistic Parent

This pattern is often reinforced by the masochistic patient's identification with a masochistic parent. In this parent, they have thus found a strong role model for overextending oneself, suffering (including tolerating abuse), and not getting one's own needs met. One patient remembered that at every Friday night dinner, her mother would cook a steak and give everyone a tender piece, leaving the fatty tail end for herself. Her mother always wore old clothes and rarely bought herself a new dress. Although this patient was financially successful, she had great difficulty spending money on herself. She also felt compelled to eat leftover food for dinner, even when it was something that she didn't want.

Triangulating the Child into Marital Problems

Masochistic patients frequently report that their unhappily married parents told the children that they remained married for the children's sake. Through such behavior, they frequently induce guilt in the child and teach the child how to induce guilt in others. Furthermore, the masochist often becomes caught in the crossfire of accusations between parents (Panken 1983) in which both parents tell the child that he or she is exactly like the other parent in some manner that they devalue. For example, one patient's father told her that she was "too sensitive, just like your mother." Her mother told the patient that she and her father "were like two peas in a pod, aggressive and self-centered." Neither parent voiced their complaints directly to the other parent.

DEVELOPMENTAL FAILURE

The primary stage of developmental arrest for the masochist is thought to be at what Mahler and colleagues (1975) refer to as the stage of "on the way to object constancy." By this stage, the child has made a symbiotic attachment to others, learned to separate self from other, has primarily integrated good and bad aspects of objects, and formed a cohesive sense of self. However, due to the child's highly ambivalent feelings toward inconsistent and predominantly hostile parents who were unable to adequately empathize with and soothe the child, the child does not experience the parent as a good-enough model with whom to complete the identification process and thus fails to internalize the parents' realistic selfobject functions. This truncation of the identification process interferes with the completion of the child's internalizations of critical soothing and esteem functions and thus impedes the child from having fully developed object constancy.

A second, less obvious, developmental failure is that due to parents' frequent abuse of the child in many forms, the masochist never really develops a sense of basic trust in other people. However, as parents were intermittently loving and abusive, and the child denied, rationalized, and internalized the parent's abusive behavior, masochists often believe that they *do* trust people. The manifestations of the masochistic patient's mistrust are more subtle than in borderline level characters, in characters on the aggressive/sadistic continuum, and even in preneurotic narcissists.

STRUCTURAL ISSUES

This developmental arrest leads to several structural deficits in the masochist. First, the parent of the masochist was unable to provide consistent selfobject functions. Second, due to the child's ambivalence toward his or her parents, he or she failed to identify with the realistic functions that the parents did provide. Having not received and internalized sufficient empathy, containment, and soothing, object constancy is incomplete. Masochists are thus often unable to soothe themselves, which leaves them vulnerable to dependency, insecurity, and depression (Horner 1979). This partially accounts for the masochist's difficulty with separation and loss as they remain dependent on external objects for gaining a sense of security that they are unable to provide for themselves.

Having received insufficient acceptance, validation, encouragement, and empathy (and not internalizing that which was provided), the masochist also suffers from unstable self-esteem and remains vulnerable to narcissistic injury. They are prone to doing what Meyers (1988) refers to as "masochistic splitting," or experiencing the self as all bad while overidealizing the significant other. The masochist thus lacks complete integration in his or her self structure.

RESULTING INTERPERSONAL STANCE

As a result of receiving intermittent reinforcement and punishment, being hurt when vulnerable and rewarded when behaving maturely, and loving but not trusting the object, masochists alternate between anxious attachments to primary objects and counterdependent behavior. Due to having been parentified at times, their counterdependence is often expressed through the excessive caregiving of others. Masochists are thus needed rather than needy. For example, one masochistic patient, in between crises with her partner, had a veritable army of people who depended on her. What she didn't have was much conflict-free leisure time with others. Relationships for masochists often resemble twelve-step programs (i.e., they are problem centered).

Furthermore, due to masochistic patients' wish to depend on, please, love, and be loved by others, and their fear of having their will squelched as it was in their family, masochists frequently find themselves in compliance-defiance conflicts. In these conflicts, they alternately submit to the wishes of the other and subtly rebel against them. For example, while one patient frequently asked the therapist for help, she rejected it when it was given. Another patient, a third-grade teacher, alternated between winning teaching awards at her school and being chastised by her principal for not making lesson plans.

Some items on the Psychodynamic Character Inventory (PCI-2) (Chapter 12) that illustrate the masochistic patient's relational stance are: (1) "I don't feel like I can count on other people to be reliable and dependable." (2) "Despite my initial intentions in a relationship, I usually find myself taking care of the other person." (3) "When I ask for advice, I usually experience a conflict between wanting to please people (i.e., taking their advice) and wanting to be my own person."

TREATMENT OF THE MASOCHISTIC PERSONALITY

In treating the masochistic personality, the following objectives are suggested. In understanding the patient's mental template and unresolved developmental issues, the therapist helps the patient to articulate and resolve the following interpersonal and structural goals.

Interpersonal Goals

Resolve Anxious Attachment

Through interpretation of the transference, therapists can help masochistic patients become aware of this particular relational stance. In essence, although masochists become intensely attached to primary objects, they don't trust them to be reliable and dependable. For example, the therapist told one masochistic patient, "While you feel very attached to me, it is difficult for you to be vulnerable with me. It would be important for us to understand this dilemma." The patient began to talk about her relationship with her mother, who would invite the patient to depend on her and then disappoint the patient for one reason or another. She described one occasion when she was ill during her second year of college and her mother suggested that the patient drive home for the weekend to let her mother take care of her. The patient did. However, when the patient arrived home, her mother was drunk, so the patient took care of herself.

While masochistic patients have great difficulty trusting other people, they often have a perception of themselves as being open, romantic, and trusting. This self-perception is ego-syntonic and accurate in regard to their conscious needs and fantasies. Masochists have a great wish for an ideal object. Due to the intensity of this wish and a certain degree of naïveté, masochists frequently make poor relationship choices. They have a tendency to choose objects who seem too good to be true rather than good enough, which is a strong factor in masochistic patients' reenactment of having experiences with Trojan horses.

The ideal object of the masochist often has regressive narcissistic proclivities. He or she thus intuitively knows what the masochist desires and is initially willing to live out the masochist's fantasy in order to seduce him or her. The ideal object then becomes resentful toward the masochist for loving his or her false self and begins to withdraw from or hurt the masochist. Masochists tend to ignore early warning signs about potential relationship problems with the ideal object. When these problems begin to be a pattern, masochists deny and rationalize the object's aggressive or rejecting behavior.

In a type of repetition compulsion, masochists tend to be attracted to interesting and seductive rather than dependable people. They become very attached to and are eventually hurt by them. This reinforces their underlying object relations template (i.e., people cannot be trusted). For example, Amy Irving's character in the film *Crossing Delancey* was far more interested in the extremely seductive, but narcissistic, Russian author than she was in the mature, kind, and loving merchant who genuinely cared about her.

Thus, an important aspect of helping masochistic patients resolve their patterns of making anxious attachments to objects involves clarifying their object relations template that determines which people they do and, more importantly, do not choose to have primary relationships with. Due to the sense of yearning established in the symbiotic stage, masochists have difficulty distinguishing between the experiences of love and longing. Like

Romeo and Juliet, in their romantic relationship masochists feel an impossible separation from an idealized object (Smirnoff 1969). In other words, they perceive an insurmountable obstacle which inevitably prevents them from getting their deepest relationship yearnings satisfied. The object, being seen as just out of reach, becomes even more desirable. What masochists have previously experienced from others, and thus have come to expect from objects, is rather intense, intermittent relatedness or excitement punctuated by feelings of frustration, loss, and emotional abandonment.

They thus often find stable, predictable people to be somewhat boring. They like the challenge of transforming a bad, but potentially good, object. When they actually do find a kind partner who returns their feelings, they are somewhat suspicious that there must be something wrong with this person if the person actually likes them. Like Groucho Marx, they don't want to be a member of a club that would have them. Thus, frequently when someone begins to return their affection, they become less interested in him or her.

Resolution of anxious attachment thus involves clarifying and interpreting the patient's relationship patterns. For example, it was important to help the patient in the previous example to understand how in her last three relationships she eventually became extremely disappointed as she chose men who were too good to be true, rather than merely good enough, and that her current partner was not like that (e.g., rather than send her two dozen roses, he helped her to plant her garden). Thus, while she was not infatuated with him, she was also less likely to become disappointed with him as she had been with previous partners.

Additionally, helping masochistic patients to resolve anxious attachments often involves providing the patient with a new, more dependable experience and helping the patient to work through his or her resistance to becoming attached to a predictable object. For example, one masochistic patient who was developing a satisfying relationship with a kind woman felt that he did not really deserve her. It was important to help this patient understand and resolve this feeling so that he did not unconsciously sabotage the relationship. This process is further addressed below (see Corrective Interpersonal Experience).

An important component of treatment involves reparation of the patient's self-esteem. Without accomplishing this latter goal, masochistic patients tend to continue to idealize people that don't like them and devalue people who do. The goal of helping masochistic patients develop more resilient self-esteem is addressed below (see Structural Goals).

Help Patients to Master Loss and Separation

Related to enabling masochistic patients to form more secure attachments is helping them to master the experiences of separation and loss. Attaching to and separating from other people are important interpersonal processes. However, as in treating impaired self-esteem, this treatment goal also involves helping patients make structural changes as well as interpersonal ones. In particular, for masochists to be able to experience the loss of significant others without becoming traumatized by this experience, they must be helped to have fully developed object constancy. One aspect of this process that is addressed in Structural Goals is helping patients internalize the therapist's selfobject functions.

Another aspect of helping masochistic patients master the process of loss and separation is teaching them to learn to tolerate separation anxiety both in the therapeutic and in other important relationships. One way of accomplishing this goal is by helping them to internalize the therapist as a comforting object.

Manageable separations are important so that the time between sessions, especially when patients are very depressed, are optimally frustrating (i.e., are not more than patients can handle while at the same time providing enough of an opportunity for mastery). We have found that twice-weekly appointments seem to provide an optimal balance for most masochistic patients who are experiencing considerable depression.

It is also important for therapists to be responsive to the masochistic patient's needs for both closeness and distance. Therapists are advised to help patients know that they can contact the therapist or someone else when they feel overwhelmed. This is particularly important when masochistic patients begin to set limits with their partners, who may initially respond to the patient's limits with verbal abuse or punishing withdrawal. Masochists must come to realize that there is not only one "mother." Rather, the world is rich with people to depend on and that, unlike their childhoods, loneliness does not have to be an interminable experience.

Masochistic patients also need the therapist's help in learning to discriminate between memory and reality. This is not an easy task, as masochists tend to relive rather than to remember painful aspects of their childhoods. For example, one high-functioning, treatable masochistic patient had the strongly held belief that no one (including the therapist) could help her. This belief was an emotional memory from childhood when her immature parents were truly not able to help her, but that realization was too painful to acknowledge. This belief thus became part of her object relations template and determined how she interpreted her current reality. An important component of mastering separation and loss is thus being able to distinguish between early losses and current losses and to be aware that losses as a child are less manageable than losses experienced as an adult who has greater internal and external resources.

Masochistic patients' mastery of the experience of separation and loss is facilitated by therapists' allowing these patients to be in control of rapprochement experiences as much as is possible in the therapeutic relationship. Thus, if masochistic patients express the need to have more frequent appointments or wish to call the therapist between sessions, therapists are advised to respond to patients' requests if they are able to do so. Unlike hysteroid patients, masochists do not overuse this privilege. Observing their own behavior in this area can have the effect of demonstrating to them that they are not bottomless pits of needs.

It is also important to support the patient moving away from or separating from the therapist. Thus, should masochistic patients request a leave of absence, even though therapy is not complete, the therapist is advised to support the patient's request rather than interpreting it as a resistance. By allowing the patient to move toward and away from the therapist, the therapist serves as a secure base from which the patient can explore the world. This therapeutic stance facilitates the patient's mastery of the rapprochement subphase of separation-individuation. If an interpretation seems necessary, therapists can respond to patients' requests by saying, "It seems important for you to try things out on your own for a while, but to know, at the same time, that I'll be here if you need me."

While the masochist's parents did not punish or intentionally withdraw from the child for separations during rapprochement, they were often unavailable for refueling the child when the child returned to the parent (due to their self-involvement and their own need for refueling). Thus, the experience of having someone who is available to return to is very reparative for masochistic patients.

It is helpful to teach patients how to master separation and loss in their primary relationships. For example, one masochistic patient's relationship was nearing the end of the courtship phase (during which both partners wanted to be together all the time). When her partner began to separate and individuate from the initial symbiotic attachment (i.e., to need more space), she became hurt and frightened about being abandoned by him. The therapist helped her to better understand the origins of her fear and suggested to the patient that if she and her partner could learn to separate in a more related manner (e.g., making their partings warm, briefly calling one another if possible on their evenings apart, giving each other small mementos before separate vacations), it might help her to feel more secure with him.

Help Patients Learn Appropriate Expression of Anger, Assertion, and Setting of Limits

Masochists have great difficulty with the appropriate expression of anger. As they were both spuriously abused by parents and punished for their own expressions of anger, masochists have come to regard anger as something dangerous. Most often they are not even aware of feeling angry. Usually they express these feelings indirectly. When they are continually pushed past their limits, masochists can lose their temper—and tend to do so with the wrong person (i.e., someone who reacts by losing his or her temper even more).

It is thus important to help masochists learn to express their anger appropriately as a viable alternative to tolerating abuse or leaving a difficult relationship (Glickauf-Hughes and Wells 1995b). It is advised, however, that this goal be addressed later in treatment, after the patient has more resilient self-esteem, is more able to self-soothe, and especially after the patient has to some extent mastered separation anxiety. Since masochistic patients are frequently involved with significant others who respond to their anger as their parents did (i.e., with escalated abuse or punishing withdrawal), it is important that masochists have developed greater ego strength before attempting this task.

In general, the therapist is advised to begin the process of helping masochistic patients to become appropriately assertive by simply helping these patients recognize their angry feelings. The therapist can watch for the masochist's indirect expressions of anger (e.g., passive-aggressive behavior) as an indicator of the patient's feelings. For example, one masochistic patient tended to complain about things that bothered her in the therapist's office (e.g., uncomfortable couch, tissues that were not soft enough) when she was angry at the therapist about something else, but not consciously aware of it. The therapist used these instances to alert the patient to her feelings of anger and helped her identify the real source of them (i.e., feeling rejected by the therapist).

After patients have learned to identify their angry feelings, they can be taught how to express them directly in a way that serves them. In general, we have found that many masochistic patients were often "truthsayers" in their families and may consequently alternate between being inauthentic (out of concern for the other's feelings or fear of retaliation) and bluntly stating what they believe is the truth. Like the child in "The Emperor's New Clothes," masochistic patients have a tendency to be honest with people when it is not in their best interest to do so. For example, one masochistic patient told a narcissistic boss that the boss was criticizing the patient because the boss was competitive with the patient. While this was probably true, the patient's comment only made his boss behave more critically toward him.

It is thus important to help masochistic patients learn to accurately assess the sensitivity (i.e., proclivity toward easily experiencing narcissistic injury) of their audience and to use that information in phrasing their confrontations. A useful guideline to teach them is that one can say almost anything to another person if he or she says it with a reasonable amount of tact. This can initially be modeled in the therapeutic relationship. For example, in the example of the patient who complained about the therapist's office, the therapist told the patient that it seemed as though she became upset about things like tissues when she was feeling frustrated with other things. The patient can also be helped to apply this principle to interpersonal difficulties with significant others in their life. For example, this same patient observed that she began to whine with her husband when she was feeling rejected by (and therefore angry at) him, which resulted in his rejecting her again.

Expression of aggression with sensitivity and tact is also a helpful guideline for masochists in determining limits to set on other people's expression of anger with them.

One masochistic patient learned to tell his wife, who viciously berated his character when she was angry at him, that he was willing to hear her complaints about him if they were expressed in a respectful manner. However, if she began to personally attack him in the process, he would not listen. From that point on, whenever she attacked or became rageful toward him, he told her, "This isn't feeling good right now. Let's talk later when we're both calmer." He then left the room.

After ten years of trying unsuccessfully to make his wife treat him better by doing thoughtful things for her, fighting with her, and placating her, he finally had an impact on her. However, he was not able to do this until his sense of object constancy was more firmly established. He previously felt terrified that she would leave him if he set limits with her. Now, he felt more confident that if she did leave him, he would be able to tolerate it. He was not, however, willing to tolerate her verbally abusive behavior toward him any longer.

Another important area in which masochists need to learn to set limits is in the amount of caregiving that they do with others. Being a caregiver is so ego-syntonic and such a large part of the masochist's identity that learning to say no to people is a difficult therapeutic objective to achieve. These patients believe that they are loved for what they do for others rather then for who they are, and they fear that people will not love them if they begin to set limits with them.

Another resistance to masochistic patients setting limits on their caregiving of others is that giving is an important way that masochists get their own dependency needs met vicariously. For example, when one masochistic patient was feeling needy and his wife was feeling irritable, he became solicitous and affectionate toward her, which was what he needed but not what she needed. It is important to help masochists learn that they can be loved for themselves and get their own needs met directly before they are able to risk setting limits with other people. A prerequisite for this is learning to trust other people.

Helping Patients Learn to Trust and Genuinely Depend on Others

Masochists are in a predicament. They are highly relational individuals, and their most compelling motive is to love and be loved. However, after a lifetime of object relationships where they were in some way "seduced" and then hurt, it is difficult for them to trust other people. They are thus in the dilemma of having important needs without any apparently safe way to meet them. The choices that they make to resolve this need-fear dilemma (e.g., counterdependency, overdetermined caregiving, help-rejecting but attention-seeking behavior, choosing bad objects who overcome their defenses and once again hurt them) are largely unsuccessful. Important objectives in treating masochistic patients are helping them (1) clarify and interpret this need-fear dilemma, (2) understand the transferential aspects of their perceptions and the repetition-compulsion involved in their object choices, and (3) experience a corrective relationship with the therapist in which they learn to trust the therapist and eventually dependable, significant others.

For example, when a masochistic patient met a new man, fell in love, and then felt terrified of getting hurt, the therapist reviewed the occurrence of this pattern with both the patient's mother and ex-husband. The therapist taught her how to evaluate whether she was having a transference reaction or if, indeed, this man was not "good enough." When he remained dependable and reliable, she found herself feeling less in love with him and craving romance and excitement with someone else. The therapist helped her to understand, rather than act out, this impulse.

Structural Goals

Resolve Masochistic Splitting

Meyers (1988) describes masochistic splitting as a somewhat primitive, and thus more simplified, intrapsychic split in which "the bad is split off from the object image which is maintained as all good while the self becomes all bad in a kind of 'identification with the aggressor.' Aggression and punishment is then directed at the bad self" (p. 181). This type of splitting provides some type of aggressive expression while preserving the relationship with the loved and needed security object. Needless to say, while this defense can serve a protective function in regard to relationships, it has disastrous consequences in regard to the patient's self, especially his or her self-esteem.

Masochistic splitting can be resolved in much the same manner as traditional splitting is resolved with borderline patients (i.e., via confrontation). For example, with one patient, the therapist recalled that last week she seemed to be feeling very positive about herself and that since she had a conflict with her partner, it seemed as though her self-perception completely changed. As in confrontation of the traditional all-good/all-bad splitting defense, this type of intervention needs to be made by the therapist on repeated occasions.

Internalizing Genuine, Reality-Based Self-Soothing and Self-Esteem

As described by Kohut (1977), the patient's self can be repaired by the therapist's providing the patient with the selfobject functions that he or she did not sufficiently receive from his or her parents. Additionally, as masochistic patients felt such ambivalence toward their parents, they were unable to internalize the realistic functions that their parents did provide, as they did not want to identify with or be like their parents in any way. Thus, by therapists' providing masochistic patients with empathy, soothing, perspective, mirroring, and esteem, the patients are given a developmental second chance to develop healthy self-esteem.

For example, one patient was very angry at himself for displeasing his critical but admired employer. The therapist shared with the patient her observations about how important receiving his boss's approval was to him and empathized with how hurt he was when he did not get it. She further observed that it seemed like it was easier for him to feel disappointed in himself for falling short in his performance (even when he realistically did not) than disappointed with his boss for being so critical. In this case, the therapist provided the patient with perspective, empathy, and esteem.

Another patient procrastinated on taking the state bar examination because she was afraid that she would fail. The therapist empathized with her fear of failure and discussed how her parents' chronic criticism contributed to her self-doubt and fear of being shamed. When the patient eventually decided to take the exam, the therapist told her, "It took a great deal of courage for you to make that decision." When she was studying for the exam and felt insecure and depleted, the therapist empathized with and soothed her. The therapist also normalized the patient's feelings by sharing her own anxiety before taking the psychology licensing examination. She told the patient that during that period, she took three baths a day in a whirlpool tub, frequently worked out, and ate a lot of Godiva chocolates. Therapist and patient both laughed. Finally, when the patient came to her therapy session and told the therapist that she passed the exam, the therapist mirrored her pride and exuberance. In this case, the therapist provided the patient with soothing, mirroring, empathy, and esteem.

As Kohut describes, in providing patients with such functions with reasonable regularity, the patient begins to internalize these functions on the occasions in which the therapist fails him or her. In one of the previous examples, the patient returned from having felt misunderstood by the therapist the previous week and set the therapist straight: "You were wrong when you said that you thought that I was hurt with my boss. I was really angry."

It is important to note when patients are not internalizing the selfobject functions that the therapist is providing. This can be observed and processed over time or in reference to a particular interchange. In the former case, the therapist observes to patients that they, for example, appear to be as self-critical as when they first came to treatment. The therapist might then suggest that the two of them explore what is occurring between the patient and the therapist that is preventing the patient from accepting the therapist's help. In one case, the patient described what we previously referred to as the Trojan horse phenomenon (i.e., the fear of allowing oneself to accept something good as it might be a trick). The therapist then discussed the transferential meaning of this belief with the patient.

In another example, during a particular session, the therapist noticed that when she empathized or soothed the patient, the patient did not respond. The therapist pointed out this process and the patient expressed her concern that the therapist was not really being authentic. Again, the transferential origins of this concern were explored.

Increase Observing Ego Functions

Helping masochistic patients learn to observe themselves and their relationships is an important aspect of treatment. A more complete description of techniques that facilitate this process is given by Glickauf-Hughes and colleagues (1996). Some approaches that they discuss for accomplishing this goal are containing the patient's affects, serving as an auxiliary ego, enabling catharsis followed by clarification, and using distancing techniques.

Containing Patients' Affects

Bion (1962, 1967, 1970) discusses the importance of mothers' bearing their children's affective expressions in order to help the child feel secure. Through such a process, children learn to tolerate their own emotions without suppressing them or inappropriately acting them out. During this process, projective processes are not damaging to mothers and introjective processes increase ego functioning in children (Glickauf-Hughes and Cummings 1995).

For example, a 2-year-old child may experience the mother (rather than him- or herself) as bad when the child is feeling excessive frustration. The child may express this by attempting to hit the mother. During the process of containing the child's feelings, the mother holds the child so that neither she nor the child is hurt by the child's aggressive acting out. She does not personalize the child's behavior or retaliate against the child. After the child's behavior is under control, she may attempt to calm the child.

Glickauf-Hughes and colleagues (1966) suggest that containing a patient's affects (particularly his or her projective identifications) is an important component of increasing patients' observing ego functions. One important aspect of this process is the therapist's not behaving reactively when the patient feels overwhelmed. Thus, a therapist listening to a masochistic patient repeatedly discuss an abusive relationship may find him- or herself internalizing the patient's feelings of anger and helplessness. When therapists are unaware of this projective identification occurring, they are prone to act out their frustration and helplessness with the patient (e.g., too quickly resorting to problem solving so the patient will stop complaining) or compensate by listening endlessly to reports of abuse inflicted on the patient. In both cases, the patient's anger is not contained.

In the first case, the therapist retaliates, and in the second case, the therapist allows him- or herself to go beyond his or her own limits of tolerating frustration (e.g., listening to the patient complain for too long without making an intervention).

A means of containing the patient's anger is for the therapist to first soothe him- or herself and then calmly discuss with the patient the therapist's observations of his or her own feelings as they speak. The therapist then asks the patient if that might be what the patient is feeling. The patient is then encouraged to directly express (rather than project) these feelings. During this process, the therapist empathizes with the patient's feelings and clarifies the patient's experience. The therapist may also wish to inquire about the patient's experience with anger in his or her own family.

When the therapist effectively contains the patient's anger, neither the therapist nor the patient is hurt by the patient's projective identification of anger. Furthermore, the patient is provided with an opportunity to identify with the therapist and internalize this process. The process of containment in the treatment of masochistic patients is subtle. Because borderline patients are more likely to act out (and what is acted out is rage rather than anger), therapists generally need to actually set limits on aggressive or self-destructive behavior.

The process of containment is particularly important with masochistic patients, as parents of masochists are prone to emotional lability and thus have difficulty containing their child's emotions. Instead, the child is often used to contain the parent's emotions. Having never had a nonreactive object respond to their emotional expressions, masochistic patients have difficulty gaining a sense of objectivity about their feelings (e.g., that just because they feel bad doesn't mean that they are bad or that their life is bad).

Catharsis Followed by Clarification

Another important means of increasing observing ego functions in masochistic patients is to follow cathartic expression with clarification. Glickauf-Hughes and colleagues (1996) believe that such an approach helps patients master affective expression, enabling them to feel less overwhelmed by their feelings. For example, after a patient cried while expressing how hurt she felt in her relationship and how insecure she felt about herself, her therapist helped the patient to understand exactly what hurt her. Encouraging catharsis and following it with clarification helps the masochistic patient learn to regress in the service of the ego.

Improve Reality Testing

Observing ego functions in masochistic patients are also improved by strengthening the patient's reality testing. In the last example, the therapist helped the patient observe that when her partner became irritable, she experienced a lowering of her own self-esteem. It is generally necessary, however, to first empathize with how the masochistic patient does perceive reality before helping him or her to see it more clearly.

Conscious Use of Dissociation

Scialli (1982) discusses the relationship between the process of dissociation and the ability to self-observe. While masochistic patients, particularly those with histories of severe abuse, have often used dissociation as a defense, they use it more automatically and as a means of escape rather than as a deliberate means of observing themselves and others more clearly. Conscious projection of the problem, use of stories and metaphors, and use of humor can all help patients get a clearer perspective on their problems (Glickauf-Hughes et al. 1996). For example, when one patient was criticizing herself for how she thought she had mishandled something at work, the therapist asked her what she would think if her best friend did the same thing under similar circumstances.

CORRECTIVE INTERPERSONAL EXPERIENCE

Varying aspects of a corrective interpersonal experience for masochistic patients have been suggested under relational and structural treatment goals. This section synthesizes the nature of this experience and discusses its overall relationship to the treatment of masochistic issues. We believe that what best allows masochistic patients to resolve developmental failures, such as lack of trust and anxious attachment, and to complete self and object constancy is the therapist's being dependable, empathic, and containing, having authentic positive regard for the patient, acknowledging therapeutic errors, supporting autonomy, and alternating between supporting the patient and confronting self-defeating behaviors (Glickauf-Hughes and Wells 1995b).

Being Constant and Nonreactive

It has been our experience in supervising therapists who are treating masochistic patients, as well as in observing our own treatment failures, that errors in not providing this type of corrective experience are common and subtle. While therapists, particularly analytic therapists who value neutrality, may not directly say to their masochistic patients "leave that horrible man/woman" or "quit that job and find a better one," they often imply such opinions through persistent questions such as "Why do you stay with someone who you think treats you so badly?" Reactivity in the therapist is also manifest by how quickly he or she begins to intervene in some fashion, rather than patiently listening to or containing the patient's affects before offering interpretions or suggestions.

In such situations, it is helpful for therapists not to overidentify with patients and thus lose their self-observing capacity. Thus, when patients' feelings dramatically fluctuate, therapists' feelings should not follow, otherwise therapists might be prompted to do something to rid themselves of the overwhelming feeling that may or may not be in the patient's best interest. This is particularly important in the process of masochistic triangulation, which is described below in the section on countertransference issues.

Genuinely Liking the Patient

Puppies and babies seem to instinctively do cute things to gain their parents' attention or to get their needs met (e.g., get the steak bone). Masochistic patients, however, were often not reinforced by parents for acting adorable and charming. Often they were the scapegoat in the family. Due to their parents' intense self-absorption, they often did not even notice the child under normal conditions. Rather, masochistic patients often gained their parents' attention by having problems. However, their parents were not effective or patient at helping the child with problems. As masochists only got attention for having a problem but do not anticipate getting genuine help with their problems, they tend to express their need for attention or help through behaviors, such as whining, that do not endear one to others, including the therapist.

Learning to endear oneself to others is an important component of change for the masochist. Patients are more than their whining. Glickauf-Hughes and Wells (1995b) believe that the therapist's genuine feeling of affinity for the masochistic patient is essential to treatment. Being able to empathize with the reasons behind the patient's self-defeating behaviors, appreciating the nonmasochistic traits in the patient, and not overly identifying with the patient's pain or having excessive subjective countertransference (e.g., being a severely masochistic parent) is very important. While ethical therapists are not directly critical, it is our experience that such attitudes are often manifested in the therapist's nonverbal behavior (e.g., tone of voice, facial expression) or even through reaction-formed excessively supportive responses. Thus, providing an authentic connection in which the therapist is reliable, dependable, and nonreactive can help increase basic trust and a secure attachment to others. Once ambivalence is more resolved and basic trust is solidified, patients can more fully identify with the therapist and complete the internalization of empathy and soothing. This process allows the patient to achieve fully established object constancy.

At this stage, the masochistic patient's self-defeating behaviors and projective identifications can begin to be confronted without endangering the therapeutic alliance or causing undue narcissistic injury to the patient. For example, at a later stage in treatment, the therapist noticed that she was having fantasies about hitting the patient while the patient was speaking. Recalling a videotape of Harold Searles (in which Searles expressed a similar fantasy to his patient), the therapist shared this fantasy with her patient (in a nonangry manner) and invited the patient to explore what it might mean to her. The patient determined that in fact she was angry at the therapist for something that the therapist had done the week before, but felt afraid to tell her about this. Thus, processing the patient's projective identifications later in treatment after trust has been established can be very useful. However, a similar intervention used earlier in treatment or with a patient that one does not like would most likely harm the patient.

DIFFERENTIAL DIAGNOSIS

In treating masochistic patients, it is important, as it is with all patients, to first arrive at an accurate diagnosis. The masochistic or self-defeating personality disorder has been particularly criticized for overlapping with other diagnostic categories. Other character disorders that share common symptomatology or developmental origins include the narcissistic personality disorder, hysteroid personality disorder, obsessive-compulsive personality disorder, and hysterical personality disorder (Glickauf-Hughes and Wells 1991b). These are the disorders that are thus most likely to be confused with the masochistic personality.

Masochistic Versus Narcissistic Personality Disorder

Masochistic and narcissistic traits have frequently been described in the literature as co-occurring in the same individual (Cooper 1988, Stolorow

1975). Similarities may result from (1) the occurrence of narcissistic pathology in parents of both types of patient or (2) their both being at the preneurotic level of ego development and object relations. Both masochists and narcissists tend to be quite perfectionistic and struggle with non-resilient self-esteem.

However, the motivation behind the perfectionistic strivings of masochists and narcissists differs. Masochists wish to be perfect in order to be loved. The form that they choose is being perfectly good, helpful, or competent. In contrast, narcissists wish to be perfect in order to be admired by others. They thus strive to be perfectly brilliant, beautiful, or talented.

Rather than striving to be admired, masochists attempt to repair their self-esteem through establishing idealizing transferences. This can make differential diagnosis between masochists and regressive narcissists very difficult. Both need the object to be ideal in order increase their self-esteem. However, masochists are more likely to ignore the ideal object's imperfections, whereas regressive narcissists quickly begin to criticize the object and seek a new object to idealize.

In general, masochists deny, rationalize, and internalize the object's problems to preserve a relationship. In contrast, narcissists are more likely to sacrifice a relationship with the object to maintain their self-esteem. When in conflict with the object, preneurotic narcissists are thus more likely to utilize defenses such as projection, devaluation, and, occasionally, projective identification and splitting. When masochists and narcissists have altercations, the masochist is the first to apologize and the narcissist rarely apologizes (Glickauf-Hughes 1994).

Masochists often have a somewhat higher level of ego development and object relations functioning than preneurotic narcissists. Masochists generally have a suppressed but cohesive self, whereas preneurotic narcissists' grandiose self often overlies a less developed and somewhat fragmented self. Borderline narcissists' grandiosity compensates for an impoverished self that lacks cohesion.

In relationships, masochists predominantly relate to others as whole objects, have a greater capacity for love and fewer problems making commitments. In contrast, even preneurotic narcissists frequently relate to others as selfobjects or a set of functions that they need rather than as a whole person whom they love. For these patients, commiting oneself to an object relationship elicits fears of engulfment. In therapy, masochists are more likely than narcissists to notice if something is wrong with the therapist (e.g., noticing a strained expression on the therapist's face) and express genuine concern. The narcissist, particularly the progressive narcissist, is more likely to notice if the therapist does something wrong (e.g., makes an empathic failure, is impinging).

Masochistic Versus Obsessive-Compulsive Personality

Due to their proclivities to struggle with autonomy issues, masochistic and obsessive-compulsive patients can have a similar presentation. Both are prone to being willful, subtly defiant, and passive-aggressive in their behavior. However, as masochists have more relational motivations, they are generally not argumentative and nitpicking. In an altercation, it is more important to masochists to resolve the tension with the object, whereas it is far more important to the obsessive to be "right."

Furthermore, masochists are typically structured at the preneurotic level of development. Due to incomplete object constancy, masochistic patients are more prone to experience separation anxiety, anxious attachment, dependency, and depression than obsessive patients. While neurotic obsessive patients are more difficult to relate to, they are more securely attached to others and genuinely self-sufficient (rather than counterdependent) than masochistic patients. Furthermore, while obsessives struggle with feelings of insecurity, they have more resilient self-esteem than masochistic patients.

Masochistic Versus Hysteroid-Borderline Patients

Masochistic patients who are experiencing a crisis can appear similar in their clinical presentation to hysteroid-borderline patients. Both struggle with intense emotions, depression, fear of separation and loss, and problems with self-soothing. However, hysteroids are organized at the borderline level of ego organization. Their general level of functioning in both work and relationships is thus much less stable than that of masochistic patients.

Hysteroid patients thus have less developed object constancy, more frequently utilize primitive defenses, and have a less cohesive sense of self. In contrast, masochists are organized at the preneurotic level of ego organization. Thus, while they often have anxious attachments to objects and problems with self-esteem regulation, they are able to relate to others more as whole objects and have more resilient self-esteem and better ego functioning. A useful way to differentiate early in treatment between the two character types is by assessing the ease with which the therapist is able to form an alliance with the patient's reality ego.

Furthermore, masochists tend to be counterdependent, caregiving, and unable to set limits, whereas hysteroids are more dependent, demanding, and have difficulty tolerating limits. Thus, masochists have great difficulty calling the therapist, whereas the hysteroid has great difficulty not calling the therapist. Hysteroid patients are frequently angry and even rageful, whereas for masochistic patients, anger is ego-dystonic.

Masochistic Versus Hysterical Patients

Masochistic patients are most often confused with hysterical patients. In fact, we first began to study masochistic character organization with patients that we initially (and inaccurately) had diagnosed as hysterical. However, we became aware of some significant differences between these groups of patients.

Both neurotic hysterical and preneurotic masochistic patients are highly relational and form a good alliance with the therapist early in treatment. This differs from both the hysteroid borderlines and sadomasochistic borderlines who are more prone to develop negative therapeutic reactions. The primary motive of masochistic and hysterical patients is to love and be loved. Both frequently seek the approval of significant objects. However, masochists are more willful than hysterics and have more of a competing need to be autonomous. They thus have a greater propensity to behave in a stubborn, passive-aggressive manner than hysterical patients who are more consciously manipulative.

Furthermore, masochists are usually structured at the preneurotic level of ego development, whereas hysterics are structured at the neurotic level. Thus, hysterical patients typically have more fully developed object constancy, more resilient self-esteem, and better ego functions.

While hysterical patients appear to be more dependent (as dependency is ego-syntonic) than masochistic patients who have a more counterdependent style, masochists are more anxiously attached to objects and have more problems with separation and loss and greater difficulty in self-soothing. Despite surface appearances, masochistic patients are more dependent than they present and hysterical patients are more capable. In difficult relationships, masochists have a much harder time leaving their partner than do hysterics.

COUNTERTRANSFERENCE ISSUES

In treating masochistic patients there are several countertransference issues that therapists are likely to experience. These include the desire to make reparation, masochistic triangulation, becoming sadistic, and feeling gratitude (Glickauf-Hughes and Wells 1995b).

Masochistic Triangulation

The most common countertransference phenomenon experienced by therapists treating masochistic patients is what Horner (1979) refers to as masochistic triangulation, in which there are three roles: (1) the victim (i.e.,
the masochist); (2) the persecutor (i.e., the masochist's partner, employer,
etc.); and (3) the rescuer (i.e., the therapist). In masochistic triangulation,
patients describe in detail a litany of transgressions committed by the bad
object in a very contained manner. During this transaction, the therapist
frequently becomes the recipient of the masochist patient's anger toward
the object. To relieve themselves of bad feelings (e.g., anger and helplessness), therapists are tempted to persuade masochistic patients to leave the
bad object.

However, having expressed and relieved themselves of their angry feelings, masochists are now less angry toward the object and more in touch
with their feelings of love and fears about separation and loss. Efforts
(subtle or otherwise) to influence masochistic patients to leave the object
(e.g., "What makes you stay with her?" "Have you considered getting a
different job?") are met with resistance, causing therapists to be even more
frustrated and patients to feel inadequate about their perceived inability
to leave the relationship.

We recommend that therapists remain conscious of this dynamic. Thus,
when therapists begin to observe that they are feeling frustrated and helpless, they can use these feelings to empathize with the incredible bind that
the patient experiences (e.g., feeling both a compulsion and an inability to
leave the relationship). Furthermore, it is often very useful for therapists to
help masochistic patients realize when these feelings are memories of childhood experiences with parents (e.g., "When you were a child, you loved and
needed your parents and were completely dependent on them. Even if they
hurt you, you could not leave. You had no alternative. It is as if your current
situation feels the same way to you. You seem to believe that you would not
be able to survive on your own.").

Desire to Make Reparation to the Patient for
Having a Traumatic Childhood

The stories of parental abuse chronically experienced by masochistic patients
are often profoundly unsettling. As previously described, one patient's
mother told her that she was a punishment from God. Another patient's
mother told him that if she had known he would be gay, she would have
had an abortion. A third patient's father repeatedly told her that she was

stupid and ugly and that no one would ever love her. When she stood up to him and said that it wasn't true, he broke her nose (see Extended Case Example, below).

Despite a history of traumatic experiences, preneurotic masochists generally develop into insecure and occasionally frustrating, but fundamentally kind, loving human beings. Having internalized their parents' hatred, they believe that the woes of the world are their fault. It is easy for therapists to wish to convince these patients that they are fine people and that things are not all their fault. Unfortunately, such convincing usually falls on deaf ears. Masochists tend to listen to the music more than they listen to the words. Thus, when one of the authors playfully agreed (in a warm tone of voice and with a twinkle in her eye) with a masochistic patient that he was indeed her hardest patient, it did more to soothe him than reassurance or even interpreting the transference behind the concern.

While a vital premise of object relations therapy underscores the importance of providing patients with corrective interpersonal experiences, we believe that therapists cannot really make it up to patients for having a traumatic childhood no matter how much therapists may wish to do so. All therapists can do is be good-enough objects in the therapeutic relationship, thus demonstrating the hope of a world that, however flawed, is still more promising than the interpersonal world that masochists first experienced.

Becoming Sadistic

The most frequent concern among therapists treating masochistic patients is becoming unconsciously induced to behave in a sadistic manner with them. In fact, in his interpersonal circle, Leary (1957) hypothesizes that masochistic (i.e., hostile-submissive) behavior induces sadistic (i.e., hostile-dominant) behavior in others.

While this is indeed a concern among therapists, we have noted that as so many therapists have masochistic proclivities themselves and thus have difficulty with their own aggression, they are usually fairly conscious of these impulses and are able to process them with patients in a constructive manner.

Nonetheless, therapists have "bad days" and patients can test therapists' patience on these days to find out if they can trust them or if, in fact, the therapist will also behave like their bad objects. On such occasions, it is important for therapists to acknowledge their feelings of irritability if they have been subtly expressed and to process the patient's response.

Feeling Gratitude

It is easy to feel grateful to patients who think so much about our feelings and concerns. It is almost diagnostic when on an initial interview the patient looks sympathetically at the therapist and says, "It must be difficult listening to people's problems all day." Masochistic patients are the first to bring the chairs into the group room (Cashdan 1988) or to bring the therapist a present for Christmas. Such behavior can be a welcome relief from the entitlement of narcissistic patients or the demandingness of hysteroid patients.

It is important, however, not to allow this behavior to go unexamined once it becomes a pattern (including the impact that is has on the therapist). It is easy for therapists not to confront patients who are so nice to them and who are treated so badly by others. However, in the same way that confrontation should be avoided when it is done from sadistic impulses, confrontation should not be avoided due to feelings of gratitude when it is in the patient's best interest to be confronted about something.

One masochistic, obsessive-compulsive patient had a strong need to control things in his life, including the therapy sessions. He brought the therapist a Christmas present at the fourth appointment, which the therapist found to be unusual so early in treatment. When the patient gave her the present, the therapist thanked him and then asked what made him decide to bring her a gift. However, when the patient said, "Oh, I just felt like it," the therapist dropped her line of questioning. Furthermore, when throughout the session the patient interrupted her and disagreed with the therapist or changed the subject after the therapist made clarifying comments, the therapist felt impolite confronting or interpreting the patient's behavior after receiving a Christmas present.

It was important to eventually interpret this patient's pattern as it was a reenactment of the very sequence of behaviors that the patient's mother did with the patient (which made the patient feel controlled by and frustrated with his mother). Thus, at a later point in treatment, the therapist commented on this pattern and asked the patient if he ever experienced anything similar. The patient associated to how his mother was always giving him things he did not want and doing things for him, and that this made it difficult to then set limits with her when she was controlling or intrusive with him.

EXTENDED CASE EXAMPLE

Lauren, a 32-year-old businesswoman, was the youngest child of a mother who was regarded as the pillar of the community and a father who "hadn't been quite right since he came back from the Korean War." She remembered that upon her father's return from the war, she heard him outside rolling around in the snow and howling. She crawled into bed with her older brother, who was very protective of her.

As a small child, Lauren was very close with her brother, mother, and maternal grandmother. When she entered treatment, she spoke of her mother adoringly and said that people thought of her mother as a saint. She was afraid to feel or express any angry feelings toward her mother with the therapist for fear that it would somehow hurt her mother.

Lauren said that she thought of her mother as quite fragile and always felt protective of her. As a small child, she remembered an incident in which she and her brother talked her mother out of a suicide attempt. Lauren said that her mother was chronically depressed and occasionally told her things such as Lauren being her mother's punishment from God. Lauren believed her mother and thought that she was bad and somehow responsible for her mother's unhappiness.

Lauren said that her mother was one of those people who was always doing good works. She was active in the church and always helping other people. Everyone respected and liked her mother and "thought that she was a wonderful person."

Lauren was described by her mother as being an active, intelligent, curious child. Her mother told her that she was "born wild"—that she didn't crawl, she walked, and that when she began to talk, she quickly talked in whole sentences. Lauren said that her mother preferred her older brother who was more compliant and who just sat there when her mother told him to.

Lauren said that she was always afraid of her father. She described him as impulsive and both physically and verbally abusive. As a small child, she began to stand up to him. When he drove her to school, he frequently berated her and told her that she was stupid and ugly and that no one would ever love her. When she finally asserted herself to him and said that this wasn't true, her father broke her nose. Lauren began to gradually become more willful. Thus, one time her father told her that if he heard one more word out of Lauren's mouth, he would hit her with a belt. Lauren predictably responded by saying, "One more word."

Lauren described both parents as being loving as well as hurtful. She said that her mother could be warm, sensitive, and understanding, and that her father was very generous and a great deal of fun. Both parents were angry at her rather than at her brother. She thus grew up believing that her parents were good and that she was bad and that if only she would change they would love her as they seemed to love her brother.

Lauren entered treatment due to depression and fairly extreme marital problems. Her husband was a professor in physics and she greatly admired his intellect and felt insecure about her own. She and her husband had a whirlwind courtship during which he was very loving and romantic.

Lauren described her husband as sullen, moody, and critical, but said that he could still be very loving and charming at times. She gained fifty pounds after she got married and her husband frequently criticized her appearance and was sexually rejecting with her.

When Lauren entered treatment, she felt very discouraged about the possibility of getting help. She said that she felt like Humpty Dumpty, and that all the king's horses and all the king's men couldn't put her together again. Early in treatment, she both idealized the therapist and projected criticism on her. For example, on the few occasions that she was late, she was terrified that the therapist would be angry with her. When she shared normal concerns, she worried that the therapist would think that she was "extremely fucked up." The first time she cried with the therapist, she profusely apologized.

Lauren felt a great sense of shame about her feelings and needs. She had internalized her immature and profoundly insecure parents' view of her, which was reinforced by the current criticism from her husband. On the other hand, while she frequently felt unhappy with her husband, she was tremendously attached to him and was frightened to leave him. She felt contempt for her own sense of dependency on him.

Other than her marriage, Lauren functioned extremely well in her life. She operated a very successful business and was well respected by her colleagues. She had several close friendships that she sustained since childhood. She also did photography as a hobby and won several awards for her work.

Within the first year of treatment, Lauren formed a stable alliance with the therapist. Each incident in which she expressed distrust (e.g., being late, crying) helped her to distinguish her transferential objects from the therapist. She progressively became more comfortable needing the therapist and asked to come to treatment two times per week. She was anxious prior to the therapist's vacations but would write to the therapist in a journal during those times. Thus, absences served as an opportunity to internalize the therapist as an empathic, friendly observer.

Periodically, Lauren came to therapy complaining about a marital crisis. She described fights with her husband that became rageful and out of control. During one of these fights, her husband threw the cat against the wall. Lauren said that her friends were tired of hearing about her problems and thought that she should leave her husband. She said that they did not understand how she remained so attached to him and confessed how frightened she was to leave him.

When Lauren discussed her marital problems with the therapist, the therapist assumed a neutral stance toward her husband despite feelings of anger inspired in the therapist toward him during the session. During this time, the therapist attempted to help Lauren objectively understand the dynamic occurring between she and her husband. For example, on one occasion when Lauren's husband had one of his articles rejected by a prestigious journal, he began to criticize the dinner that Lauren had prepared. She initially attempted to please him by cooking something else and then became angry and threw the dinner down the toilet when he remained so sullen. He became calm at this point and said that he didn't know why he stayed married to someone who was so unstable.

The therapist said that it sounded like her husband was feeling insecure about his article being rejected and that when he was insecure, he tended to be critical with her. Lauren took his criticisms literally as statements about her rather than as his feelings about his work (and himself), and thus tended to redouble her efforts to please him. When that was unsuccessful, she eventually lost her temper with him. Her husband then criticized her for losing her temper and Lauren felt ashamed.

The therapist said that this seemed to be a common pattern with them— that when Lauren's husband felt bad about himself, their interactions eventuated in Lauren feeling bad about herself. The therapist said that she thought that it was important for Lauren to be able to learn to distinguish between her husband's feelings and her own. She also told Lauren that it was important for her to learn to become aware of, rather than deny, signals that her husband was angry or struggling with feelings of low self-esteem so that she could protect herself.

Lauren began to discuss how reminiscent that this pattern was of her relationship with her parents in which there was so much yelling in the house that it was never clear who was angry at whom about what. The only thing that was agreed on by everyone was that it was almost always Lauren's fault. The therapist said that Lauren probably learned to deny danger signals with her parents, as it would have been unbearable for a child to acknowledge how often it felt dangerous. Rather, it was easier for Lauren to collude with her parents that things were her fault as that perception provided her with more hope (since she could potentially change and be "good").

Over time, Lauren slowly internalized the therapist's warm feelings toward her and the therapist's ability to step outside of a difficult situation in order to look at it more objectively. She also improved her ability to soothe and understand herself. Her self-esteem thus significantly improved and her depression abated.

Gradually, Lauren's relationship with her husband began to improve. When he snapped at her or criticized her, rather than being reactive she learned to ask him what was bothering him or to set limits on his behavior toward her (e.g., leave the room). As their arguments decreased, her husband became more depressed himself and eventually entered treatment with another therapist.

10

Object Relations Therapy of the Obsessive-Compulsive Personality: Treating Impaired Autonomy

Freud (1908, 1909) viewed the obsessive-compulsive as parsimonious, stubborn, and overly clean. Felix Unger in *The Odd Couple* epitomized the character traits of an obsessive personality. Excessively neat, correct, and inflexible, Felix was always trying to get his much more messy, "guy's guy" apartment mate Oscar to neaten up, clean up, and essentially "fly right." This behavior drove Oscar to distraction. Felix never "got it" that what he thought was the one right way to do things was often just a preference and that there were actually many right ways. Due to obsessives' attempts to perfect their self-discipline, Wilhem Reich (1933) described obsessives as "living machines," calling to mind Mr. Spock of the television and movie series *Star Trek*. However, even Spock had a human side to him beyond his ability to control. When it emerged, it caused him great distress.

Obsessive patients are confronted with an impossible dilemma, in that they have a strong need to control that which cannot and does not want to be controlled (i.e., themselves and other people). This dilemma accounts for these patients' dynamics and overt symptomatology.

DESCRIPTIVE CLINICAL OVERVIEW

In the description of the obsessive personality, we have observed three underlying themes: anxiety about the unknown, ambivalence, and issues related to autonomy. We believe that the obsessive's predominant characteristics or traits (e.g., need for control, problems with commitment and making decisions, intellectual rigidity, discomfort with affect, an excessive devotion to work, grandiosity, and a tendency to have a personality composed of unresolved dyads) are all, to some extent, related to these three underlying issues.

For example, if an individual fears the unknown (e.g., the future consequences of a decision), is frequently ambivalent, and struggles to feel a sense of autonomy (e.g., "Have I decided this because someone is pressuring me or because I think it is the right decision?"), it follows that the process of making decisions would be a painful struggle. When an individual feels grandiose and in control of a particular situation, he or she is more able to sustain the illusion of power over the unknown (and consequently feels less anxious).

The Need for Control or Being Right

The hallmark characteristic of the obsessive-compulsive is the need to be in control or to be right. Obsessive patients tend to view every human interaction as a struggle for control (John Nardo, personal communication). Thus, they frequently get into power struggles or tugs-of-war with other people. This can happen over the most trivial event. For example, one obsessive patient, who was ambivalent about what she wanted, asked her husband where he wanted to go to dinner and he said that he did not care. She told him that she would really like to hear his ideas. He suggested a neighborhood steakhouse. She said that the food at this restaurant was too high in fat. He then suggested a new restaurant that had received a wonderful review. She replied that this restaurant was too expensive. He mentioned an inexpensive Thai restaurant and she told him that she was tired of Thai food. The patient was unable to go along with any of her husband's suggestions as it compromised her sense of autonomy. Needless to say, her husband finally left the room in exasperation and said, "I don't even want to go out to dinner!"

Another manifestation of obsessive patients' need for control is their problem in communicating with others; they are sometimes difficult to follow when they are talking. Wells and colleagues (1990) attribute the obsessives' difficulty in their verbal communication with others to their unconscious need to maintain control through expressing themselves in a manner that obfuscates rather than elucidates. For example, one patient frequently changed the subject when she was asked questions that she did not wish to answer. Another patient tended to use obscure jargon and tangential talking, rather than saying things plainly, when he wished to avoid being pinned down or taking a stand on an issue.

Salzman (1980) believes that the obsessive-compulsive personality represents a style of managing anxiety about the unknown. The major purpose of obsessive-compulsive tactics is thus to provide an individual with the illusion of being in control in a world where one is not in control. For example, William Hurt's character in the film *The Accidental Tourist* is a writer of travel books for people who had to travel but did not want to. He provides his readers with helpful tips about how to keep things the same no matter where in the world one is living. (For example, in Paris one is advised to eat at Burger King and simply remove the excess pickles from one's hamburger.) Salzman believes that the obsessive style is a way of dealing with feelings of insecurity, helplessness, powerlessness, and uncertainty.

Problems with Commitment and Decision Making

Salzman (1980) notes that obsessives have problems with making commitments and decisions. Making commitments is difficult for them as they feel tied down and controlled by a decision once it is made. For example, during winter, when airfares were very low (but nonrefundable), an obsessive patient's wife suggested that they make reservations to go to San Francisco (his favorite city) for a long weekend during the spring. He told his wife that he did not want to commit to buying the tickets, explaining to her that he might not feel like going to San Francisco at that time and would then feel forced to as the tickets were nonrefundable.

As obsessives are ambivalent, fear the unknown (e.g., the future), and have difficulty with autonomous actions, they also have problems making decisions. As they fear making mistakes and do not believe that decisions are often reversible, they are afraid that they will make the wrong decision. This difficulty often causes them future problems.

For example, one obsessive patient felt extremely ambivalent about what major to choose in college. She was afraid that she would choose the wrong one and be stuck forever with her bad choice. As a result of her vacillations, she chose three majors and thus it took her eight years to graduate.

Intellectual Rigidity

Shapiro (1965) describes the obsessive's cognitive style as one that involves intellectual rigidity or vacillations between dogma and doubting. He also believes that their social reality testing is compromised at times by their single-mindedness and consequent inattention to new information or points of view. For example, one obsessive patient reported that when he was in the hospital and was told that he was delusional due to a high fever, he still felt that he was right.

Inability to Grasp the Big Picture

Another component of obsessives' cognitive style is their overattentiveness to small details and inability to grasp the big picture (Shapiro 1965). As the expression goes, they are often unable to see the forest for the trees. One obsessive patient (who was the director of a social service agency) was feeling worried about several problems in the agency. He brought a list of his concerns with him when he visited the associate director of the agency who was recuperating from surgery. He proceeded to go down the list discussing each item of concern with her until her mother said to him, "Don't you understand that they're giving her morphine and she doesn't really understand what you're talking about?"

Trial by Thought

Obsessives also have a cognitive style marked by "trial by thought" rather than "trial by action." For example, one patient spent so long thinking about and planning for the house that he wished to buy that he never bought one. Another patient obsessed about his term paper, writing and rewriting it in his mind so many times that he missed the deadline.

Lack of Spontaneity

Obsessive-compulsives approach life with a sense of dead seriousness. Due to most of the issues previously discussed (e.g., need for control, fear of making mistakes), they have a marked lack of spontaneity. Being spontaneous makes things feel too unpredictable and out of control. Obsessives would rather be safe than have fun. Thus, one obsessive patient always ate at the same restaurant (and rarely tried new foods) because she wanted to be absolutely certain she could count on eating something that she liked.

Perfectionism

Obsessive-compulsives are highly perfectionistic. It is very important to them that all the "i"s are dotted and the "t"s are crossed. Part of being obsessive-compulsive is being unable to stop doing something (or thinking about it) until it is completed and in perfect condition.

Obsessive-compulsives' perfectionism is immobilizing. It often prevents them from doing things, as they will not be able to do them perfectly. Furthermore, the awareness of how much time and work it takes to do a task perfectly makes the task undesirable. For example, one patient decided that he wanted to learn Chinese cooking, and he followed the recipes literally and precisely. He thus cut each vegetable into pieces of an exact size and boiled it separately in a pot. It never occurred to him to cut all the vegetables into pieces of any size and cook them all together. Making the meal took hours and was unsurprisingly the last Chinese dinner that he ever cooked.

Obsessives also have perfectionistic standards for the behavior of other people. They often feel free to share their ideas about these standards, usually in a manner that others experience as critical or picky. Thus, the same patient reported that his wife had gone out of her way to prepare a special meal for him. When she asked how he liked it, he told her that the meat was overdone. He told the therapist that he did not understand why she became upset, or why she asked the question if she did not really want an honest answer. This example also illustrates the obsessive patient's missing the forest for the trees.

Excessive Devotion to Work

Part of obsessives' perfectionistic tendencies is due to their harsh superegos (i.e., high moral and ethical standards). One common standard shared by many obsessive patients is a strong belief in the work ethic. They frequently bring work home. Their leisure time is often spent doing projects that accomplish something (e.g., repairing things around the house, gardening). Generally, obsessives have a very difficult time sitting still. In their internal space, while it is easy for them to obsess, ruminate, or analyze things, it is difficult for them to contemplate, fantasize, or "just be."

Discomfort with Affects

Obsessive patients often remain very busy because of their discomfort with having and expressing their feelings. One patient said that when he was feeling grief over his father's death, the rabbi told him that "motion overcomes emotion." The same is true for being intellectual and analytic. Many obsessive behaviors serve the function of helping the individual suppress the emotional side of their nature, which they experience as uncontrollable and shameful. This is discussed further in the next section.

DYADIC CHARACTER TRAITS

One reason that obsessive-compulsives are often experienced as confusing to others is that their personality is composed of dyadic traits or unresolved opposites (John Nardo, personal communication). For every trait that one observes in an obsessive-compulsive individual, one can generally observe the opposite trait over time. Some dyads that Nardo describes are (1) compliance versus defiance, (2) orderliness versus messiness, (3) conscientiousness versus procrastination, and (4) unemotionality versus overemotionality.

Compliance Versus Defiance

Obsessive-compulsives are like 2-year-old children who do not yet know what they want—only what they do not want. Any perceived injunction leaves them conflicted about what to do. Some patients behave in an overtly submissive manner (e.g., they are polite and seem cooperative), but are covertly very defiant and passive-aggressive. Such patients may seem to be saying, "I'll do anything that you tell me to" but really mean, "You can't make me do anything." For example, a therapist recommended group therapy to a rather lonely, isolated obsessive-compulsive patient. He agreed with the treatment recommendation but came late to group almost every session, rarely spoke, and tended to be a help-rejecting complainer with other group members.

In contrast, obsessive-compulsive patients can also behave in an overtly defiant, argumentative, or rebellious manner, and secretly go home and do whatever the therapist suggests. One obsessive patient felt compelled to reject every observation that the therapist made about her because it was never precise enough. If the therapist commented on the patient's perfectionistic tendencies, for example, the patient would argue by noting that it was not really perfection she sought, but the absence of mistakes. The next week, however, she would always comment on how helpful the therapist's observation had been and begin working through the interpretation that she had originally rejected.

Orderliness Versus Messiness

Steven Levy (personal communication) describes two groups that he refers to as "neat and messy obsessives." The obsessive patient's struggle with anal issues can thus manifest itself in a more retentive or more expulsive form. Most often, however, what we see are both extremes in the same person in which one tendency dominates and the other is a secret. For example, one messy obsessional patient was in constant conflict with his wife over what she regarded as his continual littering of the house. She expressed great confusion as to how he could be so sloppy around the house and yet keep his drawers and closets in perfect order (e.g., his sweaters were folded perfectly and organized according to color). In contrast, another obsessive patient who dressed immaculately and was a fanatic about the cleanliness of his home kept his desk at work so disorganized and cluttered that he had difficulty locating things. Whenever his wife would visit him at work, he tried to quickly divert her attention away from his desk area so that she could not see his mess and have the opportunity to feel critical of him.

Conscientiousness Versus Procrastination

While obsessive-compulsives are extremely conscientious and concerned about following rules, they also experience rules as injunctions to be defied. Thus, one patient spent so much time making lists of things to do, and obsessing about things that she had not done, that she rarely had time to actually accomplish anything. Each day her lists became longer and longer.

Obsessives also frequently have problems with punctuality. They worry about being on time, but are frequently late. Sometimes, they do things like arrive at the airport two hours early just to make sure that they will be on time. As authority figures, they are often very concerned that subordinates are conscientious, orderly, responsible, and prompt. Even if they are not prompt themselves, it bothers them if others are even five minutes late, and they feel critical of others when this occurs.

Unemotionality Versus Overemotionality

Obsessive-compulsives generally have a reputation for being intellectual and unexpressive. However, privately they are often dominated by feelings of shame, fear, and irritation (Wells et al. 1990). A common occurrence is the sight of an otherwise mild-mannered, contained obsessive person honking and screaming during a traffic jam.

One reason that obsessive-compulsives are so self-contained is their great concern about losing control of their privately experienced intense emotions. For example, one highly contained, rational obsessive patient, whose life was so orderly that he used the same exercise routine every morning for twenty years, lost his temper with his son and hit him so hard that it left a welt. He was filled with remorse and never hit his son again. Another pattern that is frequently observed is the obsessive patient who is highly rational and a nice guy at work, but frequently irritable with his family.

However, obsessives' fear of being overwhelmed by their feelings (causing them to do something destructive) is generally unwarranted. Obsessives have the ego-strength (e.g., frustration and anxiety tolerance, ego boundaries, object constancy, observing ego) to control their behavior, even when they are experiencing intense feelings. In fact, it is their rigid overcontrol of their feelings that is the problem. Obsessive patients need to learn how to lower their defenses and be less inhibited, rather than to build stronger defenses.

OBSESSIVE-COMPULSIVE DEFENSES

In addition to the more obvious and frequent use of obsessive thinking (e.g., rumination, intellectualization) and compulsive behavior (e.g., workaholism, exercise, cleaning), there are several other defense mechanisms that obsessive patients are prone to utilize: reaction formation, isolation of affect, and rationalization.

Reaction Formation

Obsessive-compulsives have ambivalent feelings about almost everything. Reaction formation is a way of dealing with ambivalent emotions in which the most acceptable half of the ambivalence is hypertrophied. For example, whenever one obsessive patient was angry at the therapist, he behaved unusually nice (e.g., asking her if she would rather have a check or cash in payment or asking her if he could get her a cup of tea) or polite (e.g., holding the door for her).

Isolation of Affect

Another common defense used by obsessive patients is isolation of affect in which the emotional component of an event is compartmentalized or partitioned off from the intellect. As in a nuclear device, the cognition and affect are kept apart in order to avoid a dangerous, out of control experience. Thus, for example, one obsessive patient unemotionally talked about how his employer berated him at work that day. Later that evening, he yelled at his dog and did not understand why.

Rationalization

A frequently used obsessive defense is rationalization (i.e., a pseudo-logical, private explanation for one's motivations). Most people know when they are rationalizing. Obsessive-compulsive people do not always know. To paraphrase Jeff Goldblum's character in the movie *The Big Chill*, rationalizations are more important to people than sex; when have any of us gone even a day without one?

PRESENTING PROBLEMS IN PSYCHOTHERAPY

Freud (1909) noted that obsessive patients seem to worry most often about time, dirt, and money. They thus frequently enter treatment complaining that they cannot get things done (i.e., they cannot make time bigger). As previously noted, obsessives spend so much time making lists, worrying about what is on the list, and procrastinating about doing what is listed, that they do not have time to actually perform the tasks on the list.

Problems with Time (i.e., Conscientiousness Versus Procrastination)

Obsessive patients may present in therapy complaining about problems such as procrastination, time management, and lack of organizational ability. For example, one patient in her sixth year as an undergraduate, was attempting to finish an incomplete in a course by writing over one hundred pages on a twelve- to sixteen-page paper assignment. She said she was just not quite finished with what she needed to say yet.

For obsessives, time problems are real because they try so hard to do things right (i.e., perfectly). One doctoral student wrote the first page of his dissertation over fifty times before proceeding to the second page. Another patient regularly tried to do her work while watching television, even on weekends. This compromise often resulted in this patient neither completing her work nor enjoying her television programs.

Another problem created by the obsessive's time conflicts is that spouses and employees become annoyed or put out with them for not doing something when they said that they would do it. For example, one patient told his wife that he would clean the garage the next day in order to "stop her nagging." The next day he cleaned his tools and mowed the lawn, but put off cleaning the garage, which induced his wife to nag him again. The patient was a hard worker and diligently applied himself to many household tasks. However, whenever his wife wanted him to do a particular thing (like clean the garage since it was mostly his things that took up her car's space in the garage), he tended to rebel by becoming passive-aggressive.

In constantly creating these types of conflicts, the obsessive externalizes an internal problem regarding control. For example, one patient forgot to pick up the dry cleaning when her husband needed a suit for a business trip. Another patient who was an accountant failed to turn in his reports when they were due. A third patient put off paying the bills until the telephone was disconnected. When his wife expressed frustration with him, he retorted that he was not in this world to do things on her schedule.

Problems with Dirt
(i.e., Orderliness Versus Messiness)

Another conflict area for obsessive-compulsives is dirt or mess. One couple composed of a neat obsessive and a messy obsessive had arguments about the state of the house that rivaled the couple in the Danny DeVito movie, *The War of the Roses*. She left newspapers around the house and didn't want to throw them away because she hadn't finished reading them (even newspapers that were several months old). He was unhappy if the house was not clean and neat and thus constantly nagged her about the newspapers, piled them in the corner, put the accumulated piles in her car, and occasionally threw them away (incurring her wrath). She was an avid environmentalist and recycled everything, although she procrastinated about doing so, leaving bags of bottles and cans accumulated. He criticized her relentlessly for not turning the bags in, for keeping her desk messy, and for not washing her hair frequently enough. Each thought that he or she would be happy if only their spouse would change.

Problems in Their Relationships

The obsessive style (pickiness, stubbornness, power struggles, etc.) creates frequent relational problems. Obsessives sometimes enter treatment reluctantly, sent by their exasperated spouse. As in the case of the wife who recycled, obsessive personalities tend not to see relational problems as related to their character. In fact, obsessives often think the bigger problem is that there aren't enough people like them, people who are highly moral and conscientious, and who do the right thing.

Dissatisfaction with Work

While obsessive patients are frequently referred to treatment for relationship problems experienced by their frustrated spouses or interpersonal problems experienced by their employers, they more often enter therapy on a voluntary basis due to dissatisfaction with work. While many obsessives spend most of their time working, they frequently complain that they dislike their jobs and would be happier if they did not have to work. After one obsessive patient retired, she still frequently did not have time because her list of things to do was always so staggering.

External Problems Resulting from
an Ego-Syntonic Need for Control

Overall, obsessives view every human interaction as a struggle for control (John Nardo, personal communication) and may begin treatment, even on the telephone, enacting this struggle with the therapist. They want an appointment before 8 A.M. or after 8 P.M. They need the therapist to reduce the fee, file their insurance forms by the first of every month, and not cash their co-pay check until the 15th of every month. It takes two weeks to reach them when returning their phone calls. As these struggles are so ego-syntonic, obsessive patients often seek treatment only after they have created a major problem in their life (e.g., their graduate school program has given them one year to finish their dissertation, their wife had an affair, they were fired from their job). It is difficult for them initially to understand how their character contributes to the regular occurrence of interpersonal conflicts.

ETIOLOGY

During the second year of life, the rapprochement subphase of separation-individuation comes to an end. Individuation is consolidated and the child is ready to extricate him- or herself from the matrix of the maternal relationship.

Freud (1908, 1909) described the second year of life as the anal period and viewed this as a libidinal time in which the child takes pleasure in defecating, smearing, and spreading. Erikson (1950) described the same period as one in which the central issue was autonomy versus shame and doubt. During this period, children struggle to experience themselves as the center of their actions rather than the acted upon, the latter experience leading to feelings of shame and doubt.

During the second year of life, the rapprochement subphase of separation-individuation comes to an end. The child is now ready to extricate him- or herself from the matrix of the maternal relationship, and the individuation process assumes prominence.

The Terrible Twos

Thus begins the period that is popularly referred to as the "terrible twos." During this period, the child repeatedly says no (i.e., "I'm separate from you."). What the child means by no is "I don't know what I want yet, but I don't want what you want me to want." A friend's 2-year-old child was asked by her mother if she would like some ice cream (her favorite food) and the child responded "Yes–no." The 2-year-old child is expressing the feeling of being at the center of things but not knowing what to do with it yet. By the third year, the child begins to know more about what he or she wants. The obsessive-compulsive patient is most impaired in this area.

For example, the wife of an obsessive patient repeatedly suggested movies for their agreed-upon Saturday afternoon activity. The patient rejected all of her suggestions. In exasperation, the wife finally said to him, "You pick a movie, any movie, and I'll go to it." The patient pored over the movie section of the newspaper for over an hour with no satisfactory results.

There are two trends that occur during the third year that determines whether a child becomes obsessive-compulsive or not. If parents are intolerant of the child's oppositionalism or are unable to set appropriate limits, the child is in trouble (John Nardo, personal communication).

Parental Intolerance of Oppositional Behavior

Parents must view the child's oppositional behavior as positive and as meaning "I exist." If the parent attempts to force the child to be compliant, the child learns to act compliant but remains oppositional. Such children never learn what they want, only what they do not want.

Furthermore, squelched autonomy leads to shame and rage reactions (Erikson 1950). Two-year-old children experience what Freud (1908, 1909) referred to as anal sadistic rage. They feel murderous. They step on ants. It is important for 2-year-old children to be able to express aggression openly in order to discover that it's not really murderous and can be contained by their parents.

Parental Inability to Set Appropriate Limits

Parents must set reasonable and comfortable limits for the child to bump up against. There are often two contradictory tendencies in the parenting of obsessive-compulsives. Either the child's anger is squelched or the child's murderous impulses haven't been met with something that contains them. Obsessive-compulsives are like small children with murderous, aggressive feelings inside that they repress, reaction-form against, or leak via passive-aggressive behavior. They thus develop enormous problems with limits and self-discipline.

Obsessives tend to be highly oppositional in reaction to any perceived injunction from others. However, they are severely restrictive with themselves (like a small child disciplining another child). Thus, one patient exercised two hours each day. Another patient brought his work everywhere he went, even on vacation. A third patient never permitted herself to eat any food with over 30 percent fat content. A fourth patient washed his floors every day. None knew what were reasonable gratifications of needs. When they were self-indulgent, they tended to be extremely self-indulgent.

Having an Obsessive-Compulsive Parent

Important in the history of the obsessive-compulsive patient is the presence of at least one obsessive-compulsive parent. This parent, struggling with unresolved autonomy issues with his or her own parents, overcontrols and suppresses the child. For example, one patient's mother regulated her bowel movements until age 7 or 8 and gave her enemas if she did not have a bowel movement on schedule. Meals were served at the same time each day and snacks were not permitted. She and her sister were always immaculately dressed and not allowed to run too much or play too hard. As an adult, this patient had many strictly adhered-to rituals but refused to have any of her daily habits controlled in any way by other people. For example, even on important social occasions (when there was social pressure to eat as part of the ritual, such as Christmas dinner and weddings), she would not eat any high calorie food (e.g., wedding cake) unless she really liked it and thus chose to eat it.

The second type of impact that the obsessive compulsive parent has on the child is modeling obsessive-compulsive behavior (e.g., in times of stress, one should make lists). Watching their parents, as all children do, they learn what they should and should not do (e.g., follow the rules, do not lose control, be self-contained, do not get emotional). Often one observes family rituals around rules and organization. An amusing example is the family in *The Accidental Tourist* that returns from grocery shopping and puts away the canned goods in alphabetical order.

DEVELOPMENTAL FAILURE

As a result of being overcontrolled and either having too many or too few limits, the obsessive-compulsive patient has an insufficiently developed sense of autonomy and thus frequently experiences a sense of shame and doubt. Having won too few battles in childhood, the obsessive never wants to lose a battle again, even a minor one—especially a battle with him- or herself.

As a result, the obsessive-compulsive patient's self presentation is one of pseudo-autonomy or extreme independence and self-containment of affects and impulses. However, due to an insecure sense of autonomy and parental suppression transferred onto others, the obsessive-compulsive frequently finds him- or herself in power struggles with other people (Salzman 1980).

RESULTING INTERPERSONAL STANCE

As a result of being overcontrolled and having one's feelings shamed, the obsessive patient has a pseudo-autonomous, contained presentation in the world. Obsessives often appear not to need other people and not to have emotional reactions. They form intimate relationships with individuals with hysterical proclivities who admire the obsessive's self-containment and restraint. Similarly, obsessives are often attracted to hysterics, as they make life seem more fun and help the obsessive to feel more alive. Needless to say, after this initial attraction, these two personalities begin to struggle with each other in their attempt to make the other more like themselves.

As Salzman (1985) notes, power struggles are a predominant mode of relating for the obsessive. They may occur around things as lofty as discussions regarding the meaning of life or as petty as which person has the last word in an argument. In general, obsessives relate to other people in a manner that provokes arguments. The obsessive often initiates conversations with statements like "Why did you buy the small towels?" "I got it checked out at the service station and there *was* something wrong with your engine." "Don't feed the baby fruits and vegetables at the same time." Obsessives also tend to respond to others with statements like "That's really stupid." "Yes, but . . ." or they walk away or change the subject in the middle of a conversation. As the need to be right prevails over the need to be intimate, obsessives' relationships suffer. They tend to be somewhat distant or degenerate to nitpicking.

Some items on the PCI-2 (Chapter 12) that reflect the obsessive-compulsive's interpersonal style are (1) "I have a tendency to get into struggles with people, even about little things, because I don't like feeling controlled by people (i.e., forced into doing something that I don't want to do or don't agree with)." (2) "I have been told that I'm argumentative." (3) "It is very important to me that people do things the way that I tell them to, especially when I'm quite certain that my way is the correct approach."

STRUCTURAL ISSUES

As the developmental failure in obsessive patients occurs after the rapprochement period, and as the obsessive's parents generally provide a stable environment until that time, neurotic-level obsessive-compulsive patients have developed a cohesive and integrated sense of self. As a result, they have an undisputed core identity, a sense of self continuity, and clear and stable values. However, due to the suppression of emotional expression, affects are often experienced as ego-dystonic and thus not fully integrated into the individual's core self.

Furthermore, as parents of obsessives are often described as being affectionate with infants and reasonably dependable and stable thereafter, the obsessive-compulsive generally has made an attachment to others and has securely established object constancy. However, they have an excessively harsh superego to which they frequently sacrifice interpersonal relationships.

Due to an insecure sense of autonomy, leading to a prematurely rigidified sense of identity, the obsessive's continued individuation is blunted. The obsessive patient falsely assumes that autonomy means always being in control and never allowing oneself to be overly influenced (i.e., controlled) by others. Self-restrictions prevent the obsessive from experiencing positive self-transformations or from consciously choosing at times to surrender in the world. They thus do not continue to individuate through the stages of adult development.

TREATMENT OF THE
OBSESSIVE-COMPULSIVE PERSONALITY

Overall, defensive constellations are lodged so deeply in the personality of the obsessive-compulsive patient that when they are confronted by the therapist, the patient often does not understand what the therapist means (John Nardo, personal communication). Obsessive patients often believe that their defenses are the best part of them. As we noted previously, they tend to believe that what the world needs is more, not less, highly moral, controlled, responsible people (Wells et al. 1990).

Thus, in treating obsessive-compulsive patients, therapists are advised to slowly call the patient's attention to his or her defenses (e.g., "I noticed that during every vacation you become involved in complicated, time-consuming projects and still are not able to spend time with your family as you say that you wish to"). It is important for therapists to begin to observe when obsessive patients begin to understand what the therapist is talking about. For example, the previous patient said that he noticed that last Sunday when he had nothing to do, he became vaguely anxious and began to read the newspaper and cut out coupons. When his wife sat down to talk with him, he did not want to be interrupted, although he had wished to spend time with her earlier.

With obsessive patients, it is necessary to make ego-syntonic characteristics ego-dystonic. It is important for these patients to become cognizant that the traits that they see as laudable often cause them difficulty in their life (John Nardo, personal communication). For example, the obsessive patient who recycled and was a very principled person eventually became aware that her principles were so stringent that she often felt imprisoned by them.

It is first important to help obsessives to see how these defenses hurt them and then help them to see their impact on other people. In the previous example, the patient began to see how criticized and controlled her husband felt by her and that her marriage was paying a price for her high moral values.

Progress in psychotherapy with obsessive patients tends to be slow but steady (Salzman 1980). Therapists initially may want to say more to these patients. However, it is important to hold back on making interpretations until there is an overwhelming amount of data to support one's observations and the patient's defenses are somewhat lowered.

There are frequent periods in the treatment of obsessive patients where it is unclear if therapy is even progressing. At some crucial points, we have found that it can be helpful to confront the patient's resistance by suggesting to the patient that it is possible that he or she might not want to change. For example, one patient frequently complained that he did not have enough spare time and yet persisted in overstructuring his time. The therapist suggested to the patient that maybe that was something that he didn't really want to change; nor did he really have to. The therapist said to the patient that overall his life went pretty smoothly, that he wasn't suicidal, homicidal, or psychotic. Of course, he rarely had fun, but many people didn't and maybe fun was not worth facing uncomfortable feelings to get.

Overall, however, therapists need to observe and appreciate small changes here and there with obsessive patients (Salzman 1980, Wells et al. 1990). With this in mind, we now specify the particular goals in the treatment of obsessive patients, both interpersonal and structural, and the type of corrective interpersonal experience that facilitates accomplishing these goals.

INTERPERSONAL GOALS

Increase the Value of Interpersonal Relationships Over Being Right or in Control

Dealing with Power Struggles

Obsessive-compulsive patients have a strong need to win, to be right, and to be in control. As a consequence, they frequently get into tugs-of-war with other people. For example, one couple composed of two obsessive patients frequently got into power struggles with one another in which they each fought to literally get the last word in a conversation. It is important for therapists to remember that obsessives are usually working so hard to be right or win because they desperately want to feel the security of being right or avoid the intense shame they feel when they either make a mistake or lose at something. This underlying motive is not always evident, as the obsessive is often ashamed of feeling shame or insecure and so will go to great lengths to hide this connection.

When the therapist begins to observe power struggles emerging in the therapeutic relationship, it is often helpful to make a comment such as, "It seems like we're in a tug-of-war. Let's look at what happened that made us start fighting." For example, one obsessive patient often responded to any statement that the therapist made about his needs with an intellectual argument about Zen Buddhism and needs. The therapist noted that she would occasionally get induced into debating with this patient about whether needs were good and inevitable. After she observed this pattern, she processed it with the patient and said that she thought that it would be worth understanding why the two of them seemed to argue about that topic.

In such instances, it is often helpful to retrace the steps of the conflictual interaction. During this analysis, it is useful for the therapist to acknowledge his or her own contribution to the power struggle. In the last example, the therapist noted the part of her that, at times, began to feel stubborn with the patient. In addition, it is typically useful to ask these patients to observe what they believe could be their part in the struggle.

In clarifying power struggles, it is important to help patients understand the danger underlying their defenses. In the last example, the patient felt frightened of having needs and was concerned that the therapist would force him to have them and that he would get out of control.

It is generally useful at this point to articulate the transferential origins of the fear as well as of the power struggles themselves. For example, the last patient's mother would provoke him to express needs and feelings and then frustrate or shame him.

As previously mentioned, one reason for frequent power struggles is that it is so important to obsessive-compulsives that they be right. It is thus corrective for therapists to give these patients their due when they're right and demonstrate to them that maintaining good relationships is more important than winning arguments.

Clarifying Communication

A subtle way that obsessive-compulsive patients get into power struggles with others, including the therapist, is through communication that obscures rather than elucidates (Wells et al. 1990). For example, one patient attempted to gain control of therapy sessions by switching rapidly from one topic to another. It is recommended that therapists take an active role in intervening in this process. When patients go off on a tangent, it is helpful for the therapist to comment on it and to ask patients what they were feeling before they changed the subject.

In general, it is useful to clarify for obsessive patients how circumstantial talking is a way of indirectly controlling the conversation and to let them know that if they are uncomfortable with a topic, there are other alternatives available to them besides changing the subject. For example, they can tell the therapist that they are feeling uncomfortable or directly suggest that they switch subjects. The advantage of such a process is that the relationship remains in alliance and the process of saying no is straightforwardly affirmed.

It is also important, as part of this process to discuss the transferential reasons for the patient's passive resistance. Quite often, such patients were unable to say no in their families without undue consequences. It is helpful for the therapist to affirm the patient's creative approach to affirming his or her autonomy in the face of oppression while discussing the disadvantages and lack of necessity for this behavior in the present.

Another reason for obscured obsessive communications is that such patients have great difficulty sorting out the relevant from the irrelevant. Shapiro (1965) believes that the obsessive style is to focus on details rather than the big picture, leading them at times, to miss the main point of something. Obsessive patients fear that they will not be correctly understood unless they tell the therapist every detail about events that occur. They tend to be unaware of their impact on others and thus tend to talk on and on even when they're losing their audience.

Again, an active role on the part of the therapist is recommended. Therapists must at times interrupt the obsessive patient's flow of details to point out this pattern. For example, one of the authors said to a patient, "When you give me so many details, I lose the sense of what's important to you. Does that happen with you?" (Wells et al. 1990).

It is helpful for the therapist to explain to the obsessive patient that the relationship between two people (e.g., how people are feeling while talking to each other) is as important as explaining and understanding things perfectly. Typically, family members of obsessive-compulsives competed for attention, with everyone interrupting each other and no one listening to anyone else. For example, one obsessive patient who talked nonstop during the session and interrupted almost everything the therapist said, told the therapist that in his family there were always two or three conversations going on at once.

It is important for the therapist to let obsessive patients know that as much as the therapist would like to understand these patients perfectly, he or she will probably fall short of this goal most of the time. However, unlike their family, the therapist genuinely does wish to listen to them and to understand how they are feeling.

Nonstop talking by the patient can also serve to control the therapeutic process, and thereby avoid those areas of discussion that the obsessive finds too unbearably anxious. If or when appropriate, the therapist might note that the therapist sometimes feels kept at arm's length or notices that the two of them appear to be diverted from reaching a conclusion or arriving at a certain destination by the patient's use of language. The therapist might wonder with the patient if he or she is ever aware of using words to protect him- or herself from experiencing something that could cause anxiety.

Increase Spontaneity, Affective Expression, and Playfulness with Others

A second interpersonal goal in treating obsessive patients is increasing their spontaneity, affective expression, and playfulness with others (Wells et al.

1990). Obsessive-compulsives tend to present with minimal or isolated affect. They are particularly ashamed of their tender feelings and tend to see them as weak.

Facilitating Affective Expression

A common wisdom is for therapists to behave more "hysterically" with an obsessive (i.e., in an emotional, spontaneous, and expressive manner). It is helpful for therapists to suggest that while the patient's cognitive descriptions are useful, they are leaving out an important component of their experience, their feelings.

When treating obsessive patients, therapists are advised to ask about the patient's feelings rather than their thinking, particularly when the nonverbal expression of affect is manifested. For example, while one patient was speaking logically about a problem in his marriage, his eyes begin to tear up. Rather than addressing the content of what he was saying (i.e., practical decision making), the therapist gently commented on the fact that the patient seemed sad.

Often, obsessive patients do not know what they are feeling, so that questions about their feelings are difficult for them to answer. One way of helping them to learn more about their affective experience is through the therapist's empathizing with what he or she might be feeling in a similar situation. For example, one patient was talking about a major changeover occurring at work. The therapist said that she imagined that if she were in the patient's position, she might be feeling somewhat anxious.

A second strategy is educational. Obsessives often answer questions about feelings by describing their thoughts. For example, one patient was criticized by his boss. When asked by the therapist what he felt, he said: "I feel it was inappropriate for him to say something like that to me." The therapist then asked him if he felt mad, sad, glad, or scared when his boss said inappropriate things to him. The patient responded that he felt somewhat annoyed.

The use of euphemisms helps obsessive patients begin to acknowledge feelings about which they feel shame or guilt. Euphemisms can be a means of helping obsessives understand and globally label the general category of emotion that they are feeling in a socially acceptable manner. For example, during one patient's period of depression, the therapist asked the patient if she was "feeling a bit down lately."

Often, in helping obsessive patients become aware of their feelings, therapists encounter resistance. At this point, a number of strategies are recommended. First, we advise therapists to help the patient make his or her resistance explicit rather than implicit through a reframing procedure whereby the resistance is acknowledged as a protective mechanism designed to stave off what has felt dangerous to the patient. Second, the therapist might try normalizing this process (e.g., "Everyone feels reluctant to experience things at times and they are part of what we talk about in therapy") and honoring its functionality for the patient (e.g., "Sometimes it is important to protect yourself"). Resistance may also be recognized as an attempt to be autonomous (e.g., "I will not go there just because you want me to"). In the end, it is important for both the therapist and the patient to understand why the patient's resistance is currently necessary and what the patient needs to help him or her feel safer exploring feelings.

One reason for the obsessive patients' lack of awareness of their emotions is their great fear of losing control. One patient said that every time in his life that he expressed his emotions, something bad happened (e.g., he was shamed, someone got hurt). The therapist empathized with how afraid he was that if he expressed his feelings and they got out of control, something terrible would happen to him, to her, or to their relationship. She further expressed how he had never had a relationship that allowed for losing control and making mistakes and it was difficult for him to believe that that could happen with her.

A common tendency for obsessive characters is to confuse feelings with actions. They fear that if they feel murderous rage, they will act upon it and someone will be hurt. Having never had their feelings expressed and contained, they have not had sufficient opportunity to discover that their feelings are generally harmless. This is particularly the case as obsessive patients have well-developed object constancy, good impulse control, and tend not to utilize primitive defenses such as splitting and acting out, which do, in reality, hurt other people.

Increase Spontaneity and Playfulness

One way to de-emphasize feelings is to overemphasize thinking. Obsessive-compulsive patients thus have a tendency to be overly intellectual, which leads them at times to unproductive philosophizing and dead-end investigations. They want to know and understand everything. Obsessive patients frequently ask the therapist about their theory of psychotherapy and what they can do to change some problem. In fact, they usually ask such questions several times.

It is recommended that therapists initially answer such questions, especially in the beginning of treatment (Glickauf-Hughes and Chance 1995).

After that, it is suggested that therapists explore the meaning behind the question (e.g., concerns about whether the therapist can help them, the need to be in control through intellectual understanding), and discuss with the patient his or her belief that life can be figured out intellectually, thus avoiding mistakes.

Because avoiding making mistakes is such an important goal, obsessive-compulsives tend to do "trial by thought"—they mentally rehearse upcoming activities numerous times before taking the risk to try doing them. It is helpful for therapists to encourage obsessive patients to take action with only moderate amounts of mental rehearsal.

For example, after one obsessive patient thought through whether it was a good idea to ask a woman that he met out on a date and how he might do it, the therapist interrupted his further ruminations to ask him about what feelings were stopping him at this point. After his fears had been examined, the therapist said that she thought that he had probably figured things out as well as most people do before they actually go ahead and ask someone out.

It is important for therapists to help obsessive patients to learn that anxiety is normal and universal and cannot be eliminated from life by thinking or perfect behavior (Salzman 1980). It is also often useful to encourage obsessive patients to take action and for therapists to reassure them that they will be there to help them if they make a mistake. As part of this process, it is often clarifying to discuss with them what it was like as a child when they made mistakes (e.g., how their parents were often shaming and critical with them).

For example, one obsessive patient remembered that as a small boy he was playing outside and had to go to the bathroom, and all the doors to the house were locked. As a result, he defecated in his clothing. When his mother found him, before inquiring about what happened, she said to him in a harsh voice, "I'm so disappointed in you." As a result of this and repeated similar experiences, this patient scrupulously attempted to avoid making mistakes including overcontaining his emotions and using excessive trial by thought. In treatment, it was important to help him recognize that he did not need to be perfect to be accepted.

As part of the process of confronting intellectual defenses, addressing underlying affects, and encouraging spontaneous behavior, it is important to help the obsessive patient understand the cost of these character traits. While such behaviors may provide the illusion of control and safety, they often also contribute to the experience of their lives as boring or imprisoning, with little or no warm, spontaneous connections with other people, particularly ones that are fun.

Obsessive-compulsives tend toward behaving and treating life with extreme and dead seriousness. They see everything as crucial. For example, when a small piece of jointly owned property had flooded and required replanting, an obsessive patient and his obsessive neighbor argued for months about whether to plant gardenias or camellias, and dogwoods or crepe myrtle trees.

It is often helpful to use humor with obsessive patients in order to facilitate their being better able to see how they have impossible requirements for themselves and spend an enormous amount of time worrying about things that are unlikely to have any negative consequences or that they cannot control. For example, one well-dressed obsessive-compulsive patient asked a woman out on a date. He spent approximately twenty minutes of his therapy session discussing what to wear on their first date (e.g., "Something too formal might make her think I was trying too hard; however, something too casual may communicate a lack of interest. I have a casual suit that would be perfect, but it's white and this isn't really the time of year for white."). Eventually, the patient asked the therapist what she thought he should wear. She said, "You know, I don't think what you wear is a big player in all of this—especially since whatever you wear you look like someone on the cover of *Gentlemen's Quarterly*. Maybe we can talk about what is making you nervous about this date." If patients see the therapist's use of humor as criticism, it is important to discuss the transference implications (e.g., people having teased and shamed them, how very difficult and frightening it is for them to be more playful).

In enabling obsessive patients to be more spontaneous, it is helpful here for therapists to present in a more "hysterical" way with obsessive patients. Within appropriate limits of the therapeutic role (e.g., maintaining good boundaries), it is helpful for therapists to be a bit more spontaneous and expressive when working with obsessive-compulsives than other patients.

For example, when leading a graduate student psychotherapy group, one of the authors thought of a verse from a song that succinctly described what the patient was experiencing. As the therapist was about to quote this verse to the patient, she sang it to her instead (and the therapist does not have a particularly good singing voice).

"Carpe diem" is an important concept for obsessive patients to learn and occasionally enact. Robin Williams, in the film *Dead Poets Society*, understood this and portrayed the kind of teacher and teaching that would be excellent for an obsessive individual.

Part of enabling obsessive patients to better "seize the day" involves helping them to focus more on the present, particularly what is happening between the therapist and the patient, than on the future and what they should do to control it. For example, as one obsessive patient was complaining in a therapy group about being bored with his wife and not having enough fun with her, the therapist asked him if he was having fun in the group at that moment.

STRUCTURAL GOALS IN TREATMENT

As previously discussed, obsessive-compulsive patients tend toward a neurotic level of ego development and object relations. Thus, they primarily have a cohesive sense of self, good self-other differentiation, and fully developed object constancy. However, due to the excessive use of criticism and control in their families, obsessives tend to have an excessively harsh superego and a cohesive but rigid and pseudoautonomous sense of self. We believe that self development continues across the life span. As obsessive patients' sense of self (while cohesive) becomes rigidified and they do not truly feel secure in their sense of autonomy, their senses of self and superego do not continue to undergo transformations through maturity. Thus, structural goals for obsessive patients include (1) softening their harsh superego, (2) furthering individuation and developing a genuine sense of autonomy (rather than the sense of pseudoautonomy that is achieved through reactiveness and power struggles), and (3) integrating affect into their core self experience.

Soften Harsh Superego

Because of obsessive-compulsive patients' harsh superego, they tend to be both highly self-critical and frequently critical of other people for being less moral and righteous than they believe they themselves are. An important treatment goal is thus to soften their harsh superego (i.e., help them to be less rigid and critical and more accepting of both themselves and other people).

An important means of accomplishing this objective is for the therapist to empathize with obsessive patients when they are being self-critical and to help let them "off the hook." It is important for these patients to understand that what they are ashamed of doing, feeling, and thinking is explainable human behavior. It is helpful to make them aware of the normal, understandable motivations behind their less than perfect behavior.

For example, one obsessive patient felt highly self-critical because she broke her diet and ate two cookies the previous evening. In hearing about the patient's day, the therapist said that it sounded like she had an exceptionally demanding day and was consequently feeling especially needy, so that it was understandable that she had done something to soothe herself.

As part of softening obsessive patients' superegos, it is important to teach them to have more lenient, achievable standards for themselves (e.g., "It is okay to eat a few cookies on a diet, now and then, just not two boxes of cookies every night"). Having achievable standards helps obsessives to feel more in charge of their activities and less controlled by an unreasonable superego and its projections upon others.

Another aspect of helping obsessive patients to be less concerned about doing things right or perfectly is for the therapist to be willing to make and acknowledge mistakes with the patient (Wells et al. 1990). For example, after the therapist and an obsessive patient discussed the patient's feeling misunderstood when the therapist made an incorrect interpretation, the therapist acknowledged that she had not in fact understood her.

The obsessive patients' overly harsh superego, need to do things perfectly, and fear of making mistakes are strongly related to one of their classic symptoms —difficulty making decisions and commitments. Ruminating is obviously one of the hallmark symptoms of this character style. The obsessive ruminates in an attempt to find the right or perfect decision and thus avoid making a mistake and feeling humiliated. For example, the patient who wished to ask a woman that he had met out on a date believed, at some level, that if he only could think things out clearly enough ahead of time, she would not turn him down.

It is important for therapists to talk with obsessive patients about their great fear of making mistakes and the reversibility of most decisions (i.e., that one can usually change one's mind). In the history of many obsessive patients there is often an instance of one "wrong" decision over which they feel enormous guilt.

For example, when one 35-year-old patient was 18, his girlfriend became pregnant. The two of them jointly decided she would have an abortion. When he spoke with his father, his father expressed subtle disapproval and became more remote with him afterward. He and his father never discussed this event again. Seventeen years later, the patient still ruminates about whether or not he made the right decision. It is important in such instances to help patients to work through their feelings about choices that they have regrets about and to forgive themselves so that they can learn to be less anxious about making decisions and taking action.

Further Individuation

Helping Them to Understand Their Response to Rules

As previously described, like a 2-year-old child, the obsessive-compulsive patient has a sense of pseudoautonomy that he or she maintains through power struggles and saying no. Obsessive patients tend to be highly sensitive to rules, and any perceived rule throws them into a conflict between compliance and defiance. These patients then react to other people's perceived rules or against other people's value system rather than following their own impulses and wishes.

The way that this dynamic is likely to manifest itself in psychotherapy is in the obsessive patient's vigilance about and reaction to implied rules of the therapist. It is recommended in working with obsessive patients that therapists attend to patients' struggle with rules and help them better understand their ambivalent feelings about them (e.g., "On the one hand, rules provide you with a feeling of certainty about what's expected; on the other hand, you can feel forced and resent them"). It is also important to help them determine what they want, rather than merely reacting against the rule.

Thus, in treating obsessive patients, therapists are advised to minimize rules and maximize an interpersonal exchange in which the rights and needs of both parties are considered.

One of the authors was treating a Hispanic patient with obsessional dynamics who came late to appointments on a regular basis. As the therapist attributed this behavior to cultural norms, she did not interpret it to the patient. However, over time, the therapist noticed that she, too, was beginning to come late to therapy sessions and began to question the countertransferential implications of her own behavior. She decided to explore this with the patient and said, "I've noticed that you frequently come late to therapy and wondered whether your being late was cultural." The patient said that it was not, but rather that she just didn't like following the rules. The therapist said that she could appreciate that sentiment; however, the therapist noticed that as she did not expect the patient to be there on time that she, too, was arriving late to sessions, saying to herself such things as, "Susan probably won't be there so I might as well do this errand on the way to the office." The therapist told the patient that she did not mind her coming to the session when she wished; however, she would prefer a flexible rule for both of them. She suggested to the patient that she choose a time range during which they would both agree to begin (e.g., 9:00 to 9:05, 9:00 to 9:20, etc.). The patient liked the idea and selected 9:00 to 9:05 as a starting time and never arrived later than 9:05 after they mutually arrived at this time. This is an example of what Renik (1993) describes as the emotionally corrective value of countertransference enactment.

As part of this process, it was important to discuss with the patient the process in which rules were made and enforced in her family. In this patient's case, her father was very autocratic, and the only way she was able to get some semblance of autonomy was indirectly (i.e. through noncompliance). The therapist understood how important noncompliance was to her (in allowing her to feel some semblance of autonomy) but helped her examine the cost of this behavior to her now (e.g., the therapist arriving to sessions late).

Learning to Say Yes

As obsessives have a reactive sense of autonomy, they have a strong need to win or dominate in interpersonal situations and thus frequently become engaged in tugs-of-war.

One patient refused to talk in a therapy group even after she had been a member for six months. As the therapist had initially misdiagnosed her as schizoid, she had interpreted her nonparticipation as being due to anxiety or shyness. When another group member confronted the patient about her silence, the patient said that no one could force her to talk.

In processing this encounter, the patient shared with the group that she never felt more alive than when she was in a good power struggle. The therapist told the patient that it was true that there was probably some implicit group pressure to participate and that she could understand her feeling some pressure to talk, but her silence, while reaffirming her autonomy, was leaving her out of the group.

The therapist encouraged the patient to pay attention to her own feelings about whether she wanted to talk so that she could govern her participation in accordance with her needs rather than in reaction to group pressure. If she was in a reserved mood, the therapist supported her nonparticipation. However, the therapist suggested that it seemed like a waste of valuable resources not to participate in the group in sessions that she actually wished to do so just because the group wanted her to participate. By helping this patient become aware of her reactive tendencies and helping her to determine and act upon her own wishes, this patient began to feel a more solid sense of autonomy.

It is, thus, important in treating obsessive patients to help them learn what they want besides "not what other people want me to want."

As obsessives become less reactive and more genuinely autonomous, their need to defend themselves against external controls or influence begins to fade. As they develop greater awareness and acceptance of their emotions and desires, their sense of self may begin to undergo a second blossoming. At such times obsessive patients often reexamine life decisions (e.g., being excessively devoted to work) and beliefs (e.g., "It is bad to be self-indulgent") and may begin to make new choices that redirect the shape of their lives.

CORRECTIVE INTERPERSONAL EXPERIENCE

In treating obsessive-compulsive patients, the therapist is encouraged to behave in a manner that permits the development of genuine autonomy rather than to merely help the patient understand that and why he or she isn't autonomous. While recommendations for a corrective interpersonal experience have been implied throughout the previous section, they will be summarized here. They include (1) being warm, spontaneous, and emotionally expressive; (2) modeling appropriate risk taking; and (3) being nondirective and nonauthoritarian.

Being Warm, Spontaneous, and Emotionally Expressive

The value of therapists' behaving in a more "hysterical" manner with obsessive patients is clinically well known (Wells et al. 1990). Obsessives are frequently drawn to warm, spontaneous, expressive people who possess what they are deficient in and need to develop for themselves. This, in part, accounts for the high incidence of obsessive-hysterical marriages (Barnett 1971). In such relationships, each partner wishes to learn what the other has mastered.

In the film *The Accidental Tourist*, William Hurt's character is followed to Paris by a dog trainer (Geena Davis) whom he is dating. She joins him for lunch at Burger King. As he recommended in his book, William Hurt takes the excess pickles off his hamburger to keep it the same as an American hamburger. Without thinking, Geena Davis takes the pickles and puts them on her own sandwich. Later, when explaining to his ex-wife (who is more similar to him) why their marriage would never have worked, he tells her that while it is important whom we are with, it is sometimes more important who we are when we are with them. Although his match with the dog trainer is not as socially appropriate as his match with his wife was, he is livelier, more fun, and more emotional with her.

The same principle holds true in psychotherapy. Very obsessive therapists are often not as effective with obsessive patients. They may intellectually understand them but it is difficult for them to help obsessive patients resolve developmental issues that to some extent remain a problem for the therapist, including modeling more spontaneous, expressive behavior. This is, in part, why Gestalt therapy has been regarded as a useful form of treatment for obsessive-compulsive patients. Gestalt therapy is centered on increasing awareness of affect and values spontaneity and present experience. It may be, too, that therapists with less obsessive character structures are drawn to this particular treatment modality.

We have observed that certain "incidental" behaviors seem to be curative for obsessive-compulsive patients. These include gestures such as taking off one's shoes, having candy in the office, and getting the date wrong on receipts. One could argue that such behaviors promise too much libidinal gratification or not enough constancy. However, we have observed that while such behaviors might need to be monitored with borderline patients due to their potentially adverse effects, we believe that this is not the case with neurotic patients who have obsessive dynamics.

With obsessive patients, as much as it is possible, therapists should make therapy fun, as fun is what obsessives are missing in their lives (e.g., laughing at one's foibles, seeing the irony in life's frustrations). We would like to distinguish here between the type of joking or banter that is used to avoid feelings or express aggression indirectly and humor that comes from simultaneous perspective on life's difficulties or one's conflicts and a cathartic release (i.e., representing a regression in the service of the ego). We believe that if an empirical study investigated the amount of time the therapist and the obsessive-compulsive spent laughing and correlated it with therapeutic outcome, the results would be significant.

In a therapy group that was run by both authors, there was a ritual upon termination in which the therapist, and any member who wished to do so, gave the departing group member a small, symbolic gift. When one formerly very obsessive patient was leaving the group, the therapist gave her a large bag of penny candy including flying saucers made from wafers and rows of sugar dots attached to strips of paper. Such a gift validated this patient's newfound discovery of the pleasures of being like a child at times.

Thus, like characters we adore in films (e.g., Ruth Gordon in *Harold and Maude*, Jason Robards in *A Thousand Clowns*, Robin Williams in *Dead Poets*

Society), a good therapist experientially teaches the obsessive-compulsive patient the concept of regression in the service of the ego. The obsessive patient learns this concept in therapy in a very different fashion than does the borderline patient for whom the emphasis is on ego rather than on regression.

As previously described, obsessive patients tend to fear giving up control due to prior experiences of being criticized, shamed, or in some way hurt when doing so. They thus never learned to get the sense of a loving parent watching the child play while ensuring that he or she does not get hurt while having fun.

Obsessive patients are frightened—both of their impulses and feelings and of the world's response to them when they are expressed. However, unlike borderline patients, obsessive patients don't use splitting and other primitive defenses, experience more modulated affects (e.g. anger rather than rage), and, thus, need not realistically fear the experiencing and expression of their emotions as much as they do.

It can be useful in treating obsessive patients for therapists to model this behavior at times. From our experience, we have found that it is not harmful for the therapist to express occasional annoyance toward an obsessive patient (as it might be toward a narcissistic patient).

Obsessive patients are not fragile. They in fact require encounters with real human beings for their emotional growth. Discovering that the therapeutic relationship can tolerate both the patient's and the therapist's feelings is usually a liberating experience for them.

Good differential diagnosis is important to ensure that one is not treating a borderline or narcissistic patient with obsessive defenses. If the therapist is at all in doubt, he or she is advised to be conservative.

Model Appropriate Risk Taking

Appropriate risk taking is a form of regression in the service of the ego. One thus first checks the water to determine its depth and find out if there are sharks or sharp rocks before one dives in. Therapists can help obsessive patients learn appropriate risk taking through teaching, self-disclosure, and modeling risk-taking behavior in the therapy situation.

In the first instance (i.e., teaching), the patient describes a risk that he or she wishes to take and the therapist discusses the pros and cons of taking that risk with the patient. For example, one patient was chronically angry at her employer for giving her contradictory messages. The therapist and patient explored together what the advantages and disadvantages would be in her discussing her concerns with him.

Therapists can also do nonjudgmental "postmortem examinations" with obsessive patients on failed adventures to help them learn from their mistakes. For example, the last patient decided to speak with her employer and he became defensive. Afterward, she learned through the grapevine that he had recently been confronted by a number of dissatisfied employees. She decided that keeping up with the grapevine before taking such actions in the future would likely be to her advantage.

A second method of teaching appropriate risk taking is through the therapist's self-disclosure about both successful and failed risks. For example, the therapist shared with the previous patient what she had learned from a similar disaster with her own employer and how it had helped her better gage things in the future.

The most powerful and therefore convincing means of teaching risk taking is encouraging or modeling it in the therapy session. Thus, some of the previous examples (e.g., singing in the group, confronting a patient's lateness) exemplify the need for therapists themselves to take some emotional risks. In like fashion, the therapist can encourage the patient to take similar risks (e.g., sharing anger or tender feelings with the therapist).

Being Nondirective and Nonauthoritarian

Obsessive patients are accustomed to being controlled and directed by early caregivers and transfer an image of a controlling object onto almost everyone in their lives, only to then resist their control. For example, every time that the wife of an obsessive patient asked for his help with housework, he experienced her as being domineering and refused to participate.

Many psychotherapies, particularly psychoanalysis and client-centered therapy, provide a naturally corrective experience in that they are by nature nondirective. The attitude of neutrality in psychoanalytic treatment is extremely important in treating obsessive patients because by not providing the patient with a direction to resist, he or she must determine his or her own. Steven Levy (personal communication) says that in analysis we repair the engine of a patient's car, but we do not become invested in where the patient drives it.

A disadvantage, however, of traditional psychoanalytic treatment with obsessive patients is that, when executed inflexibly, it tends to convey the impression of the analyst as an authority figure, so that the patient's responses to the analyst as such are not entirely transferential. Rules in the psychoanalytic situation are generally firm and nonnegotiable.

For example, many analysts have the policy that sessions are to be paid for whether or not the patient attends. It is encouraged that patients take their vacations when the analyst does and there are financial consequences for not doing so. Furthermore, some analysts interpret the patient's taking a vacation at a different time as an indication of resistance to treatment.

This condition potentially sets up a situation in which the patient's behavior revolves around the analyst's needs. It is recommended in treating obsessive patients that more flexible policies be used that take both parties' needs into account. For example, one analyst allowed his patients to cancel sessions during their vacations if they gave him several months' notice.

A further way that therapists are encouraged to be nonauthoritarian with obsessive patients is to avoid being subtly insistent on the patient's accepting the accuracy of the therapist's interpretations. This can become an important area in which power struggles can be enacted between therapist and patient, as being right is so important to the obsessive.

For example, one of the authors suggested to an obsessive patient that it seemed like she was angry at her friend as she was perceiving her to be critical (as she had experienced her mother). The patient rejected this interpretation and said that she wasn't angry with her friend and that her friend was not at all like her mother, and she proceeded to document all the ways that she was different. The therapist, feeling confident about her interpretation, found herself inclined to point out the ways in which the patient had described her friend as being similar to her mother, but fortunately resisted. Rather, she asked the patient how she felt about her interpretation and then stated how important it was for the patient to have a mind of her own.

It is important for therapists to convey an attitude about their interpretations that they are offering one potential hypothesis to be explored rather than "the truth," which, if not accepted by the patient, must be treated as resistance. It is not implied that patients, particularly obsessive patients, don't resist accurate interpretations, but rather that automatically analyzing the patient's behavior in this direction implies a self-righteousness on the part of the therapist that is often a repetition of the behavior of the obsessive's transferential object (e.g., "Your parents are always right").

DIFFERENTIAL DIAGNOSIS

In creating appropriate treatment strategies for obsessive patients, it is important that an accurate diagnosis be made. This does not imply that individuals do not have mixed personality disorders, which most people do, but that as obsessive defenses can be so prominent, a determination needs to be made whether the patient primarily has a neurotic obsessive character structure or another character structure, particularly a lower level one, and obsessive defenses.

It is important to first determine whether a patient has a neurotic level of ego organization and object relations development (e.g., a cohesive sense of self, fully established object constancy, good reality testing, etc.). This is particularly important as the strategies that are recommended for treating obsessive patients often promote regression and would thus be untherapeutic for a borderline patient with obsessive defenses. For example, offering candy to a borderline patient might promote too much fantasy about merging with and being gratified by an all-good object.

There are three character styles that tend to present differential diagnosis problems with the obsessive personality due to either similar symptomatology or underlying developmental issues: the schizoid personality, the narcissistic personality, and the masochistic personality. This section offers some guidelines for differentiating obsessive patients from related disorders.

Differentiating the Obsessive from the Schizoid Personality

Differentiating an obsessive from a high-functioning schizoid patient is often a diagnostic challenge as they have many common features. Both obsessives and schizoids tend to have overcathected intellects and are thus often cut off from their affective experience. Both character styles tend to be more introverted and withdrawn.

However, the schizoid character is typically organized at the borderline level of ego development and object relations functioning. Thus, in spite of a similar surface presentation, the two personality styles have quite different structural organizations. The obsessive patient has a cohesive sense of self that is never totally lost in spite of frequent battles for a sense of autonomy. The obsessive has fully developed object constancy and is thus able to integrate good and bad characteristics of others and to self-soothe when alone. Furthermore, the neurotic-level obsessive seldom, if ever, utilizes primitive defense mechanisms. In contrast, borderline-level schizoids, who lack object constancy, have not developed a cohesive sense of self and manifest underdeveloped ego functions. Thus, to expand Levy's metaphor, obsessives' engines are in reasonably good condition. They just do not know where to drive (and are afraid to step on the gas). In contrast, schizoid patients are not stalled due to mere confusion about where to go. Rather, their engines need major repair (and their gas tank may be near empty).

Obsessive and schizoid patients are both afraid that their anger could get out of control and be hurtful to others. However, this is not a realistic danger with obsessive patients as it is with schizoid patients who have suppressed rage and insufficient ego functions to contain this feeling when the patient reexperiences it.

Furthermore, obsessives tend to have more stable work and relationship histories and have a greater proclivity to get into control struggles than schizoid patients who tend to retreat rather than engage in conflict. Finally, although both tend toward introversion, the obsessive is more generally object related than the schizoid patient although he or she is often ambivalent toward others. Obsessives experience love for others but feel embarrassed about expressing it.

Differential Diagnosis Between the Obsessive and the Masochistic Personality

Masochistic and obsessive patients can appear similar at times as both have strong compliance-defiance conflicts. Both obsessives and masochists struggle with conflicting needs to please others and to assert their will. This manifests itself in both personalities in passive-aggressive behavior and help-rejecting complaining. However, in obsessive patients the need to assert their will or autonomy outweighs the need to please others. Thus, obsessive patients tend to be more directly argumentative and confrontational than masochists.

In a related vein, while both obsessive and masochistic patients have tendencies to be stubborn, the masochist's need to be liked by others modulates his or her expressions of stubbornness, whereas it is generally more important to obsessives to be in control or to be right than to be liked (Wells and Glickauf-Hughes 1993, Glickauf-Hughes and Wells 1995b). Overall, masochists tend to be warmer and more field dependent, whereas obsessives tend to be more reserved and field independent.

Furthermore, obsessives who are structured at the neurotic level have fully developed object constancy and more highly developed ego functions than the preneurotic masochist. Thus, despite the obsessives' ambivalence, they have more secure attachments and a greater sense of basic trust than masochistic patients. Furthermore, while obsessives struggle with shame and doubt, they have more stable self-esteem than masochistic patients.

Differentiation Between Obsessive and Narcissistic Personalities

It is easy for clinicians to confuse narcissistic and obsessive patients. This is particularly difficult as there is some tendency for these traits to coexist in the same individual (Glickauf Hughes and Wells 1995a). One important commonality between these two styles is the proclivity toward perfectionism.

The difference between these two character organizations is that narcissistic patients want to be perfect (e.g., smart, beautiful), whereas obsessive-compulsive patients want things to be perfect (e.g., clean, orderly) (John Nardo, personal communication). Narcissists are preoccupied with themselves, whereas obsessives are preoccupied with rules. Narcissists are motivated to live up to their ego-ideal, whereas obsessives are driven to please their superego. Narcissists thus have an inordinate need for admiration from others, whereas obsessives wish to please their moral introject and live up to its values.

Narcissistic patients tend to be organized at a borderline or preneurotic level of ego development and object relations, whereas obsessives tend to be neurotically organized. The narcissistic patient is thus more likely to have an underdeveloped sense of self, whereas the obsessive patient has a suppressed or rigidified sense of self. Thus, while it is not always easy for obsessive patients to know what they feel or want as they so often are in a reactive mode, they are able to become aware of preferences more readily than the narcissist when encouraged to do so. Furthermore, while the ruminating, anxious obsessive appears to be more insecure than the narcissist, in reality he or she has far more resilient self-esteem.

COUNTERTRANSFERENCE FEELINGS

Needless to say, as obsessive patients have been compared at times to children going through the terrible twos, one would expect therapists to have a variety of both objective and subjective countertransference reactions to these patients. The objective countertransference responses most often experienced by therapists include power struggles, remaining too intellectual, feeling bored and frustrated with the patient, and prematurely forcing patients into cathartic expression. To the extent that therapists have parents with obsessive traits or have obsessive characteristics themselves, these responses will be subjective as well as objective and thus intensified.

Power Struggles

A proclivity to engage in struggles for power and control with a patient, however subtle, is almost diagnostic of working with an obsessive patient. If

one isn't careful or has obsessive tendencies oneself, therapy can degenerate into nitpicking. For example:

Therapist: You sound frustrated.
Patient: I'm not frustrated. I'm irritated.
Therapist: And how are the two experiences different from each
             other?
Patient: They just have a different quality.
Therapist: Can you describe that difference for me?

In this example, the obsessive patient, splitting hairs, substitutes his own term
(*irritated*) for the therapist's term (*frustrated*). The therapist, feeling frustrated at having his statement rejected, attempts to make the obsessive patient prove that his term is really different and thus more accurate than the
therapist's. On the surface, this example may seem like what is occurring is
the therapist's attempting to understand and clarify the patient's experience.
However, what is really occurring is a contest about whose word is right.

It is easy to get into control struggles at almost every level with obsessive
patients. For example, obsessives can even struggle with feeling compelled
to both comply and resist the implicit "demand" to talk in therapy. As a result,
the patient may begin sessions in a "silence showdown" with the therapist
to determine who will talk first. In another example, a statement from the
therapist that the time is up invariably elicits a continued explanation of what
the patient was describing. When the patient asks the therapist a question
and the therapist doesn't answer it directly, the obsessive patient can begin
a struggle to get the therapist to answer his or her question while the therapist valiantly resists being coerced into doing so. When therapists do answer
obsessive patients' questions, these patients frequently interrupt the therapist's response. This can elicit the therapist's raising his or her voice to talk
over the patient and finish his or her answer.

It is almost impossible not to get into a power struggle at some point with
obsessive patients. It is important for therapists to remain aware of this tendency so they can attempt to prevent it whenever possible and to process it
with the patient when it does occur. In the dialogue cited above, the therapist would be advised to stand corrected. After noting several indices of similar behavior, the therapist might explore with the patient how important it
is for him or her to be understood perfectly or to state things in his or her
own language. In the event that the therapist does get hooked, as in the
example, he or she might say, "It seems as though we're in a struggle, now.
It might be helpful for us to try to understand it better." What is important

here is to attempt for the countertransference response to be a regression in the service of the ego so that it can be consciously used rather than acted upon indefinitely.

In the example, the therapist noting and then distancing himself from his response might have playfully said to the patient, "No. My word is better!" as a way of illustrating the patient's struggle. It is our experience that when there is a reasonable alliance with patients, the latter type of response can provide a corrective experience and turn a deadly serious tug-of-war into good-natured playfulness. Such an intervention indirectly demonstrates the importance of having a relationship as well as being right.

Remaining Overly Intellectual

Getting into a pattern of nonproductive, intellectual analysis is always a potential danger in treating obsessive patients, as all therapists have some graduate school degree and are thus likely to have intellectual proclivities themselves. After having their hysteroid borderline patient from the previous hour flood therapists with his or her primitive defenses, questions from the obsessive patient such as "Why do people get depressed?" or "How will my understanding this be helpful?" can provide a welcome relief. Obsessive patients often become obsessive in part because they are intelligent, and obsession, rationalization, and intellectualization are all natural defense mechanisms for intelligent people to use.

While discussions with obsessive patients can be frustrating, they can also be interesting. Furthermore, both patient and therapist can unconsciously collude that their relationship cannot tolerate the expression of affect. Thus, it is less controversial to answer the question "How will my understanding this be helpful?" than to address the potential negative affect that underlies it (e.g., "Why aren't you helping me instead of making me understand things that I don't want to?").

It is not bad to intellectualize with an obsessive patient and it can occasionally be useful. Initially, it may be important as a means of forming an alliance by speaking the same language as the patient (i.e., thinking rather than feeling). Ultimately, however, intellectual analysis with an obsessive patient is not a corrective experience and does not help him or her with the ego-dystonic world of affect. Therapists should thus try to resist the pull toward excessive analysis, however seductive it might seem. Furthermore, when they observe that this is occurring, it is useful to comment on it and to explore with the patient the components of his or her experience that are not being adequately addressed.

Feeling Bored and/or Frustrated

Boredom and frustration are common affective responses to the obsessive patient's lack of affective expression and frequent bids for power struggles. When therapists feel bored with obsessive patients, it is easy to dissociate and internally obsess oneself (e.g., "If you don't listen to me, I won't listen to you") or to guiltily compensate for feeling bored by redoubling one's efforts to be helpful. Neither strategy helps the obsessive patient. Rather, it is more useful when the therapist tactfully enables the obsessive patient to acknowledge and understand his interpersonal impact on other people (e.g., "Sometimes you tell me things as though you really don't expect me to be listening to you. I think it would be important for us to understand this"). Similar feelings of frustration are often cues to impending power struggles that can be processed as described in the previous section.

Prematurely "Forcing" Obsessive Patients to Experience and Express Affects

As therapists, we are trained that it is positive when patients express their emotions. We have noted that new therapists in particular often feel pleased about therapy sessions in which patients cry, interpreting this as a sign that the therapy is progressing. Expressing feelings is initially very difficult for obsessive patients. To the extent that they sense that therapists want them to express their emotions (i.e., that this is the mark of a good patient), obsessive patients are even more likely to resist affective expression. When therapists have countertransference reactions to this (e.g., feel ineffective or sabotaged by the patient), they can unconsciously double their efforts to break down the patient's defenses when it is premature to do so. Getting the obsessive patient to express emotion can thus become a challenge for the therapist and a seduction of the patient that is in the therapist's, not the patient's, interest. It is thus important for therapists to note when they are overzealous in their use of techniques to facilitate catharsis or overcome resistance with obsessive patients. These patients must feel free to not feel as well as to feel and make a conscious choice about what they want the most.

EXTENDED CASE EXAMPLE

Brian is a 34-year-old unmarried history teacher. His father was a country doctor and his mother was a first-grade teacher. He was the middle child in the family and described his family as very close and his parents as very good people. His older sister was a nurse who followed in her father's footsteps (although her parents did not encourage her to be a doctor because she was female) and his younger brother was an artist and a rebel. Brian reported that his sister was anorexic when she was an adolescent.

Brian was expected to be a physician as his father was, but he did poorly in his science and math courses when he went to college. His parents were displeased with Brian about this as they had him tested in high school and were told that he had an I.Q. of 145. They therefore believed that he had the ability to be a doctor.

Brian developed an interest in history, particularly Asian history. He enrolled in a Ph.D. program that he completed with the exception of his dissertation, which he started six years before. He supported himself by teaching history in a private high school but felt like a failure and was perceived as such by his parents for not completing what he started.

Brian entered treatment when his advisor called him and told him that his graduate program would terminate him from the program if he did not complete his dissertation in two years. Other complaints were insomnia, difficulty getting along with the principal of his school, and a desire for a relationship with a woman.

Brian frequently asked the therapist how long treatment would take and if they were making progress. He often asked how therapy would help him with his problems and wondered what the point of talking about his childhood was. He asked the therapist if there was some medication that he could take that might increase his motivation. When he asked these questions, the therapist processed them with Brian to help him to explore his underlying feelings.

Furthermore, when Brian described events in his life to the therapist, he did so without affect and in precise detail. He had a tendency to go off on tangents, especially in response to questions, so it was difficult, at times, to understand him.

The therapist observed to Brian that when she asked him questions, he often changed the subject. She asked him what he made of that. Brian said that he guessed he didn't want to answer her questions but didn't want to be impolite. The therapist said that it seemed like he thought that he didn't have the option of saying no, and Brian said that he knew the therapist was trying to help him and that he didn't want to be uncooperative.

The therapist asked Brian how his parents responded when he said no to them. He said that he had no memories of saying no to his parents, that his younger brother was kind of a rebel and was always arguing with his mother but that he didn't want to hurt her like that. His only memory of disagreeing with his mother was when he was shopping for clothes with her as an adolescent. Brian said that to this date his mother criticized his clothing and was always telling him how to dress.

The next time the therapist asked Brian a question and he changed the subject, the therapist asked Brian how he felt about answering the question that she had just asked him. Brian said that it made him uncomfortable. The therapist suggested to Brian that if she asked him questions that he preferred not to answer, it was fine for him to say that he preferred not discussing that now.

In general, the process of passive resistance was monitored and processed in therapy and in Brian's life. The therapist helped him to examine the activities that he did not finish (e.g., his dissertation) to understand the underlying dynamics. Brian became aware that he was content teaching high school and that the only reason that he pursued a Ph.D. was to please his parents (i.e., so that he would be some sort of doctor). He did not feel that choosing not to complete his Ph.D. was a genuine option as he believed that it would disappoint his parents enormously.

Brian began to observe a similar pattern between himself and the principal of his school (i.e., the principal would ask him to do things and he would agree and then not complete the tasks). In addition, he said that he and his principal frequently argued about issues ranging from student management to politics, much as his younger brother had done with his mother. He said that he found himself arguing with the principal at times when he didn't even really disagree with him. The therapist said that it seemed like it was important for Brian to be able to say no as well as yes to people.

Over time, the therapist observed that Brian spoke with her in a more straightforward, less tangential manner. Brian also reported that his relationship with the principal was becoming more cooperative. He decided not to finish his dissertation as it was a lot of work for something that wasn't meaningful to him. When he told his parents about his decision, they told him that he never finished anything. He told them that in fact he was finishing it as far as he wanted to—that he felt good enough about what he was doing now and that he had achieved as much as he needed to for himself.

At this point in treatment, Brian began to learn more about what he wanted to do—not just what he did not want to do. He became aware of how much he enjoyed fishing and began to do more of it. He began to consider the possibility of moving to the country, but as it came time to make a decision about buying a house he ruminated to the point of indecision. After this happened a number of times, the therapist observed this pattern to him and said that it seemed to be difficult for him to make a decision. He said that every time he thought about the pros and cons of purchasing a house, there were always some things wrong with each house. He loved one house but thought that it was a bit overpriced. Another house needed a new roof, and a third house had a lot of potential and was a good price but needed a great deal of cosmetic work and he did not really enjoy that process.

The therapist asked him whether he thought he needed to make a perfect decision and he said that he did. He associated to a time when he was an adolescent and his girlfriend became pregnant. He talked with his father about what to do and he and his girlfriend decided to have an abortion, which he asked his father to arrange. However, he felt that he had truly disappointed his father in making that decision and that their relationship had never been the same after that incident. The therapist said that it seemed as though he learned from that experience that there was one right decision and that if you didn't make it, it was catastrophic and that this belief interfered with his ability to decide upon anything.

The therapist put a piece of paper in her hand and said to Brian, "In my hand, there is a piece of paper. On this paper, God wrote down which house is the right one for you to buy. You have 5 seconds to tell me what you hope is on this paper." He said "the expensive house" and they both laughed.

The therapist asked him what stopped him from buying that house. Brian said that the house was just what he wanted, that he could afford it, and that it wasn't really overpriced—it just wasn't a bargain, and his father always told him that he should buy things that were a very good value. He described how his parents never really bought themselves exactly what they wanted in spite of their prosperity. Brian decided that he did not want to live his life that way and that as he would have no difficulty making payments on this house, there was no good reason not to buy it.

Brian reached a state of reasonable contentment in his life. He enjoyed his work and new home, began dating a new woman, and said that most nights he slept well—that he didn't stay up worrying like he used to. He said that he had been thinking about terminating therapy, but that he did not want the therapist to feel hurt. He was also aware that he still had some issues, but felt that "this is as good as I get for now."

The therapist commented on how much clearer Brian seemed about his choices—including the decision not to be a perfect person. She said that the goal of therapy was not to make perfect people but to help people so that they pretty much handled things in their life well enough and that Brian seemed to believe that he did. She told him that if he ever needed to return that he could always call her.

They both talked about how Brian had learned to live the rest of his life in a manner that was similar to how he went fishing—more simply, more in the present, and with more clarity. She said that while there were always new things for a fisherman to learn, he did not need to stay home to learn them but could learn them in the world.

11

Object Relations Therapy of the Hysterical Personality: Supporting Initiative, Appropriate Self-Assertion, and Authentic Mutuality

Like the character Scarlett O'Hara in *Gone with the Wind*, the hysterical personality is emotional, provocative, and overly romantic. Scarlett used her social charms and sexual attractiveness to command the center of attention, particularly the attention of men. Scarlett also learned to feign helplessness in order to be perceived as nonthreatening (and thus more desirable) to men. Although she was resilient, successful, and a woman to be reckoned with, she felt insubstantial without a man. Her life primarily revolved around yearning for and attempting to seduce two men when they were unavailable. In addition, Scarlett felt particularly jealous and competitive with any woman whom she considered a rival for the affection of these men.

Like Scarlett O'Hara, the prototypical female hysteric behaves in an exaggerated presentation of the traditional female role. Both male and female hysterics often appear to be living out the lead role in a romance novel, eroticizing relationships in both idealized and melancholic forms.

DESCRIPTIVE CLINICAL OVERVIEW

Many of the characteristics of hysterical patients are related to their unconscious conflict between their wish for and fear of having a romantic relationship with an object who resembles the favored parent. These characteristics include (1) stereotyped sex role behavior, (2) search for the romanticized parental object, (3) relationship-oriented style, (4) field dependence, (5) superficiality, (6) myth of passivity and feelings of helplessness, (7) dependence–independence conflicts, (8) dramatic style, (9) excessive need for attention, (10) global impressionistic style of thinking, (11) a flighty, irresponsible persona, (12) trial by action, (13) lack of self-awareness, (14) hyperemotionality and pseudoemotionality, and (15) triangular relationships.

Stereotyped Sex Role Behavior

Hysterical personality disorders frequently manifest exaggerated characteristics of femininity or masculinity as espoused by the hysteric's culture, subculture, or parent with whom the child was aligned. Consequently, if the culture (and favored parent) value women being coy, seductive, and charming, the heterosexual hysterical woman is prone to act like a southern belle. If the culture (and favored parent) values machismo and sexual prowess in men, then the heterosexual hysterical man may act strong, heroic, and charming with women. If the culture (and favored parent) values more androgenous, sensitive men, then the heterosexual male hysteric may become someone that women can talk to who is able to express his and understand their feelings. If the lesbian subculture (and preferred parent) value masculine behavior, then the lesbian hysteric may act more butch. Thus, the hysterical patient's sex role behavior is both an adaptation to the culture or subculture with which he or she is identified and the gender and values of the parent the patient is most identified with or attached to.

Search for the Romanticized Parental Object

While acting seductive is the hysteric's predominant way of beginning a relationship, it is merely a vehicle to obtain a romantic relationship with a love object. For example, one hysterical patient who was "daddy's girl" during childhood (only to be rejected at puberty), wished to recapture her father's love with a romantic partner. Her flirtatious, provocative style reflected how she learned to behave to get her father's attention as a little girl rather than a strong sexual drive. This behavior then generalized to other objects.

Hysterical patients often believe that when they find their fantasy object that they will finally receive the exclusive love and attention that they always wished for. However, since they tend to be attracted to objects who are only partially available to them (e.g., because, like their fathers or mothers, they are already married, workaholics, and/or self-absorbed), their search becomes an exercise in repetition compulsion.

Furthermore, hysterics often learned about relationships from reading fairy tales and watching romantic movies. They know how to capture the object and believe that once they do, they will live happily ever after. However, they were never taught to develop and sustain a relationship. Thus, like the final scene in the film *The Graduate*, they do not quite know what to do with the object once they have him or her.

Relationship-Oriented Style

While they are not skilled at it, having loving relationships is very important to hysterical patients. While their dramatic, attention-seeking style gives others the impression that, like narcissists, they are very self-centered, their focus is on gaining the object's attention, and their underlying wish is to get and give love. They generally behave in an engaging, responsive, and genuinely warm manner. Thus, while hysterics, like narcissists, are frequently manipulative and attention seeking, their aim is to gain the object's love rather than the object's admiration.

Field Dependence

As a result of wanting to be liked or loved, hysterics tend to be field dependent (Witkin 1965, Witkin et al. 1954). They are thus willing to change their appearance, opinions, or values in order to appear more desirable to significant others. For example, one young adult patient, who was raised in an upscale, culturally snobbish family that valued propriety, social grace, and classical music, fell in love with a singer in a band and completely changed her physical presentation (e.g., from stylish to grunge), her professed preferences (e.g., from classical music to rock), and elements of her interpersonal style (e.g., from proper to brash). Her changes were aimed at increasing her appeal to her new lover, which was far more important to her than superficial values.

Because hysterics are so sensitive to their culture, they are often aware of or anticipate new trends before anyone else. As a result, they appear on the cutting edge of what is fashionable or trendy. More business-minded hysterics often have a remarkable intuitive feel for what is going to be a hot item or a popular property. If they are ambitious, they are often successful.

Superficiality

While hysterical individuals are relationship oriented, their relationships appear somewhat superficial. They are frequently easy to like but difficult to truly know because of their focus on captivating the other's attention rather than on expressing their real self and knowing the other. For example, one hysterical patient was very verbal, smiled a great deal, talked about how much she liked the therapist and how much she was learning about herself, but was hard to reach. Unlike the narcissistic patient, when the therapist shared this observation with her and talked about the pressure the patient felt to act "on" all the time in order to be liked, the patient expressed amazement that there was another option.

Myth of Passivity and Feelings of Helplessness

Hysterical patients frequently manifest a hallmark characteristic described as the "myth of passivity" (Krohn 1978). They believe that the love object demands that they behave in a submissive, weak, or passive manner, sacrificing their self-assertion and initiative. Hysterics often believe they must act charmingly incompetent in order to enhance the love object's feelings of power or strength. To avoid outperforming their love objects and potentially bruising their self-esteem, hysterics hide their intellectual ability and competence. Unfortunately, they eventually come to believe that their persona is their real self. They begin to underestimate their ability and eventually feel insubstantial and insecure. This leads them to overrely on others for reassurance.

For example, one female patient, who was exceptionally intelligent and athletic as a child, learned that her accomplishments made boys uncomfortable with her. As winning their approval was her primary goal, she learned to act stupid and let the boys win at sports. Eventually, she gave up her athletic interests and lost confidence in her intellectual ability. A male patient who lost his father received love from a dominating mother and aunt by being charming and compliant. In so doing, he was able to twist them around his fingers. As an adult, he continued relating this way to the strong women to whom he was attracted, However, he resented and behaved passive-aggressively toward them. Both these patients eventually came to believe that the role they initially assumed in order not to threaten the love object was their real self.

These examples demonstrate how the hysteric's learned helplessness is not reality based. In addition, passivity is enacted with underlying resentment and is often employed to aggress as well as seduce. For example, one patient agreed with each of the therapist's interpretations, remarking on how brilliant they were, but neither acted on these interpretations nor used them to further the exploratory process. The patient's lip service without follow-through reflected a passive-aggressive reaction to the therapist, who the patient thought underestimated her ability to figure things out for herself. She, thus, thought he "needed to be taken down a peg or two."

Dependence-Independence Conflicts

Despite hysterical patients' dependent persona, they want neither to be controlled by the dominant parent nor to be like the submissive parent. While they believe that their dependent woman-child or man-child persona is required in relationships with significant others to enhance the object's self-esteem, they resent being condescended to as they were in their families. They are thus in a constant dependence-independence conflict.

Furthermore, while illness was often reinforced by one of their parents (who usually manifested psychosomatic tendencies themselves), they often feel contempt for that parent, who they view as ineffectual. One patient who somaticized her conflicts and used illnesses to get attention, became outraged when people implied that she was in any way undependable. Couldn't they see she was resourceful and could always pull it off? This patient, who stayed out of work for 4 weeks with back problems, simply held court from her bedroom everyday, having people bring each day's assignments to her and using the phone to maintain communications.

Dramatic Style

Hysterics engage others through their dramatic, exhibitionistic, and entertaining style of relating. Their lively, energized state of mind also inhibits or diverts depressed or angry feelings. For example, one hysterical patient told absorbing stories that were very entertaining and even touching. As the patient told his story, he would act out the different people, changing accents and mannerisms as he colorfully mimicked their essential traits. Only through perseverance did the therapist discover that the patient was really experiencing considerable depression. It was the anniversary of his father's death in an accident in the patient's car. Due to feeling responsible for his father's death, this patient's sense of loss and guilt were overwhelming to him.

Excessive Need for Attention

As hysterics like to be on center stage, they develop many techniques to enter-tain, impress, and engage others. In addition to being dramatic, they are hyperemotional, seductive, provocative, exhibitionistic, and sexually attrac-tive. Their desire to be the center of attention often draws them to individu-als who are flattering and responsive, even when they are inappropriate.

For example, one young hysterical patient, who looked like a woman-child (with a small devil tattooed on her ankle and a tiny tank top), began danc-ing with her boyfriend at a local club. Once on the dance floor, her friend's date leaned over and whispered to her that she looked fantastic. She re-sponded by dancing provocatively with him, going back and forth between the two men until her friend left the dance floor, feeling that she just couldn't compete.

Global, Impressionistic Style of Thinking

In contrast to the overly detailed thinking style of the obsessive, hysterics have a cognitive style that is global, vague, and impressionistic (Shapiro 1965). Patients with this impressionistic style often rely on intuition. They see the big picture but, to turn a phrase, can't see the trees for the forest.

One 40-year-old hysterical patient, who was beginning to experience menopause symptoms, expressed fears about not being able to remember details and wanted a neuropsychological examination. The therapist asked her to look over a complicated painting and then to close her eyes. While they were shut, the therapist asked her what she remembered, and she re-sponded, "A big, red ball."

When discussing important events, hysterics remain vague about the details and are often unable to connect their emotional impressions with corresponding ideation. While they may express strong global opinions, they are generally unable to back up their opinions with facts or rational, logical thinking. They thus have difficulty determining if their impressions are accurate.

A Flighty, Irresponsible Persona

Josephs (1995) believes the hysteric's style of talking in broad generalities and social clichés can give the appearance of irresponsible flightiness. Cre-ating the impression of being flighty is another way that these patients indi-cate to their love object that they are not a threat to their dominance and narcissistic needs. Creating this impression comes easily to these patients due to their global thinking and their tendencies to dissociate and forget details when stressed. Their proclivity to deny and repress their motives, feelings, and impulses adds to their appearance of being irresponsible. Hysterics experience the world as happening to them. As one patient often said, with a somewhat dazed expression, "Something just made me do it. I don't know how it happened."

While hysterics often are very responsible in many areas of their life, they tend to avoid assuming responsibility for anything that might generate disapproval or elicit feelings of guilt and anxiety. They have learned that being responsible under certain conditions (e.g., getting narcissistic gratification from dancing seductively with her friend's date) can lead to overwhelming guilt. Thus, awareness of their underlying motive is repressed or denied.

Trial by Action

Another means of avoiding being responsible is determining things by using trial by action (i.e., behaving without thinking things through). Unlike narcissists, hysterics genuinely do care about the object's feelings. Thus, if they did think things through, they might find a reason not to do something. In the earlier example, if the patient who danced provocatively with her friend's boyfriend thought about it before she did it, she probably would not have done it, since she would not have wanted to hurt her friend.

Trial by action also has positive aspects as it leads to more creative behavior. For example, one patient (who was a wonderful cook) hated following recipes. He just put things together. Some of his concoctions were inspired, while others tasted awful. If they were awful, he just ate ice cream for dinner.

Because of the hysteric's proclivity to act without thinking, therapists can at times better understand these patients by observing what they do rather than by only listening to what they say. Hysterical patients' memories are often discovered by observing their action patterns. For example, one hysterical patient rubbed the back of her neck every time she talked about her father. While she verbally insisted that she had a wonderful childhood and a great dad, she expressed the problematic part of her relationship with her father through her nonverbal and somaticizing behavior. From the time she reached puberty, the patient's father had been a "pain in the neck" (e.g., he became overly critical of how she dressed, conducting daily inspections, making her button the collars on her shirts, and waiting up for her to return from dates). In this case, the therapist observed that when the patient talked about her father, she always rubbed her neck. The therapist asked the patient if she was aware of this behavior and what she made of it.

Lack of Self-Awareness

Another hallmark of the hysterical character style is their rather impressive lack of self-awareness regarding the impact of their behavior on other people. Their use of denial and externalization and their global style of thinking allows them to remain oblivious to their manipulative behavior. However, in contrast to narcissistic patients, when hysterical patients are in a nonjudgmental therapeutic relationship that encourages objective self observation, they can be surprisingly introspective, and are capable of having considerable insight into their behavior. In fact, we have generally found, that they find learning to understand themselves without judgment to be a very positive experience.

In their social life, hysterics appear quite motivated to remain unconscious of their motives and unaware of their impact on others. For example, one hysterical patient who said that she had a very good husband who she loved very much, somehow just happened to begin a lesbian affair with her best friend, who appeared to manifest significant hysteroid traits (e.g., she frequently threatened to tell her husband about the affair or kill herself if the patient did not comply with her wish for the patient to leave her husband). The patient said that she loved them both and did not want to leave her husband. The patient was a psychiatrist on an inpatient unit (and thus understood borderline dynamics), but for months she would begin sessions by smiling and looking down and saying, "Ann was very depressed this week and called me to ask me to come over. I felt so sorry for her, that I went over there. She kept saying to me 'Why don't you leave Andrew?' I tried to tell her that I love him." She then looked up at the therapist seductively (twirling a strand of long hair over her fingers) and said, "We ended up making love. I don't know how that happened. What do you think I should do?" For this patient, lack of self-awareness helped her to obtain forbidden gratification and reenact a similar dynamic between herself, her mother, and her father as well as deny and suppress her anger at her mother and her husband and avoid feeling guilty.

Hyperemotionality and Pseudoemotionality

The concept of hysteria has been closely associated with the expression of theatrical emotionality, which is why hysterics are called *hysterical*. The term *hyperemotionality* refers to the fact that hysterics exaggerate expression of feelings or substitute one feeling for another and then hypertrophy the substitute feeling. These patients exaggerate the expression of their emotions rather than truly experiencing them. As a result, they are often confused about what they really do feel.

For example, one patient who felt guilty over her brother's death (she had a big fight with him just before he was run off the road by a drunk driver) would act out exaggerated feelings of seemingly unending grief in order to avoid her real feelings of genuine remorse, guilt, loss, and especially anger. She could only feel a caricature of her loss and was totally unaware of her guilt and anger at him for not being more careful with himself (e.g., he tended to speed, which contributed to the fatality).

The term *pseudoemotionality* refers to the propensity of hysterical patients to enact rather than experience their feelings. They can thus quickly change what they are feeling, sobbing hysterically one moment and acting cheerful the next. The result of their pseudoemotional style is that hysterics often seem inauthentic because they are acting a role rather than genuinely expressing themselves.

Exaggerated, quickly changing feelings are used to divert attention away from a threatening feeling to a nonthreatening one. For example, one hysterical patient who was afraid that her criticism would hurt her boss's feelings and make her seem unladylike, generally transformed her critical feelings into sadness, crying when she really felt angry and wanted to confront him. Her expression of poignant distress was intended unconsciously to buffer the impact of what she had to say and to elicit protective feelings in the authority figure.

Triangular Relationships

Hysterics have a history of being used by one parent against the other parent (e.g., a mother spending time with her son to make her husband jealous). As adults, hysterics thus frequently engage in or create triangular relationships in which they feel competitive and jealous toward others who they experience as potential rivals.

For example, one patient became obsessively jealous of the therapist's husband during the winter that the therapist got married. He had daydreams in which he was waiting with the other guests at the therapist's wedding reception to celebrate her marriage. The patient then looked out the window and noticed the therapist driving by with her new husband. The patient remembered feeling upset and jealous, hating being left behind and wanting to be the most special person in the therapist's life.

Another patient frequently told the therapist about things other people had said about the therapist. One time the patient told her that one of the patient's friends lived in the therapist's neighborhood and had seen her running with her dog. The patient noted with some distress that her friend had said the therapist "ran funny with the dog" (the therapist neither had a dog nor ran).

MALE VERSUS FEMALE HETEROSEXUAL
HYSTERICAL PATTERNS

Many manifestations of the hysterical personality are culturally determined. Both male and female hysterics are primarily motivated by the desire to have an exclusive, romantic relationship. However, because of the different gender-related behaviors required for acceptance from the culture or subculture to which they belong, men and women manifest different external presentations. Some theorists believe that the most common male counterpart to the female hysteric is the hypermasculine, heterosexual male hysteric (Blacker and Tupin 1991). Hypermasculine male hysterics may more directly express aggression and bravado while hyperfeminine, heterosexual female hysterics often manifest more hyperemotionality and pseudodependency.

What is important to remember with regard to diagnosis is that while the superficial presentation can vary considerably, the underlying structure, dynamics, and motivations of male and female hysterics are similar. More specifically, the male hysteric has all of the essential features relevant to diagnosing the female hysteric. "Thus, the conflict, defensive structure, cognition, perception, and interpersonal styles are the same in males and females, but the most common behavioral manifestations are mirror images, pseudofemininity in the female, and pseudomasculinity in the male" (Blacker and Tupin 1991, pp. 47–48).

The authors, however, have noticed that a preponderance of their male, hysterical, heterosexual patients manifest a social presentation that is a less dramatic version of female hysterics. That is, they are charming and compliant, feel insubstantial, and experience difficulty taking initiative. We believe that the social style or superficial presentation exhibited by the hysteric depends on the behaviors reinforced by their primary attachment figure. Thus, if a girl is attached to a father who wants her to act like a flirtatious, entertaining young lady, she will adopt an exaggerated feminine presentation. On the other hand, if the father reinforces a more reserved, intellectual, and instrumental (e.g., athletic, academic) persona, then the girl's superficial presentation will look quite different. Furthermore, a boy whose primary attachment is to a father who thinks men should act like "real men" is likely to adopt an exaggerated masculine presentation. However, if the boy's father had valued sensitivity and the aesthetics, particularly if the culture or subculture supported it, this boy's presentation would be very different.

HYSTERICAL DEFENSES

Repression: The Primary Defense

Repression or motivated forgetting is the most common defensive mechanism employed by the hysterical patient. The origin of repression in the hysterical patient is thought to begin with the oedipal situation (Mueller and Aniskiewitz 1986). Because the child's normal libidinal wishes to be the partner of one of the parents were encouraged through flirtatious play with that parent, and because the incest taboo and the imagined retaliation by the other parent are so strong, such forbidden feelings and motivations immediately leave the child's awareness. As an adult this defense, coupled with an impressionistic thinking style that loses details, serves the purpose of allowing forbidden activities (e.g., flirtatious play with someone who is married).

Dissociation, denial, and cognitive fog are closely related defenses, which also support the hysteric's tendency to keep forbidden experiences and ego-dystonic motivations unconscious. Hysterics use all these defenses to disconnect ideational linkage with their respective feeling states in order to defend against the awareness of needs, wishes, and desires that are too threatening (Allen 1991).

In a classic example of the hysteric's use of repression and denial, one patient reported her surprise and then her outrage that her boss called her competitive and not a team player. The patient thought she had, in fact, been quite the opposite. "I do a lot of work that is really his and do it better than he does. He just doesn't get it. I know what corporate headquarters wants from us, so I'm not going to sit on my thumbs. If that's not team playing I don't know what is." This patient was unable to understand how she subtly communicated her disrespect toward her boss through her attitude. She thus denied his accusations of her competitiveness and repressed her unconscious motivation to "show him up for the blow-hard he really is."

This patient's father was a braggart, who would talk endlessly at the dinner table, exaggerating his achievements and expecting everyone, especially his "favorite little girl," to listen in admiration. She consciously remembered her family as "wonderfully close knit, with real family dinners every night." Because her father was so domineering and "wouldn't allow back talk," this patient had to repress her aggressive feelings and deny the negative thoughts about her father that would induce them.

Secondary Defenses

Related defenses include displacement, externalization, affect storms, acting out, and reaction formation (Kernberg 1992). Hysterics are known for acting out their unconscious conflicts through displacement and externalization. In the example just cited, the patient was displacing her unconscious conflict with her father onto her boss and acting it out. As an authority figure with a dominant personality, her boss became the father substitute. However, the acting out of the hysteric is much less primitive and destructive than that of the hysteroid. Since hysterics generally have the depressive position, their major motivation (i.e., to maintain relationships) outweighs the urge to protect themselves. With hysteroids, the primary desire to protect themselves leaves the killer instinct unmediated. Thus, the hysterical patient in the last example eventually tried to reconnect with her boss.

Instead of indirectly acting out their aggression, hysterics often use reaction formation (e.g., behaving excessively sweet and expressing exaggerated concern). The patient cited above became scared that her boss felt as critical of her as she did of him and sent him, as a gift, a Waterford pen (that he once admired) and a very charming card that told him how much she admired his forthrightness, his ability to see the big picture, and his business savvy. She expressed deep concern that he would think she had intended to undermine him, as she very much wanted to have a good working relationship with him.

Character Defenses

Many of the hysteric's character traits work together with the hysteric's defenses to serve protective functions. We have already alluded to the defensive function of such characteristics as superficiality, vague and impressionistic thinking, an innocent persona, and a flighty style. These traits allow the hysteric to avoid taking responsibility for his or her actions. For example, a therapist asked a hysterical patient if she ever felt competitive with the therapist. The patient, who struggled with her weight and body image, brought a large box of chocolates to the therapist when the therapist lost weight, talked about how she wished her office was also located in the trendy neighborhood in which the therapist's office was located, and expressed her preference for pure bred dogs over mongrels (when the patient knew that the therapist had mixed-breed dogs). The patient replied, with wide-eyed innocence, exaggerated distress, and an apologetic tone: "Oh, I'm just a blabbermouth, saying whatever comes to mind. I just really like your office and admire how down to earth you are. I wouldn't ever say anything if I thought you'd get your feelings hurt. You know I'm so very sorry if you took me the wrong way." Acting out exaggerated remorse distanced her from her real feelings of guilt for having felt and behaved competitively with the therapist.

The hysteric's self-image of helplessness and insubstantiality often serves as a defense against feeling guilty for being too powerful (e.g., the oedipal victor) and unseating one of the parents. Hysterics, thus, feel afraid of their aggressive impulses and adopt a character trait that is intended to deny the truth. The hysteric unconsciously realizes that it may be smart to play stupid at times if that is what will help to maintain a relationship in an environment in which one parent feels competitive with the child and the other parent derives narcissistic gratification from his or her relationship with the child at both the child's and the partner's expense.

PRESENTING PROBLEMS

The hysteric typically enters therapy with one or more of a number of common complaints, including (1) problems with romantic relationships, (2) somatic complaints, (3) problems related to acting without thinking, and (4) sexual problems.

Problems in Romantic Relationships

Hysterics often enter treatment with global complaints of ungratifying, distressing relationships or intimacy patterns that the hysteric feels helpless to change. "It just keeps happening to me with every guy I get involved with. Maybe I should just become a lesbian." These patients may have just ended a relationship because they felt controlled. They often long for someone who is not really available (e.g., by being committed to another, a workaholic, or self-absorbed). They often complain that the significant other is self-centered and critical.

Above all, they do not feel valued as a strong, independent, intelligent person (even when they clearly have those characteristics). They do not understand why significant others do not take them seriously. As one patient noted, "I can always get his attention. Just put on my teddy and shake my bootie. But when I try to make a serious point and be heard, he just talks over me or says something like 'Yeah, yeah honey' and ignores me to watch a football game. He doesn't treat other men like that."

After a sustained period of feeling ignored or devalued in their primary relationship, hysterics frequently seek an extramarital relationship to enhance their self-esteem and gratify their wishes for love and attention (Josephs 1995), re-creating familiar triadic tensions. Many hysterical patients enter therapy in the midst of an affair, feeling a mixture of guilty pleasure, anxiety, and guilt.

Somatic Complaints

Hysterical patients frequently somaticize their anxiety. They thus enter treatment with various physical complaints, including allergies, chronic fatigue syndrome, arthritic-like pains, fibromyalgia, and colitis. One hysterical patient noted that she seemed to develop crippling joint problems just when she had determined to try something new that would require an emotional risk.

This patient's pattern was to go to a series of doctors to get their various expert opinions, only to be told that they could not find any medical explanation for her discomfort. She recognized that she enjoyed their concern and their failure. Her father had been a very popular physician in a small town and she relished saying, "Medicine can't do everything." Somaticization thus provided many secondary gains for this patient.

The hysterical patient's somatic complaints can also reveal important information about his or her dreams. For example, one hysterical patient who felt overburdened by her father's criticism during her teenage years, developed back pain that would put her to bed. She eventually associated her back pain with criticism from her boss, her own criticism of his incompetence, and her wish to be taken care of. Her illness elicited sympathy from her husband and gave her temporary relief from burdensome responsibilities at work. Her body expressed what she could not verbalize (i.e., "Get off my back").

Problems Associated with Acting Without Thinking

Hysterics have the proclivity to be more impulsive, global, and prone to acting out when they are under interpersonal stress and feeling needy and angry.

However, acting impulsively to gratify narcissistic needs (e.g., extramarital affairs, alcohol abuse, buying sprees) causes problems. For example, every time one hysterical patient broke up with her boyfriend, she would mediate the stress she felt by blowing her budget on expensive clothes in the latest slinky fashion, which helped her feel more desirable.

Sexual Problems

Because of their unresolved oedipal issues leading to feelings of guilt about sexual feelings and confusion over their needs for sex versus affection, hysterics often enter therapy with sexual complaints. For the hyperfeminine hysterical patient, these complaints typically revolve around feeling treated like a sexual plaything by the romantic partner, feeling sexually unattracted to this partner, experiencing low sexual desire, and/or being inorgasmic. One hysterical patient who spent considerable time and attention on her appearance in order to be sexually appealing, complained that she never wanted to have sex when her husband did. She thought that he seemed as "unattractive as a horny dog, wanting sex day and night. It turns me off." The only time this patient could have sex with her husband was on her initiative and through mutual masturbation rather than sexual intercourse. This was the only way she believed that he was responding to her needs rather than solely to his own. "I just don't want to be his personal sex toy that scratches his itch." Furthermore, she found it easier to have sex in the beginning of romantic relationships or with anonymous lovers when sexual contact did not seem so incestuous.

ETIOLOGY

For the most part, hysterics appear to come from intact families with substantially adequate early mothering and relatively stable family histories (Lazare 1971). The primary problem for the hysteric is not deficits in ego functioning, but an injunction not to use their ego functions. Hysterics also have many unconscious conflicts which develop in response to specific parental behaviors.

The Female Hysteric

Relationship with the Mother

While the mothers of female hysterics can demonstrate substantial effectiveness and responsibility both at home and work, they behave in a submissive way with their husbands. They also want their daughters to be submissive, resenting the child's assertive, lively behavior because it makes them feel anxious and insecure. The hysteric experiences her mother as ineffectual in the face of the father's controlling behavior and insubstantial in terms of helping to protect her from the father's provocative behavior. If the female hysteric has male siblings, she often feels unrecognized and unimportant to the mother, who treats male children as if they were more competent and desirable (Mueller and Aniskiewicz 1986). The mother conveys to her daughter in a number of different ways that males are the dominant, competent, and important people, and the role of women is to be attached and subservient to them. Even when the father is somewhat inadequate, the family colludes that he is really the Wizard of Oz (e.g., "Your father is the best salesman in the city of New York").

In addition, female hysterics often experience their mothers as self-indulgent as well as envious of and subtly competitive with their fathers (Celani 1976). The daughter, sensing the mother's inadequacy in being able to provide her with genuine, sustained warmth, affection, and attention, turns to her father, not as a father but as a substitute mother.

Relationship with the Father

Fathers of the female hysteric are often described as behaving in an over-stimulating, seductive manner with their daughters while espousing puritanical attitudes with them (Celani 1976). More specifically, the father's seductive interest in his daughter during her childhood typically changes to prohibitions against her sexual and romantic involvements with boys during her adolescence. In some cases, lectures about the dangers of men and sex begin sooner. For example, at the age of 10, one patient was warned by her father that men were animals who only wanted *one thing*.

In general, fathers of female hysterics are described as superficially charming, overpowering, self-centered, relatively immature, and controlling. These fathers tend to be overprotective of their daughters, not trusting them to learn from their mistakes. They are frequently infantilizing with their daughters, and use them to provide gratifications withheld by the mother (e.g., narcissistic gratification, affection, sexual validation). The daughter's only power in the family is through her alliance with her father, whose need to dominate her significantly interferes with the development of her sense of initiative (Mueller and Aniskiewicz 1986).

Although these fathers were gratified by their daughter's entertaining flirtations with them, they did not father them. That is, they did not seriously pay attention to and help their daughters work through their conflicts and problems, providing them with mature guidance in the world. Instead, these fathers focused on their daughter's performances and left her with the feeling that she was valued for her ability to be charming, cute, and undemanding, rather than intrinsically valuable for the evolving nature of her character, capabilities, and initiative (Mueller and Aniskiewicz 1986). As a result, hysterical patients often enter adulthood feeling unprepared for life.

The daughter thus learns that she is operating in a manipulative marketplace (Kell and Mueller 1966) where sexual attractiveness and being used to gratify the other's needs are bartered for love and maternal nurturance. The hysterical patient often experiences both her parents as giving contingent love, and consequently learns that she must perform a certain role if she is to obtain the love that she needs (Celani 1993).

Three Stages in the Development of the Hysterical Personality in Women

There are three predominant stages in the development of the female hysterical personality: (1) the first years of life (primarily spent with the mother), (2) the oedipal stage until puberty (spent primarily with the father), and (3) the postpuberty stage of "orphanhood."

The Preoedipal Stage: The Hysteric's Relationship with Her Mother

During the symbiotic stage of development, the mother of the hysteric is sufficiently gratifying and attuned with the child to develop an attachment. However, due to her own lack of confidence and discomfort with females, she is not sufficiently demonstrative to create a sense of security in the child that her needs can be met in the world. In part, the mother's inattentiveness results from denying her own anxiety and insecurity about being a mother and treating the baby as if everything is fine when the mother feels quite differently (Mueller and Aniskiewicz 1986). However, the mother's lack of confidence and discomfort with affection is not due to major deficits in attachment or severe problems in self-esteem regulation. Rather, it is usually developed from the mother having a mother whose character was similar to her own. Thus, the hysteric leaves the symbiotic period with a number of oral issues related to excessive neediness, greed, coveting what others have, and fearing the loss of opportunity for gratification.

During the postsymbiotic period, because the mother is not sufficiently attached to or involved with her daughter, the mother does not interfere with the separation-individuation process. Nor is she psychotic or abusive. This is particularly important to note in understanding the more advanced development of the hysteric. The mother does not have inadequate ego functions. Rather, like the daughter, she has been reinforced by cultural norms for not using them, for being subservient to men and not being assertive. Thus, the mother fails to provide a sufficient model with which her daughter can identify. The mother unconsciously encourages her daughter to use denial (e.g., "Do as I do—pretend everything is fine when it isn't") (Mueller and Aniskiewicz 1986).

Additionally, the hysterical patient's mother often only attends to her daughter when she is ill or in crisis because the mother's solicitous behavior at these times enhances her image of herself as a good mother both to herself and to others (Josephs 1995, Mueller and Aniskiewicz 1986). Furthermore, mothers of hysterics often feel more confident in this area of parenting. Thus, one hysterical patient reported that most of her good childhood memories with her mother were when the patient was sick. During these times, her mother would let her sleep in her bed and make her favorite foods for her.

However, these mothers have a difficult time consistently responding to the more mundane, daily needs of their children since such activities offer fewer possibilities for self-enhancement (Mueller and Aniskiewicz 1986). Furthermore, the mother generally feels inadequate as a mother. From such interactions, the hysterical patient learns to behave dramatically, passively, and helplessly in order to get attention.

The Oedipal Period Through Puberty: Relationship with the Father

For females, sufficient rejection by an insecure, reserved mother who is uncomfortable and competitive with other females during the first years of life leads the child to turn to the father for maternal supplies (Mueller and Aniskiewicz 1986). This period represents the second stage of development. The hysteric's father (who has narcissistic issues, but not necessarily a narcissitic personality disorder) tends to be charming, overstimulating, and self-centered. He thus responds to his daughter with seductive playfulness, teaching her to develop a flirtatious, entertaining style in order to get his attention. This is partially due to the father's unconscious needs to be acknowledged as a desirable man, which are not met by his wife. The daughter (who is sensitive to interpersonal cues) learns that in order to obtain the maternal gratifications she now seeks from her father, she must gratify the father's needs for self-affirmation by behaving in a seductive and submissive manner. As neither parent supports the child's strivings for self-assertion, the child's development of initiative is undermined.

Typically a collusive relationship develops between daughter and father, with the daughter unseating and disparaging the mother (e.g., for not sufficiently meeting the father's needs). The father demands his daughter's undivided loyalty and appears to enjoy mother and daughter competing for his attention. The daughter's alliance with her father thus becomes an identification with the aggressor, laying the pattern for interactions with other men and women later in her life (Josephs 1995, Mueller and Aniskiewicz 1986).

In this type of family system, mothers experience feelings of inadequacy and ambivalence about their daughters due to their own semi-denigration of women and women's roles. Consequently, they eventually resign themselves to a collusive role, abandoning their daughters to the father's influence. Often the mother does not really like the father and withdraws into illness to avoid him, has an affair, or becomes very involved in community work. In the case of the latter, the daughter is often confused by her mother's inattentiveness to her as the mother obviously is "such a good person." The daughter thus takes the father off the mother's hands. She then internalizes her mother's passive or indirect way of gaining control, making it one of her own defenses in later life.

Because of his possessiveness and needs for narcissistic gratification, the hysteric's father fosters an unhealthy dependency in his daughter during her childhood. However, for various reasons, the father is really repelled by dependent women. Thus, while the father creates dependency in his daughter, he also has contempt for it (Mueller and Aniskiewicz 1986).

Although the father previously reinforced his daughter's flirtatious behavior, when she reaches adolescence he begins to feel uncomfortable with the sexual undercurrents in their relationship and often emotionally abandons her. An additional contributor to the father's rejection of his daughter during puberty is that the father feels more intense sexual arousal toward her and recognizes the need for the firmer boundaries that were previously upheld by his daughter's physical and emotional immaturity as a sexual being. To some extent, this demonstrates the greater ego strength of the hysteric's parents (as compared to the hysteroid's parents, who are more likely to inappropriately act out sexual impulses).

Postpuberty

At puberty, which heralds the third stage of development for the hysteric, the father thus becomes critical of his daughter, condemning the seductive behaviors he has previously reinforced (Mueller and Aniskiewicz 1986). He now interprets the daughter's sociability as sexually motivated and becomes rejecting, intrusive, and even more controlling with her. Fights erupt between father and daughter over curfews, clothes, and dates. One hysterical patient reported that her father, who had always called her his little princess during her childhood, made her feel like a slut (even though she was a virgin) during her adolescence. Common results of these fights is for the daughter to run to her room and slam her door or for the father to leave the house, slamming the door behind him. Slamming of doors is symbolic as well as literal, indicating the re-erection of a boundary that should have been established much earlier.

The daughter thus begins to establish an identity at this time, breaks her pact with her father, asserts her will, and no longer bolsters his ego or centers her undivided attention on him. The father threatens the daughter with rejection and appears to stop loving her. Her mother tries to rebind the daughter to the father and colludes with the father in attempting to control the daughter (Mueller and Aniskiewicz 1986). Essentially, the mother tells the daughter to submit to her father's will as the mother has done.

Mueller and Aniskiewicz (1986) have observed that the daughter attempts to renegotiate with the parents by trying to make the mother into someone who is a stronger role model with whom she can identify. She attempts to get her father to stop rejecting her and also tries to get more power with him. When these attempts fail, the hysteric transfers her conflicts (e.g., fear of betrayal, rejection, possessiveness, and being controlled) to her relationships with other men. The adult female hysteric views men as self-centered and narcissistically inclined, but all-important.

Neither father nor mother ever accept responsibility for the problems in their marriage. Quite often, they covertly, if not overtly, blame the daughter for their troubles (Josephs 1995). The hysteric internalizes this perspective and feels intensely guilty as well as resentful. Having bargained for security at the expense of fulfillment, the hysteric feels robbed and relatively unprepared for life.

The Male Hysteric

The etiology of the male hysteric (Samuel Brown, personal communication) differs to some degree from that of the female hysteric. Most often, the male hysteric is an oedipal victor, thus unseating one parent to become the other's partner. For example, the mother feels disappointed in the father and rejected by his extreme preoccupation with work. She thus simultaneously infantilizes her son (as she values compliance) and uses him as a substitute husband. These mothers often enjoy being entertained and wooed by their son and in turn excessively dote on him. Additionally, they use their son as a confidant to discuss their problems, especially problems with their hus-- band. Frequently the hysterical male is an only child or the youngest child with many siblings to care for him (and no older brother to teach him to be an assertive, independent male). Being little and doted on thus becomes ego-syntonic. The hysteric's mother remains his main attachment figure. However, unlike the mother of the hysteroid, she does not prevent his becoming involved in separate activities or having peer relationships.

Mother and son develop a collusion against the father, who tends to be a passive peacemaker, rejecting toward his son, and resentful of the mother's relationship with the son as it interferes with the father–son relationship. However, fathers of hysterical men do not necessarily want to reject their sons. Rather, their characterological passivity prevents them from fighting with the mother to renegotiate the situation or they are too preoccupied with work. If the father is quite successful, the son often feels inadequate by comparison, believing that he will be unable to live up to his father's suc- cess. The son does not seek the father out as a mentor and the father mis- understands his son's behavior, feels rejected, and fails to assume his respon- sibility to teach his son how to become a mature male in the world.

Less is known about the etiology of the second type, the hypermasculine male presentation, than about the more compliant, androgenous one (Blacker and Tupin 1986). Although our familiarity with the hypermasculine hysteric is more limited, we have observed a tendency for their mothers to be emotionally cold, distant, and controlling. The mother's coldness to the son is thus often based on a distrust of men that began with her husband, and sometimes with her own father.

In contrast, the hypermasculine hysterics' fathers tend to be warmer and are often charming, romantic rogues. While they have a very masculine persona, they are often inadequate. The wife is usually the strong, compe- tent one who keeps the family together. The father often has several affairs (which he frequently discusses with his son), relying on his ability to charm and seduce women to gratify his narcissistic needs. The father is usually vain, appearance-conscious, hyperemotional, impressionistic, and flirtatious. The son identifies with the father (who has both hysterical and narcissistic fea- tures) and becomes a "lady's man." In reality, while both father and son appear to be strong, confident, and competent, it is only their false-self pre- sentation. Underneath, they believe that women have the power and their means of gaining power is to seduce them. While these fathers initially present in a charming, jovial manner, their other feelings are close to the surface and can erupt into an affect storm if they are frustrated or hurt. Unlike hysteroid males, however, they do not use splitting. Their anger is thus short-lived and less hurtful.

Developmental Arrest

The major developmental fixation for the hysteric occurs during the oedipal stage of psychosexual development. The classic oedipal fantasy of the heterosexual child is to win the opposite-sex parent away from the same-sex parent, thus replacing him or her as the opposite-sex parent's partner. At the same time, the child fears provoking the same-sex parent's retaliation.

The heterosexual hysterical child is thus made the oedipal victor by the same-sex parent's abandonment of the child to the opposite-sex parent and the opposite-sex parent's flirtatious possession of the child. In the case of the hypermasculine, "Don Juan" male hysteric, the scenario is somewhat different, although the desire is the same. While he wishes to seduce his mother from his father, his mother is unseducible for the boy and his father. The father thus teaches him how to seduce and be taken care of by other women.

Furthermore, we have observed a similar pattern in gay and lesbian patients, although the pattern is reversed (i.e., the child wishes to win the same-sex parent from the opposite-sex parent). In normal development, children realize that the mother and father are married. They thus develop an identification with the rival parent so that when they become adults, they can marry someone similar to the desired parent. With hysterics who are oedipal victors, the appropriate limits and identifications do not occur, leading to a lifetime struggle with triadic issues such as triangulation and jealousy.

The oedipal period coincides with what Erikson (1950) refers to as initiation versus guilt. Hysterics thus demonstrate guilt over aggression, difficulty taking initiative, and a propensity to wish to depend on a fantasized romantic object. This is due to fear of hurting the rival parent with their aggression and having their initiative suppressed by the desired parent.

RESULTING INTERPERSONAL STANCE

As a result of the child's sociability, the preferred parent's domination of the child, and reinforcement of his or her charming and seductive behavior, hysterics develop a pseudodependent interpersonal stance. The hysteric behaves in a passive-compliant manner and manifests a childlike helplessness that induces others to take care of or direct them. Hysterics enact a fragile, innocent, and pleasing persona that belies their true resourcefulness and inner strength. While they consciously identify with the submissive parent, they often have made an unconscious identification with the dominant parent and have the ego resources and self development to function autonomously. However, they believe that if they are competent and powerful, they will not be loved.

The main motive of hysterics is to love and be loved rather than to be competent. They have learned that behavior such as seductiveness elicits the illusion of love from others. Thus, hysterics both consciously and unconsciously relate to potential love objects in a provocative and seductive way that, unfortunately, does not really accomplish their goal. Hysterics do not understand that seduction and manipulation do not lead to intimacy. Furthermore, their interpersonal stance with potential sexual rivals is one of jealousy and competition. They never learned that these rivals are another source of love and intimacy.

Some items from the Psychological Character Inventory (PCI-2) that illustrate the hysterical patient's interpersonal stance are (1) "While I find triangular relationships to be very difficult (e.g., having two friends that know each other well, having a partner with an extremely close friend that I feel competitive with), I often find myself in these types of situations." (2) "I have been told that I behave seductively and have been surprised, as that wasn't my intention." (3) "I need a lot of reassurance." (4) "While I have emotional outbursts, I don't stay mad for long and am able to apologize to or forgive the person that I'm mad at."

STRUCTURAL ISSUES

Cohesive but Suppressed Sense of Self

Hysterics have an essentially intact and integrated sense of identity and object constancy, but self expression is suppressed in conflictual areas of their lives. For example, one hysterical patient was very capable of initiating projects at work, but was unable to self-initiate at home with her husband. Due to his responses to her self-assertions and his own need to feel like the boss, she was compliant and pleasing with him at the expense of her self-initiation.

She was very adept at helping him to implement his dreams. For example, she essentially ran the campaign that put him in local political office. She

stood by his side for hours of campaigning, applying her sociability and enticing charm to winning over voters. But her efforts were always applied to his
dreams, not hers. Thus, in this relationship, only part of her self was expressed.

Underuse of Well-Developed Ego Functions

While hysterics have well-developed ego functions, they believe that using
them (and therefore appearing strong and capable) will eventuate in the
loss of the love object's approval. Hysterics thus learn to act as though they
are unable to think things through, get perspective, understand certain
aspects of reality, or recover from a temporary regression. After many years
of underusing their cognitive capabilities, they began to believe the persona
that they show to the world (e.g., they are inadequate, are not resilient, and
cannot solve their problems).

Because of their dependent, dramatic, emotional persona, and their tendency to catastrophize and let themselves feel overwhelmed, hysterics may
appear to be lacking ego functions. However, as they are structurally very
solid, their defenses may be interpretively resolved.

At ten minutes before the end of the session, one hysterical patient broke
down in tears. She realized that she forgot to tell the therapist how badly
her partner had treated her that week. She told the therapist that she
needed more time or she would not be able to return home as the situation there was so awful (i.e., her boyfriend had gone on a spending spree
after his promotion had been postponed, instead of taking her out to
dinner as he had promised). She told the therapist that she was so upset
that she thought she would need to stay at a girlfriend's house until her
next appointment unless she could talk to the therapist and get her advice about what to do. Her boyfriend made her crazy and she felt at her
wit's end. She said that she felt desperate and just had to have more time.

However, as the therapist believed that the patient had the resources
to manage her situation over the next week, rather than running over
the time limit, she offered a correct interpretation of the patient's underlying motivations (e.g., "Sometimes you catastrophize and let yourself feel
overwhelmed as a way of inviting me to take over for you so you can feel
taken care of. This will be a good thing for us to talk about next session.").
The patient sat up, inhaled a large breath of air, and replied, "You hit
the nail right on the head. I really wish you would figure this out for me
but I know I need to take the night off and think about what I really want
from Ben." She then said, "See you next week" and left the office.

In many ways the hysteric is one of the healthier personality disorders or character styles, manifesting many ego strengths (e.g., observing ego, object constancy) upon which both patient and therapist can rely during the therapeutic process.

Stable Observing Ego

Most significant for therapeutic work, hysterics have the capacity to self observe (even when it's not in use). They are thus capable of joining the therapist in observing, exploring, and working through their conflicts. While their capacity for self observation is often not readily apparent, therapists who resist colluding with the patient's belief in his or her weakness, can rely on the hysterical patient's ego to join the therapist in understanding the underlying motivations of the patient's behavior.

One patient, after missing a session with the therapist, reported that she had "felt blown off" by her boyfriend over the weekend and had then forgotten to call him back when she was supposed to. When he finally reached her and asked her what the matter was, she replied that she must have just been preoccupied. The therapist asked the patient if she thought there was any way that missing her last session was related to having felt "blown off" by the therapist? The patient was able to reflect on possibilities with the therapist and eventually became aware that she was angry at the therapist for giving her such short notice of a schedule change. She interpreted the therapist's behavior as an indication that the therapist thought that her time was more valuable than the patient's time. While the patient felt anxious about expressing her irritation with the therapist, she was able to observe as well as experience herself and able to join the therapist in analyzing the process as it developed between them.

Acting Out

Since the hysteric's parents were somewhat immature and self-indulgent, inconsistent with discipline, and reinforced tantrums by their tendency to attend only to the child's dramatic behaviors, the hysterical patient has relatively low frustration tolerance and a proclivity to act out. Acting out, especially enacting emotions, helps distance the hysteric from what he or she fears is dangerous or overwhelming. Thus, the hysteric can practice expressing emotions without actually experiencing them and being vulnerable. For example, one patient behaved like a petulant child and then watched carefully for the therapist's reaction, to see whether or not it was "really okay to be so rip-roaring mad that I wanted to spit."

The hysteric also acts out what they are unable or unwilling to remember. Thus, due to one patient's paternal transference with the therapist (including incestuous wishes), when the therapist left town the patient had an affair with a man who had the same name as the therapist. In this action, the patient unconsciously expressed her desire to seduce the therapist and her deeper wish to seduce her father. However, while the hysteric's acting out is, at times, inappropriate, it is not self destructive. In contrast, the hysteroid's acting out is more extreme, sadistic, and uncontained.

Object Constancy

As the hysterical patient has fully developed object constancy, the therapist can more easily develop a therapeutic alliance with his or her observing ego to examine the more regressive, inappropriate aspects of the patient's behavior. It is very important for therapists to remember that hysterics frequently exaggerate their feelings. Thus, when they make statements such as "I really hate him," they are often exaggerating and being dramatic rather than splitting. Since hysterics have object constancy, they do not need extra appointments or phone calls (although they are likely to be requested). Gratifying these requests infantilizes patients and colludes with their illusion of insufficiency.

TREATMENT GOALS

In treating the hysterical patient, the following interpersonal and structure building goals are recommended. The focus of treatment with hysterical patients is on developing a process to resolve conflicts, restore self-initiative, and develop the patient's ability to establish and maintain intimate, egalitarian relationships based on mutuality.

Interpersonal Goals

Develop Appropriate Self-Initiation and Assertion

One of the most important goals in working with hysterical patients is to help them develop appropriate self-assertion, self-initiative, and independent actions. These patients tend to resist this development, however, by repeated attempts to induce the therapist into taking over for them, as their father (or mother) did. They relate to the therapist as the expert with all the answers and often ask the therapist to tell them what to do. The therapist often feels pressured to do something or to give wise answers.

Therapists can help these patients develop initiative by (1) resisting the temptations to take over (including giving advice and answering questions); (2) empathically confronting their portrayal of themselves as helpless, incompetent, and passive; (3) supporting their autonomous strivings; and (4) interpreting their ambivalent feelings about being autonomous. For example, one patient had a habit of pursuing a line of thought and then trailing off, ending with "Oh, I don't know" and looking up at the therapist. The patient appeared to turn off his thinking process just before arriving at a conclusion. After noticing the development of this pattern, the therapist observed, "Sometimes, when you seem to get on a roll, you then pull back, just before you arrive at your destination and you turn to me to provide you with the conclusion. What do you make of this?"

When patients do assert themselves or begin to find direction in their life, the therapist needs to be supportive and watch for their proclivity to self-sabotage.

One patient ended a session with an insight about herself that was quite powerful. She noted how she had loved playing the drums when she was a child, but had given them up for the piano because her father wanted her to play a more "ladylike" instrument. She became genuinely excited about picking up the drums again and left the session saying she was going to go out and buy a used drum. The therapist noted that her depression appeared to lift as she experienced a sense of initiative and that this connection might be important for them to track.

Over the next session, the patient never returned to this topic and when the therapist finally expressed curiosity about this, the patient simply said, "Oh yeah. It was just a flash in the pan, I guess. Just like me, isn't it?" The therapist then noted how the patient seemed to be dismissing herself and inviting the therapist to do the same. The therapist wondered what had happened to the patient's interest in pursuing her genuine interests. Eventually, the patient understood how she tended to squelch her own initiative before anyone else could as a way of avoiding the anxiety that she felt about being criticized and rejected when she pursued what she wanted.

Help Patient Distinguish Between Sexual and Affectional Needs

A second goal is to help hysterical patients learn to distinguish between their needs for sex and their needs for affection and comfort. When discussing the patient's reports of troublesome dating experiences or marital interactions, the therapist can help clarify when the patient develops a conflict with a partner or feels unfulfilled or used. For example, one patient had a stressful day at work and wanted comfort. When her husband came home, she was wearing a seductive nightgown and had music on and he attempted to seduce her. The patient felt angry that her husband wasn't responding to her needs. The therapist asked what she needed and she said love. The therapist asked how she wanted her husband to demonstrate that he loved her and she said she wanted him to hold her. The therapist asked her whether a big terry cloth bathrobe or flannel nightgown might have conveyed that message better. The patient laughed and said, "I see what you mean." The therapist and patient then discussed the origin of her confusion about what she needed and how and why she conveyed the wrong idea about what she needed to men.

Another important means of clarifying the hysterical patients' confusion about what they need, how they communicate what they want, and the etiology of this pattern is in working through the erotic transference with the therapist.

In the previous example of the patient who was a married psychiatrist who was having a lesbian affair, the patient said that she loved her husband, and the affair "just happened." The patient said that she felt confused by and uncomfortable with her situation, which the therapist saw as egodystonic for her; the patient said she did not want to hurt anyone.

The patient said that she got married very young and that her family (which was very close) had extremely conservative values. She said that this friend was the first woman that she felt attracted to. She'd had many experiences with male lovers but no experiences with female lovers. The therapist initially conceptualized the patient's problem as the patient's denial of her lesbian proclivities due to her fear of parental rejection. While the therapist kept this as an alternative hypothesis, as she learned more about the patient the question of diagnosis and underlying conflicts became more complicated.

The therapist began to observe the patient behaving in a seductive way with the therapist (e.g., twirling her long hair, leaning over and looking intently at the therapist, smiling coquettishly, then shyly looking down). The therapist additionally observed that the patient behaved this way with her when she seemed to be feeling particularly insecure and needful.

During the beginning of treatment, the patient's seductive behavior was not addressed. Rather, the therapist attempted to get a clearer picture of the patient's current life and family history. She thus learned that while the patient thought that her husband was a kind person and she felt genuinely sexually attracted to him (particularly at the beginning of their relationship), he was not affectionate or emotional, did not express his appreciation, love, and need for her, and was not tender or romantic during sex. In contrast, the woman that she was having an affair with was intensely loving, affectionate, and maternal, and due to her borderline proclivities expressed her love for and need of her with great intensity (e.g., threatening suicide if she did not leave her husband).

As the therapist began to ask the patient questions about her family history to understand the relationship between her previous experiences and her current problem, she discovered that the patient's mother was preoccupied and self-absorbed but that her father seemed warm and loving (as well as very needy and sexually exploitative with the patient). The patient eventually told the therapist that she and her father had an intensely flirtatious and eroticized relationship for many years (e.g., they had given each other long sensuous foot rubs and whispered secrets in each other's ear in front of the mother). The father terminated this relationship abruptly when the patient turned 16 and started dating. The patient had conflictual feelings about this experience as she had enjoyed her father's undivided attention and affectionate contact, but she also felt they "were doing something wrong" that hurt her mother. She was, however, devastated when her father ended these experiences and behaved in a more remote and critical manner with her.

The therapist began to discuss the patient's confusion between sexuality and mothering. She told the patient that she thought that what she really wanted from both her father and her lover was mothering. However, in both instances the relationship became sexualized. The therapist told the patient that she wondered whether she thought that she had to be seduced or to seduce someone to get love and affection.

Later in treatment, the therapist began to gently confront the patient's seductive behavior toward the therapist. The patient initially denied that she was behaving this way and told the therapist that she was misinterpreting her. However, as the patient continued to behave in a seductive manner with the therapist, she eventually began to observe this behavior in herself. The therapist asked the patient if she was feeling a need for mothering from the therapist at that moment.

The patient thought about it and said that maybe she was. She reported that this week both her husband and her lover were very demanding and withholding with her. The therapist asked if she might be feeling a bit mad at them, and she said that she probably was feeling that way. The therapist asked her if she might have also felt mad at her mother for being so rejecting with her when she had tried so hard to have a relationship with her. The patient said she felt guilty when she thought about being angry with her mother.

The therapist also talked with the patient about having to cross a boundary to receive love and affection in her relationship with her father, by having an affair with her best friend (who spent time with she and her husband) and being seductive with the therapist. The therapist and the patient discussed her feeling of excitement about doing something forbidden. She began to realize that in addition to not being affectionate, her sexual relationship with her husband had waned since they were married as it was no longer forbidden. She said that she frequently had dreams about making love with her priest or one of her married professors.

Thus, through making a connection between the patient's current relationships, her family relationships, and her relationship with the therapist, the therapist and patient jointly unraveled the motivations behind her presenting problem. Furthermore, in the relationship with the therapist, the patient discovered that sexuality and nurturance do not necessarily have to go together.

It is important for therapists to help hysterical patients become more aware of their dependency needs (e.g., needs for affection, reassurance, tenderness, empathy). As seductive behavior and needs for maternal comfort became confused in their early attachment experiences, they continue to be confused in their current relationships. They do not believe they can trust other people to simply comfort them without having ulterior motives.

For example, one patient could not believe that her boyfriend really loved her beyond gratifying his sexual and narcissistic needs. She resented feeling like his sexual trophy, the beautiful woman that he showed off to his buddies, and yet she knew that this was how she had originally won him away from the woman he had previously been dating. Even when he was genuinely and platonically affectionate with her, she would suspect that what he really wanted was sex and would either eroticize his advances or rebuff him in her resentment.

Once the eroticization of needs for nurturance is recognized, the hysterical patient can begin the process of rediscovering and clarifying what their interpersonal needs really are at any given point in time. Hysterics are more likely to get their interpersonal needs met when they have greater clarity about what their needs really are.

Help Patients Learn to Express Needs and Feelings Directly

It is important to help hysterical patients learn to express their needs and feelings directly and appropriately rather than through seduction and manipulation. It is particularly useful to attend to the patient's indirect communications to the therapist (e.g., the patient brings up problems in outside relationships that apply to how the patient is feeling with the therapist), to understand the patient's fears and fantasies about direct communication, and to encourage the patient's direct verbalizations regarding his or her concerns.

Structural Goals

Hysterics do not have poor ego functions. Rather, for these patients using ego functions is ego-dystonic. Thus, the therapist needs to foster the patient's use of these functions and enhance the areas that were not sufficiently encouraged by their parents. The hysterical personality's three areas of structural weakness are (1) the ability to integrate thinking and feeling, (2) the ability to think before acting, and (3) the ability to gain perspective on competing needs or underlying motivations. Related to these weaknesses is the hysteric's vague, impressionistic cognitive style.

Perhaps, one of the best examples of turning off the ego is the hysteric's overuse of global, impressionistic thinking. This is not to say that there are not positive things about this style, but rather that it needs to be balanced with logical thinking and attention to detail. The creative process has been viewed as a type of regression in the service of the ego in which individuals vacillate between what is currently described as right and left brain thinking. Thus, all the following goals are to some extent related to learning this ability (e.g., integrating thinking and feeling, thinking before acting on impressions).

Treating Global, Impressionistic Thinking Style

Therapists are advised to resist directly confronting the patient's global, impressionistic cognitive style in the first phase of treatment (Josephs 1995). Instead, the patient's attention needs to be directed toward their ego-dystonic affects. The therapist begins by remaining in the area of emotional relating, where the hysterical patient is most comfortable. The therapist, therefore, helps the patient to recognize and work through pseudoemotional defenses so that the patient can relate more authentically without enacting a role. This includes helping the patient understand the etiology of his or her ego-dystonic feelings (i.e., the ones they don't want to express).

As patients begin to develop a more authentic therapeutic alliance, the therapist can then help them understand how their impressionistic cognitive style (combined with their hyperemotionality) tends to make them feel insubstantial and contributes to faulty conclusions. In particular, the therapist can show patients how they have combined impressionistic thinking with a tendency to idealize (or use "rose-colored glasses") in order to support their illusion of a wonderful childhood or fantasy about an ideal romantic object. Many hysterical patients enter therapy describing their parents and their childhoods as "American as apple pie." However, they are unable to remember any details about what actually happened (Josephs 1995). Asking the patient who talks impressionistically to fill in details and make ideational connections can be very helpful in grounding and clarifying the hysteric's thinking (e.g., "What are some particularly good childhood memories for you?" "What were you angry at each other about?"). This point was pressed with one patient who had described her family as very close; she then recalled that in third grade, she asked to live for one year with her aunt and uncle who lived across the country. The patient said that she never thought about this and the therapist told her that she thought that this experience would be very important for them to understand.

Another patient talked about her upcoming wedding as a "disaster in the making with everyone at each other's throats." When the therapist asked the patient for details about whom, specifically, she was worried, the patient was able to more accurately discuss her difficulties with her future mother-in-law, who was trying to run the show by giving the patient advice that she did not want. The therapist then discussed the patient's difficulty setting appropriate limits with her future mother-in-law and the triangle that the patient experienced between her fiancé, his mother, and herself.

Integrating Cognition with Affect

The therapist can further encourage the integration of the patient's cognitions and emotions as well as promote the patient's ability to integrate related ideas by (1) encouraging the patient to think through events rather than glossing over them, and (2) helping hysterical patients make relevant cognitive connections whenever they seem to be emotionalizing or defensively employing cognitive fog rather than thinking clearly. In addition, the therapist can help hysterical patients recognize that they have a good brain upon which they can rely and that it is acceptable, appealing, and fun to be smart.

For example, one hysterical patient who was extremely bright and creative, quickly felt overwhelmed with learning basic computer skills, believing that her brain "just didn't work that way." It did not matter to her that she was excelling in her graduate program and had won several academic awards. She fully believed that she was almost incapable of learning how to master basic commands without deleting something really important and so had to rely on the kindness of her friends. In therapy, this patient came to understand how she found ways to downplay her intelligence and play up being inept in order to assure being accepted by her peers and, in particular, her boyfriend, who felt competitive with her.

The therapist's integration of his or her own cognitive and affective experience as expressed through emotional empathy for the patient also helps the hysterical personality to experience and witness a working model of integration in action (Mueller and Aniskiewicz 1986). This is especially important as the hysteric has not really had the opportunity to interact on a genuine and intimate basis with a significant other who was comfortable with combining expressive and instrumental traits or aspects of experience. In the previous example, the therapist modeled being both empathic and analytical as she helped the patient understand why she felt insecure about using computers.

Becoming Cognizant of Competing Needs and Aims

One of the hallmark characteristics of hysterics is their struggle with unconscious competing needs or aims and the dilemmas they experience as a result of these conflicts. It is useful for the therapist to help the patient uncover for examination each pole of their conflict and develop a process for becoming aware of and better understanding their conflicts. The traditional psychoanalytic techniques of confrontation, clarification, and interpretation are useful for this process.

For example, one patient persistently pressured the therapist to "tell me what to do." To acknowledge the polarity represented by both the spoken and unspoken press, the therapist said, "Part of you wishes that I knew what would be best for you and was willing to direct your actions like your father did. However, we know from previous experience that there is another part of you that resents feeling underestimated or treated like a child. And telling you what to do would prevent us from getting to know you better."

Once patients become aware of or acknowledge conflicting needs or motivations, the therapist may help them to understand the origin of the conflict (e.g., different messages from their mother and father, conflicts between what they want and their moral values). In addition, the therapist can help patients see how their two internal voices do not mediate or influence each other, thus truncating and recycling the conflict instead of arriving at a more satisfying conclusion. At this point, the therapist can help patients utilize their observing ego functions to mediate the conflicts. For example, in one situation the therapist asked a patient, "If you were a mediator, and your conflicting feelings were two people, what would you think and how would you advise them?"

Learning to Think Before Acting

Therapists can help hysterical patients in a number of ways learn how to thoughtfully reflect on their feelings before acting on them. For example, instead of jumping to immediately assist a patient (e.g., answering his or her question), the therapist can model taking a minute or so to think about how he or she would like to respond. Even commenting on this process can sometimes be helpful; the therapist might say, "I'm not asleep over here—I'm just letting things simmer around to give that question its due."

In addition, John Nardo (personal communication) talks about the fine art of "playing dumb doctor" with patients, as a way of inviting them to reflect on their process. For example, one patient complained of feeling "used and abused" by her mother-in-law, who told long-winded stories about herself and appeared to want the patient's undivided attention while the patient was both trying to prepare a family meal and tend to her 6-month-old infant. On automatic, the patient would cut her mother-in-law off with some lame excuse that usually backfired and made her husband angry. When the patient asked what she should do, the therapist responded by asking the patient what she thought of throwing up on her mother-in-law's feet. The patient laughed, and said she would love to. The therapist then said, "It sounds like you feel more permission to throw up on her or cut her off than you do to just tell her what you need from her . . . like watching the baby or cutting up the vegetables. What do you think stops you?" The patient then began to talk about how she felt resentful about being unable to be direct with her own mother as a child, due to her mother's seeming fragility.

Therapists can also help hysterics learn to think before acting by first helping them to recognize when they do not think things through. It is useful to explore with them both the advantages, in terms of spontaneity, and disadvantages, in terms of unforeseen or unwanted consequences, of acting without thinking.

CORRECTIVE INTERPERSONAL EXPERIENCE

Hysterical patients have experienced frequent conflicts around (1) responsibility–irresponsibility, (2) power–powerlessness, (3) dependence–independence, (4) love and sexuality, and (5) substantiality–insubstantiality. As a child, the hysterical patient was not sufficiently attended to by one parent and infantalized or dominated by the other. Thus, it is important that the therapist treating hysterical patients does not take over for them. Rather, it is useful to allow them to experiment and make their own mistakes, providing them with help when needed.

In providing hysterical patients with a corrective therapeutic relationship, it is recommended that therapists be nondirective, nonexploitative (while setting reasonable limits to avoid being exploited), warm (without being subtly seductive), and appropriately thoughtful. The therapist helps the patient to make ideational connections while offering emotional empathy, and always invites the patient's observing ego to join the therapist in the continuing exploration of the patient's self experience. The corrective therapeutic stance thus requires the therapist to be authentic, self-aware, nondirective, and nondefensive. Most importantly, the therapist must relate to the hysterical patient as an intelligent adult.

In particular, the therapist needs to resist being seduced into being the expert (i.e., the one who has the insights; being narcissistically gratified by the patient's progress). Rather, the therapist must allow the hysterical patient to struggle on his or her own and reflect back to the patient his or her own efforts and contributions. This is more complicated than it seems since hysterical patients can literally shape the therapist's behavior in this direction (e.g., "You were so helpful today").

In treating hysterical patients, therapists are thus advised to encourage the patients' evolving investigatory process, to facilitate their capacity for self-reflection, and to help them develop their own insights and increase their understanding of themselves and others in a more complex and transference-free manner. In large measure the therapist facilitates these goals by allowing hysterical patients the opportunity to experience their anxiety while helping them "to discover its sources and disabling manifestations in relationships" (Mueller and Aniskiewicz 1986, p. 115).

Therapist Must Be Authentically Warm, Particularly as the Relationship Develops

The therapist's authentic expressions of warm feelings are especially important because as a child the hysterical patient did not receive warmth from one parent and received it with conditions from the other parent (e.g., be my substitute spouse, be my mirror). Warmth includes affection, tenderness, empathic responsiveness to the patient, genuine interest in his or her development, and authentic regard for the patient's best interests. Warmth resides in the heart and sits on the face as an expression of caring, respect, and faith in the personhood of the patient. It is particularly important when hysterical patients are seeing a therapist who is the same sex as the rejecting parent.

Therapist Must Not Be Seduced by or
Get Angry at the Hysteric's Seductive Behaviors

Therapists must be tolerant of seductive (and competitive) transferences without exploiting or reacting to the patient. It is important that therapists do not personalize the patient's seductive behavior or in some way participate in the patient's cycle of acting out, gratification, fear and rejection, punitive anger, guilt, and suffering (Josephs 1995).

Clarifying the real underlying needs being expressed in an erotic transference requires the therapist to (1) tolerate his or her uncomfortable feelings as the erotic transference develops; (2) resist colluding or acting out on erotic feelings with the patient (e.g., not subtly flirting with the patient); (3) treat the erotic transference like any other, which means encouraging verbalized exploration of what is being conveyed through the development of the transference relationship; and (4) clarify the real needs and motivations that underlie the patient's transactions. Understanding how the patient came to confuse lust and love and empathizing with how the patient learned that sexuality (e.g., flirting, seductive flattery) needed to be bartered for maternal nurturance (e.g., affection, empathy, soothing, warmth, caring concern) can be clarifying.

The therapist needs to be cautious about exploring the erotic transference, especially in the first phase of treatment. Josephs (1995) warns therapists to minimize direct attention to the hysteric's sexual provocativeness in favor of exploring the hysteric's underlying needs for affection and intimacy, which fuels this symptom. Josephs (1995) believes that if the patient's sexually provocative behavior is confronted too soon, the hysterical patient may become more defensive or terminate prematurely. Direct explorations and interpretations are often most effective once these patients have started to comment on this behavior themselves (e.g., noting how they behave flirtatiously at times when they do not mean it).

Pseudoerotic defenses against aggressive impulses are also common and require the therapist to help the patient understand what she or he is really trying to communicate and why. One patient would tell the therapist in detail how he wanted to find a woman just like her, kind and gentle and sensitive, but also emotionally strong and wise. As he talked he would spread his legs wide apart, run his fingers through his hair, bite his lower lip, and caress his hands in a suggestive manner. The more he talked the more uncomfortable the therapist became, until she finally realized that he seemed to engage in this pseudoerotic sequence of behavior directly after the therapist made an interpretation that appeared to offend or distress the patient in some way. The therapist asked the patient if he were trying to communicate more than one message to her at the same time. She wondered if while one part of the patient was expressing appreciation of her, perhaps another part was expressing some discomfort. The therapist noted that the patient's flattering and somewhat provocative response to her began after her last comment about how intrusive and yet needed his mother was to him as a child. In this example, it was particularly important that the therapist contain her responses to the patient, rather than directly or indirectly express her discomfort.

Once again, these exploratory speculations must be offered with care after a genuine alliance has been secured. Hysterical patients will feel exposed and ashamed when confronted with the possibility that they are trying to convey their real feelings through indirect or manipulative means. It is thus important for the therapist to watch carefully for patients' shame reactions and attend to them with empathy. Explaining to the hysteric that most people develop indirect modes of expression because direct modes were unsuccessful (e.g., were punished or shamed) can help normalize their behavior and lead them to feel understandable.

Therapist Must Resist Being Overwhelmed by the Patient's Hyperemotionality

It is important for the therapist to resist becoming overwhelmed by the patient's frequent expressions of a "sea of affects" and thus not drown in them. While hysterical patients grew up feeling that they could only get attention for being dramatic and hyperemotional, they also often believe and were told by their parents that they and their feelings "are too much" for other people. It is, thus, important for the therapist neither to give extra attention nor to subtly withdraw from the patient at these times.

It is also necessary for therapists to distinguish between the hysterical patient's genuine feelings and their exaggerated, acted-out emotions. The function of the latter is often the avoidance of something uncomfortable for the patient, often a different feeling. Therapists' genuine interest and patience in learning about the patient's authentic feelings provides an attitude with which the hysterical patient can begin to identify.

After an alliance is formed, this process can be directly addressed and explored, particularly when the patient is expressing exaggerated, enacted emotions. For example, the therapist warmly said to a patient, "Sometimes I get the sense that you don't really believe that I'll listen to you, unless you turn the music way up—that you don't expect me to be listening for your quiet sounds. Is this a familiar experience for you?" "It is as if you expect me to respond like your mother (father)."

Therapist Must Resist Being Overly Entertained or Too Self-Disclosing

Therapists must also resist letting themselves be overly entertained by the patient's charming ways or succumbing to the pull to self-disclose too much in response to the patient's press to make the relationship less threatening before understanding the threat. All of our patients are not charming and funny. When such patients enter treatment, it can be a welcome relief just to relax and enjoy them. The therapist is not advised to act like a blank slate, never laughing or smiling (i.e., using reaction formation against his or her natural proclivity). Rather, what is important is that the therapist does not use the relationship to get his or her own narcissistic needs met or that enjoying the patient does not become a primary way of relating. If this does occur, the therapeutic relationship will recapitulate the patient's collusion with the seducible parent.

For example, one South American hysterical patient spoke in a manner that was reminiscent of a Gabriel García Marquez novel. She was bright, whimsical, and creative. She frequently told the therapist stories in a delightful manner with a charming accent such as, "Although I describe myself as a vegetarian, I really don't like vegetables. I am, more accurately, a non-flesh eater. What I really feel passion for is chocolate." She then began to tell a very amusing story about an elderly, eccentric aunt in South America who only ate chocolate. On another occasion, she told the therapist: "Before I die, I have two wishes: to touch the tongue of a whale and to swim with the manatees. Carlos [her husband] told me 'Aida, you better not tell anyone that.'" After a sufficient period of time to establish that this behavior was a pattern, the therapist told her that while she enjoyed her stories and found them delightful, it was important to understand why she was paying the therapist to entertain the therapist. The therapist said that she also sensed that there were important feelings that the patient needed to discuss with the therapist, but was afraid to.

In the beginning phase of treatment, therapists are also advised to resist the urge to overcome the hysteric's inhibitions, resistances, or narrow thinking through self-disclosure or giving the patient glimpses of the therapist's own life experiences (i.e., to enable them to acknowledge a feeling in themselves). Although hysterics may feel vulnerable, alone, and embarrassed, and may have difficulty with one-sided self-disclosure (Mueller and Aniskiewicz 1986), the therapist is advised to interpret the unconscious resistance to enduring the anxiety about experiencing the conflicted areas of their childhood. "The patient feels vulnerable, but exactly to what the patient does not know" (Allen 1991, p. 159).

As reciprocity is important for the hysterical patient to develop, once the patient's transference to the therapist is understood and resolved, self-disclosure in response to the patient's questions that are not defensively based or too personal is not problematic. It is important, however, for hysterical patients first to understand why they do not feel like the therapist's equal before helping them to feel that way.

Therapist Must Support Initiative, Competence, and Appropriate Assertion

The hysteric has no model for appropriate assertion and the healthy expression of initiative. Generally one parent modeled passivity while the other parent suppressed assertive behavior. The latter parent's need was to dominate the patient, requiring the child's compliance instead of supporting the child's initiative.

In the beginning of treatment, one patient kept requesting authoritative guidance from the therapist by asking if he could talk about a particular topic, bring a drink into therapy, or tell the therapist about his dreams. In some ways this patient was testing the therapist (i.e., checking out the therapist's control needs before entrusting himself to the therapeutic relationship). The therapist understood this and helped the patient to explore his underlying conflicts with authority that compelled him to ask so many of these questions.

It is important for the therapist to be very nondirective with hysterical patients to allow them to find their own direction. Furthermore, when the hysteric does find it, and takes initiative, it is advised that the therapist support the patient's own good feelings about taking a risk and being successful rather than verbally rewarding taking initiative. The latter has the potential of transforming the patient's initiative into a compliant enactment (i.e., of the therapist's advice to take the initiative). This can inadvertently support the hysteric's ego-syntonic stance of passivity.

DIFFERENTIAL DIAGNOSIS

Hysterical Versus Hysteroid Personalities

While the hysterical and hysteroid personality superficially seem to share a number of characteristics, including heightened emotionality, seductiveness, and a theatrical, dramatic style of relating, they also manifest distinct differences, most markedly in terms of underlying structural issues that affect their level of object relatedness. The behavior of hysterics, while exaggerated, is constrained by social roles, while hysteroids' behavior is not. Hysterics may allow themselves to feel overwhelmed by emotions, but they have the ego strength (e.g., ego controls, tolerance of anxiety, object constancy, observing ego) to regroup, which hysteroid-borderlines do not. Hysterics rarely have unconstructive regressions because they can mediate or contain their emotions when needed, whereas hysteroids generally are unable to do so.

In addition, the hysteric's tendency to polarize and act out extreme emotional states may superficially look like splitting. But the hysteric's polarities really represent a struggle with ambivalence or a conflict between needs rather than splitting. Hysterics are thus able to emotionally recognize the relevance of both poles. Furthermore, their intense expression of affect is often exaggerated to have an impact on others rather than as an expression of true primitive feelings.

Hysterics generally have well-developed ego functions. As a result, the therapist can rely on their observing ego to join in the investigatory process. They are thus generally able to see the reality of the therapist as well as experience their transference feelings. In contrast, hysteroids cannot differentiate transference from reality or join in observing the interactions occurring between the therapist and the patient.

Furthermore, hysterics have stable object constancy and whole object relations. They thus do not primarily relate to others as selfobjects. While they may act very needy and demanding, they are able to tolerate not getting their needs met while maintaining positive feelings toward the object. They are also able to empathize with the object's needs and feelings.

Hysterics also have a developed sense of self. While they may act like they do not know what they want and have difficulty asserting themselves to obtain what they want, they do generally know what they need and feel (except in specific areas such as confusing sex with affection or being uncomfortable with aggression).

The aims of the hysteroid and hysteric are distinctly different. The hysteroid's primary aim is to protect the self or merge with a maternal object, while the hysteric's primary aim is to maintain a loving relationship where his or her independence is encouraged.

Hysterical Versus Narcissistic Personalities

The hysteric's public style is similar to the narcissist's presentation. Both personalities are attention-seeking, and thus often charming and exhibitionistic around potential love objects. The underlying aims, however, are very different. The hysteric's wish is to be loved and appreciated in a mutual (e.g., give and take), exclusive relationship with a whole object. In contrast, the narcissist's underlying aim is to be admired and adored in a unilateral relationship (e.g., the narcissist takes, the other gives) with a selfobject.

Despite their inappropriate object choices, the neurotic-level hysteric, with whole, integrated object relations, is thus able to love others for who they are, as separate individuals, and want to be loved back as an independent, thinking person. In contrast, preneurotic narcissists, with more compromised object relations, are generally still searching for someone who provides a mirroring or idealizing selfobject relationship rather than an intimate relationship with a separate person. Although hysterics are very attracted to romantic fantasy, they have less difficulty giving up their illusions than narcissists, as the illusions don't compensate for inadequate internal structures. They can also distinguish between their transferential fantasies and the real relationship in which they are involved. The narcissist has much more difficulty with this distinction.

Hysterical Versus Masochistic Personalities

Both hysterical and masochistic personalities are other-oriented and concerned about relationships, and they tend to idealize the love object. While hysterics often manifest mild masochistic tendencies because of having been overpowered by one of their parents, their interpersonal style and underlying aims differ considerably from those of masochists. Hysterics attempt to

seduce the romantic object through sexual attractiveness, flirtatious entice-
ments, and being adorable and adoring and clever. In contrast, masochists
attempt to guarantee a relationship with an idealized security object by taking care of the object and making him- or herself indispensable to or needed
by the object. While the hysteric's style is dramatic and entertaining, the
masochist's style is sensible and caring.

Both personality types have unsatisfying romantic relationships, but hysterics participate in creating the relational turbulence while masochists live
a life of quiet desperation. Furthermore, hysterics are often the ones to leave
a relationship or have an affair when it is unsatisfying, while masochists simply endure the painful relationship (believing that they have no other option). For example, one hysterical patient who was in an abusive relationship told her partner: "Either you stop talking to me like that or I'm out of
here." In contrast, masochistic patients, in a similar situation, would be likely
to think that their partner's behavior was their fault and would try harder
to please the partner.

COUNTERTRANSFERENCE ISSUES

The therapist who is helpful to hysterical patients must be able to allow
countertransference reactions to develop, using them to understand the
patient at a deeper level. Countertransference reactions often give the
therapist a glimpse of the hysterical patient's underlying motivations or
intentions with the therapist. It is important that the therapist's countertransference responses be experienced as a regression in the service of
the ego.

Being Induced to Taking Over (i.e., Fostering
Too Much Dependency, Infantilizing the Patient)

As we have previously noted, the hysterical patient typically makes implicit
or explicit bids for the therapist's advice, as if the patient were inadequate
and needed the expertise of the powerful, all-knowing therapist. Even when
hysterical patients have an insight of their own, they may often turn to the
therapist to ask, "Do you think I'm right?" The hysteric may tell therapists
what a great help their comments are to the patient and how much the
patient appreciates their guidance. Or the patient may just stop before finishing his or her sentences, nonverbally inviting the therapist to finish the
patient's ideas (Mueller and Aniskiewicz 1986). Therapists often begin to

feel impressive, effective, competent, and an especially good match with the hysteric patient.

If therapists are insecure or have their own need to be in control, they may succumb to the patient's bid. In such cases they begin to regularly give the patient advice or habitually finish the patient's sentences. Unfortunately, this behavior reinforces patients' beliefs about their insufficiency. It also supports their belief that relationships are contingent on their willingness to relinquish their power to the love object. In such circumstances, therapists will often notice that while hysterics initially seem appreciative of the therapist's advice, they really only use the advice that supports them doing what they want. In such cases, therapists may begin to feel frustrated with the patient.

Furthermore, if hysterical patients sense that the therapist is getting excessive narcissistic gratification about being experienced as omnipotent, they feel betrayed and offended. They often frustrate the therapist's attempts to help them, indirectly pulling the pedestal out from under him or her. This often engenders the therapist to experience the hysterical patient's feelings of inadequacy and helplessness. Under such conditions, therapists may feel narcissistically injured and experience feelings of shame about themselves or anger toward the patient.

Most importantly, when therapists give advice to hysterical patients (as the parent did), it impedes the development "of a clearly delineated transference that can be made conscious to the patient and then interpreted" (Allen 1991, p. 162). In other words, if therapists introduce themselves into the mix (i.e., behave like the transferential object), discerning what is transference and what is real is a far more difficult task.

When hysterical patients confront a therapist who has unconsciously behaved in an arrogant or authoritarian way (even if this behavior was largely induced by the patient), therapists are advised to acknowledge their contribution and empathize with the patient's response. Hysterical patients first need to have the validity of their perceptions acknowledged. At that point, therapists may gently suggest that the patient may also be sensitive to these issues because of his or her history and that, as a team, they may want to explore how these issues are played out in the patient's relationship with the therapist and other important people in the patient's life. If therapists attempt to diffuse the intensity of these patients' anger with the therapist by prematurely connecting the present relationship issues to the past, patients will sense that the therapist is trying to manipulate them into squelching their anger by blaming them in some way, and the therapeutic alliance will be jeopardized.

Getting Seduced by the Patient

Since the hysterical patient is skilled at the art of seduction, the therapist needs to be particularly cautious about subtly acting on eroticized impulses or fantasies. If the therapist joins patients in their flirtations, allows him- or herself to be overly entertained, subtly flirts back with the patient, or accepts the patient's gifts without processing the meaning, the therapy may be derailed. The therapist must also resist succumbing to the patient's many efforts (e.g., flattery, appreciativeness, friendliness, acting cooperative) to convince the therapist that this is going to be an easy, enjoyable therapeutic relationship (Mueller and Aniskiewicz 1986). This attitude oversimplifies the complexity of hysterical patients' struggles and misses their investment in role playing and impression management.

Hysterical patients are adept at inducing narcissistic collusions with seductive undertones. Playing the role of the good patient, like the good daughter or son, comes naturally. Unlike in the narcissist, however, this process is much more conscious in the hysteric.

Consequently, therapists may notice that they are really looking forward to the session with the patient and/or they may not consult about the patient with a colleague since everything seems to be going so well. It is important for therapists to recognize these telltale signs, use their consulting relationships to sort out the patient's impact, and, when appropriate, discuss with the patient how difficult it might be for the patient to let him- or herself step out of the "good patient" role.

Therapists who are threatened by their own reactions to the erotic transference can become angry with the patient about feeling manipulated, or they may be afraid of their own sexual feelings or of being sued for something that they did not do. A common way therapists enact these feelings is by withdrawing from the patient or behaving in a passive-aggressive manner (e.g., not returning phone calls promptly).

Hysterical patients often sense this reaction and either try to submit to the therapist's wishes or rebel. They may feel ashamed, emotionally withdraw, or escalate their seductive behaviors, affect storms, and acting out. A premature termination may occur. As with all defensive behavior, therapists need to acknowledge their contribution and understand the patient's response.

Being Triangulated

Hysterical patients tend to develop or involve themselves in triangulated relationships both in and out of therapy. Within the therapeutic relationship the patient may attempt to induce triangulation either by telling the therapist about what someone else has said about them, or by comparing the therapist directly or by implication to others. Triangulation often induces feelings of jealousy, competition, and anger in therapists.

One patient who was a professional counselor came to session after session talking about how his supervisor had been so incredibly helpful to him in understanding his relationship with his wife. He extolled the wisdom of his supervisor's concrete advice and suggestions about how to handle various difficult interactions. The patient then talked about how he realized therapy could not give him the same kind of help as supervision (although his marital relationship was one of the major therapeutic issues discussed). The therapist began to feel competitive with the supervisor and subtly critical toward the patient.

A more helpful intervention would be for the therapist to observe to the patient how he came to her for help with his marriage and was recently discussing how much more helpful the supervisor was in helping him with this problem. The therapist might say, "I'm aware of feeling like I'm in a triangle with your supervisor where we're competing to be the most helpful to you. Do you ever feel this way with people?"

Anger at Feeling Manipulated

Therapists can become angry with the hysterical patient in reaction to feeling controlled or maneuvered. Therapists with subjective countertransference (who experience countertransference reactions out of their own related histories of having controlling, manipulative parents) can be particularly sensitive to the patient's manipulations, feel angry, and respond to the patient in a somewhat defensive or guarded way.

Appreciating these patients' history of being dominated and reinforced for expressing their needs indirectly can facilitate both the therapist's and the patient's understanding of the patient's underlying motivations, including its causes. Therapists can also use their anger diagnostically; they can explore with the patient if the patient ever felt angry at being maneuvered. As with all countertransference responses, therapists are encouraged to treat it as information, and attempt to resist acting it out.

Being Reactive to the Hysteric

Hysterical patients' tendency to catastrophize and act out can at times be overwhelming to a therapist, particularly if the therapist's parents did not contain their own or the therapist's emotions when he or she was a child. It is very important, however, not to get hysterical with hysterics. Reactivity re-inforces these patients' tendency to exaggerate and catastrophize and leads them to feel like neither they nor the therapist is a grown-up. Rather, it is advised that the therapist quietly listen to the patient's emotions and then respond to the patient in a manner that clarifies and increases the patient's perspective. Once an alliance is established, humor can be an important tool to increase the ability to self-observe (Glickauf-Hughes et al. 1996).

For example, one patient came in complaining (1) about how she had an argument with her boyfriend and she was sure that he did not love her anymore, (2) that her parents were laying a guilt trip on her for not visiting them over spring vacation, (3) that an insect bit her and she might have Lyme disease, (4) that she was too stupid to pass her statistics course and probably should drop out of school, and (5) she ate a hot fudge sundae after an argument with her boyfriend and was thus getting obese. The therapist responded, "Whew! A real bad hair day!"

SPECIAL ISSUES IN TREATMENT RELATED TO THE GENDER OF THE THERAPIST AND PATIENT

Female Heterosexual Patient with Female Therapist

Confront and Interpret Competition and Oedipal Issues

One female hysterical patient initially expressed her unconscious feelings of jealousy and competition with the therapist through her dreams. The patient described one dream in which the female therapist had a perfect husband and was telling him that she was pregnant. In exploring the dream the patient realized that she felt jealous of the therapist's relationship with her husband, wishing that she, too, could have a perfect husband. The pa-tient also felt competitive with the therapist's "wisdom and perceptiveness." The patient was aware that the therapist was writing a book and thus "preg-nant" with creative ideas, while she felt unable to tap her own creativity because it was hard to be reflective or trust herself. The therapist responded to the dream by noting how it was "difficult not to feel a little mad or com-petitive when someone else had what you wanted—especially if you were afraid that you might never get it." She then asked the patient how com-petitive feelings were expressed and responded to in her family.

Be a Strong Identification Figure

In general, therapists who are warm, compassionate, assertive, thinking, and independent provide hysterical patients with the type of female role model that they never experienced and thus did not identify with. These behaviors can be expressed in a number of ways: (1) alternating between empathy and confrontation, (2) modeling the integration of feeling and thinking, and (3) keeping a good balance between accepting the patient and providing appropriate limits. Most important, however, is the therapist's genuine comfort with being a woman and rapport with other women.

Avoid Focusing on Dependency Issues to the Exclusion of Sexual and Aggressive Issues

Female therapists with female patients may overly focus on the patient's needs for affection to the exclusion of exploring sexual and aggressive issues (Samuel Brown, personal communication). The patient may in fact divert the therapist from these explorations because, as one patient said, "I just could never talk about sex with my mother. We would have both died in shame." Any topic that is actively avoided needs to be noted. In this example, talking about shame issues may need to precede discussions of sex and aggression.

Female Heterosexual Patient with a Male Therapist

Provide a New Experience with a Man Who Does Not Dominate and is Not Self-Centered

The male therapist treating a female hysteric needs to provide a relationship with the patient that does not use her to gratify his narcissistic needs even though she plays up to those needs and expects him to respond (Mueller and Aniskiewicz 1986). The male therapist needs to treat the patient as an independent, intelligent, thinking individual who has a good mind worth understanding and getting to know. He needs to resist taking over for her and, instead, clarify her struggles between power and powerlessness, substantiality and insubstantiality as is appropriate.

Process the Erotic Transference

The male therapist needs to first help the patient to understand the underlying aims that propel the erotic transference (e.g., the need for affection and maternal nurturance). Then, preferably after the patient has commented on her seductive behavior with men, the therapist needs to process it within and outside the therapeutic relationship, helping the patient to make the historical links that put her behavior in perspective and help to make it understandable (Josephs 1995). Most important, if the therapist is aware of being attracted to the patient, he must use this as information rather than being subtly seduced by the patient or reacting to her in a reaction-formed manner.

Encourage Relationships with Women

An important issue for male therapists to address with a female hysterical patient is her need for mothering (Josephs 1995). Clarifying needs for maternal nurturance and encouraging relationships with women who can gratify these needs in friendship is especially healing for hysterical patients since their fathers were subtly or more openly denigrating of their mothers. Treating the patient and discussing other women in a respectful manner can be an important adjunct to this process.

Male Heterosexual Patient with Female Therapist

Support Independence Without Being Rejecting or Critical

Since the male hysteric was inappropriately seduced into excessive dependency and overinvolvement with his mother, replacing his father as her partner, the patient needs to experience a woman who invites him to engage in independent thinking and action without shaming him for his dependency needs. For example, one patient continually asked the therapist for her advice, opinions, and interpretations. The therapist responded by saying that she was aware of how his mother liked him to rely on her that way, and that while she did not mind answering his questions, she thought that it was not in his best interest as it kept him from discovering his own capabilities and from finding out whether the therapist would still like and accept him as an assertive, competent man.

Avoid Infantilizing the Patient

The mother of the male hysterical patient infantilized her son, treating him as a child even as he matured into adulthood. The therapist thus must be sensitive to and address the patient's feelings in this area. The female therapist is advised to treat the patient like a capable adult despite the patient's frequent regressions to behaving in a boyish and cute manner. For example, one patient brought in party hats and cupcakes for his birthday, inviting the therapist to sing a childhood party song in celebration with him. The therapist, feeling in a bind, told the patient that she was aware of wanting to join the patient in the fun of celebrating. However, she was also curious about the meaning such a celebration with the therapist would have for the patient. The therapist explained that it was sometimes important to understand the meaning behind our impulses before we took action so that the meaning of what we decide to do would be clearer. The therapist then invited the patient to explore how his birthdays had gone in the past and what this celebration might mean today.

By introducing a process of thoughtful reflection between the patient's impulse and action, the therapist attempts to help the patient understand what he is about to enact as well as exercise the ability to think things through. Such an approach also avoids treating the patient as if he could not bear anything but the therapist's compliance with his invitation and its enactment, and thus treats him like the adult he is.

Support Relationships with Men

The female therapist should also support the patient's development of relationships with men since the mother interfered with the patient's relationship with his father, essentially keeping her son to herself. Through friendships with other men the patient can learn more about how to be a man in the world of men. It is important that the female therapist talk respectfully about men.

Male Patient with Male Therapist

Allow Competition

The male therapist with a male hysterical patient needs to be able to allow competitive feelings and behaviors, including exploring healthy ways to compete and express ambitious strivings with other men. Furthermore, it is sometimes important to acknowledge to the patient when he has won the competition with the therapist.

Serve as a Male Role Model

Since the father of the hysteric did not have time for his son and did not teach him more instrumental skills in the world, the male therapist needs to serve as a model and a guide for the patient. This involves both being independent as well as relational and helping the patient with authentic deficiencies in his learning that are not an expression of pseudohelplessness (e.g., providing the patient with a simple guide to interviewing for jobs or a place to get help with this when he genuinely does not understand the process). This is particularly important when the patient is young and has not had adequate opportunity to receive guidance from alternative male objects such as teachers or coaches.

Treating Gay and Lesbian Hysterical Patients

While this issue cannot be sufficiently addressed here, as to do so would involve writing another book, we would like to discuss a few issues and concerns. The first is that the guidelines (e.g., male therapist with male patient) outlined above do not apply to gay patients because the desired object and the rival object are different. This is based on our belief and on current research (Minton and McDonald 1985) that indicates that sexual preference is generally a biological phenomenon rather than a reaction to particular family patterns (e.g., dominant mother, absent father). Thus, one would expect the same type of oedipal issues to occur and be thwarted with gay and lesbian patients, only with the different-sex parents. Complicating the situation, however, is the fact that parents may not intentionally be behaving in a seductive way intended to stimulate the child. For example, one lesbian patient remembered feeling aroused when her mother took her clothes off in the locker room. In this case the patient's mother believed and was behaving toward her daughter as though she were heterosexual.

It is important in diagnosing gay and lesbian patients' behaviors to resist automatically interpreting extremely masculine or feminine behaviors as a manifestation of the hysterical personality. This is particularly true with gay men who manifest a theatrical, extremely feminine presentation. While they may, in fact, have a hysterical personality disorder, they could also be manifesting a hysterical style with an underlying narcissistic or borderline personality.

SUMMARY

The hysterical personality is characterized by a relational orientation, and polarized conflicts between insubstantiality and substantiality, irresponsibility and responsibility, passivity and action-oriented, powerlessness and power, dependence and independence. Depending on which sex role characteristics are reinforced by the parent whom the hysteric favors, his or her external presentation can vary. The underlying conflicts and dynamics will remain similar, however. Treatment should focus on helping the hysterical patient develop a process for managing competing needs and motives, authentic self-expression, mutuality in relationships, and clarification of underlying needs.

EXTENDED CASE EXAMPLE

Lee, an attractive, vivacious, engaging, emotionally expressive, and well-attired 25-year-old, single Caucasian woman, worked as an airline cabin attendant. She was a middle child, with a sister two years older and a brother six years younger. Lee noted that her sister and "baby brother" were close with her mother, while she was "Daddy's girl" until she started dating a 23-year-old Hispanic man when she was 16. "At that time my father went ballistic and never came back to earth." She was currently involved in a serious relationship with a pilot who was seven years her senior.

Lee presented in therapy with problems of low self-esteem, difficulty with initiative, and conflicts about sexuality with her boyfriend. She had not realized that she had low self-esteem or difficulty acting on her own independent thinking until she had taken a psychology course at a local community college "just for fun." She could see herself in the examples illustrated in the assigned textbook and realized how dependent all the women in her family, including her grandmothers and aunts, were. She described them as centering their lives around men and being catty about women.

Lee's low self-esteem resulted, in part, from her negative identity as a woman. She viewed women as inferior to men and thus disparaged herself as weak and not intelligent enough. She tended to underestimate her goals, becoming an airline attendant instead of a veterinarian. Although Lee had the intellectual ability (e.g., she was valedictorian of her class) to compete in veterinary school, she doubted her intelligence (e.g., "I grew up in a small town where anyone could have been valedictorian"), and she heeded her mother's advice (e.g., "Men with anything on the ball are not going to want to marry girls who work with smelly animals all day"). Her mother, who disparaged their small town life, had once mused about how romantic it would be to marry a pilot and travel all over the world. Lee was making her mother's dream come true.

In addition to devaluing women, Lee felt extremely jealous of and competitive with other women, whom she saw as rivals. She viewed men as the source of all important emotional supplies (e.g., affection, adoration) and women as competitors for these supplies. She had few female friends and invested most of her energy in pursuing romantic relationships. When a man asked her out on a date, she frequently canceled plans with female friends.

Her current conflicts with sexuality revolved around her realization that while she knew how to catch a man, she did not have the slightest idea what to with him once he was in love with her. Most disconcerting, she was aware that she became less sexually attracted to men after she was in a committed relationship and she did not understand why. She had previously found a reason to dump them, but now wanted to understand better why this occurred, as her current boyfriend was "such a good guy. I don't want to just dump him even though I don't feel that sexually interested anymore."

Lee described her mother as "a very attractive woman and a social climber who liked the country club lifestyle and wanted everything to be okay." Lee experienced her mother as competitive, rejecting, and cool with her. Her mother had experienced a difficult labor with her first child and had only wanted a second child in order to have a boy. When the mother delivered her second daughter, she was thus disappointed. In their family, bearing male children brought status to a mother that female children did not. As a result, while her mother pretended everything was fine, she actually felt overwhelmed and anxious about her status in the family (both the mother's sisters had male children as their firstborn). As a result of her mother's cooler response to her, Lee, who was a responsive, cuddly, beautiful child, quickly turned to her father once she could walk and thus "dance for him."

She experienced her father as much warmer than her mother, "more charming and much more fun." He seemed more interested in her and she looked to him for the affection for which she longed from her mother. She also saw him as more powerful and "the last word on anything important in the family. Mother never could stand up to him." By age 4, Lee had become her father's "little princess" and spent time with him while her mother spent time with her older sister. When Lee's baby brother was born two years later, her mother devoted herself to her son. Lee's older sister secured her place in the family by being "mother's helper," but her mother's heart belonged to her baby boy. As her brother got older, Lee felt jealous of the attention and privileges accorded to her brother by both parents due to his male status.

Lee was particularly aware of feeling competitive with her mother and sister in getting her father's attention. Her father seemed to relish having three women vie for his attention and encouraged the competitive nature of their interactions with him. For example, every Sunday when they were all getting ready for church, each of the females would parade their outfits in front of him for his approval and he would select the "belle du jour." Lee was often the winner, which afforded her the prized seat beside him in the front of the car. Such favoritism drew further resentment and jealousy from her mother and sister. The patient was thus primarily rewarded for her social skills and physical beauty, which furthered the emotional distance between Lee and her mother and sister.

During adolescence, Lee felt betrayed and emotionally abandoned by her father when she began to date boys. She rebelled by dating older men because she knew they would draw particular disapproval. There began to be a great deal of uproar at home. Her father came home less, stayed at work late, and began an affair with a co-worker. Her parents divorced two years later. Lee blamed herself for this as her father's affair appeared to be in reaction to her growing up and rebelling against his control.

While Lee had achieved object constancy, a cohesive sense of self, and an observing ego, she behaved like a seductive, dependent woman-child rather than developing mutual, interdependent relationships with men. Furthermore, she struggled with(1) conflicts between opposing needs or desires (e.g., complying because she wanted others to like her but rebelling because she did not want to be controlled), (2) sexualizing her needs for maternal nurturance, and (3) issues related to her confusing relationship with her father. In particular, Lee needed a reparative relationship that would clarify her underlying needs for affection and nurturance, support the development of appropriate self-assertion and initiative, and help her develop a relationship based on authentic mutuality.

While Lee seemed to quickly form an attachment with the therapist (e.g., "You are so helpful. I really like coming here to talk to you."), she tended to enact the roles of patient and competitor rather than relating authentically with the therapist. Thus, while Lee expressed appreciation of the therapist, she also subtly devalued the therapist's comments and behaved in a competitive manner with her (e.g., the therapist dressed casually and the patient said, "I really prefer a more sophisticated corporate look"). Throughout the course of therapy, she discussed the possibility of switching to a male therapist, whom she felt would be more helpful. When discussing the reasons behind this desire, she talked about (1) men being more intelligent; (2) feeling competitive with the therapist because she was educated, attractive, and had "a perfect husband"; and (3) feeling "women don't really care about you anyway."

During the first phase of treatment, the therapist focused on Lee's need for mothering due to the distance she felt with her mother. The therapist helped Lee to become more cognizant of her needs for respect, affection, authenticity, and reciprocity in her relationships. Lee noted how she "liked or didn't like someone right away" rather than allowing trust and affection to develop as she began to really know others and found out that they were able to work through interpersonal differences. Lee and the therapist began to understand Lee's interpersonal style as it manifested in treatment and outside relationships. Lee also began to understand that her threats to leave the therapist for a male therapist was a test to see if the therapist would easily abandon her (like her mother) or would need to control her in some way (like her father did). During this phase of treatment, it became clearer to Lee that she was searching for affection without exploitation, nurturance without infantilization, and affection without guilt. As Lee began to better understand her underlying needs, she became more skilled in getting them gratified by others, and thus felt stronger, more impactful, and better about herself.

Lee became aware that she was searching for a female role model who was strong and capable, yet warm, sensitive, and feminine. The therapist, to some extent, provided this model by allowing Lee's competitive transferences to develop without reacting to or squelching them. Instead, the therapist was able to empathize with how Lee tended to cast women into either the role of rival or a devalued, ineffectual being who could not really be of any help or consequence. The therapist said that she imagined it must be hard for Lee to view women this way as Lee was a woman and it reduced both her self-esteem and her proclivity to turn to women for help. Eventually, Lee made a connection between this transference proclivity and the feelings of disparagement that she felt about herself. Over time, the therapist's acknowledgment of Lee's strengths (e.g., intelligence, sense of humor, and curiosity) and her resourcefulness began to modify Lee's self-concept and therefore her self-esteem.

The second phase of treatment focused on Lee's need for the functions provided by a good-enough father. Lee needed the therapist to do what her father had not: (1) to express an active interest in her, (2) to listen to what she had to say without telling her what to do, (3) to help her be and feel effective in the world. This latter aim was accomplished, in part, by helping Lee work through conflicts with others. In particular, Lee needed assistance in clarifying her conflicts regarding her feelings of responsibility for her parent's discord and divorce. Helping Lee develop a process for understanding conflicts (e.g., self-reflection, gaining objective perspective) also enabled her to better understand her sexual problems. She became aware that once men committed to her she felt overly responsible for the relationship and afraid that she would be dominated by them as she was by her father. In addition, she became aware of the underlying sexual tension between herself and her father (due to her mother's neglect of both of them). Thus, when she became more involved with a man, sexuality began to feel incestuous, leading her to feel guilty and lose her sexual desire. As she began to separate from her partner (who was neither dominating nor her father), her sexual desire began to return.

Furthermore, helping Lee understand the different ways that men and women are taught to behave in this culture, enabled her to further differentiate her partner from her father. For example, she noticed that her partner tended to problem-solve whenever she brought up a concern. She interpreted his response as infantilizing, feeling that he treated her as though she didn't have a brain in her head and was contemptuous of her emotions. She wanted her partner to just listen to her and understand what she was feeling—not tell her what to do, as she realized that she was capable of doing that herself.

The therapist discussed with Lee how, in general in this culture, men tended to think their job was to solve problems while women tended to want empathy and affection. Lee began to understand how they both felt frustrated with these interactions and began to tell her partner more directly what she wanted.

The therapist also assisted Lee in becoming aware of her ambitions by expressing interest in Lee's own ideas and intuitions (e.g., related to her veterinary school dreams) and resisting her clever bids to take over for her or tell her what to do. It was difficult at first for Lee to know what she did think or want; but over time it became clearer as the therapist and Lee developed a supportive exploratory process of Lee's inner life.

Next, the therapist worked with Lee on helping her to understand what kept her from initiating and accomplishing her goals. Lee struggled between her fear of failure (being inadequate like her mother) and her fear of success (which might threaten men and cause them to reject her). As she became more aware of these struggles, Lee was better able to become aware of and to consciously choose what action she wanted to take.

Finally, Lee began to work through issues related to her romantic choices (e.g., triadic jealousies, needs for exclusivity, and fear of commitment). Choosing a pilot seven years her senior had initially reflected her desire to be taken care of as well as her oedipal strivings to be "Daddy's girl" again. As Lee began sharing more of her real desires and ambitions with her partner and he responded in a supportive manner, their relationship matured (e.g., they developed more mutual respect and intimacy with each other). Lee realized she had unconsciously wanted a man who her mother would like (e.g., a pilot and traveler) as well as a man like her father (e.g., successful, charming) and that her current partner was that man. However, she also discovered that she really loved him and that, unlike her father, he loved her for being herself and was eager to support her independent strivings (e.g., he encouraged her decision to go to veterinary school).

As termination was considered, Lee began to have fantasies about becoming friends with the therapist. Lee's fantasies were reexamined in terms of termination stirring up old feelings about maternal abandonment and confusing boundaries with her father. The therapist also expressed to Lee that she thought that a very positive aspect of her fantasies about their becoming friends was that it seemed as if Lee now viewed women as good people with whom to have relationships.

12

The Psychodynamic Character Inventory: A Tool For Helping Therapists Assess Personality Style and Disorders

Many readers, particularly new clinicians or psychotherapists who are less familiar with psychodynamic theory, may find themselves feeling somewhat overwhelmed at this point by the amount of information in this book. They may be wondering how they can possibly remember it all, let alone apply it to the treatment of their patients. As previously stated, we believe that treatment plans must be individualized according to the patient's unique combination of characterological issues. Therefore, obtaining an accurate diagnostic picture of the patient as soon as possible provides psychotherapists with an invaluable guide in the development of their treatment goals and informs them when to make a referral.

HISTORY OF THE PSYCHODYNAMIC CHARACTER INVENTORY

As teachers, when our students presented cases to us, they often asked us how we knew something about one of their patients. In an attempt to help them benefit from our experience and teach them the difficult process of making a discerning differential diagnosis, we developed an instrument called the Psychodynamic Character Inventory (PCI), a 139-item, true-false test with seven scales that measures paranoid, schizoid, masochistic, hysteroid, narcissistic, obsessive-compulsive, and hysterical personality disorders.

Each scale has twenty-four items. Each category has a number of items that overlap with other categories. Test-retest reliability of this instrument is 0.89. Inter-item correlations on each scale, however, are somewhat low as there are too many variables per scale to correlate highly with each other. For example, in the *DSM-IV* there are several categories for each diagnosis and it is not necessary for a patient to have all the behaviors and/or characteristics in each category to receive a diagnosis. To increase the inter-item correlation, it was necessary to remove 0.5 to 0.7 of the items on each scale. We believe that while this improved the scale statistically, it detracted from its richness and from our original purpose, which was not just assigning patients a score but helping student therapists understand how to make a differential diagnosis and learn to recognize the characteristics of each personality disorder that applied to their patients.

We, thus, decided to revise the scale (PCI-2) and use it with a different intention, as a type of written semistructured interview rather than a statistically sound, objective personality measure. When we revised the PCI, we decided to make several changes: (1) we eliminated the items that did not seem to discriminate between groups (e.g., "I have strong reactions to things"), (2) we eliminated the paranoid scale to keep it consistent with the categories that are used in this book, (3) we removed all items that overlapped with another scale, and (4) we added some new items or modified the wording of old ones.

For example, some items were eliminated because they were either over- or underendorsed and didn't discriminate between groups. These include (1) "I have strong reactions to things" (Hysteroid scale—overendorsed), (2) "I am more comfortable with animals than people" (Schizoid scale—overendorsed), and (3) "I am terrified at times of being annihilated" (Schizoid scale—underendorsed).

Other items were modified to make them more precise or to make a stronger statement: (1) "I have intense moods that change rapidly" was changed to "I have very intense moods that change rapidly" (Hysteroid scale); (2) "Separations from people that I'm attached to are difficult for me" was changed to "Separations from people that I'm attached to are almost unbearable for me" (Hysteroid scale); (3) "I frequently make lists to organize my activities" was changed to "I frequently make lists to organize my activities but have difficulty completing the things on the list according to schedule" (Obsessive scale); (4) "I secretly feel proud of my self sufficiency" was changed to "I secretly feel proud of my extreme self sufficiency" (Schizoid scale);

(5) "My same-sex parent was cold, uninterested, and/or uninvolved with me but my opposite-sex parent was more involved with me, warmer, and was someone who other people experienced as funny, charming, or even somewhat flirtatious (if heterosexual)"; we added "if gay or lesbian this situation was reversed" as we believe that the oedipal dynamics do not create sexual preference but that as sexual preference is to a large extent biologically determined (Minton and McDonald 1985), it influences who the child experiences as the exciting object (Hysterical scale); and (6) "It is important to me that my partner is attractive, successful, and intelligent" was changed to "It is very important to me that my partner is intelligent, attractive, appreciative of me, and a good listener" (Narcissism scale). The latter item was changed to include the mirroring as well as idealizing aspects of the narcissistic transferences.

Furthermore, some new items were added to the PCI-2: (1) "I have a tendency to get in struggles with people, even about little things, because I don't like feeling controlled by people (e.g., forced into doing things that I don't want to do or don't agree with)" (Obsessive scale); (2) "The emotion that I feel most often is a combination of rage and self-hatred" (Hysteroid scale); (3) "While I have never made suicide attempts or would kill myself, on a number of occasions I've wanted to die just to end my feelings of pain" (Masochistic scale); and (4) "While I find triangular relationships to be very difficult (e.g., having two friends that know each other well, having a partner with an extremely close friend that I feel competitive with), I often find myself in these types of situations" (Hysterical scale).

THE PSYCHODYNAMIC CHARACTER INVENTORY-2

The Psychodynamic Character Inventory-2 (PCI-2) is a 90-item paper and pencil, semistructured interview that is designed to help inform clinicians about their patients' characterological issues. We have found that in written interviews patients are more likely to endorse ego-dystonic feelings or behaviors than in a face-to-face interview. The PCI-2 has six scales with fifteen items per scale that represent the six personality styles/disorders described in this book. Rather than using exact scores from each scale to make a statistically accurate diagnosis (e.g., this patient scores higher on scale 1 than 80 percent of the population), the purpose of the PCI-2 is to help therapists understand their patient's underlying characterological issues, including the defenses, behaviors, and developmental issues that accompany each diagnostic category. As there are no validity scales, the clinician must remember that a patient's endorsement of an item doesn't ensure that it is true. Rather, it provides the therapist with a potentially important area to investigate with the patient in a subsequent session.

In this chapter, we first present and explain each of the six scales individually, and demonstrate how patients' particular developmental, structural, or interpersonal issues can be assessed from individual (or a constellation of) items. Next the PCI-2 is presented in a form that can be given to patients, if the therapist so desires. A scoring sheet is provided. Therapists can then refer back to particular chapters in the book if they wish to review the dynamics and treatment of each disorder that patients check a significant number of items on. Even if patients endorse only a few salient items on a scale, if these issues are verified by the patient in a follow-up interview, the therapist can turn to the relevant chapter to better understand and treat that particular issue in the patient.

When a patient has endorsed many items on multiple scales, the therapist will have the challenge of developing a treatment plan for a mixed personality disorder, which we believe describes most people. In such cases, an important guideline is that structural issues take precedence over other issues (Horner 1979). Thus, in treating a patient who has checked many items on the Hysteroid and the Obsessive-Compulsive scales (uncommon but not impossible), the therapist's primary goals would be to establish a therapeutic alliance, develop object constancy, establish a cohesive sense of self and increase ego functions such as integration, differentiation, and reality testing (i.e., issues associated with a borderline level of functioning). Secondary goals would be working on issues such as needs for control, developing spontaneous and appropriate self-expression, and softening the patient's harsh superego (i.e. neurotic level goals for patients with obsessive dynamics).

Guidelines for Administration of the PCI-2

The following guidelines are suggested for administering the PCI-2 to a patient. First, recommending to a patient that he or she take a test is an event that has meaning to the patient. Therefore, we suggest that therapists primarily give the PCI-2 to new patients at the time of intake with the explanation that the therapist routinely administers this test at the beginning of treatment to help him or her to understand the patient more quickly. The patient is asked to bring the questionnaire home to fill out and to return it to the therapist at the next session. Any patient reactions regarding this event should be explored and the patient reassured that the information is confidential, that this is a voluntary activity, and that the therapist will be glad to provide the patient with feedback about his or her test responses if the patient desires (an example will be provided later in this chapter regarding how to do this).

If the therapist is experiencing diagnostic confusion or a stalled psychotherapy with a patient whom the therapist has already been treating for a significant period of time, we suggest that the therapist tell the patient, "I have the sense that things have been stuck in our work together recently (or lately, I have felt confused about _____). I have a questionnaire I would recommend that you take that may help us to clarify things." Sometimes, the mere act of the therapist's addressing the therapeutic impasse leads to a clarifying discussion between therapist and patient so that taking the PCI-2 is no longer necessary.

THE SIX SCALES OF THE PSYCHODYNAMIC CHARACTER INVENTORY-2

We present each of the six scales of the PCI-2 separately to provide the readers with an explanation of the issues that each scale and the individual items in that scale attempt to address. We then point out how some items use slightly different wording to discriminate between how, for example, noncompliant behavior may reflect different phenomena in the narcissist, the masochist, and the obsessive-compulsive patient.

The Schizoid Scale

4. I have a tendency to be absentminded.
14. I spend most of my time daydreaming and having fantasies.
19. I am an objective, neutral observer of life.
20. I have been described as eccentric.
27. I feel secretly proud of my extreme self-sufficiency.
28. I frequently feel detached from my needs and feelings.
29. I am painfully shy.
44. I don't enjoy eating as much as other people seem to (i.e., I eat to live rather than live to eat).
49. I live by myself and have few, if any, relationships.
57. I feel detached from other people.
58. Life often feels futile, meaningless, and unreal.
64. Given a choice, I value spiritual pursuits over pleasure in daily living.

73. I have felt, at times, that I had no right to exist.
79. I would like to live alone somewhere that is remote and peaceful.
89. People say that they experience me as cool and aloof.

In general, items on the Schizoid scale assess detachment, unrelatedness, withdrawal from relationships with other people to internal objects, lack of cathexis to real objects (e.g., people, food, daily pleasures in the world), and existential concerns. For example, item 73 is based on Fairbairn's (1954) theory that as the schizoid individual was not wanted by parents, he or she does not feel like he or she has the right to exist. Items 4 and 14 reflect the schizoid patient's withdrawal from external to internal objects. Items 29, 49, 57, 79, and 89 illustrate the schizoid's difficulty having relationships with other people. Items 58 and 73 reflect concern about existential issues. Items 19, 20, 27, and 64 reflect the schizoid's sense of superiority about being self-sufficient or above involvement in the mundane concerns of the world. Items 28 and 44 address the schizoid patient's detachment from sensory and affective experiences.

The Hysteroid Scale

5. Separations have always been extremely difficult for me (e.g., starting school, going to high school, leaving home, graduating college, leaving a job or relationship).
12. Spending time all alone is very difficult for me.
13. I have extremely intense moods that seem to change rapidly.
18. I often feel terrified, "like a baby alone in space."
21. I don't have any idea about who I really am inside, what I want, or what is truly important to me in life.
30. When I am rageful or depressed, I have done things to hurt myself physically (e.g., suicide attempts, self-mutilation).
34. My relationships generally tend to be short and intense.
41. I was physically and/or sexually abused as a child to an extreme degree.
42. I often feel panicked that people will abandon me.
48. At times, I have had strange and unusual experiences (e.g., seeing or hearing things that are not there, believing things that no one else believed).
51. As a child, when I went off and played by myself or made friends with other children, my mother acted rejecting toward me.
63. Things feel black and white to me. When I like and feel supported

by someone, I think that they're absolutely perfect. When they disappoint me and I get angry at them, its difficult for me to remember anything good about them.

80. Separations from people that I am attached to are almost unbearable for me.
82. I often have the experience of being "one" with important people in my life. When I do, I both like it and feel frightened by it.
83. The emotion that I feel the most frequently is a combination of rage and self-hatred.

In general, the Hysteroid scale measures problems with impulse control (item 30), reality testing (item 48), trauma history (item 4), difficulties with separation (items 5, 18, 42, 51, and 80), and individuation (item 80), and a lack of a sense of self (item 2) and object constancy (items 12, 13, 34, 63, and 83). The most important item on this scale is item 63, which attempts to determine whether the individual uses defensive splitting.

The Narcissistic Scale

7. My family is very proud of my talents and special abilities.
10. I get very angry when I feel criticized.
15. I feel either very important or very unworthy.
23. When I put aside my accomplishments, I am not really sure who I am.
24. I have a very hard time apologizing.
38. It is very important to me that my partner is attractive, intelligent, appreciative of me, and a good listener.
40. I frequently feel bored and empty inside.
43. My physical appearance is very important to me.
50. I expect a great deal from people, have difficulty taking no for an answer, and persist in my attempts to get what I want. If people do not eventually go along with what I want, they can be replaced.
53. I am the happiest when I have a relationship with someone (e.g., friend, teacher, partner) that I greatly admire and identify with.
68. What a talented person can accomplish in this world is unlimited.
69. It's hard for me to do things for other people that I do not want to do without feeling like I'm giving a part of myself up.
77. People tend to like me because I know how to make them feel really important and special.
78. I tend to adore/admire people at first and to then get very disillusioned in them.

87. I don't believe that people will respect or be interested in me unless I'm perfect (i.e., brilliant, exceptionally attractive, thin, successful).

The Narcissistic scale attempts to measure traits such as a propensity toward perfectionism and an unrealistic ego ideal (items 7, 43, and 68), conditional love and disregard for real needs (items 7 and 87), defenses against threats to the narcissist's self-esteem (items 10 and 24) and sense of self (item 69), problems with experiencing their true self (items 23 and 40), being demanding and entitled (item 50), idealization and devaluation (item 69), regressive narcissism (items 53 and 77), and use of other people as selfobjects (items 38, 50, and 53). In particular, item 68 attempts to indirectly measure grandiosity. We have found this to be a diagnostically important, infrequently endorsed item (i.e., it is mostly endorsed by individuals with strong narcissistic dynamics or naive, enthusiastic adolescents and young adults).

The Masochistic Scale

3. I don't feel like I can count on the people to whom I am attached to be reliable and predictable.
8. I'm having a hard time leaving a relationship or job where I feel criticized, rejected, devalued, and/or hurt.
9. I have a tendency to think that problems with other people are all my fault.
25. While I never have made suicide attempts or would kill myself, on a number of occasions I've wanted to die just to end my feelings of pain.
35. I'm afraid that deep down, people like me for the things that I do for them rather than for who I am.
36. My parents paid the most attention to me when I had some sort of problem (e.g., misbehaved, was ill).
37. Despite my initial intentions in a relationship, I usually find myself taking care of or being responsible for the other person.
39. When I ask people for advice, I experience a great conflict between wanting to please them so that they will like me (i.e., taking their advice) and wanting to be my own person (i.e., making my own decisions).
47. Losing a relationship with someone that I love would be more painful to me than anything else.
52. I was the scapegoat (e.g., my family thought that I was "bad" or "screwed up") or the caretaker (e.g., I was one of my parent's confi-

dants, I was given too much responsibility for a child my age) in my family.

59. In sexual relationships, I have a tendency to be attracted to people who initially appear to be particularly loving, romantic, and/or seductive but then begin to frequently behave in a cruel or rejecting manner toward me.

67. I frequently struggle with feelings of low self-esteem, especially when someone important to me is critical of and/or angry at me.

70. One or both of my parents (or a sibling) was quite unpredictable in their behavior toward me (i.e., alternated from being very loving, attentive, and/or fun to be with to being moody, critical, withdrawn, or even abusive).

81. Sometimes, when I feel like I'm trying my very best to be nice and cooperative, people seem to get irritated with me and I don't really understand why.

88. I believe that I could get what I need from my parent(s) or partner if only I could figure out the right thing to do.

The Masochistic scale attempts to measure overdetermined caretaking (items 35, 57, and 52), the conflict between asserting one's will and gaining approval (items 39 and 81), problems with anxious attachment, separation, and loss (items 3, 8, 47, 59, and 70), the experience of being scapegoated (items 36 and 52), severe depression (item 25), problems with self-esteem (item 67), and tendencies toward internalizing relational problems (items 9, 67, and 88). We have noticed that items 8, 47, and 59 are commonly endorsed by these patients.

The Obsessive-Compulsive Scale

1. I am more aware of what I think than what I feel.
11. I have great difficulty making decisions.
17. I strive "never" to make a mistake.
26. I have been told that I'm argumentative.
31. I have a tendency to get into struggles with people, even about small things, because I don't like feeling controlled by people (i.e., forced into doing something that I don't want to do or don't agree with).
45. I tend to do things to an extreme (e.g., I'm either very messy or very neat, very rational and logical or lose my temper, etc.).
54. I value work and productivity over spending time in leisure activities or with other people.

56. I have high moral standards and try to be conscientious.
60. I feel driven at times to accomplish my goals, even when I know that it is not in my best interest.
65. It is very important to me that people do things the way that I tell them to do them, especially when I'm quite certain that my way is the correct approach.
71. Sometimes when I speak, although I'm quite logical, other people seem to have difficulty following my ideas.
76. Being right (especially when other people acknowledge it) is very important to me.
84. I have difficulty compromising, especially when I know that my way is the right way.
85. I tend to notice details and can lose sight of the big picture at times.
90. I frequently make lists to organize my activities but have difficulty completing things on the list according to schedule.

The Obsessive-Compulsive scale attempts to measure a proclivity toward being detail oriented (item 85), overreliance on cognitive capacities (item 1), lack of ability to be spontaneous and enjoy life (items 11, 54, 60, and 90), perfectionism (items 11 and 56), and the excessive need to be right or in control (items 26, 31, 65, 71, 76, 84, and 90). The reason that item 71 measures control issues is that obsessives have a proclivity to unconsciously use circumstantial talking as a means of preventing conversations from being directed to an area that they do not want to discuss. While the latter items reflecting issues with control may look similar to items on the Narcissistic and Masochistic scales, there are subtle differences. Items 65, 76, and 84 unambivalently express the need for control unlike a similar item on the Masochistic scale in which the need to express one's will conflicts with the need to be liked (item 39). Furthermore, similar items on the Narcissistic scale (items 50 and 69) measure the need for control due to low frustration tolerance and as a means of protecting an enfeebled sense of self (which the obsessive-compulsive does not have).

The Hysterical Scale

2. I have difficult believing that I'm competent even when I'm successful.
6. I have a tendency to get jealous that my partner will love someone else more than me.

16. I have been told that I behave seductively and have been surprised as that wasn't my intention.

22. While I find triangular relationships to be very difficult (e.g. having two friends that know each other well, having a partner with an extremely close friend with whom I feel competitive), I often find myself in these types of situations.

32. I have been told that I'm dramatic.

33. I need a lot of reassurance.

46. My sexual fantasies are almost always about doing something forbidden.

55. I am more emotional than analytical or logical.

61. While people find me likable and entertaining, I don't really have intimate relationships with friends, excluding a parent or partner (i.e., people with whom I frequently spend leisure time, who I can share things that I feel embarrassed or guilty about, who are very important to me and that I can depend on).

62. I feel guilty and/or embarrassed about my sexual fantasies and desires.

66. I have been told that I have an innocent or childlike manner.

72. My same-sex parent was somewhat cold, uninterested, and or uninvolved with me, but my opposite-sex parent was more involved with me, warmer, and was someone other people often experienced as funny, charming, or even somewhat flirtatious (if heterosexual). If gay or lesbian, the situation is reversed.

74. I tend to look at the big picture. I am not at all a detail person.

75. While I have emotional outbursts, I don't stay mad for long and am able to apologize to or forgive the person that I'm mad at.

86. I tend to act somewhat impulsively and to think about it afterward. However, this doesn't usually cause me great harm.

The Hysterical scale attempts to measure oedipal issues (items 6, 22, and 72), a tendency toward overemotionality (items 55 and 75), attention-seeking behavior (items 32 and 33), a belief in or self presentation of insufficiency (items 2, 33, and 66), a propensity toward global thinking (item 74), sexual conflicts (items 16, 46, and 62), trial by action (item 86), and superficiality (item 61). In particular, items 75 and 86 should help clinicians differentiate the hysterical from the hysteroid patient (i.e., the hysteroid remains angry and has difficulty apologizing and forgiving, and the hysteroid's acting out causes greater harm).

PSYCHODYNAMIC CHARACTER INVENTORY-2

The following questions are designed to help your therapist gain a better understanding of your character. Though you may find some of these statements difficult, please try to respond to them as honestly as possible. While this checklist might seem lengthy, most people are able to complete it relatively quickly. Check each item as either T (for True or Mostly True) or F (for False or Mostly False).

_____ 1. I am more aware of what I think than what I feel.

_____ 2. I have difficulty believing that I am competent even when I'm successful.

_____ 3. I don't feel like I can count on the people to whom I'm attached to be reliable and predictable.

_____ 4. I have a tendency to be absentminded.

_____ 5. Separations have always been difficult for me (e.g., starting school, going to high school, leaving home, graduating college, leaving a job or a relationship).

_____ 6. I have a tendency to get jealous that my partner will love someone else more than me.

_____ 7. My family is proud of my talents and special abilities.

_____ 8. I'm having a hard time leaving a relationship or job where I feel criticized, rejected, devalued, and/or hurt.

_____ 9. I have a tendency to think that problems with other people are all my fault.

_____ 10. I get very angry when I feel criticized.

_____ 11. I have great difficulty making decisions.

_____ 12. Spending time all alone is very difficult for me.

_____ 13. I have extremely intense moods that seem to change rapidly.

_____ 14. I spend most of my time daydreaming and having fantasies.

_____ 15. I feel either very important or very unworthy.

_____ 16. I have been told that I behave seductively and have been surprised as that was not my intention.

_____ 17. I strive "never" to make a mistake.

_____ 18. I often feel terrified, like a "baby alone in space."

_____ 19. I am an objective, neutral observer of life.

_____ 20. I have been described as eccentric.

_____ 21. I don't have any idea about who I really am, what I want, or what is truly important to me in life.

_____ 22. While I find triangular relationships to be very difficult (e.g., having two friends that know each other well, having a partner who has an extremely close friend with whom I feel competitive), I often find myself in these types of situations.

_____ 23. When I put aside my accomplishments, I am not really sure who I am.

_____ 24. I have a very hard time apologizing.

_____ 25. While I never have made suicide attempts or would kill myself, on a number of occasions I've wanted to die just to end my feelings of pain.

_____ 26. I have been told that I'm argumentative.

_____ 27. I feel secretly proud of my extreme self-sufficiency.

_____ 28. I frequently feel detached from my needs and feelings.

_____ 29. I am painfully shy.

_____ 30. When I am rageful or depressed, I have done things to hurt myself physically (e.g., suicide attempts, self-mutilation).

_____ 31. I have a tendency to get into struggles with people, even over small things, because I don't like feeling controlled by people (i.e., forced into doing something that I don't want to do or don't agree with).

_____ 32. I have been told that I'm dramatic.

_____ 33. I need a lot of reassurance.

_____ 34. My relationships generally tend to be short and intense.

_____ 35. I'm afraid that, deep down, people like me for the things that I do for them, rather than for who I am.

_____ 36. My parents paid the most attention to me when I had some sort of problem (e.g., misbehaved, was ill).

_____ 37. Despite my initial intentions in a relationship, I usually find myself taking care of or being responsible for the other person.

_____ 38. It is very important to me that my partner is attractive, intelligent, appreciative of me, and a good listener.

_____ 39. When I ask people for advice, I experience a great conflict between wanting to please them so that they will like me (i.e., taking their advice) and wanting to be my own person (i.e., making my own decision).

_____ 40. I frequently feel bored and empty inside.

_____ 41. I was physically and/or sexually abused as a child to an extreme degree.

_____ 42. I often feel panicked that people will abandon me.

_____ 43. My physical appearance is very important to me.

_____ 44. I don't enjoy eating as much as other people seem to (i.e., I eat to live rather than live to eat).

_____ 45. I tend to do things to an extreme (e.g., I'm either very messy or very neat, very rational and logical or lose my temper).

_____ 46. My sexual fantasies are almost always about doing something that is forbidden.

_____ 47. Losing a relationship with someone that I love would be more painful to me than anything else.

_____ 48. At times, I have had strange and unusual experiences (e.g., seeing or hearing things that are not there, believing things that no one else believes).

_____ 49. I live by myself and have few, if any, relationships.

_____ 50. I expect a great deal from people, have difficulty taking no for an answer, and persist in my attempts to get what I want. If people don't eventually go along with what I want, they can be replaced.

_____ 51. As a child, when I went off and played by myself or made friends with other children, my mother acted rejecting toward me.

_____ 52. I was the scapegoat (e.g., my family thought that I was "bad" or "screwed up") or caretaker (e.g., I was my parent's confidant, I was given too much responsibility for a child my age) in my family.

_____ 53. I am the happiest when I have a relationship with someone (e.g., friend, teacher, partner) that I greatly admire and identify with.

_____ 54. I value work and productivity over spending time in leisure activities or with other people.

_____ 55. I am more emotional than analytical or logical.

_____ 56. I have high moral standards and try to be conscientious.

_____ 57. I feel detached from other people.

_____ 58. Life often feels futile, meaningless, and unreal.

_____ 59. In sexual relationships, I have a tendency to be attracted to people who initially appear to be particularly loving, romantic, and/or seductive but then begin to frequently behave in a cruel or rejecting manner toward me.

_____ 60. I feel driven at times to accomplish my goals, even when I know it is not really in my best interest.

_____ 61. While people tend to find me likable and entertaining, I do not really have intimate relationships with friends (i.e., people with whom I frequently spend leisure time, who I can share things that I feel embarrassed or guilty about, who are very important to me and that I can depend on).

_____ 62. I feel guilty and/or embarrassed about my sexual fantasies and desires.

_____ 63. Things feel black and white to me. When I like and feel supported by someone, I think that they're absolutely perfect. When they disappoint me and I get angry at them, it's difficult for me to remember anything good about them.

_____ 64. Given a choice, I value spiritual pursuits over pleasures in daily living.

_____ 65. It is very important to me that other people do things the way that I tell them to do them, especially when I'm quite certain that my way is the correct approach.

_____ 66. I have been told that I have an innocent or childlike manner.

_____ 67. I frequently struggle with feelings of low self-esteem, especially when someone important to me is critical and/or angry at me.

_____ 68. What a talented person can accomplish in this world is unlimited.

_____ 69. It's hard for me to do things for other people that I do not want to do without feeling as though I am giving a part of myself up.

_____ 70. One or both of my parents (or a sibling) was quite unpredictable in their behavior toward me (i.e., alternated from being very loving, attentive, and/or fun to be with to being moody, critical, withdrawn, or even abusive).

_____ 71. Sometimes when I speak, although I'm quite logical, other people seem to have difficulty following my ideas.

_____ 72. My same-sex parent was somewhat cold and uninterested in me but my opposite-sex parent was more involved with me, warmer, and was someone who other people experienced as funny, charming, or even somewhat flirtatious (if heterosexual). If gay or lesbian, the situation is reversed.

_____ 73. I have felt, at times, that I had no right to exist.

_____ 74. I tend to look at the big picture. I am not at all a detail person.

_____ 75. While I have emotional outbursts, I don't stay mad for long and am able to apologize to or forgive the person that I'm mad at.

_____ 76. Being right (particularly when other people acknowledge it) is very important to me.

_____ 77. People tend to like me because I know how to make them feel really important and special.

_____ 78. I tend to adore/admire people at first and to then get very disillusioned in them.

_____ 79. I would like to live alone somewhere that is remote and peaceful.

_____ 80. Separations from people that I am attached to are almost unbearable for me.

____ 81. Sometimes, when I think that I'm trying my best to be nice and cooperative, people seem to get irritated with me and I don't really understand why.

____ 82. I often have the experience of being "one" with people in my life. When I do, I both like it and feel frightened by it.

____ 83. The emotion that I feel the most frequently is a combination of rage and self-hatred.

____ 84. I have difficulty compromising, especially when I know that my way is the right way.

____ 85. I tend to notice details and can lose sight of the big picture at times.

____ 86. I tend to act somewhat impulsively and to think about it afterward. However, this doesn't usually cause me great harm.

____ 87. I don't believe that people will respect or be interested in me unless I'm perfect (e.g., brilliant, exceptionally attractive, thin, successful).

____ 88. I believe that I could get what I need from my parent(s) or partner, if only I could figure out the right thing to do.

____ 89. People say that they experience me as cool and aloof.

____ 90. I frequently make lists to organize my activities but have difficulty completing things on the list according to schedule.

SCORING SHEET

1. *Schizoid scale:* Items 4, 14, 19, 20, 27, 28, 29, 44, 49, 57, 58, 64, 73, 79, 89
2. *Hysteroid scale:* Items 5, 12, 13, 18, 21, 30, 34, 41, 42, 48, 51, 63, 80, 82, 83
3. *Narcissistic scale:* Items 7, 10, 15, 23, 24, 38, 40, 43, 50, 53, 68, 69, 77, 78, 87
4. *Masochistic scale:* Items 3, 8, 9, 25, 35, 36, 37, 39, 47, 52, 59, 67, 70, 81, 88
5. *Obsessive-Compulsive scale:* Items 1, 11, 17, 26, 31, 45, 54, 56, 60, 65, 71, 76, 84, 85, 90
6. *Hysterical scale:* Items 2, 6, 16, 22, 32, 33, 46, 55, 61, 62, 66, 72, 74, 75, 86

CASE EXAMPLE OF USE OF THE PCI-2

Information from Initial Interview

The patient is a 40-year-old married male physician, with one child, who has been practicing medicine for ten years. His presenting problem was difficulty experiencing sexual pleasure with his wife (of seven years) to the point of feeling repulsion toward her and rarely having sex with her. While he had fantasies about having extramarital affairs, he had only one brief affair and felt quite guilty about it. He said that he very much wanted to resolve their sexual problems as, while sex wasn't really that important to him, he loved his wife and the absence of a sexual relationship made his wife feel unhappy, rejected, and undesirable.

This patient had a prior history of enjoying sex, including a period of extreme promiscuity when he was abusing drugs and alcohol. He felt shame and guilt about his behavior during this period. When asked what made sex with his wife difficult, he said that while he thought that she was a wonderful person, he found her unattractive, especially since she had gained a bit of weight when their child was born. When asked, he said that they had a passionate sexual relationship during courtship.

This patient also said that he was a recovering addict. The drugs that he had used most frequently were amphetamines and cocaine. He reported doing illegal things at times to obtain these drugs (i.e., forging prescriptions).

One of the reasons that he used these particular drugs is that he was very concerned about his physical appearance and thought that his own body was very out of shape (it was not) and at times felt repulsed by it. He said that he had prior cosmetic surgery on his nose and worked out regularly. Thus, while he was quite attractive, well dressed, seductive, and charming, he still felt that he had not achieved his standards for attractiveness.

This patient was born to a Southern Baptist family in a small town where his father was a minister who was well liked and respected in the community. He described having a close relationship with his father. On the one hand he admired his father for "being good to the point of being saintly." On the other hand, he somewhat disrespected his father for being passive, somewhat unmanly, and not standing up to his mother. In contrast, he felt very angry toward his mother (with whom he now had little involvement). He described her as perfectionistic, critical, controlling, charming, and seductive. He reported that when he was very young, he was very close with her and had warm memories of sitting on her soft lap and playing games with her. He said that he enjoyed watching her put on her beautiful dresses and wonderful perfume. She used to call him her handsome young man. However, when he got older, his mother became increasingly critical and rejecting toward him. As an adolescent, he remembered her speaking contemptuously about his father and confiding in him about her extramarital affairs. He said that she was more interested in the men that she was having affairs with than in him.

Other than participating in a drug and alcohol program, the patient reported one previous experience of psychotherapy that he did not find helpful. He said that he never really had confidence in this therapist as he had only a master's degree and he didn't think that the therapist was strong or smart enough to help him.

The patient said that something about being with this therapist made him feel like a "bad boy." Midway through treatment, the therapist suggested that he take the Minnesota Multiphasic Personality Inventory (MMPI). When giving the patient feedback about the test results, he told the patient that his test results indicated that he was psychopathic.

Initial Diagnostic Impression

The therapist found this patient somewhat diagnostically confusing. From the information obtained on the first interview, if forced to make a diagnosis, the therapist would have been inclined to underscore the patient's narcissistic issues. This impression was based on (1) his extreme concerns about his appearance (including almost compulsive exercising, the use of illegal drugs to help with weight loss, and cosmetic surgery when he was 21 years old); (2) his criticism of his wife's physical appearance; (3) his history of acting out (including illegal acting out); (4) his reported high score on psychopathic deviance on the MMPI; (5) his charming, engaging social presentation; and (6) the therapist's initial impression that he was not sexually attracted to his wife because she was not an ideal object (e.g., thin, beautiful, charming) but relied on her mirroring selfobject functions (e.g., she frequently told him that he was handsome and brilliant, and he described her as very understanding).

However, the therapist did not feel confident about this diagnosis. Some impressions that contradicted it were that the therapist didn't feel related to by the patient as a selfobject but rather experienced an authentic connection with the patient. The patient was not generally blaming of others (as narcissists are) but rather seemed to accept more than his share of responsibility for relational problems. He loved his family, was able to make commitments, and was aware of his feelings, values, and goals, indicating a cohesive sense of self.

A potential alternative diagnosis was hysterical personality due to (1) sexual problems, (2) a more affective manner of self expression, and (3) a history of having been his mother's favorite until he matured. However, he was appropriately assertive and was able to be logical and analytical, and, most important, the therapist felt that there was insufficient information to warrant this diagnosis. The same was true for masochistic personality. Although this patient had some traits from this area (e.g., a proclivity to internalize and be self critical), he did not have anxious attachments or separation anxiety, and didn't appear to have compliance-defiance conflicts.

Patient's PCI-2 Profile

Items endorsed on the Schizoid scale: 0.
Items endorsed on the Hysteroid scale: 0.
Items endorsed on the Narcissistic scale: 3.

38. It is very important to me that my partner is intelligent, attractive, appreciative of me, and a good listener.
43. My physical appearance is very important to me.
87. I don't believe that people will respect or be interested in me unless I'm perfect (e.g., brilliant, exceptionally attractive, thin, successful).

Items endorsed on the Masochistic scale: 4.

9. I have a tendency to think that problems with people are all my fault.
37. Despite my initial intentions in a relationship, I usually find myself taking care of the other person.
59. In sexual relationships, I have a tendency to be attracted to people who initially appear to be particularly loving, romantic, and/or seductive but then begin to frequently behave in a cruel or rejecting manner.
60. I frequently struggle with feelings of low self-esteem, especially when someone important to me is critical and/or angry at me.

Items endorsed on the Obsessive-Compulsive scale: 0.
Items endorsed on the Hysterical scale: 9.

2. I have difficulty believing that I am competent even when I'm successful.
16. I have been told that I behave seductively and been surprised as that wasn't my intention.
32. I have been told that I'm dramatic.
33. I need a lot of reassurance.
46. My sexual fantasies are almost always about doing something forbidden.
47. I am more emotional than analytical or logical.
61. While people find me likable or entertaining, I don't really have intimate relationships with friends (i.e., people with whom I frequently spend leisure time, who I can share things that I feel embarrassed or guilty about, who are really important to me and that I can depend on).
62. I feel guilty and/or embarrassed about my sexual fantasies and desires.

75. While I have emotional outbursts, I don't stay mad for long and am
able to apologize to or forgive the person that I'm mad at.

Interpretation

After reviewing this patient's responses on the PCI-2, the therapist revised
her initial diagnostic impression. The therapist's initial hypothesis had been
based on the patient's description of some glaring narcissistic symptomatology (e.g., obsession with physical appearance, history of drug abuse and
forging prescriptions, reported MMPI score) as well as the unfortunate tendency to overdiagnose men as narcissistic and women as hysterical.

Upon reconsideration, the therapist's next hypothesis was that this patient had a neurotic-level hysterical personality with narcissistic and masochistic features. It is important to remember that these diagnostic formulations
are always only considered to be tentative hypotheses until accumulated
information solidly supports a particular diagnostic picture.

The primary diagnosis (i.e., character style) of hysterical personality was
based on a number of observations on the patient's PCI-2 responses: (1) the
predominant number of items endorsed were on the Hysterical scale, including characteristics such as emotionality, frequent sexual conflicts, a lack of
awareness of a conscious intent behind dramatic, seductive behavior, and
an illusion of incompetence; (2) items both endorsed on the Hysterical scale
and not endorsed on other scales pointed to a neurotic-level ego structure,
including self and object constancy, lack of splitting, and good reality testing (which the narcissistic personality does not have); and (3) important
items were not endorsed that are highly diagnostic of narcissistic issues such
as grandiosity, fear of engulfment, and entitlement.

In rethinking the information gathered on the initial interview, the therapist again noted her previous concerns about viewing this patient's primary
character style as narcissistic (e.g., ability to love and make commitments).
Furthermore, the oedipal dynamics in the patient's family now seemed more
apparent than they previously had as a potential explanation for the patient's
lack of sexual feelings toward his wife. For example, while he attributed his
lack of sexual attraction to his wife's decline in appearance, his lack of attraction could alternately be attributed to the fact that he now experienced sex
with his wife as inducing more incestuous feelings in him due to the increased intimacy in their relationship and due to his wife becoming a mother.
His feelings of inadequacy, while partially narcissistic (due to his mother's
admiring and devaluing of him and his father), could also be explained by
an identification with a father that he and his mother viewed as weak, and

being rewarded for behaving in a more boyish, less assertive way with his mother. His drug history (which correlated with his period of sexual promiscuity) could be viewed as a way to overcome sexual guilt (due to unconscious sexual desires toward his mother and a strict religious upbringing) rather than a lack of ability to self-soothe and poor impulse control. His emphasis on attractiveness also may have been more related as a means of obtaining love rather than admiration.

Initial Treatment Goals

Based on the above diagnostic formulation, initial treatment goals would include (1) helping the patient to develop insight into the relationship between Oedipal issues with his mother and his current lack of sexual desire for his wife; (2) providing him (if the therapist is male) with or encouraging him to find a strong male role model to identify with; (3) clarifying with him whether he thought that his wife's physical appearance was objectively unattractive or whether his lack of attraction toward her might be due to something else; (4) generally clarifying his thinking by helping him become more conscious and directing his attention to facts and thought processes rather than impressions; (5) assuming a nondirective stance with him and interpreting maternal (i.e., critical, seductive, rejecting) and paternal (i.e., weak, "too good," not manly enough) transferences; (6) softening his harsh superego (hysterical issue) and unrealistic ego ideal (narcissistic issue), particularly in reference to sexual guilt and physical appearance; (7) helping him to objectively observe rather than internalize relational problems (masochistic issue); and (8) helping him understand if there are other interpersonal difficulties between he and his wife that might be effecting their sexual relationship (e.g., anger leading to withdrawal).

PROVIDING THE PATIENT WITH FEEDBACK REGARDING HIS OR HER PCI-2 RESPONSES

In general when providing the patient with feedback from the PCI-2, therapists are advised to integrate the data into general themes or impressions. Statements to patients are best made tentatively and tactfully as possibilities to be accepted or rejected by the patient. At the end, it is often useful to ask the patient how he or she is currently feeling. The following is an example of the type of feedback that a therapist might give to the patient in the case previously discussed:

"Some initial impressions that I have from your responses to this questionnaire and our first session is that your relationship with your mother and father was complicated and confusing and may in some way be affecting your sexual relationship with your wife. Also, it seems as though feelings of guilt and shame about having sexual feelings might be a broader concern for you than in this particular situation with your wife.

"You also seem to underestimate yourself and blame yourself when things go wrong. I think that loving relationships are important to you and my guess is that love, sex, and physical attraction are a bit confused for you. I think that it might be important for us to understand more about this confusion.

"The last thing is that it seems like in spite of your having previously abused drugs, and done illegal things, you have a number of strengths that you do not give yourself credit for, including being a pretty solid guy, having a strong sense of who you are, and being able to love, forgive, and be giving to other people. You might feel a stronger need to be giving than is in your best interest—*I'm not sure about this*—but I think it would be worth our exploring. I think it would also be worth our talking about the period during which you behaved in a way that I think you experienced as 'not you.'

"Do you have any feelings, thoughts, or questions about the feedback I gave you? What seems to fit and what seems off?"

The above manner of understanding patients and giving them feedback is a natural entrée into the process of beginning to make treatment contracts and goals. Obviously, the more severe the patient's pathology, the more caution and tact that is required from the therapist in this process.

13

Conclusion

Object relations therapy is an approach to diagnosis and treatment based on principles of object relations theory as described by members of the British school, such as Fairbairn, Guntrip, and Winnicott, and by members of the American school, such as Mahler, Kohut, and Kernberg. In diagnosis, an emphasis is placed on understanding developmental deficits, structural issues, and resulting interpersonal styles.

Treatment in this model involves traditional approaches (e.g., confrontation, clarification, and interpretation) to increasing patients' insight regarding their underlying dynamics. What is interpreted, however, is perceptions of and relationships between self and objects rather than conflicts regarding unconscious drives and defenses against them.

Through interpretation, therapists hope to enable patients to become more consciously aware of their mental template of self and others. This includes facilitating an understanding of how this template was initially formed (i.e., through important experiences with significant objects from the past) and how this template is used as a lens through which current experience is viewed.

It is important to help patients change their template of self and others so that it more accurately reflects their current social reality. For this to occur, in addition to giving patients interpretations leading to greater insight, therapists must also provide patients with a corrective interpersonal experience. The entirely neutral, abstinent therapist is not really a blank slate upon which to project. Rather, it is a particular type of object relationship (e.g., cool, nonresponsive, nonimpinging) that is more or less useful to different patients. The traditional psychoanalytic stance provides a particular stimulus for patients to respond to rather than no stimulus (i.e., a blank slate). Behaving in ways other than as a blank slate does not seem to significantly reduce transference. In fact, patients who perceive the therapist accurately (e.g., perceive support as support and criticism as criticism) are usually less in need of treatment.

What constitutes a corrective interpersonal experience for patients is a relationship that helps the patient master his or her unresolved developmental issues, further develop deficient psychic structures, and evolve a flexible, adaptive, and authentic interpersonal style. It is an intellectual challenge for therapists to determine what this entails for each patient, and it depends on making a complex and accurate structural and developmental diagnosis. An important factor in treatment is the interpersonal flexibility of therapists and their ability to acknowledge their own limits.

Current relationships in one's social world can be therapeutic and provide individuals with corrective experiences. When they are, individuals don't usually seek treatment. More often, however, they are not.

Current relationships are often not corrective interpersonal experiences for patients because of repetition compulsions and transference. Because of repetition compulsion, individuals have a proclivity to choose new objects in their lives who are similar to their old exciting or rejecting objects. These objects seem familiar and are thus comfortable for people in their own way. They provide a known painful experience over which they may feel an illusory sense of control.

Furthermore, individuals often have a deep wish to make the bad object into a good object. These clients may unconsciously believe they have to cure the object or entice the object to have fun or take care of themselves before the client can have fun or be taken care of. This strategy usually does not work. Rather, history repeats itself and an old wound is reinjured or the individual is merely disappointed.

Even when individuals have the foresight or good luck to choose new objects with which a reparative experience is possible, a corrective experience is still unlikely, as many individuals have the propensity to transfer their old experiences of self and objects onto new objects. Friends, teachers, husbands, and wives are often perceived as, for example, critical and controlling, when they are not.

As adults it is difficult to find individuals with whom we can have corrective experiences in a sustained fashion, quite simply because other people have their own needs and their own unresolved developmental issues. The good-enough mother is devoted to her child. Particularly during infancy, the child's needs generally take precedence over her own. She thus attempts to be attuned to the needs of the infant (which often involves paying almost constant attention to him or her) when the infant is having needs. Furthermore, she tries not to impinge when the infant is content, sometimes denying her own needs for contact with the infant. The good-enough husband, wife, or friend does not behave in this manner. Rather, he or she may be preoccupied or have needs of his or her own that at times assume greater importance.

However, individuals still have unresolved issues in areas such as basic trust, autonomy, and self development that cause them considerable problems in many areas of their lives and motivate them to seek treatment. To some extent, therapists can provide patients with these experiences.

Such experiences are necessary for helping patients develop a more accurate template of self and others. Traditional analytic theory states that we help patients learn about their transference (i.e., template of self and others) by providing them with a blank slate on which they project their interpersonal templates. In contrast, we believe that patients can be helped to be aware of and change their mental template by providing them with new experiences and observing how they distort them due to their experiences from the past.

Thus, over time patients begin to observe how they misperceive the therapist due to past experiences with parents and how they do the same thing with other people in their life. In addition, the relationships with the therapist and eventually with other people begin to provide them with new experiences with which they begin to revise their mental template of self and others.

This approach to treatment is not intended to be used as a cookbook. It is useful to conceptualize patients' problems with theories that help us better understand them and organize the material that patients present us with. However, patients are complex and their dynamics must not be oversimplified.

Diagnosis is thus intended to be used as a starting point—as a hypothesis to be accepted, rejected, or modified with further information about the patient. It is important to be open to changing our conceptualizations of patients as we get to know them better rather than trying to make our patients fit our diagnoses in order to prove that we were right.

We could as easily skip diagnostic categories altogether and discuss corrective interpersonal experiences for patients with different developmental issues, structural deficits, and interpersonal styles. Diagnoses are really a constellation of behaviors that reflect issues in these three areas.

Despite the often antiquated meaning of terms such as *schizoid, masochistic,* and *narcissistic,* we have chosen to use diagnostic categories because they reflect the nomenclature that is currently used and because we have personally found them to be helpful, especially when one is willing to make a diagnosis of a mixed personality disorder, which while less simple is also generally a more accurate picture of an individual's dynamics.

However, for those therapists who dislike the use of diagnostic labels because of their pejorative and categorical nature, it is possible to adapt this theory of treatment. Diagnoses may be bypassed and patients may be viewed with regard to their developmental, structural, and interpersonal issues. If, for example, a therapist hypothesizes that a patient has unresolved issues with autonomy, an underdeveloped sense of self, and a reactive, oppositional, and passive-aggressive interpersonal style, the therapist can individually construct a corrective experience for such a patient that is geared to helping him or her resolve these issues (e.g., attunement, being nondirective, confronting and interpreting passive-aggressive behavior). Indeed, in many ways this is what we do.

A potential criticism from therapists with a more traditional psychoanalytic orientation might be that this is just supportive psychotherapy or that people don't change by just being nice to them. While we are not advocating being "mean" or unsupportive, we believe that the relational experiences that we are suggesting are more complex than the term *support* implies. Furthermore, the goal of treatment is to change underlying character structure, not to prop patients up or help them to temporarily cope with life better.

Thus, as indicated in Chapter 4, the type of developmental goals that a therapist might address with a particular patient are forming an attachment, furthering individuation, and developing initiative. The type of structural goals might be developing a sense of self, developing resilient self-esteem, and increasing observing ego functions. The type of interpersonal goals are increasing appropriate assertiveness, and helping an individual learn to be more vulnerable with other people. These three types of goals are related. Thus, for example, it may be necessary to increase basic trust in order to help a patient learn to be vulnerable with others or to develop a sense of self in a patient in order to help them to be more assertive.

There is a growing zeitgeist in psychoanalysis and in psychotherapy at large toward developing more relational approaches to treatment including the Sullivanian-interpersonal school, the British object relations theorists, self psychology, and the feminist object relations theorists. We offer our theory of object relations therapy as one model to be tested alongside the other relational theories of psychotherapy that have been and are currently being developed.

Finally, we do not mean to imply here that we believe that all aspects of character are environmentally determined. However, we are currently just beginning to learn about the biological determinants of psychopathology. We suspect that over the next century this knowledge will increase exponentially, with a corresponding rise in biological methods of treatment.

We do, however, believe that humans are relational creatures and are, thus, enormously influenced by their interactions with others, including the psychotherapist. Thus, while at times the judicious use of medication may be an important adjunct to treatment, we do not believe that it can replace the relational component of the psychotherapeutic process that we have emphasized in this work. Ultimately, however, the respective usefulness of both biological and relational theories of treatment will be empirically determined by the clinicians who utilize them and the scientists who attempt to measure their impact on patients.

References

Adler, G. (1974). Regression in psychotherapy: Disruptive or therapeutic? *International Journal of Psychoanalytic Psychotherapy* 3(3):252–263.

——— (1985). *Borderline Psychopathology and Its Treatment.* New York: Jason Aronson.

Ainsworth, M. D. S., Bell, S. M., and Stayton, D. J. (1969). Individual differences in strange situation behavior of one-year-olds. In *The Origins of Human Social Behavior*, ed. H. R. Schaffer, pp. 17–57. New York: Academic Press.

Alexander, F., and French, T. M. (1946). *Psychoanalytic Therapy.* New York: Ronald.

Allen, D. W. (1991). Basic treatment issues. In *Hysterical Personality Style and the Histrionic Personality Disorder*, ed. M. Horowitz, pp. 147–192. Northvale, NJ: Jason Aronson.

American Psychiatric Association (1980). *Diagnostic and Statistical Manual of Mental Disorders, Third Edition (DSM III).* Washington, DC: American Psychiatric Association.

——— (1987). *Diagnostic and Statistical Manual of Mental Disorders*, 3rd ed., rev. (*DSM-III-R*). Washington, DC: American Psychiatric Association.

——— (1994). *Diagnostic and Statistical Manual of Mental Disorders*, 4th ed. (*DSM-IV*). Washington, DC: American Psychiatric Association.

Arieti, S. (1955). *Interpretation of Schizophrenia.* New York: Brunner/Mazel.

Avery, N. D. (1977). Sadomasochism: a defense against object loss. *Psychoanalytic Review* 64:101–109.

Azrin, N. H., and Holz, W. C. (1966). Punishment. In *Operant Behavior: Areas of Research and Application*, ed. W. K. Honig. New York: Appelton, Century, Croft.

Bach, S. (1985). *Narcissistic States and the Therapeutic Process.* New York: Jason Aronson.

462   REFERENCES

Bach-y-Rita, G. (1974). Habitual violence and self-mutilation. *American Journal of Psychiatry* 131(9):1018–1020.

Barnett, J. (1971). Narcissism and dependency in the obsessional hysterical marriage. *Family Process* 10:75–83.

Baron, M., Gruen, R., Rainer, J. D., et al. (1985). A family study of schizophrenic and normal control probands: implications for the spectrum concept of schizophrenia. *American Journal of Psychiatry* 142:447–454.

Basch, M. F. (1981). Psychoanalytic interpretation and cognitive transformation. *International Journal of Psycho-Analysis* 62(2):151–175.

——— (1983). Empathic understanding: a review of the concept and some theoretical considerations. *Journal of the American Psychoanalytic Association* 31(1): 101–126.

Beier, E. G. (1966). *The Silent Language of Psychotherapy: Social Reinforcement of Unconscious Processes.* Chicago: Aldine.

Benjamin, L. S. (1979). Structural analysis of differential failure. Use of structural analysis of social behavior (SASB) and Markov chains to study dyadic interactions. *Journal of Abnormal Psychology* 88:303–319.

——— (1993). *Interpersonal Diagnosis and Treatment of Personality Disorders.* New York: Guilford.

Berliner, B. (1947). On some psychodynamics of masochism. *Psychoanalytic Quarterly* 16(4):459–471.

Bion, W. (1962). *Learning from Experience.* New York: Basic Books.

——— (1967). *Second Thoughts: Selected Papers on Psycho-Analysis.* London: Heinemann.

——— (1970). *Attention and Interpretation: A Scientific Approach to Insight in Psychoanalysis and Groups.* London: Tavistock.

Blacker, K. H., and Tupin, J. P. (1991). Hysteria and hysterical structures: developmental and social theories. In *Hysterical Personality Style and the Histrionic Personality Disorder*, ed. M. Horowitz, pp. 15–66. New York: Jason Aronson.

Bowlby, J. (1969). *Attachment and Loss: Vol. 1. Attachment.* New York: Basic Books.

——— (1973). *Attachment and Loss: Vol. 2. Separation: Anxiety and Anger.* New York: Basic Books.

Bradley, S. J. (1979). The relationship of early maternal separation to borderline personality in children and adolescents: a pilot study. *American Journal of Psychiatry* 136:424–426.

Brende, J. O., and Parson, E. R. (1985). *Vietnam Veterans: The Road to Recovery.* New York: Plenum.

Brenner, C. (1959). The masochistic character: genesis and treatment. *Journal of the American Psychoanalytic Association* 7:197–226.

Briggs, D. (1979). The trainee and the borderline client: countertransference pitfalls. *Clinical Social Work Journal* 7(2):133–146.

Brody, S. (1982). Psychoanalytic theories of infant development. *Psychoanalytic Quarterly* 51:526–597.

Bromberg, W. (1955). Maternal influences in the development of moral masochism. *American Journal of Orthopsychiatry* 25:802–812.

Buie, D. H., and Adler, G. (1982). Definitive treatment of the borderline personality. *International Journal of Psychoanalytic Psychotherapy* 9:51–87.

Caplan, P. J. (1984). The myth of a woman's masochism. *American Psychologist* 39: 130–139.

Carpy, D. V. (1989). Tolerating the countertransference: a mutative process. *International Journal of Psycho-Analysis* 70:287–294.

Cashdan, S. (1988). *Object Relations Therapy.* New York: Norton.

Celani, D. (1976). An interpersonal approach to hysteria. *American Journal of Psychiatry* 133:1414–1418.

———— (1993). *The Treatment of the Borderline Patient: Applying Fairbairn's Object Relations Theory in the Clinical Setting.* Madison, CT: International Universities Press.

Chessick, R. D. (1985). *Psychology of the Self and the Treatment of Narcissism.* Northvale, NJ: Jason Aronson.

Cohen, J. (1980). Structural consequences of psychic trauma: a new look at "Beyond the Pleasure Principle." *International Journal of Psycho-Analysis* 61:421–432.

———— (1981). Theories of narcissism and trauma. *American Journal of Psychotherapy* 35:93–100.

Cohen, L. (1991). I'm your man. Cassette. Los Angeles, CA: Leonard Cohen Stranger Music.

Cooper, A. M. (1988). The narcissistic-masochistic character. In *Masochism: Current Psychoanalytic Perspectives,* ed. R. A. Glick and D. I. Meyers. Hillsdale, N.J.: Analytic Press.

Cooper, A. M., and Fischer, N. (1981). Masochism: current concepts. *Journal of the American Psychoanalytic Association* 29:673–688.

Detrick, P. W. (1985). Alter ego phenomena and the alterego transference: some further considerations. In *Progress in Self Psychology,* vol. 1, ed. A. Goldberg. New York: Guilford.

———— (1986). Alter ego phenomenon and the alterego transference: some further considerations. In *Progress in Self Psychology,* vol. 2, ed. A. Goldberg. New York: Guilford.

Dolan, R., Arnkoff, P., and Glass, C. (1993). Client's attachment style and the therapist's interpersonal stance. *Psychotherapy* 30(3):408–412.

Druck, A. (1989). *Four Therapeutic Approaches to the Borderline Patient.* Northvale, NJ: Jason Aronson.

Dryden, W. (1991). *Therapist's Dilemmas.* London: Harper & Row.

Easser, B. R., and Lesser, S. R. (1965). Hysterical personality: a re-evaluation. *Psychoanalytic Quarterly* 34:390–415.

Edward, J., Ruskin, N., and Turrini, P. (1991). *Separation-Individuation: Theory and Applications.* New York: Gardner.

Egeland, B., and Farber, F. (1985). Infant-mother attachment: factors related to its development and changes over time. *Child Development* 55(3):753–771.

Epstein, L. (1977). The therapeutic function of hate in the countertransference. *Contemporary Psychoanalysis* 13:442–461.

Erikson, E. H. (1950). *Childhood and Society.* New York: Norton.

———— (1956). The problem of ego identity. *Journal of the American Psychoanalytic Association* 4:56–121.

Fairbairn, W. R. D. (1941). A revised psychopathology of the psychoses and psychoneuroses. In *An Object-Relations Theory of the Personality.* New York: Basic Books, 1952.

———— (1944). Endopsychic structure considered in terms of object relationships. In *Psychoanalytic Studies of the Personality*, pp. 82–135. London: Routledge and Kegan Paul, 1952.

———— (1952). *An Object-Relations Theory of the Personality*. New York: Basic Books.

———— (1954). Observations on the nature of hysterical states. *British Journal of Medical Psychology* 27:105–125.

Fenichel, O. (1941). *Problems of Psychoanalytic Technique*. Albany, NY: Psychoanalytic Quarterly.

———— (1945). Neurotic acting out. In *Collected Papers of Otto Fenichel*, vol. 2, pp. 296–304. New York: Norton, 1954.

Finell, J. S. (1987). A challenge to psychoanalysis: a review of the negative therapeutic reaction. *Psychoanalytic Review* 74:487–515.

Fisher, A. E. (1955). *The Effects of Differential Early Treatment on the Social and Exploratory Behavior of Puppies*. Unpublished doctoral dissertation. University Park, PA: Penn State University.

Fliess, R. (1953). Countertransference and counteridentification. *Journal of the American Psychoanalytic Association* 1:268–284.

Franklin, D. (1987). The politics of masochism. *Psychology Today* 21:52–57.

Freud, A. (1936). *The Ego and the Mechanisms of Defense*. New York: International Universities Press.

Freud, S. (1905). Three essays on the theory of sexuality. *Standard Edition* 7:125–245.

———— (1908). Character and anal erotism. *Standard Edition* 9:169–175.

———— (1909). Notes upon a case of obsessional neurosis. *Standard Edition* 10:65–68.

———— (1910). The future prospects of psycho-analytic therapy. *Standard Edition* 11:139–151.

———— (1912). The dynamics of transference. *Standard Edition* 12:97–108.

———— (1914). Remembering, repeating, and working through. *Standard Edition* 12:145–156.

———— (1915). Repression. *Standard Edition* 14:143–158.

———— (1919). A child is being beaten. *Standard Edition* 17:175–204.

———— (1921). Group psychology and the analysis of the ego. *Standard Edition* 18:65–143.

———— (1923). The ego and the id. *Standard Edition* 19:1–66.

———— (1924). The economic problem of masochism. *Standard Edition* 19:157–170.

———— (1926). Inhibitions, symptoms, and anxiety. *Standard Edition* 20:75–175.

———— (1937). Analysis terminable and interminable. *Standard Edition* 23:209–253.

———— (1940). An outline of psycho-analysis. *Standard Edition* 23:141–207.

Friedman, R. (1991). The depressed masochistic patient: diagnostic and management considerations: a contemporary psychoanalytic perspective. *Journal of the American Academy of Psychoanalysis* 19:9–30.

Gear, M. C., Hill, M. A., and Liendo, E. C. (1983). *Working Through Narcissism: Treating its Sadomasochistic Structure*. New York: Jason Aronson.

Geisel, T., and Geisel, A. (1988). *Green Eggs and Ham*. New York: Random House.

Ghent, E. (1983). Masochism, submission, and surrender. *Contemporary Psychoanalysis* 26:108–136.

Giovacchini, P. L. (1989). *Countertransference Triumphs and Catastrophes*. Northvale, NJ: Jason Aronson.

Glick, R. A., and Meyers, D. I., eds. (1988). *Masochism: Current Psychoanalytic Perspectives.* Hillsdale, NJ: Analytic Press.

Glickauf-Hughes, C. (1988). *The psychodynamic character inventory.* Unpublished manuscript.

———— (1994). Dynamics and treatment of the narcissistic-masochistic couple. *Psychoanalysis and Psychotherapy* 2(1):34–46.

———— (1996). Sadomasochistic interactions. In *Handbook of Relational, Diagnoses, and Dysfunctional Family Patterns,* ed. F. Kaslow, pp. 270–284. New York: Wiley.

———— (In press, a). Masochism, authenticity, and will. *Issues in Psychoanalytic Psychology.*

———— (In press, b). Etiology of masochistic and narcissistic personalities. *American Journal of Psychoanalysis.*

Glickauf-Hughes, C., and Campbell, L. (1991). Experiential supervision: applied techniques for a case presentation approach. *Psychotherapy* 28(4):625–635.

Glickauf-Hughes, C., and Chance, S. E. (1995). Answering client's questions. *Psychotherapy* 32:375–380.

Glickauf-Hughes, C., and Cummings, S. (1995). Use of containment in supervising couples therapy. *The Family Journal* 3:149–152.

Glickauf-Hughes, C., and Mehlman, E. (1995). Narcissistic issues in therapists: diagnostic and treatment considerations. *Psychotherapy* 32:213–221.

Glickauf-Hughes, C., Riviere, S., Clance, P., and Jones, J. (1997). An integration of object relations theory and gestalt techniques to facilitate structuralization of the self. *Journal of Psychotherapy Integration* 6(1):39–69.

Glickauf-Hughes, C., and Wells, M. (1991a). Current conceptualizations on masochism: genesis and object relations. *American Journal of Psychotherapy* 45:53–68.

———— (1991b). Differential diagnosis of the masochistic personality. *Journal of Psychoanalysis and Psychotherapy* 9(2):167–176.

———— (1995a). Narcissistic characters with obsessive features: diagnostic and treatment considerations. *American Journal of Psychoanalysis* 55:129–143.

———— (1995b). *Treatment of the Masochistic Personality: An Interactional-Object Relations Approach to Psychotherapy.* Northvale, NJ: Jason Aronson.

Glickauf-Hughes, C., Wells, M., and Chance, S. (1996). Techniques for strengthening clients' observing ego. *Psychotherapy* 33(3):431–440.

Glickauf-Hughes, C., Wells, M., and Genirberg, R. (1987). Psychotherapy of gifted students with narcissistic dynamics. *Journal of College Student Psychotherapy* 1(3):99–115.

Goldstein, W. N. (1985). *An Introduction to the Borderline Conditions.* Northvale, NJ: Jason Aronson.

Gordon, R. M. (1990). *The Structure of Emotions: Investigations in Cognitive Philosophy.* New York: Cambridge University Press.

Grayer, E., and Sax, P. (1986). A model for the diagnostic and therapeutic use of countertransference. *Clinical Social Work Journal* 14:295–309.

Greenberg, J. R., and Mitchell, S. A. (1983). *Object Relations in Psychoanalytic Theory.* Cambridge, MA: Harvard University Press.

Greenson, R. (1967). *The Technique and Practice of Psychoanalysis.* Madison, CT: International Universities Press.

Grinberg, L. (1993). Countertransference and the concept of projective counteridentification. In *Countertransference: Theory, Technique, Teaching*, ed. A. Alexandris and G. Vaslamatzis, pp. 47–65. London: Karnac.

Grinspoon, L. (1990). Self-defeating behavior and masochism. *The Harvard Mental Health Letter* 6(9):1–4.

Grotstein, J. (1982). The significance of Kleinian contributions to psychoanalysis. III: The Kleinian theory of ego psychology and object relations. *International Journal of Psychoanalytic Psychotherapy* 9:487–510.

Groves, J. E. (1978). Taking care of the hateful patient. *New England Journal of Medicine* 298:883–887.

Gunderson, J. G., Zanarini, M. C., and Kisiel, C. L. (1995). Borderline personality disorder. In *The DSM-IV Personality Disorders*, ed. W. J. Livesley, pp. 141–157. New York: Guilford.

Guntrip, H. (1961). *Personality Structure and Human Interaction: The Developing Synthesis of Psychodynamic Theory*. New York: International Universities Press.

——— (1969). *Schizoid Phenomena, Object Relations, and the Self*. New York: International Universities Press.

Hamilton, G. (1988). *Self and Others: Object Relations Theory in Practice*. Northvale, NJ: Jason Aronson.

——— (1995). *From Inner Sources: New Directions in Object Relations Therapy*. Northvale, NJ: Jason Aronson.

Harlow, H. (1958). The nature of love. *American Psychologist* 13:683–685.

Hartmann, H. (1939). *Ego Psychology and the Problem of Adaptation*. New York: International Universities Press.

——— (1950). *Essays in Ego Psychology*. New York: International Universities Press.

——— (1952). The mutual influences in the development of the ego and id. In *Essays on Ego Psychology*. New York: International Universities Press, 1964.

Havens, J. (1978). *A Fifth Yoga: The way of relationships*. Wallingford, PA: Pendle Hill.

Havens, L. L. (1976). *Participant Observation: The Psychotherapy Schools in Action*. New York: Jason Aronson.

Hearst, L. E. (1988). The restoration of the impaired self in group psychoanalytic treatment. In *Borderline and Narcissistic Clients in Therapy*, ed. N. Slavinska-Holy, pp. 123–142. Madison, WI: International Universities Press.

Hedges, L. (1983). *Listening Perspectives in Psychotherapy*. New York: Jason Aronson.

Hegel, G. W. (1967). *The Phenomenology of the Mind*. New York: Harper & Row.

Herman, J. L. (1992). *Trauma and Recovery*. New York: Basic Books.

Herman, J. L., Perry, J. C., and van der Kolk, B. A. (1989). Childhood trauma in borderline personality disorder. *American Journal of Psychiatry* 146:490–495.

Horner, A. (1979). *Object Relations and the Developing Ego in Therapy*. Northvale, NJ: Jason Aronson.

——— (1991). *Psychoanalytic Object Relations Therapy*. Northvale, NJ: Jason Aronson.

Horney, K. (1939). *Neurosis and Human Growth*. New York: Norton.

Horowitz, M. J. (1992). *Stress response syndromes*. Northvale, NJ: Jason Aronson.

Horowitz, M. J., Marmar, C., and Weiss, D. S. (1984). Brief psychotherapy of bereavement reactions. *Archives of General Psychiatry* 41:438–448.

Jacobs, T. (1993). *On beginnings: alliances, misalliances, and the interplay of transferences in the opening phase*. Paper presented at the American Psychoanalytic Association Seminar for Clinicians, Atlanta, GA, August.

Jacobson, E. (1964). *The Self and the Object World.* New York: International Universities Press.

Johnson, S. (1985). *Characterological Transformation: The Hard Work Miracle.* New York: Norton.

—— (1987). *Humanizing the Narcissistic Style.* New York: Norton.

Jones, R., and Wells, M. (1996). Research on parentified personalities. *American Journal of Family Therapy* 24(2):145–152.

Josephs, L. (1995). *Character and Self-Experience.* Northvale, NJ: Jason Aronson.

Kainer, R. G. (1977). Beyond masochism: the relationship of narcissistic injury to will. *Journal of Otto Rank Association* 12(2):21–28.

Kalus, O., Bernstein, D. P., and Siever, L. J. (1995). Schizoid personality disorder. In *The DSM-IV Personality Disorders,* ed. John Livesley, pp. 58–70. New York: Guilford.

Karterud, S. W. (1990). Bion or Kohut: two paradigms of group dynamics. In *The Difficult Patient in Group: Group Psychotherapy with Borderline and Narcissistic Disorders,* ed. B. E. Roth, W. N. Stone, and H. D. Kibel. Madison, WI: International Universities Press.

Kell, B. L., and Mueller, W. J. (1966). *Impact and Change: A Study of Counseling Relationships.* Englewood Cliffs, NJ: Prentice-Hall.

Kernberg, O. (1965). Notes on countertransference. *Journal of the American Psychoanalytic Association* 13:38–57.

—— (1970). A psychoanalytic classification of character pathology. *Journal of the American Psychoanalytic Association* 18:800–802.

—— (1974). Further contributions to the treatment of narcissistic personalities. *International Journal of Psycho-Analysis* 55:215.

—— (1975). *Borderline Conditions and Pathological Narcissism.* New York: Jason Aronson.

—— (1976). *Object Relations Theory and Clinical Psychoanalysis.* New York: Jason Aronson.

—— (1978). The diagnosis of borderline conditions in adolescence. *Adolescent Psychiatry* 6:298–319.

—— (1980). *Internal World and External Reality.* New York: Jason Aronson.

—— (1982). Self, ego, affects, and drives. *Journal of the American Psychoanalytic Association* 30:893–917.

—— (1984). *Severe Personality Disorders: Psychotherapeutic Strategies.* New Haven, CT: Yale University Press.

—— (1992). *Aggression in Personality Disorders and Perversions.* New Haven, CT: Yale University Press.

Kernberg, O. F., Selzer, M. A., Koenigsberg, H. W., et al. (1989). *Psychodynamic Psychotherapy of Borderline Patients.* New York: Basic Books.

Klein, D. (1970). Psychotrophic drugs and the regulation of behavioral activation in psychiatric illness. In *Drugs and Cerebral Function,* ed. W. L. Smith. Springfield, IL: Charles C Thomas.

—— (1977). Psychopharmacological treatment and delineation of borderline disorders. In *Borderline Personality Disorders,* ed. P. Hartocollis, pp. 365–383. New York: International Universities Press.

Klein, M. (1929). Infantile anxiety-situations reflected in a work of art and in the creative impulse. In *Contributions to Psychoanalysis, 1921–1945*. New York: McGraw-Hill, 1964.

——— (1935). A contribution to the psychogenesis of manic-depressive states. In *Contributions to Psychoanalysis, 1921–1945*. New York: McGraw-Hill, 1964.

——— (1948). On the theory of anxiety and guilt. In *Envy and Gratitude and Other Works, 1946–1963*, pp. 25–42. New York: Delacorte, 1975.

——— (1952a). The origins of transference. In *Envy and Gratitude and Other Works, 1946–1963*, pp. 48–56. New York: Delacorte, 1975.

——— (1952b). The mutual influences in the development of ego and id. In *Envy and Gratitude and Other Works, 1946–1963*. New York: Delacorte, 1975.

——— (1957). Envy and gratitude. In *Envy and Gratitude and Other Works, 1946–1963*. New York: Delacorte, 1975.

Kohut, H. (1968). The psychoanalytic treatment of narcissistic personality disorders. *Psychoanalytic Study of the Child* 23:86–113. New York: International Universities Press.

——— (1971). *The Analysis of the Self*. New York: International Universities Press.

——— (1977). *The Restoration of the Self*. New York: International Universities Press.

——— (1984). *How Does Analysis Cure?* Chicago: University of Chicago Press.

Krafft-Ebing, R. F. (1895). *Psychopathia Sexualis*. London: F. A. Davis.

Kretschmer, E. (1925). *Physique and Character*. London: Kegan, Paul, Trench, and Trubner.

Krohn, A. (1978). *Hysteria: The Elusive Neurosis*. New York: International Universities Press.

Lasch, C. (1979). *The Culture of Narcissism*. New York: Norton.

Lawy, F. H. (1970). The abuse of abreaction: an unhappy legacy of Freud's cathartic method. *Canadian Psychiatric Journal* 15:551–565.

Lazare, A. (1971). The hysterical character in psychoanalytic theory. *Archives of General Psychiatry* 25:131–137.

Lazarus, A. (1993). Tailoring of the therapeutic relationship, or being an authentic chameleon. *Psychotherapy* 30(3):404–407.

Leary, T. (1957). *Interpersonal Diagnosis of Personality*. New York: Ronald.

Levy, S. (1990). *Principles of Interpretation: Mastering Clear and Concise Interventions in Psychotherapy*. Northvale, NJ: Jason Aronson.

Little, M. I. (1951). Counter-transference and the patient's response to it. *International Journal of Psycho-Analysis* 32:32–40.

——— (1957). "R"—the analyst's total response to his patient's needs. *International Journal of Psycho-Analysis* 38:240–254.

Lowen, A. (1985). *Narcissism: Denial of the True Self*. New York: Collier.

Luborsky, L., Crits-Christoph, P., and Mintz, J. (1988). *Who Will Benefit from Psychotherapy?* New York: Basic Books.

Magnavita, J. J. (1997). Treating personality disorders: psychotherapy's frontier. *Psychotherapy Bulletin* 32(1):23–28.

Mahler, M. (1965). On the significance of the normal separation-individuation phase: with reference to research in symbiotic child psychosis. In *Drives, Affects, Behavior*, vol. 2, ed. M. Schur. New York: International Universities Press.

——— (1968). *On Human Symbiosis and the Vicissitudes of Individuation.* New York: International Universities Press.

Mahler, M. S., and Furer, M. (1968). *On Human Symbiosis and the Vicissitudes of Individuation.* New York: International Universities Press.

Mahler, M., Pine, F., and Bergman, A. (1975). *The Psychological Birth of the Human Infant.* New York: Basic Books.

Mahrer, A. (1993). The experiential relationship: Is it all purpose or is it tailored to the individual client? *Psychotherapy* 30:413–416.

Margulies, A. (1984). Toward empathy: the uses of wonder. *American Journal of Psychiatry* 141:1025–1033.

Marmar, C. R., Weiss, D. S., and Gaston, L. (1989). Toward the validation of the California Therapeutic Alliance Rating System. *Psychological Assessment: Journal of Consulting and Clinical Psychology* 1:46–52.

Marmor, J. (1953). Orality in the hysterical personality. *Journal of the American Psychoanalytic Association* 1:656–671.

Masterson, J. F. (1972). *Treatment of the Borderline Adolescent: A Developmental Approach.* New York: John Wiley (Wiley-Interscience).

——— (1975). The splitting defense mechanism of the borderline adolescent: developmental and clinical aspects. In *Borderline States*, ed. J. Mack. New York: Grune & Stratton.

——— (1976). *Psychotherapy of the Borderline Adult.* New York: Brunner/Mazel.

——— (1981). *Narcissistic and Borderline Disorders: An Integrated Developmental Approach.* New York: Brunner/Mazel.

——— (1993). *The Emerging Self.* New York: Brunner/Mazel.

——— (1996). *The Borderline Personality Disorder: Diagnosis and Treatment.* Unpublished manuscript.

McClure, M., and McClendon, R. (1989). The self-contained therapist. *Psychotherapy Patient* 4:29–37.

McCormack, C. (1984). The borderline/schizoid marriage: the holding environment as an essential treatment construct. *Journal of Marriage and Family Therapy* 15:299–309.

Meissner, W. (1984). *The Borderline Spectrum: Differential Diagnosis and Developmental Issues.* New York: Jason Aronson.

——— (1988). *Treatment of Patients in the Borderline Spectrum.* Northvale, NJ: Jason Aronson.

——— (1992). *Ignatius of Loyola: The Psychology of a Saint.* New Haven, CT: Yale University Press.

Merrikangas, K. R., and Weissman, M. M. (1986). Epidemiology of *DSM-III* Axis II personality disorders. *Psychiatric Update: The American Psychiatric Association Annual Review*, vol. 5, ed. A. J. Frances and R. E. Hales. Washington, DC: American Psychological Association.

Meyers, H. (1988). A consideration of treatment techniques in relation to the functions of masochism. In *Masochism-Current Psychoanalytic Perspectives*, ed. R. Glick and D. Meyers. Hillsdale, NJ: Analytic Press.

Miller, A. (1981). *The Drama of the Gifted Child.* New York: Basic Books.

Miller, R. (1990). Projective identification and the therapist's use of self. *Journal of Contemporary Psychotherapy* 20(1):63–73.

Millon, T. (1981). *Disorders of Personality DSM-III: Axis II*. New York: Wiley.
——— (1985). *Personality and Its Disorders: A Biosocial Learning Approach*. New York: Wiley.
Minton, H., and McDonald, G. (1985). Homosexual identity formation as a developmental process. In *Origins of Sexuality and Homosexuality*, ed. J. DeCecco and M. Shively, pp. 91–104. New York: Irvington.
Modell, A. (1968). *Object Love and Reality*. New York: International Universities Press.
Moore, B. E., and Fine, B. D. (1990). *Psychoanalytic Terms and Concepts*. New Haven, CT: American Psychoanalytic Association and Yale University Press.
Moras, K., and Strupp, H. H. (1982). Pretherapy interpersonal relations, patients' alliance, and outcome in brief therapy. *Archives of General Psychiatry* 39:405–409.
Morrison, A. P. (1987). The eye turned inward. In *The Many Faces of Shame*, ed. D. Nathanson, pp. 271–291. New York: Guilford.
——— (1989). *Shame: The Underside of Narcissism*. Hillsdale, NJ: Analytic Press.
Mueller, W. J., and Aniskiewicz, A. S. (1986). *Psychotherapeutic Intervention in Hysterical Disorders*. Northvale, NJ: Jason Aronson.
Nichols, M. P., and Kolb, L. C. (1986). Catharsis: clinical applications. In *Basic Techniques in Psychoanalytic Psychotherapy*, ed. M. P. Nichols and T. Paolino, pp. 103–126. New York: Gardner.
Norcross, J. (1993). Tailoring relational stances to clients' needs: an introduction. *Psychotherapy* 30(3):402–403.
Ogden, T. H. (1979). On projective identification. *International Journal of Psycho-Analysis* 60:357–373.
——— (1982). *Projective Identification and Psychotherapeutic Technique*. New York: Jason Aronson.
Orlinsky, D. E., and Howard, K. I. (1986). Process and outcome in psychotherapy. In *Handbook of Psychotherapy and Behavior Change*, ed. S. L. Garfield and A. E. Bergin. 3rd ed. New York: Wiley.
Ornstein, P. A. (1978). *Memory Development in Children*. New York: Halsted.
Overholser, J. C. (1989). Differentiation between schizoid and avoidant personalities. An empirical test. *Canadian Journal of Psychiatry* 34(8):785–790.
Panken, S. (1983). *The Joy of Suffering*. New York: Jason Aronson.
Patton, M., and Robins, S. (1982). Kohut's self-psychology as a model for college student counseling. *Professional Psychology* 13(6):876–888.
Peterfreund, E. (1978). Some critical comments on psychoanalytic conceptualizations of infancy. *International Journal of Psycho-Analysis* 59:427–441.
Piaget, J. (1936). *The Origins of Intelligence in Children*. New York: International Universities Press.
Pine, F. (1993). A contribution to the analysis of the psychoanalytic process. *Psychoanalytic Quarterly* 2:185–205.
Piper, W. E., Azim, H. F. A., Joyce, A. S., and McCallum, M. (1991a). Transference interpretations, therapeutic alliance, and outcome in short-term individual psychotherapy. *Archives of General Psychiatry* 48:946–953.
Piper, W. E., Azim, H. F. A., Joyce, A. S., et al. (1991b). Quality of object relations versus interpersonal functioning as predictors of therapeutic alliance and psychotherapy outcome. *Journal of Nervous and Mental Disease* 179:432–438.
Piper, W. E., De Carufel, F. L., and Szkrumelak, N. (1985). Patient predictors of

process and outcome in short-term individual psychotherapy. *Journal of Nervous and Mental Disease* 173:726–733.

Poggi, R. G., and Ganzarain, R. (1983). Countertransference hate. *Bulletin of the Menninger Clinic* 47:15–35.

Racker, H. (1953). A contribution to the problem of countertransference. *International Journal of Psycho-Analysis* 34:313–324.

—— (1960). *Estudios Sobre Tecnica Psicoanalitica.* Buenos Aires: Paidos.

Rehm, L., and Mehta, P. (1994). Depression. In *Advanced Abnormal Psychology*, ed. V. B. Van Hasselt and M. Hersen. New York: Plenum Press.

Reich, A. (1951). On counter-transference. *International Journal of Psycho-Analysis* 32:25–31.

Reich, W. (1933). *Character Analysis.* New York: Farrar, Straus & Giroux, 1972.

Reiser, D. E., and Levenson, H. (1984). Abuses of the borderline diagnosis: a clinical problem with teaching opportunities. *American Journal of Psychiatry* 141: 1528–1532.

Renik, O. (1993). Countertransference enactment and the psychoanalytic process. In *Psychic Structure and Psychic Change*, ed. M. Horowitz, O. Kernberg, and E. Weinshel. New York: International Universities Press.

—— (1996). The perils of neutrality. *Psychoanalytic Quarterly* 65(3):495–517.

Rinsley, D. B. (1977). An object relations view of borderline personality. In *Borderline Personality Disorders: The Concept, the Syndrome, the Patient*, ed. P. Hartocollis, pp. 47–70. New York: International Universities Press.

—— (1982). *Borderline and Other Self Disorders: A Developmental and Object-Relations Perspective.* New York: Jason Aronson.

Rogers, C. (1942). *Client Centered Therapy.* Boston: Houghton Mifflin.

—— (1965). *On Becoming a Person.* Boston: Houghton Mifflin.

Rothenberg, A. (1987). Empathy as a creative process in treatment. *International Review of Psychoanalysis* 14:445–463.

Rucker, H. (1968). *Transference and Countertransference.* New York: International Universities Press.

Salzman, L. (1980). *Treatment of the Obsessive Personality.* New York: Jason Aronson.

—— (1985). Psychotherapeutic management of obsessive-compulsive patients. *American Journal of Psychotherapy* 39:323–330.

Salzman, L., and Thaler, F. M. (1981). Obsessive-compulsive disorders: a review of the literature. *American Journal of Psychotherapy* 38:286–296.

Sandler, J., and Rosenblatt, B. (1962). The concept of the representational world. *Psychoanalytic Study of the Child* 17:128–145. New York: International Universities Press.

Sartre, J. P. (1943). *The Age of Reason*, trans. E. Sutton. London: Hamilton, 1947.

Scharff, D. E., and Scharff, J. S. (1987). *Object Relations Family Therapy.* Northvale, NJ: Jason Aronson.

—— (1991). *Object Relations Couple Therapy.* Northvale, NJ: Jason Aronson.

Scharff, J. S., and Scharff, D. E. (1992). *Scharff Notes: A Primer of Object Relations Therapy.* Northvale, NJ: Jason Aronson.

—— (1994). *Object Relations Therapy of Physical and Sexual Trauma.* Northvale, NJ: Jason Aronson.

Schultz, R., and Glickauf-Hughes, C. (1995). Countertransference in the treatment of pathological narcissism. *Psychotherapy* 32(4):601–607.

Scialli, J. (1982). Multiple identity processes and the development of the observing ego. *Journal of the American Academy of Psychoanalysis* 10:387–405.

Segal, H. (1981). *The Work of Hanna Segal: A Kleinian Approach to Clinical Practice.* New York: Jason Aronson.

Seltzer, M. (1983). Preparing the chronic schizophrenic for exploratory psychotherapy: the role of hospitalization. *Psychiatry* 46:303–309.

Shapiro, D. (1965). *Neurotic Styles.* New York: Basic Books.

Slipp, S. (1984). *Object Relations: A Dynamic Bridge Between Individual and Family Treatment.* New York: Jason Aronson.

Smirnoff, V. (1969). The masochistic contract. *International Journal of Psycho-Analysis* 50:665–671.

Soloff, P., and Millward, J. W. (1983). Developmental histories of borderline patients. *Comprehensive Psychiatry* 24:574–588.

St. Clair, M. (1996). *Object Relations and Self Psychology: An Introduction.* Pacific Grove, CA: Brooks/Cole.

Sterba, R. F. (1934). The fate of the ego in analytic therapy. *International Journal of Psycho-Analysis* 15:117–126.

Stern, D. N. (1985). *The Interpersonal World of the Infant.* New York: Basic Books.

Stolorow, R. D. (1975). The narcissistic function of masochism (and sadism). *International Journal of Psycho-Analysis* 56:441–448.

Stone, M. H. (1987). Psychotherapy of borderline patients in light of long-term follow-up. *Bulletin of the Menninger Clinic* 51:231–247.

Sullivan, H. S. (1924). Schizophrenia: its conservative and malignant features. In *Schizophrenia as a Human Process.* New York: Norton, 1962.

——— (1938). The data of psychiatry. In *The Fusion of Psychiatry and Social Science.* New York: Norton, 1964.

——— (1940). *Conceptions of Modern Psychiatry.* New York: Norton.

——— (1953). *The Interpersonal Theory of Psychiatry.* New York: Norton.

——— (1954). *The Psychiatric Interview.* New York: Norton.

——— (1972). *Personal Psychopathology.* New York: Norton.

Sutherland, J. P. (1989). *Fairbairn's Journey in the Interior.* London: Free Association Books.

Trull, T. J., Widiger, T. A., and Frances, A. (1987). Analysis of paragesia. *American Journal of Orthopsychiatry* 9:767–771.

Ulman, R. B., and Brothers, D. (1988). *The Shattered Self: A Psychoanalytic Study of Trauma.* Hillsdale, NJ: Analytic Press.

van der Kolk, B. A. (1989). The compulsion to repeat the trauma: revictimization, attachment, and masochism. *Psychiatric Clinics of North America* 12:389–411.

——— (1994). The body keeps score: memory and the evolving psychobiology of PTSD. *Harvard Review of Psychiatry* 1:253–265.

van der Kolk, B. A., Hostetler, A., Herron, N., and Fisler, R. E. (1994). Trauma and the development of borderline personality disorder. *Psychiatric Clinics of North America* 17(4):715–730.

Varga, M. P. (1985). An object relations perspective on dealing with depressive masochistic character resistances. *Issues in Ego Psychology* 8(1):59–62.

Weinshel, E., and Renik, O. (1992). Treatment goals in psychotherapy. In *The Technique and Practice of Psychoanalysis, Vol. 2: A Memorial Volume to Ralph R. Greenson,* ed. A. Sugarman, R. Nemiroff, and D. Greenson, pp. 91–99. Madison, CT: International Universities Press.

Weiss, J. (1993). *How Psychotherapy Works.* New York: Guilford.

Wells, M., and Glickauf-Hughes, C. (1986). Techniques to develop object constancy with borderline clients. *Psychotherapy* 23(3):460–468.

———— (1993). A psychodynamic object relations model for differential diagnosis. *Psychotherapy Bulletin* 28(3):41–49.

Wells, M., Glickauf-Hughes, C., and Beaudoin, P. (1995). An ego/object relations approach to treating childhood sexual abuse survivors. *Psychotherapy* 32(3): 416–429.

Wells, M., Glickauf-Hughes, C., and Buzzell, V. (1990). Treating obsessive-compulsives in psychodynamic-interpersonal group therapy. *Psychotherapy* 27(3): 366–379.

Willi, J. (1982). *Couples in Collusion.* New York: Jason Aronson and Hunter House.

Winnicott, D. W. (1945). Primitive emotional development. In *Collected Papers: Through Paediatrics to Psychoanalysis,* pp. 145–156. London: Tavistock.

———— (1949). Hate in the countertransference. *International Journal of Psycho-Analysis* 30:69–74.

———— (1951). Transitional objects and transitional phenomenon. In *Through Paediatrics to Psycho-Analysis,* pp. 145–156. London: Hogarth, 1975.

———— (1958a). The capacity to be alone. In *The Maturational Process and the Facilitating Environment,* pp. 29–36. New York: International Universities Press, 1965.

———— (1958b). *Through Paediatrics to Psychoanalysis.* London: Hogarth, 1965.

———— (1959). Classification: Is there a psycho-analytic contribution to psychiatric classification? In *The Maturational Process and the Facilitating Environment,* pp. 124–139. New York: International Universities Press, 1965.

———— (1960). Ego distortion in terms of true and false self. In *The Maturational Process and the Facilitating Environment,* pp. 140–152. New York: International Universities Press, 1965.

———— (1962). Ego integration in child development. In *The Maturational Process and the Facilitating Environment,* pp. 56–63. New York: International Universities Press, 1965.

———— (1963). From dependence to independence in the development of the individual. In *The Maturational Process and the Facilitating Environment,* pp. 83–99. New York: International Universities Press, 1965.

———— (1965a). *The Maturational Process and the Facilitating Environment.* New York: International Universities Press.

———— (1965b). The mentally ill in your caseload. In *The Maturational Process and the Facilitating Environment,* pp. 217–229. New York: International Universities Press.

Witkin, H. (1965). Psychological differentiation and forms of pathology. *Journal of Abnormal Psychology* 70:317–336.

Witkin, H., Lewis, H., Hertzman, M., et al. (1954). *Personality Through Perception.* New York: Wiley.

Young, D. M., and Beier, E. G. (1982). Being asocial in social places: giving the client a new experience. In *Handbook of Interpersonal Psychotherapy,* ed. J. C. Anchin and D. J. Kiesler. New York: Pergamon.

Zetzel, E. R. (1956). Current concepts of transference. *International Journal of Psycho-Analysis* 37:369–376.

Index

Identification, defined, 8–9
Incorporation, defined, 7
Intellectualization
  obsessive-compulsive personality,
    337–338
  schizoid personality, 137
  schizoid personality and, 130
Internalization
  Kernberg and, 43–44
  masochistic personality, 299
Interpersonal relationships
  hysterical personality, 389–390
  hysteroid-borderline personality,
    190–191
  masochistic personality, 308–309
  narcissistic personality, 252–253
  obsessive-compulsive personality,
    348–349
  schizoid personality, 126, 139
Interpretation, object relations therapy,
    59–60
Introjection, defined, 7–8, 43

Jacobs, T., 60, 100
Jacobson, E., 4, 23, 39
Johnson, S., 75, 127, 130, 137, 138, 139,
    140, 142, 146, 152, 153, 159, 238,
    241, 243, 244, 247, 262, 268, 273,
    281, 302, 303
Jones, R., 306
Josephs, L., 382, 390, 394, 395, 396, 412,
    423, 424
Judging component, countertransfer-
    ence, 114

Kainer, R. G., 292
Kalus, O., 156, 157
Karterud, S. W., 48
Kell, B. L., 393
Kernberg, O., 1, 8, 13, 15, 23, 27, 38–46,
    77, 78, 79, 82, 83, 90, 112, 169, 170,
    174, 175, 179, 186, 187, 188, 191,
    194, 214, 217, 229, 230, 231, 233,
    237, 238, 249, 251, 279, 280, 283,
    388
Klein, D., 128, 133, 168

Klein, M., 13, 19–24, 116, 169, 170, 218
Kohut, H., 2, 4, 5, 6, 13, 46–52, 60, 62,
    64, 67, 107, 182, 230, 232, 234, 237,
    238, 239, 244, 245, 247, 248, 253,
    255, 257, 263, 273, 278, 279, 282,
    317
Krafft-Ebing, R. F., 290
Kretschmer, E., 132, 134
Krohn, A., 81, 82, 90, 214, 380

Lasch, C., 229
Lawry, F. H., 206
Lazare, A., 391
Lazarus, A., 61
Leary, T., 63, 65, 328
Lesser, S. R., 82, 90, 169, 170
Levenson, H., 218
Levy, S., 13, 192, 340
Libidinal ego, 25, 28
Little, M. I., 112
Lowen, A., 231

Mahler, M., 5, 12, 15, 33–38, 44, 65, 113,
    186, 246, 307
Manipulation, narcissistic personality,
    232
Margulies, A., 113
Marmor, J., 169
Masochistic personality, 289–333
  case example, 330–333
  corrective emotional experience,
    321–323
  countertransference issues, 326–329
  defenses, 298–300
  developmental failure, 307–308
  differential diagnosis, 323–326
  etiology, 302–307
  hysterical personality compared,
    417–418
  hysteroid-borderline personality,
    215–216
  interpersonal goals, 309–317
  interpersonal stance, 308–309
  narcissistic personality compared,
    275–276

Searles, H., 323
Segal, H., 112, 282
Self, defined, 4–5
Self-absorption, narcissistic personality, 232
Self-esteem
　masochistic personality, 301
　narcissistic personality, 252
Self-expression, hysteroid-borderline personality, 172–173
Selfobject, defined, 6
Self psychology, object relations theory, 46–52
Self-reflection, schizoid personality, 126
Self-sacrifice, masochistic personality, 290
Self-sufficiency, schizoid personality, 127
Seltzer, M., 208
Sensitivity
　narcissistic personality, 230
　schizoid personality and, 131–132
Separation anxiety, hysteroid-borderline personality, 173
Separation-individuation
　hysteroid-borderline personality, 182–184, 194–196
　masochistic personality, 295–298, 303
　narcissistic personality, 257–259
　object relations theory, 33–38
　obsessive-compulsive personality, 360–362
Sex role, hysterical personality, 378
Sexuality
　gender of therapist, hysterical personality, 422–426
　hysterical personality, 391
　object relations theory, 2
Shame, narcissistic personality, 231
Shapiro, D., 209, 241, 278, 337, 338, 353, 382
Slipp, S., 62, 184
Smirnoff, V., 311
Soloff, P., 185
Somaticization
　hysterical personality, 390
　narcissistic personality, 241

Spitz, R. A., 38
Splitting, defined, 15
Sterba, R. F., 100
Stern, D., 38
Stolorow, R. D., 93, 323
Stone, M. H., 178, 185
Subjective countertransference, described, 119–120
Sullivan, H. S., 2, 4, 53–55, 60, 65, 66, 218
Superego, obsessive-compulsive personality, 358–359
Superiority, schizoid personality and, 128
Sutherland, J. P., 102, 145
Symbiosis
　hysteroid-borderline personality, 181–182
　masochistic personality, 302–303
　narcissistic personality, 245–246
Symbiotic stage, described, 34–35

Therapeutic alliance, defined, 16–17
Transference, defined, 17
Transference acting out, defined, 17–18
Transitional object, defined, 6–7, 31
Transmuting internalization, defined, 13
Trauma, hysteroid-borderline personality, 185, 209–210
Treatment contracts, 99–109
　developmental-interpersonal contract, 106–107
　first session, 105–106
　object relations therapy and, 100
　overview, 99–100
　problematic contracts, 102–105
　translation of bad to good, 108–109
　treatment rationale, 100–102
Trull, T. J., 157
Tupin, J. P., 386, 397
Twinship selfobject relationship, described, 48

Ulman, R. B., 176